Production Management Systems

An Integrated Perspective

SECOND EDITION

Production Management Systems

An Integrated Perspective

SECOND EDITION

JIMMIE BROWNE

University College Galway

JOHN HARHEN

SmithKline Beecham

JAMES SHIVNAN

MBA candidate
MIT Sloan School of Management

With Case Studies by Michael S. Spencer

The University of Northern Iowa

ADDISON-WESLEY PUBLISHING COMPANY

Harlow, England • Reading, Massachusetts • Menlo Park, California
New York • Don Mills, Ontario • Amsterdam • Bonn • Sydney • Singapore
Tokyo • Madrid • San Juan • Milan • Mexico City • Seoul • Taipei

Cover designed by Crayon Design of Henley-on-Thames
and printed by The Riverside Printing Co. (Reading) Ltd.
Line diagrams drawn by Chartwell Illustrators.
Typeset by Meridian Phototypesetting Limited, Pangbourne.
Printed in Great Britain by Biddles of Guildford.

First printed 1996

ISBN 0-201-42297-2

British Library Cataloguing in Publication Data
A catalogue record for this book is available from the British Library.

Library of Congress Cataloging in Publication Data
Browne, Jimmie.
    Production management systems : an integrated perspective / Jimmie
    Browne, John Harhen, James Shivnan ; with case studies by Michael S.
    Spencer. -- 2nd ed.
        p.   cm.
    Includes bibliographical references and index.
    ISBN 0-201-42297-2 (alk. paper)
    1. Production management--Data processing. 2. Computer integrated
manufacturing systems. I. Harhen, John. II. Shivnan, James.
III. Title.
TS155.6.B76   1996
658.5--dc20   95-26032
                                                                   CIP

To: Maeve, Lorcan, Shane, Ronan, and Fergus
  Anna, Aoife, Dearbhla, Aodhán, and Síle
  Marcella

Preface to the second edition

Since the publication of the first edition of this book in 1988, recognition of the importance of the manufacturing function has increased significantly. The value of managing the extended enterprise from suppliers, through production to the eventual customers can easily be seen from a review of today's manufacturing and business press. Computer Integrated Manufacturing (CIM) and Production Management Systems (PMS) are important components in effectively running the ever more complex manufacturing systems throughout the extended and integrated enterprise. This book deals with the components and operation of PMS in an integrated environment.

This second edition retains the five-part structure of the first edition. Part I describes the development of manufacturing and the increased use of computers in the competitive environment. CIM and Production Activity Control (PAC) have emerged as key strategies for firms as they compete in developing and maintaining competitive manufacturing advantages. Part I also looks to other recent developments such as lean production, the importance of the extended enterprise, and the emergence of environmental concerns.

Parts II, III, and IV concentrate on three distinct production management systems: Materials Requirements Planning (MRP), Just in Time (JIT), and Optimized Production Technology (OPT). These parts have been expanded to include significant new quantitative sections such as MRP forecasting and scheduling techniques. Parts II and III also include new case studies on the production management and manufacturing operations of two companies illustrating many of the issues discussed in the main text.

Part V presents our view of and a detailed architecture for a hybrid production management system that builds on the strongest aspects of MRP, JIT, and OPT. We describe in detail the tactical and operational issues of this architecture as well as specific issues for the smaller firm.

The audience for the book is unchanged from the first edition. It is primarily targeted at professionals in industry, students, and those taking specialized industrial training or certification courses. However, with the addition of questions at the end of each chapter, problems at the end of the book, and case studies at the end of Parts II and III, the second edition is much more useful for students. Graduate and undergraduate students of industrial engineering and manufacturing systems courses as well as MBA students concentrating on operations management will find the questions, problems, and case studies invaluable in developing a clear understanding of production management systems.

The style of this edition is very much in the same vein as the first and our goal continues to be one of facilitating the transition from theory to practice in production and inventory management.

Jimmie Browne, John Harhen, James Shivnan
January 1996

Preface to the first edition

Increasing emphasis is being placed on the manufacturing function in the competition between industrial firms. In order to compete successfully in global markets, firms must achieve excellence in managing their manufacturing operations. Computer Integrated Manufacturing (CIM) is seen as one of the key strategies that firms should adopt in their efforts to achieve manufacturing excellence. CIM involves the integrated application of computer technology to achieve the firm's business objectives. At the very heart of the CIM system lies the Production Management System (PMS), which regulates the pulse of the manufacturing firm through its decisions of what and when to buy and make. It comes as no surprise, therefore, that an effective production management system is essential for the firm in its efforts to achieve CIM and boost its competitiveness. This book is concerned with the various production management approaches available to firms engaged in discrete parts manufacturing.

The five-part structure of the book is illustrated in Figure 1. In Part I we discuss the new competitive manufacturing environment in which firms find themselves and the emergence of CIM as a means to respond to this environment. This is the context in which future production management systems will operate. In industry, three distinct production management system strategies have emerged, which are seen to be competing. These strategies are Manufacturing Resource Planning (MRP II), Just in Time (JIT), and Optimized Production Technology (OPT). In the central sections of this book we take each of these strategies in turn, discuss its underlying philosophy and try to outline the basic techniques that it uses. Thus Parts II, III, and IV deal with the MRP II, JIT, and OPT approaches, respectively, and each may be read in isolation.

Part V seeks to offer a critical overview of the three approaches and to present some ideas for the design and operation of PMS systems in a CIM environment. In particular, we argue for an approach that puts equal emphasis on the social and technical subsystems in the design of production management systems. Furthermore, we believe that a hybrid production management system, which draws on the best insights from JIT, MRP, and OPT, is likely to offer the best solution in the factory of the future. We present a preliminary sketch of what that hybrid system might look like.

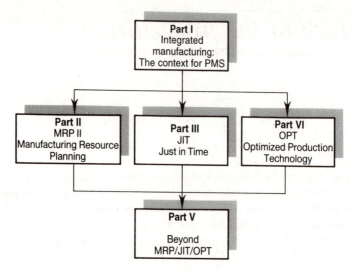

Figure 1 The structure of the book.

The book is aimed primarily at three types of reader. Firstly, those professionals in industry, i.e. managers, engineers, and production management personnel, who wish to explore the fundamentals of the various alternative and competing production management strategies for discrete parts manufacturing and who wish to develop ideas that can be used to good effect in their own firms. Secondly, students in industrial/ manufacturing systems engineering and business schools, i.e. those involved in final year undergraduate and postgraduate industrial engineering and manufacturing engineering courses; also MBA students who are interested in the practice of production and operations management and manufacturing systems design. Finally, those taking specialized training for production management and manufacturing systems certification programs and those involved in industrial training courses in production and inventory management.

In writing this book, we have adopted an informal (i.e. non-mathematical) approach and have been guided constantly by the realization that, given the nature of production management, any proposed advances are only useful in so far as they find successful application in manufacturing industry. We believe that this book should help facilitate the transition from theory to practice in production and inventory management – at least that was our intention in writing it.

Acknowledgments

The journey toward writing this book involved many people over the last few years. We acknowledge our debt to those who helped us along the way and influenced the formation of our understanding of production management systems and their role within CIM systems.

We thank our colleagues at Digital Equipment Corporation, John McCahill, Manus Harley, Ed O'Connell, Dennis O'Connor, and Bob Haynes, for the support that they have given us over that time. We thank Pat Galvin for his invaluable insights into the practice of production management. We particularly thank Richard Joyce, who made a very valuable contribution in the early stages of the formulation of this book.

We thank our colleagues within the Department of Industrial Engineering at University College Galway, in particular Dr Richard Gault, Mr John Roche, and Professor M. E. J. O'Kelly for the many insights we have gained from them over the years. We are grateful to the Computer Services Department within UCG for their technical support in preparing the original manuscript.

We acknowledge the insights we have gained from many formal and informal discussions with colleagues from various European industries, universities, research institutes, and the Commission of the European Community working within the ESPRIT programme of the European Economic Community. In particular those colleagues involved in COSIMA and other related ESPRIT CIM projects, who have offered us useful insights into the nature of production control problems in advanced manufacturing systems; also Professor Guissippe Menga (from the Politecnico di Torino, Alfred Bauer from Digital Equipment Corporation in Munich, Germany, Dick Davies from Digital Equipment Corporation in Reading, UK, and Eric Gerelle from Digital Equipment Corporation in Geneva, Switzerland.

We also acknowledge the significant influences of our colleagues in IFIP Working Group 5.7, in particular Professors Peter Falster in Denmark, Asbjorn Rolstadas in Norway, John Burbidge in England, Guy Doumeingts in France, and J.C. Worthmann in the Netherlands. We also thank those who have influenced our thinking over the years, including Professor John Davies and Dr Harry Jagdev of the University of Manchester Institute of Science and Technology, UK, Professor Andrew Kusiak in the University of Manitoba, Canada, Professor Kathryn Stecke in the University of Michigan, USA, and Professor Keith Rathmill, UK.

We especially thank Professor Robert Graves from the University of Massachusetts for his very helpful criticism of the first draft of this book.

A special thanks goes to the researchers at the CIM Research Unit of University College Galway, particularly John Lenihan, Richard Bowden, Subhash Wadhwa, and Jim Duggan, for their contribution to our understanding of CIM problems.

We thank Simon Plumtree, Allison King, Tim Pitts, Sheila Chatten, and Margaret Conn from Addison-Wesley for their continuing patience and help as the manuscript developed.

We acknowledge the many authors whose work we have consulted in the preparation of this book and whom we have referenced in the manuscript. In particular we acknowledge Yasuhiro Monden for his book *Toyota Production Systems* from which we learned much about Just in Time, and Robert E. Fox whose articles were a clear presentation of the underlying concepts of Optimized Production Technology.

Last, but not least, we thank Maeve, Anna and Ann for suffering without complaint through this book's lengthy gestation period and without whose support we could not have continued.

Jimmie Browne, John Harhen, James Shivnan
January 1988

Publisher's acknowledgments

The publisher would like to thank the following for giving their permission to reprint their material:

Harvard Business Review for excerpts from (i) 'The Focused Factory' by Wickham Skinner (May–June 1974). Copyright © 1974 by The President and Fellows of Harvard College; all rights reserved. (ii) 'Plan for Economies of Scope' by Joel D. Goldhar and Mariann Jelinek (Nov.-Dec. 1983). Copyright © 1983 by The President and Fellows of Harvard College; all rights reserved. (iii) 'Manufacturing – the Missing Link in Corporate Strategy' by Wickham Skinner (May–June 1969). Copyright © 1969 by The President and Fellows of Harvard College; all rights reserved.

Elsevier Science Publishers for excerpts from (i) Primrose, P. and Leonard R. (1986) 'Conditions Under Which Flexible Manufacturing is Financially Viable' in *Flexible Manufacturing Systems: Methods and Studies* edited by A. Kusiak. (ii) Rosenthal, S. and Ward, P. (1986) 'Key Managerial Roles in Controlling Progress Towards CIM' in *Manufacturing Research: Organizational and Institutional Issues* edited by A. Gerstenfeld, H. Bullinger and H. Warnecke. (iii) Burbidge, J. (1985a) 'Automated Production Control' in *Modelling Production Management Systems* edited by P. Falster and R. Mazumber. (iv) for excerpts, and Figures 2.1 and 2.2 and Table 2.1, taken from figures in Harhen, J. and Browne, J. (1984) 'Production Activity Control: A Key Node in CIM' in *Strategies for Design and Economic Analysis of Computer Supported Production Management Systems* edited by H. Hubner. (v) Shivnan, J., Joyce, R. and Browne, J. (1987) 'Production and Inventory Management Techniques – A Systems Perspective' in *Modern Production Management Systems* edited by A. Kusiak.

Pergamon Journals Ltd for an excerpt from Spur, G. (1984) 'Growth, Crisis and the Factory of the Future', *Robotics and Computer Integrated Manufacturing*, **1**(1), 21–37.

Computer Aided Manufacturing International, Inc. for an excerpt from CAM-I Factory Management Project, PR-82-ASPP-01.6.

Taylor & Francis for an excerpt from Meredith, J. and Suresh, N. (1986) 'Justification Techniques for Advanced Manufacturing Technologies', *International Journal of Production Research*, **24**(5), 1043–57.

American Production and Inventory Control Society, Inc. for excerpts from *Production and Inventory Management:* (i) Vollman, T. E. (1986) 'OPT as an Enhancement to MRP II', **27**(2), 38–46; (ii) Swann, D. (1986) 'Using MRP for Optimized Schedules (Emulating OPT)', **27**(2), 30–37; (iii) Galvin, P. (1986) 'Visions and Realities: MRP as System', **27** (3); (iv) Hinds, 5. (1982) 'The Spirit of Materials Requirements Planning', **23** (4), 35–50; (v) Latham, D. (1981) 'Are You Among MRP's Walking Wounded?', **22**(3), 33–41; (vi) Safizadeh, M. and Raafat, F. (1986) 'Formal/Informal Systems and MRP Implementation', **27**(1); (vii) Benson, P., Hill, A. and Hoffman, T. (1982) 'Manufacturing Systems of the Future: A Delphi Study', **23**(3), 87–106; (viii) Mather, H. (1985), 'Dynamic Lot Sizing for MRP: Help or Hindrance', **26**(2); (ix) St. John, R. (1984) 'The Evils of Lot Sizing in MRP', **25** (4); (x) DeBodt, M., van Wassenhove, L. (1983) 'Lot Sizes and Safety Stocks in MRP', **24**(1). Also for an excerpt from Wallace, T. (1980) ed. *APICS Dictionary* 4th edn.

IFS (Publications) for Figure 2.4 based on a figure from *The FMS Magazine*, April 1984; IFS (Conferences) for Figure 16.4 based on a figure from the 4th Automan Conference Proceedings.

Dow-Jones Irwin for an excerpt from Hall, R. W. (1983) *Zero Inventories*.

Butterworth Scientific Ltd for an excerpt from Gallagher, C. C. and Knight, W. A. (1973) *Group Technology*.

Society of Manufacturing Engineers for an excerpt from Laszcz, J. Z. (1985) 'Product Design for Robotic and Automatic Assembly', in *Robotic Assembly* edited by K. Rathmill, IFS Publications Ltd. Copyright © 1984, from the Robots 8 Conference Proceedings.

Institute of Industrial Engineers for (i) an excerpt from and (ii) Figures 15.1, 15.2 and 15.3 based on figures taken from Jacobs, F. R. (1984) 'OPT Uncovered: Many Productions Planning and Scheduling Concepts Can Be Applied With or Without the Software', *Industrial Engineering*, **16**(10). Copyright Institute of Industrial Engineers, 25 Technology Park/Atlanta, Norcross, GA 30092. (iii) for Figures 12.9, 13.4 and 13.25 based on figures taken from *Toyota Production Systems,* Monden, Y. Copyright 1983 Institute of Industrial Engineers.

Penton Publishing for an excerpt from (1981) 'Implementing CIM', *American Machinist*, 152–74.

W. H. Freeman and Company for an excerpt from Gunn, T. (1982). 'The Mechanization of Design and Manufacturing', *Scientific American*, **247** (3), 87–110.

Institute of Electrical and Electronics Engineers, Inc. for an excerpt from Cortes-Comerer, N. (1986) 'JIT is Made to Order', *IEEE Spectrum*, September, 57–62.

Auerbach Publishers, Inc. for an excerpt from Gold, B. (1986) 'CIM Dictates Change in Management Practice', *CIM Review*, **2**(3), 3–6.

Wright Publications and R. E. Fox for (i) Figures 14.2, 14.3 and 14.6 taken from figures in Fox, RE. (1982) 'OPT – An Answer for America' Part II, *Inventories and Production Magazine*, Nov.–Dec. 1982. (ii) for an excerpt from 'MRP, Kanban or OPT. What's Best?', *Inventories and Production Magazine*, July–Aug. 1982.

About the authors

Professor Jim Browne is Director of the CIM Research Unit at University College Galway in Ireland. He received his Ph.D. degree from the University of Manchester for work on the simulation of manufacturing systems and his D.Sc. degree from the same university for published work on the design and analysis of manufacturing systems. His research work has focused on production management systems, computer integrated manufacturing, and more recently the extended enterprise. He has authored and co-authored over 100 scientific publications and is an active member of IFIP Technical Committee 5 and Working Group 5.7. In recent years he has been engaged in a number of large industrial R&D projects funded by the European Commission under its ESPRIT and BRITE–EURAM programs.

Dr John Harhen works for SmithKline Beecham's consumer healthcare manufacturing facility in Dungarvan, Ireland. John's responsibilities include operations management for packed product production, information technology management, and has also included logistics management. Prior to this, he worked for 13 years at Digital Equipment Corporation, in a variety of locations in Ireland and the US. John's responsibilities in Digital included management of a corporate strategic management service offering, based on innovative technology, and prior to that, research into artificial intelligence applications for management. He also worked in a variety of information systems and engineering roles. John holds a Ph.D. in industrial engineering/operations research from the University of Massachusetts, Amherst, and holds a masters degree in industrial engineering, from University College Galway. He is also a certified Fellow of the American Production and Inventory Control Society (APICS).

James Shivnan is currently pursuing an MBA from the Sloan School of Management at MIT in Cambridge, MA where he is specializing in strategy, information technology, and operations. Previous activities during his seven years with Digital Equipment Corporation include consulting to Digital's customers on their strategic planning systems and infrastructure, applying knowledge based approaches to the strategic decision process in the manufacturing function at Digital, and using simulation and production activity control systems within a CIM environment. James has publications in the areas of production management systems, simulation, and AI applications. He holds a Master of Engineering Science degree in industrial engineering from University College, Galway.

Contents

PART I

Integrated manufacturing: the context for production management

Overview

Production management takes place in a context. This context comprises both the nature of discrete parts manufacturing itself, as well as the technological framework in which the Production Management System (PMS) finds itself, namely integrated manufacturing. Part I of this book is devoted to discussing the context in which PMSs operate while focusing on discrete parts manufacturing firms. It is structured as follows.

Chapter 1 discusses the emerging competitive pressures that are acting upon the discrete parts manufacturing firm. Various organizations of the manufacturing process are possible in this mode of manufacturing. These are jobbing shop production, batch production, and mass production. We will also try to differentiate between manufacturing systems by looking at the nature of their interface with the customer. In discussing the features of, and differences between, these types of manufacturing organization, we will highlight the changes brought about by the new emphasis on competitiveness in manufacturing.

In Chapter 2, the development of automation in discrete parts manufacturing is discussed. The various stages on the road to Computer Integrated Manufacturing (CIM) are identified. Significant islands of automation are described. Particular attention is devoted to a discussion of Flexible Manufacturing Systems (FMS). An examination of the history of the development of manufacturing automation should provide us with an understanding of the current emphasis on achieving integrated manufacturing. All of this serves to set the stage for a discussion of CIM.

In Chapter 3, CIM is examined from various viewpoints, such as the engineering perspective and the production management perspective. CIM is described in the narrow sense as **four walls** CIM. Also in Chapter 3 the role of production management within the CIM system is discussed. The structure of the PMS itself is examined, and several different levels are identified. Production management is identified as a central function within CIM. Some attention is then devoted to the relationship between

1

the PMS and the nature of the manufacturing process. The execution level, Production Activity Control (PAC), is seen as the gateway between the higher level planning modules within the PMS and the process technology of the shop floor, and thus is key to the achievement of CIM at the factory floor or operational level.

In Chapter 4 we look beyond CIM, initially at Computer Integrated Business (CIB), which takes a broader view of CIM as the integration of factory CIM with the rest of the business. Both the single plant and multi-plant cases of CIB are discussed. We also look at the emerging approach in manufacturing systems which seeks to achieve integration across the whole value chain and includes consideration of the supply chain. This approach we term the **extended enterprise**.

Because the PMS is at the heart of integrated manufacturing, it is very important to the competitive operation of the firm. The choice of an appropriate production management strategy can determine the success or failure of the firm. For this reason, we propose to examine in detail three important alternative strategies for production management. These are Manufacturing Resource Planning (MRP II), Just in Time (JIT), and Optimized Production Technology (OPT). This comprises the material for the next three parts of this book. Finally, in Part V, we compare and contrast the assumptions, approaches, and strategies implicit in the use of these techniques and offer an overview of a complete PMS, taking into account many of the ideas presented in the earlier parts of this book.

CHAPTER ONE

The new manufacturing environment

1.1 Introduction

Writing in the *Harvard Business Review*, Skinner (1969) pointed to the unusual position of manufacturing within the business environment at that time. He wrote:

> "A company's manufacturing function typically is either a competitive weapon or a corporate millstone. It is seldom neutral . . . Few top managers are aware that what appear to be routine manufacturing decisions frequently come to limit the corporation's strategic options, binding it with facilities, equipment, personnel and basic controls and policies to a non-competitive posture which may take years to turn around."

Recent developments, particularly the success of Japan in world markets and the feeling that this success has been derived, to a significant degree, from superior manufacturing systems, have changed people's perception of the role and importance of the manufacturing function in the industrial firm. Business managers and business authors, such as Hayes and Wheelright (1984), now regard manufacturing as a competitive weapon in the market-place and recommend that each company include in their business plans specific goals in the area of achieving manufacturing excellence. Manufacturing is now an equal partner at the corporate boardroom. The focus in manufacturing is competitiveness, and the emphasis is on integration and the factory of the future as the means of achieving it.

Skinner, writing in 1985, acknowledged the new situation:

> "After years of neglect, top management's attention has been captured . . . the action in manufacturing has been extraordinary in these last five years."

3

1.2 The new environment for manufacturing

Manufacturing is therefore seen as the new competitive weapon and, as a result, manufacturing firms find themselves in a totally changed environment. This change is not confined to any one industry, and evidence of it can be seen in such varied industries as the automotive industry, consumer goods, electronics, and white goods. Management faced with rapid changes must devise new strategies to deal with the competitive nature of this new environment. The old strategy of mass production derived from notions of economies of scale is no longer seen as valid and is being discarded in favor of a strategy that facilitates **flexibility**, reduced **design cycle time**, reduced **time to market** for new products, and reduced **order cycle time** to the customer for existing products.

Some important characteristics of this new environment are:

- Increased product diversity.
- Greatly reduced product life cycles.
- Increased awareness and understanding of the environmental impact of manufacturing systems and their products.
- Changing cost patterns.
- Great difficulty in estimating the costs and benefits of integration technology.
- Changing social expectations.

Each of these factors will now briefly be discussed in turn.

Increased product diversity
The market is no longer satisfied with a mass produced uniform product. Manufacturing firms must now compete by offering variety. The age of the personalized consumer product seems to be approaching rapidly. This represents a much changed situation from earlier in this century (see Figure 1.1). The explosion of product variety is particularly evident in the automobile and computer industries. However, product variety dramatically increases the complexity of the tasks of process design and production management. For instance, frequent process changeover can be a significant burden. Offering increased choice at reduced cost thus poses significant challenges for the manufacturing firm that is attempting to achieve or maintain competitiveness.

Greatly reduced product life cycles
The life cycle of a product falls naturally into several phases. In simple terms, these are the design phase, the manufacturing phase, and the end-of-life phase. The complete product life cycle, in simplified form, is

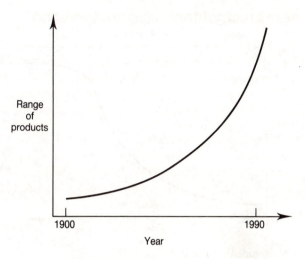

Figure 1.1   Increasing product diversity.

represented by Figure 1.2. Demand is light and grows very slowly in the initial periods, during which the manufacturer can establish the product design and production method. The second stage is one of a mature product enjoying high stable demand. The third and final stage sees the gradual decline in demand for the product. The costs incurred during the early part of the design cycle include the design costs and the costs associated with developing and installing the production process.

In the old way of doing business, the design cycle and the manufacturing cycle were separated and occurred *sequentially*. A product design was *proven* before it entered production. There was thus a significant amount of time available for production methods to be established prior to volume production of the product. The situation is illustrated in Figure 1.3. Once

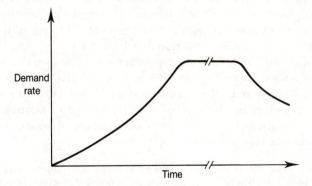

Figure 1.2   Traditional product life cycle.

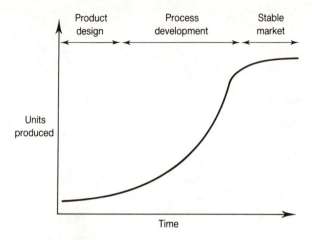

Figure 1.3   Development of market.

the product was established in the marketplace, the manufacturer could look forward to a relatively high demand for a number of years before the product became obsolete. The many years of high, stable demand enabled the costs incurred in the early stage of product and process development to be recovered.

The difficulty in today's manufacturing environment is that manufacturing can no longer look forward to many years of stable high demand. This is because product redesign is happening continuously, and a product's useful life in the marketplace is constantly under attack from improved versions incorporating the latest design features. Moreover, due to the pressures of competitiveness, firms must strive to get their products to the marketplace in ever shortening times. All of this means that manufacturing must put processes in place that are sufficiently flexible to accommodate new product designs rapidly without incurring large process introduction costs. Otherwise the costs incurred in the product design and process development phase will be too large to be recovered over the much shorter peak demand phase of the product life cycle. The cost distribution over this shortened life cycle is illustrated in Figure 1.4.

Because of the compression of product life cycles, manufacturing firms can no longer expend huge resources on developing a dedicated production capability, since the product design is likely to change before that production facility has been paid for. The concept of **economies of scale** has been replaced by the notion of **economies of scope**. Goldhar (1983) explains that economies of scope exist:

> "when the same equipment can produce the multiple products more cheaply in combination than separately. A computer controlled machine does not care whether it works in succession on a dozen different product designs – within,

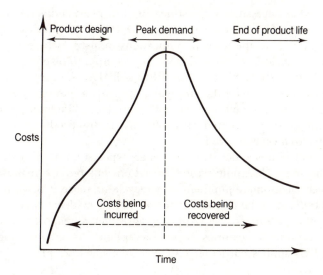

Figure 1.4 Distribution of cost over product life cycle.

of course, a family of design limits. Change-over times (and therefore costs) are negligible, since the task of machine set-up involves little more than reading a computer program."

Moreover, this has implications for investment appraisal procedures since companies must now put in place flexible production facilities, which will be used not only on existing product designs but also on future redesigns of these products. In summary, the combination of greater product diversity, shortened product life cycles and pressures for faster time to market have given rise to the need for economies of scope.

Increased awareness of the environmental impact of manufacturing
systems and their products
Public opinion is increasingly aware of the environmental impact of manufacturing processes and, indeed, the products of manufacturing. Legislation is increasingly constraining product and process design in terms of energy utilization, the required use of recyclable material and the reuse of products at the end of their life. Essentially, society is putting pressure on manufacturers to create products and to operate processes that are neutral with respect to the environment. Legislation in almost all parts of the industrialized world imposes severe constraints on manufacturers and requires, for example, that noxious substances not be emitted to the atmosphere or released into the water system. The use of certain materials – for example, asbestos – is severely curtailed. In the automotive industry in Germany, it is clear that legislation requiring the use of water-soluble

spray paints has necessitated investment in new plant and added considerably to the cost of a new car (see Warnecke 1993). Another example, also from Germany, is in the telecommunications industry, where suppliers of large Public Branch Exchanges (PBXs) are required to dispose, in an environmentally friendly fashion, of the PBX that they are replacing. Within the European Union (EU) the emphasis, in terms of emerging legislation, is on the prevention of pollution caused by products. "Polluter pays" seems to be emerging as an accepted principle; that is, the producer is liable for the final disposal costs of products.

In the electronics industry there is an expectation in the USA and in Europe that new electronic waste legislation will require manufacturers to take back electronic equipment and recycle or reuse it or dispose of it properly. Indeed, in the electronics sector there is evidence that some large multinational customers are requiring agreements regarding reuse and return of product accessories before acceptance as a totally approved supplier. This applies particularly to such items as laser printer toner kits and associated parts.

Increasingly, large multinational corporations, aware of the trend in legislation and, indeed, of the requirements of their customers are adapting an environmentally friendly approach to the design of their products and processes. More frequently one comes across references to "design for sustainable development." Companies seek to decrease the amount of materials and components in products without sacrificing functionality, performance, or quality. The end result is fewer waste by-products. Manufacturers also seek to design products that can be disassembled easily (**design for disassembly** will soon be as important as **design for assembly**). This facilitates the separation of components from products at the end of life, and allows the possibility of the recovery and reuse of suitable materials.

Design for disassembly also facilitates maintenance and mid-life refurbishment of products. In fact, it seems paradoxical that at a time when market forces and technological developments facilitate customized products and short production life cycles, there is at the same time pressure for extended product field life and, where possible, recycling of products and components at the product disposal stage. We will return briefly to this topic in Chapter 4.

Changing cost structure

Authors such as Goldratt (1983), Kaplan (1984), and Umble and Srikanth (1990) have argued strongly that existing cost accounting systems are inappropriate to the cost analysis and management of advanced manufacturing systems. Kaplan (1984) goes so far as to suggest that "yesterday's accounting undermines production." Umble and Srikanth (1990) indicate that "the basic argument is that the standard cost procedures and the performance measures supported by these cost systems all too often trigger dysfunctional actions within the organisation in general and specifically within the manufacturing system." Later, in Part IV, we will give an example of this, when we come to discuss the so-called "hockey stick" phenonenon.

Traditionally, manufacturing costs have fallen under three headings: material cost, labor cost, and overhead. Furthermore, labor hours were used in many industries as a base for *recovering* overhead. Bonsack (1986) points out that "current overhead accounting most often uses the full absorption method which assigns all factory overhead to units of production based on the labour costs incurred."

What happens when direct labor costs fall to a very small fraction of total cost – to below 5%, as is the case in very many factories today? A manager in the electronics industry made the following observation, quoted by Gould (1985): "Direct labour used to account for almost half of production costs; in today's electronics, it accounts for 5% to 8%. For example IBM's direct labour cost is about 4%; at Apple's new Macintosh plant, it is 1%." In the factory of the future, where almost unmanned manufacturing will be the norm, it seems obvious that direct labor cost can no longer be the foundation of a standard costing system. Bonsack (1986) speculates that it is likely that "the direct labour cost category will eventually be eliminated entirely in many automated work cells by the incorporation of all costs except material in overhead." Innovative costing methods will undoubtedly have to be developed that allocate this overhead cost against meaningful measures of output.

It can be argued that since integrated manufacturing systems will incorporate sophisticated data capture technology at each production stage, this consequently will facilitate the association of cost with individual items – whether components, subassemblies or finished products – at the point of time at which the cost is incurred. This, however, ignores the issue of how to value a machine hour in an environment of rapid technological and product change, where there is great difficulty in predicting the useful life of the machine and, equally importantly, the life cycle of the products that are processed on it.

An alternative to the standard cost system, which seems to be finding increasing favor, is the **Activity Based Costing** (ABC) system. ABC, sometimes known as transaction based costing, seeks to allocate overhead to product in a manner that accurately reflects the amount of overhead consumed by the product. ABC identifies cost activities from the finished product down to the individual components within the product, and the processes and activities used to design, procure materials, manufacture, assemble, and so on, those components. Costs are tracked and assigned to where they actually occur. The ABC approach identifies the various activities that take place, traces costs to these activities, then uses cost drivers to trace the cost of activities to components and ultimately to the final product.

Although ABC has been slow to gain widespread acceptance by manufacturing industry, it is clear that many large companies are aware of its potential and are beginning to test its application in practice (see Nicholls 1992).

The difficulty of estimating the costs and benefits of integration

It is often very difficult to justify investment in integration technology using traditional investment appraisal methods. This problem can be understood in the context of the economies of scope ideas proposed by Baumol and Braunstein (1977) and Goldhar and Jelinek (1985) and discussed above. Gold (1986) claims that "field studies of several industries suggest that the fundamental reason that so many companies have failed to exploit the potential of integration technology is that management has generally assumed that the new technologies are no different than the traditional equipment acquired to improve production efficiency." He goes on to say that when a company appraises large technology acquisition proposals, it often makes some false assumptions, including:

- "The prospective equipment will affect only a narrow range of production activities.
- The capabilities of the equipment are known and will not change significantly (except for gradual decline) after installation.
- The acquisition's contribution to the effectiveness of operations and cost reductions can be estimated with reasonable accuracy . . ."

Clearly, for integration technology these assumptions are dubious. For example, integration equipment is extremely flexible, so the limits of its capability and its application are difficult to define. Meredith and Suresh (1986) suggest using differing justification strategies corresponding to the different levels of automation under consideration. Economic justification procedures are appropriate when a company is involved in straightforward replacement of old equipment such as the purchase of a Numerically Controlled (NC) lathe to replace an existing conventional lathe. "However with systems approaching full integration, clear competitive advantages and major increments towards the firm's business objectives are usually being attained. Here strategic approaches are needed that take these benefits into consideration, although tactical and economic benefits may be accruing as well."

Primrose and Leonard (1986), talking in terms of Flexible Manufacturing Systems (FMS) which can be seen as mini-CIM systems, point out that: "Because of the company-wide implications of introducing FMS, many authors have suggested that the benefits are considerable but intangible, with the word *intangible* being regarded as synonymous with *unquantifiable* . . . Because the inclusion of the intangibles significantly influences the viability of a proposed FMS . . . [it becomes] necessary to develop techniques to enable all of the potential benefits of such a system to be both quantified and included in an evaluation."

Changing social expectations

Today, many important social influences are impacting on the manufacturing environment. The age profile of the population is changing; in general, the population is becoming older and more experienced and may have greater difficulty in adapting to change. Further, there seems to be some difficulty in attracting large numbers of intelligent young people into manufacturing. For many young people manufacturing engineering, compared to, for example, design engineering, is not seen as a rewarding career path. The working week is getting shorter. The availability of advanced information technology and telecommunications systems supports distributed and home based working.

We have now identified a number of important characteristics of this new emerging competitive environment. This environment has significant implications for the manner in which industrial firms organize their manufacturing processes. We will now discuss traditional styles of manufacturing organization, methods of categorizing manufacturing systems and their effect on manufacturing competition. Later, in Chapter 4, we will see how the competitive environment described here leads to the concepts of customer driven manufacturing, world class manufacturing, lean production, and the extended enterprise.

1.3 Manufacturing process organization for discrete manufacturing

Manufacturing systems analysts, such as Wild (1971), have identified two basic categories of industrial plant, namely continuous process industries and discrete parts manufacturing. Continuous process industries involve the continuous production of product, often using chemical rather than physical or mechanical means (e.g. the production of fertilizers or sugar). Discrete parts production involves the production of individual items and is further subdivided into mass, batch, and jobbing shop production, as illustrated in Figure 1.5. Our focus in this book is on discrete parts manufacturing.

Now we will consider the main attributes of jobbing shops, batch, and mass production systems. Later we will review a somewhat different mechanism for categorizing discrete parts manufacturing systems, namely a mechanism that distinguishes **Make to Stock** (MTS), **Assemble To Order** (ATO), **Make To Order** (MTO) and **Engineer To Order** (ETO) systems. In our view this approach is more useful in terms of understanding the production management needs of manufacturing companies.

1.3.1 Jobbing shop production

The main characteristic of jobbing shop production is very low volume production runs of many different products. These products have a very

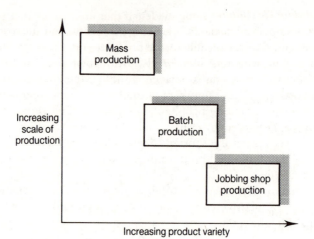

Figure 1.5 Classification of discrete production.

low level of standardization in that there are few, if any, common components. To produce the different products, the manufacturing firm requires a highly flexible production capability. This implies flexible equipment capable of performing many different tasks, as well as a highly skilled work force. Jobbing shops normally operate an MTO or ETO inventory policy. A typical example of the jobbing shop is a subcontract machine shop.

1.3.2 Batch production

Batch production's main characteristics are medium volume production runs of a medium range of products. Batch production is defined as the production of a product in small batches or lots by a series of operations, each operation typically being carried out on the whole batch before any subsequent operation is started.

The production system must be reasonably flexible and uses general purpose equipment in order to accommodate varying customer requirements and fluctuations in demand. Batch production can be seen as a situation which lies between the extremes of the pure jobbing shop and pure mass production, where the quantity required is insufficient to justify mass production. Batching, however, offers economies in terms of amortizing set-up cost. Because of the large variety of jobs involved, batch production has much of the complexity of the jobbing shop. A typical example of batch production is the manufacture and assembly of machine tools.

Batch production represents a sizable element within the total manufacturing base of developed economies. Gerwin (1982) cites statistics which claim that batch production represents more than 35% of the US manufacturing base, and constitutes 36% of manufacturing's share of the GNP.

Furthermore, there is some evidence that companies that previously used mass production methods are being forced by the pressures of the market to adopt more flexible batch production oriented systems, i.e. systems capable of dealing with relatively small quantities of a variety of products. This is particularly true of the automotive industry and manufacturers of consumer goods.

1.3.3 Mass production

The major characteristics of mass production are large volume production runs of relatively few products. All products are highly standardized. Typically, demand is stable for the products and the product design changes very little over the short to medium term.

The production facilities consist of highly specialized, dedicated machines. Although these machines are extremely expensive, the cost is amortized over very long production runs. The term **hard automation** or **Detroit style automation** was coined to describe the type of automation associated with mass production. It is *hard* in the sense that the automation is dedicated and very inflexible. The classic example of mass production used to be automotive manufacture and assembly, hence the term Detroit style automation. Nowadays, for reasons which will briefly be explored later, the automobile industry is no longer solely bound to mass production strategies.

1.4 Comparing the types of manufacturing process organization

The three categories of mass, batch, and jobbing shop production have been discussed as if they represented a clear picture of the categories of discrete parts manufacturing, into which all discrete parts manufacturing systems could be neatly slotted. The reality of manufacturing, of course, is somewhat more complicated. Manufacturing exists on a continuum between two extremes – jobbing shops and pure mass production – and the majority of discrete parts manufacturing facilities lies somewhere along that continuum, not fitting into a well-defined category. In many cases, differing and hybrid manufacturing process organizations can be found in the same production facilities. Nonetheless, the important characteristics of the three types of discrete parts manufacturing are given in summarized form in Figure 1.6.

The extremes of mass production versus jobbing shop can also be explored in terms of the difference between manufacturing process organization based on product flow and manufacturing process organization based on the commonality of process equipment, as discussed by Rolstadas (1986). Traditionally, the process layout, which involves organizing the plant in terms of individual processes or operations, has been associated

	Mass production	Batch production	Jobbing shop production
Production volumes	High	Medium	Low
Labor skills	Low	Medium	High
Specialized equipment and tooling	High	Medium	Low

Figure 1.6 Characteristics of types of process organizations.

with batch production and jobbing shops, and results in great flexibility but long throughput times. The product oriented approach, which involves laying out the plant to correspond to the flow of products through the processes they require, has traditionally been associated with mass production systems and has, in recent years, through the development of group technology principles, begun to be applied to batch production systems. Product flow layouts are somewhat less flexible than the process oriented approach, but result in greatly reduced throughput times. These issues will be considered in more detail in Part III, when JIT (Just in Time) approaches to manufacturing problems will be discussed.

Because of today's competitive pressures, product diversity is now the norm and manufacturing companies that may previously have used a mass production strategy are now having to move into a more batch oriented environment. This is to achieve more flexibility in product introduction and production scheduling. The automotive industry, which will now be considered briefly, illustrates this trend very well.

1.4.1 Changing trends in the automotive industry

When people think of mass production, the manufacture of cars in the early part of this century often springs to mind. The attitude of car manufacturers at that time was epitomized by Henry Ford. His byword that "the customer could have any color car he liked as long as it was black" offers an insight as to why the manufacture of automobiles was oriented to mass production. The automobile companies standardized their product to facilitate the manufacturing process. This philosophy allowed the manufacturers to use dedicated, specialized machines, with a relatively low skilled work force. Based on economies of scale, the car manufacturers could produce highly standardized cars in large volumes, at a price that potential customers could afford to pay. The classical example of mass production automation was, and remains, the transfer line. This particular example of hard automation was, and is still, widely used in the manufacture and fabrication of components and subassemblies in the automotive industry.

However, over the last 30 years, there have been many changes. Customers, perhaps encouraged by sophisticated marketing and sales campaigns, are demanding greater choice when buying cars, not only as regards the color but also with respect to the degree of interior luxury, the number of doors (whether two door, four door or hatchback), the engine size, manual or automatic gearbox, etc. This has resulted in each manufacturer being forced to offer a range of cars with a variety of models for each segment in the range. Also each model must be upgraded each year and major model changes are very frequent.

For these reasons, automobile production has shifted away from a mass production activity and is rapidly assuming the characteristics of batch production. Manufacturers can no longer standardize on a particular design and tool up their plants in anticipation of long product life cycles. The strategy of investing heavily in specialized (in a product model sense) equipment in anticipation of recouping this investment over a long production run is no longer seen as appropriate. The reader interested in a discussion on the consequences of programmable automation for the automotive industry is referred to Gerwin and Tarondeau (1986).

1.5 Customer order driven and stock driven systems

An alternative method of categorizing discrete parts manufacturing systems is to distinguish between **stock driven** and **order driven** systems. This leads to the identification of the four categories of system mentioned earlier, namely Make To Stock (MTS), Assemble To Order (ATO), Make To Order (MTO), and Engineer To Order (ETO).

Customization to customer needs is an emerging trend. This implies close contact between the customer and the supplier. Whereas in traditional systems the supplier or manufacturer might be able to forecast market requirements, build and stock finished products in anticipation of customer need, in today's environment this is frequently not possible. Typically, it is no longer possible to build for stock and supply customers from a finished goods buffer, as shown in Figure 1.7. The situation depicted in Figure 1.8, namely customer order driven production, is more usual.

1.5.1 Make to stock

MTS describes a manufacturing system where the demand for clearly defined product is very well known and predictable. In this situation the production volume of each sales unit tends to be high and, in general, direct interaction between the manufacturer and the customer tends to be very low. In fact, customer delivery is determined by the availability of product

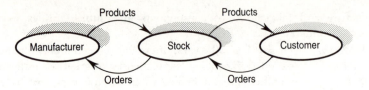

Figure 1.7   Stock driven production.

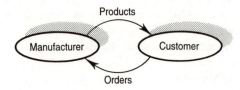

Figure 1.8   Customer driven production.

in the finished goods buffer or warehouse. In effect, the finished products warehouse acts as a buffer against the possibility of uncertain demand. Clearly inventory carrying costs can be high and the manufacturer runs the risk of the product becoming obsolete. However, the customer lead time from order to delivery is normally very low.

1.5.2   Assemble to order

In an ATO manufacturing system, products are configured or assembled to customer order from a set of core subassemblies and components. A typical example of an ATO product is a minicomputer, the precise config-uration of which – size of memory, number of input and output ports, number of peripheral devices and so on – is determined by individual customer order, but which is assembled from a set of core modules and subassemblies. In ATO the customer makes contact with the manufacturer through the sales organization, which then configures the customer order into suitable orders for the manufacturing plant. The lead time to delivery of the order is dependent on the availability of the key core subassemblies and components. No buffer of finished products exists because assembly of the finished product only takes place on receipt of a customer order.

1.5.3   Make to order

In an MTO manufacturing system, products are selected by customers based on, perhaps, a catalog of available designs. Office or kitchen furniture might be made to order. The important point is that a customer order must be received before processing can take place. The American Production and Inventory Control Society (APICS) offers an interesting definition of MTO, which includes a reference to the distinction between MTO and ATO:

> "An MTO product is finished after receipt of the customer order. Frequently long lead time components are planned prior to the order arriving in order to reduce the delivery time to the customer. Where options or other subassemblies are stocked prior to customer orders arriving, the term 'assemble to order' is frequently used. "
>
> APICS (1987)

In one sense, MTS and MTO can be considered to be reasonably well-defined categories, while ATO represents a hybrid of MTO and MTS. See Wemmerlov (1984) for a more detailed discussion of these issues.

1.5.4 Engineer to order

ETO describes a manufacturing system where the customer order requires that a new engineering design be developed. Essentially, the product is designed to a customer specification. As APICS (1987) points out, each customer order results in a unique set of part numbers, bills of materials, and process routings. ETO products are one-of-a-kind products (see Wortmann 1992).

In fact, very few manufacturing companies are strictly MTS, ATO, MTO, or ETO. Many companies involve elements of all of these categories. Also, it could be argued that these four categories exist on a continuum and that the differences between some of these categories – say, for example, MTO and ATO or MTO and ETO – is sometimes one of degree (Figure 1.9). Further, thinking back to our earlier discussion on trends in manufacturing and the move towards customized products, we can argue that the evolution of manufacturing systems is away from MTS and towards ATO, MTO, and, indeed, ETO systems. In fact, ATO, MTO, and ETO are, to different degrees, customer order driven systems.

As we move from MTS to ETO environments, the **customer order decoupling point** (CODP) defines the point after which material is dedicated to a particular customer order. The positioning of this point is vital, because it defines the parts of the process that are driven by customer orders and the parts that are driven by forecasts (Van Veen, 1992). Figure 1.10 illustrates the positioning of the CODP in the different manufacturing environments. In general, the coupling point between the forecast driven and sales driven operations is tending to move towards earlier stages of the manufacturing process. Later, in Chapter 17, we will see that the CODP is a useful idea when it comes to dealing with the selection of items for master scheduling purposes.

As stated earlier, many companies are now moving towards a hybrid form of manufacturing environment. Consequently, flexibility in dealing with the positioning of the CODP is essential. An example of the flexibility

Figure 1.9 Manufacturing as a continuum.

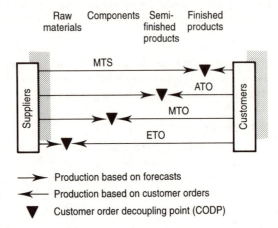

Production based on forecasts
Production based on customer orders
Customer order decoupling point (CODP)

Figure 1.10 Customer order decoupling point.

required could be the use of the master schedule to plan at an option† level and then the use of JIT principles to create the final assembly schedule for production. In this case the customer order could enter the system at two different levels – that is, customer orders come in at the MPS level but also at the shop floor level in the case of hybrid "push"/"pull" environments, where some components of the products are customized and some are standard. The possibilities here suggest the need for a new approach to PMSs.

1.6 Conclusion

We have seen that competing through manufacturing is a new and essential feature of industrial competition. We have identified what we consider to be the important characteristics of the new environment in manufacturing, namely increased product diversity, significantly reduced product life cycles, an increasing awareness of the environmental impacts of manufacturing processes and products, changing cost structures, difficulties of understanding the costs and benefits of the new technology, and changing social conditions. This is having profound implications for the way in

† The word *option* in this context means a choice or feature offered to customers for customizing the end product. In many companies the term *option* may mean a mandatory choice between a series of alternatives.

which manufacturing processes are organized. In particular, there is a trend away from pure mass production process organization and towards batch oriented systems in order to provide a greater diversity of products to an increasingly demanding marketplace. Also, we have reviewed a typology of manufacturing systems based on a distinction between stock driven and customer driven systems. Later, in Part V, we will see that this typology is useful in terms of describing the production management needs of manufacturing enterprises. The issue of manufacturing process organization will be briefly discussed again in Chapter 3, where the consequences of the nature of process organization for production management will be examined.

Questions

(1.1) What impact have reduced product life cycles had on manufacturing firms?

(1.2) "It seems paradoxical that at a time when market forces and technological developments facilitate customized products and short production life cycles, there is pressure for extended product field life and recycling of products and components at the product disposal stage." Discuss.

(1.3) How might the standard cost system trigger dysfunctional behavior?

(1.4) Differentiate clearly between economies of scale and economies of scope.

(1.5) Distinguish clearly between mass, batch, and jobbing shop production systems.

(1.6) "Today we are witnessing a move away from stock driven systems towards customer or order driven systems." Discuss.

(1.7) Distinguish clearly between Make To Order (MTO), Assemble To Order (ATO), and Engineer To Order (ETO) systems.

(1.8) What do you understand by the term *customer order decoupling point*?

CHAPTER TWO

Development of automation in manufacturing

2.1 Introduction
2.2 Mechanization
2.3 Point automation
2.4 Islands of automation
2.5 The role of computers in manufacturing
2.6 Flexible manufacturing and assembly systems
2.7 Conclusion
Questions

2.1 Introduction

Computer Integrated Manufacturing (CIM) can be viewed as the culmination of a long and ongoing effort in the application of automation in the manufacture of discrete parts. Table 2.1 presents a view of this evolutionary process as comprising four stages – mechanization, point automation, islands of automation, and CIM (Harhen and Browne 1984). This chapter briefly describes the history of the automation effort and, in so doing, sets the stage for the discussion of CIM in Chapter 3. Readers interested in a more detailed statement of the history of the development of mechanization and automation are referred to Hitomi (1979).

2.2 Mechanization

The search for better ways to manufacture components was always the main driving force behind automation. The industrial revolution was largely concerned with the replacement of human labor by machines. This replacement of human physical labor is the primary characteristic of the mechanization phase. In the early decades of this century, F.W. Taylor and others introduced many new techniques to help standardize the operations and work methods in manufacturing. Taylor is well known as the father of scientific management (and industrial engineering). His approach was to systematically divide the manufacturing operation into smaller and smaller elements and then to concentrate on improving each element in turn. Such an approach facilitates the mechanization and later automation of specific operations. However, this reductionist approach is not

Table 2.1 Stages of manufacturing automation.

Stage	Features	Examples	Date
Mechanization	Replacement of human labor by machine	Lathe Power Conveyors	1775
Point automation	Replacement of human control of machine by automatic control	NC/CNC MRP	1960
Islands of automation	Integration of point automation within its local environment to manage part of the manufacturing process	MRP II FMS CAD/CAM	1970
Computer integrated manufacturing	The integrated application of computer based automation and decision support systems to manage the total operation of the manufacturing system	The automated and the automatic factory	1990

adequate for the complexity and competitive nature of today's manufacturing.

Culture may have played a significant part in the evolution of manufacturing automation by constraining the approach of engineers and managers to various problems and process developments. This is certainly an important consideration in the discussion of Just in Time (JIT) as a production management approach. It is also a consideration when discussing approaches to the automation of manufacturing. For this reason, it is useful to make a small digression to ponder some differences between Eastern and Western thinking.

Western society has tended to adopt the world view of scientific method, which is reductionist, quantitative, and analytic in nature. The major tenet of this approach is that the whole can be reduced to its constituent parts and each examined on its own. In this manner, it is assumed that the system itself is also understood. Such thinking is evident in the work of Adam Smith, who laid the basis for the division of labor at the beginning of the industrial revolution, and more particularly so in the case of F.W. Taylor and his approach to management at the beginning of this century. If one accepts this argument, then the approach of Western manufacturing systems experts can be seen as the focused examination of well-defined areas, without giving due consideration to the overall system. For example, many of the efforts of quantitative Operations Research (OR) have not had significant impact on the practice of production scheduling (see King 1976; Solberg 1989), despite the fact that great energy has been expended over the last 30 years, since those initial influential formulations of scheduling problems in the 1960s by researchers such as Conway *et al.*

(1967). Moreover, writers such as Burbidge (1986) have reiterated this theme by taking issue with the overspecialized nature of manufacturing personnel and in particular manufacturing systems research.

In contrast, Eastern society seems more often to adopt a **systems perspective** of the world. This world view holds that the whole is greater than the sum of its parts and so recognizes the importance of interaction between the constituent subsystems. In such a **holistic** approach, each subsystem is seen as having a certain autonomy, while still operating within the overall goals of the system. The most important aspect is that no subsystem proceeds with an action which is detrimental to other subsystems. This style of thinking is exhibited frequently in the JIT approach to production management in Japan. For example, Shingo (1981) writing on Kanban at Toyota, declares, "the following is considered quite important: (to) acknowledge the conception of **Toyota production system**, its techniques and besides the systematic relationship between each technique."

The Western approach is perhaps best exemplified by so-called **mechanistic** work organization and work structures, where individual operators tend to be assigned to a few very specialized repetitive tasks in a hierarchical supervisory environment. The alternative approach, the so-called **organic** work organization, is characterized by multiskilled operators working in relatively autonomous work groups and under a less rigid control and supervisory organization. In the authors' experience, the latter approach seems more appropriate, particularly in modern manufacturing systems. The reader interested in more detailed discussion of these issues is referred to Nanda (1986), Bullinger and Ammer (1986) and Cross (1984). A parting comment is that since the CIM problem is primarily about integration, it follows that a holistic approach using organic work structures may well be necessary to attain an effective solution.

2.3 Point automation

With the introduction of control technology to the factory in the 1950s and 1960s, the human control of some machines was replaced by numerical or computer control. For example, conventional lathes could be replaced by Numerical Control (NC) and later by Computer Numerical Control (CNC) lathes.

NC is a form of programmable automation where the operation of a machine is controlled by numbers or symbols. A collection of numbers forms a program that drives a machine to produce a part. When a new part is to be produced, a new set of program steps is used. This ability to change the program, rather than the machine, is the source of the greater flexibility that is characteristic of computer based or **soft** automation. The term *soft* refers to the fact that the device is under program or software control.

There is thus a clear contrast between hard automation, which is very inflexible, and soft automation, which is more flexible. Hard automation involves a situation where the configuration of the equipment determines the feasible set of operations. If the range of products changes or new operations are required, hard automation is unable to cope without extensive reconfiguration. Early approaches to automation were typically of the hard variety, the archetypical example being the transfer line (Groover 1980).

With soft automation, the set of possible operations is not determined by the configuration of the machine, but by the limits of the available programs. NC and CNC are examples of such automation. The distinction between hard and soft automation can be seen in the differing roles of Swiss type automatic screw machines and CNC lathes. Swiss type automatics are special purpose lathes with automatic bar stock feeding, designed to produce minute rotational parts in very large production runs, normally in excess of 100 000. In effect, they are dedicated lathes, designed to operate in a mass production environment. CNC lathes, on the other hand, can be reprogrammed to machine a wide variety of parts automatically and are economical for small batch production.

The automation of manufacturing was not solely concerned with the production process itself. In fact, the earliest manufacturing applications of computers were primarily in the administrative and financial areas of the factory. Systems such as payroll and invoicing were among the first computer applications. The fact that these transaction oriented procedures were already well understood greatly facilitated their early automation through computerization. An important example was the first Material Requirements Planning (MRP) system, which linked a bill of material processor to files describing product structure and inventory status, in order to automate the function of planning material requirements.

These developments in manufacturing automation were concerned with either one individual machine or one specific function within the organization. Hence the term, **point automation**. There was no explicit strategy to integrate these point solutions or make them accessible to other point solutions. With the introduction of affordable and more powerful computers in the 1970s, the possibility of tackling larger problems presented itself. This led to the expansion of these point solutions to more integrated islands of automation.

2.4 Islands of automation

Islands of automation represent automated integrated subsystems within the factory. The initial point solutions in the previous phase were expanded to tackle ancillary or adjacent functions. Instances of such functional expansion include the emergence of production management systems, such as Manufacturing Resource Planning (MRP II), integrated material handling and storage systems, flexible manufacturing systems, and various computer aided engineering systems.

The initial point solutions, which were in place to plan material requirements (MRP), were expanded to MRP II systems. These systems had a set of modules to manage the full range of production and inventory management functions in a manufacturing plant, and all were built around a common set of files or database. MRP II will be dealt with in detail in Part II.

Within the production process, developments such as Flexible Manufacturing Systems (FMS) and Direct Numerical Control (DNC) represent the integration of some point automation solutions into islands of automation. For example, DNC describes a system where a number of machines in a production system are controlled by a single computer in real time through direct communication. The individual machines in the system are NC or CNC machines, and the part programs required to machine a particular component are downloaded on request from the DNC computer to the controller of the individual machine.

Islands of automation represent the current state of manufacturing integration. The proliferation of such locally expanding islands of functional automation has given rise to the CIM problem. These islands are now beginning to overlap and compete with each other. Before proceeding to a discussion of CIM in Chapter 3, the rest of this chapter will be devoted to describing several of the important islands of automation seen in industry today. This description covers computer aided process planning, automated storage and retrieval systems, robotics, macroplanning systems for manufacturing, Computer Aided Design (CAD), and flexible manufacturing systems. Production management is left to later sections of the book. This discussion begins by presenting a framework for examining the various roles that computers play in manufacturing.

2.5 The role of computers in manufacturing

Various schemes can be used to categorize the role of computers in manufacturing. One such scheme is to consider the nature of the computer interface to the production process. This interface may be **indirect**, with the computer's role being that of an information and decision support system, without any capability to sense the process directly. In this case, the computer system manipulates information that humans have extracted from the manufacturing process and fed into the computer. Alternatively, the interface between the production process and the computer may be **direct**, with the computer directly monitoring and actively controlling sections of the manufacturing process.

Examples of direct applications of the computer include CNC, DNC, and robotics. On the other hand, Computer Aided Process Planning (CAPP), computer assisted numerical control programming, and computerized production management are typical examples of indirect applications.

	Indirect application	Direct application

Plant level	Macro planning models
	Accounting systems
	Production management
	  systems
	Computer aided design
		Computer aided warehousing
		Direct numerical control
		Flexible manufacturing
		  systems
		Automatic storage and
		  retrieval system

Operation level	Computer aided
	  process planning
	Computer aided work
	  measurement
	Computer aided NC
	  programming
		Computer aided testing
		Computer numerical control
		Computer based automatic
		  assembly machines
		Robots

Figure 2.1   Role of computers in manufacturing.

The distinction between direct and indirect applications of the computer in manufacturing is useful in that it serves to help illustrate a common misunderstanding about the potential of the computer in manufacturing. Gunn (1982) points out that:

"The opportunities for mechanization in the factory have been greatly misunderstood. The emphasis has been almost exclusively on the production process itself, and complete mechanization has come to be symbolized by the industrial robot, a machine designed to replace the production operator one by one. Actually the direct work of making or assembling is not where mechanization is likely to have the greatest effect. Direct labour accounts for only 10 to 25% of the cost of manufacturing, . . . The major challenge now, and the major opportunity for improved productivity is in organizing, scheduling and managing the total manufacturing enterprise, from product design to fabrication, distribution and field service."

and his comments remain valid today.

A second scheme of classifying the role of computers in manufacturing is to distinguish between applications at the **plant level** and those at the **operation level**. Applications at plant level include computerized production management, computerized financial and accounting systems, and Automatic Storage and Retrieval Systems (AS/RS). Applications at the operations level include CNC machines, computer supported work measurement systems, computer based semiautomatic and automatic assembly equipment, for example VCD (Variable Center Distance), DIP (Dual In-line Package), and robotic equipment for inserting components into printed circuit boards in the electronics assembly industry.

Using these two axes, namely the nature of the computer interface to the process and the level of application, a matrix of computer applications in manufacturing can be drawn up. This matrix is presented in Figure 2.1.

An interesting aspect of this framework of computer applications in manufacturing is that it also roughly defines the traditional responsibility

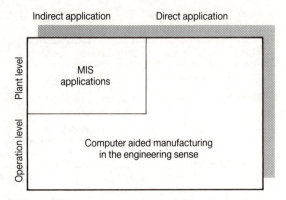

Figure 2.2 Traditional responsibilities for CAM.

within manufacturing plants for various computer based applications. This is illustrated in Figure 2.2. Traditionally MIS (Management Information Systems) or DP (Data Processing) departments have had responsibility for indirect applications at plant level, while engineering groups, both product and manufacturing, have assumed responsibility for the other areas. This has led to the frequent use by engineers of the term "Computer Aided Manufacturing" (CAM) to mean only those manufacturing areas in which engineers are involved. Perhaps this explains a frequently met view that integration is achieved when CAD/CAM integration has been realized. Seen from the perspective of the above framework, this is a narrow engineering viewpoint.

Rosenthal and Ward (1986) support this point by commenting that in many companies there are two groups:

> "(1) computer aided manufacturing (CAM) and (2) integrated manufacturing information systems for planning and control, commonly called manufacturing planning and control systems. An understanding of the nature of these sub-fields, as well as the requirements in combining them to form CIM, raise a number of . . . key implications for management . . . CAM and manufacturing planning and control systems have different organizational roots and technical orientations . . . Further, CAM and manufacturing planning and control systems are beginning to overlap in many manufacturing organizations . . . the traditional differences between MIS and CAM initiatives are beginning to be felt . . . Top management must begin to encourage an integrated response despite these traditional differences."

Leaving this discussion aside, and returning to the matrix of Figure 2.1, which included many islands of automation, we will now briefly examine some of the more important of these. Given the significant investment that these applications represent, it follows that the CIM design process must involve the recognition that these applications will not be discarded. Because of its special significance for CIM, the concept of flexible manufacturing will be discussed in greater detail in Section 2.6.

Macro planning models

At the boardroom level, corporate planning models have been used for some time. From a manufacturing point of view, these models have been developed to allow top management to understand the impact of changes in key manufacturing variables, including, for example, the level and mix of output, labour skills, new product introduction rates and levels of productivity. These models tend to represent the manufacturing system at a highly aggregated level. They can be implemented in distributed spreadsheet tools.

A typical application area for these models is Long Range Production Planning (LRPP). LRPP is concerned with "the determination, acquisition and arrangement of all of the facilities necessary for the future production of products" (Wild 1971). The output from the LRPP process would typically be a series of plans, which might list requirements for products per unit time, working capital, capital equipment, headcount in terms of quantity and skill level, space, and facilities. Such plans are frequently developed using spreadsheet tools, which allow the analyst or manager to play out various "what if" scenarios. For example, the planner might look at the requirements for labor based on a particular prediction of market demand, and analyze whether that demand could be met using overtime or subcontracting and outsourcing.

Special purpose modeling languages and packages are also available, for example, systems such as the systems dynamics approaches of Jay Forrester (1961), Roberts (1978), and Lyneis (1980). Systems dynamics uses quantitative means to investigate the dynamic behavior of systems and has been reasonably widely applied to the analysis of manufacturing problems. Towill (1991), for example, showed how systems dynamics could be used to analyze the impact of demand fluctuations on the supply chain. The model, as well as providing quantitative forecasts of the performance of the suppliers, also enabled the evaluation of possible methods for the improvement of system performance, i.e. the reduction of supply lead times and the removal of unnecessary links in the chain. Software tools, many implemented on PCs, are now widely available to support analysis using the systems dynamics approach.

Current research in this area includes the application of knowledge based approaches to this problem (see Harhen *et al.* (1987), Jackson and Browne (1992) and Kerr (1991), for example). The knowledge based approach is interesting because the process of strategic planning and, indeed, long range planning frequently involves dealing with qualitative as well as quantitative data. Decisions are frequently based as much on intuition and experience as on logic and rationality. Qualitative knowledge is extremely difficult to encode using traditional database technology and algorithmic programming languages. Thus, computer based techniques that facilitate the capture of non-numeric data and knowledge are likely to be useful. Jackson (1991) describes a system that allows high level decision makers to encapsulate their knowledge of strategic decision making in the form of a qualitative knowledge base or mind map. Relationships between objects in the knowledge base are expressed both numerically and linguistically, and include associated degrees of credibility or confidence in the relationships. Further, an inference engine was developed, which performs aggregation and subsequent propagation of qualitative relationships and their associated degrees of confidence throughout the knowledge base. The system was designed to be used in a decision support mode.

It is perhaps worth concluding this very short discussion on macro planning models and strategic planning models with a quotation from a very early paper by Little (1974), who warned against developing very complex models. Little argued that

> "We should not be surprised if he [the manager] prefers a simple analysis that he can grasp, even though it may have a qualitative structure, broad assumptions and only a little relevant data, to a complex model whose assumptions may be partially hidden, or couched in jargon and whose parameters may be the result of obscure statistical manipulations."

Computer aided process planning (CAPP)

CAPP is a computer application that supports the development and creation of the technological plan required to produce a given part. It is an important application from an integration perspective because it is a key interface between CAD and CAM. The resulting process plan consists of a statement of the sequence of operations necessary to manufacture the part, the identification of the machines on which these operations should be carried out, and the operation times. Special tooling and set-up procedures are also identified.

Until now, the majority of the work done on CAPP, has been oriented towards metal cutting applications. According to Chang (1990), the process planning function may involve several or all of the following functions:

- The selection of the appropriate machining operations.
- The sequencing of these machining operations.
- The selection of the corresponding cutting tools.
- The determination of set-up procedures.
- The calculation of the cutting parameters, including the tool speed, the tool feed rate, the use of cutting fluids, and the depth of cut.
- The planning of tool paths and the generation of part programs for the numerically controlled machines.
- The design of tools and fixtures.

Clearly, the automation of the process planner's task is by no means trivial, and currently available computer based systems are unable to deliver all of the functionality identified in the above list. Essentially, existing CAPP systems are able to offer decision support in many of the tasks identified above. In fact, there are two approaches to developing CAPP systems:

(1) The variant approach.

(2) The generative approach.

The variant approach involves the preparation of a process plan through the manipulation of a standard plan or the plan of a similar part. The process plan for the master composite part is stored in the computer and used in the planning of subsequent parts. The master part is a composite of all features likely to be seen on the parts to be planned. The variant approach uses parts classification techniques to identify features on parts and match them to equivalent features on the master part. In practice, variant process planning is implemented by using a technique known as **group technology** to identify families of parts that share similar design and manufacturing attributes. Group technology, which is discussed in some detail in Chapter 11, is an approach to manufacturing in which subsets or families of parts are grouped together to take advantage of their similarities in manufacturing and/or design. Group technology part families are often defined by using parts classification and coding systems. Essentially similar parts will have similar codes. In variant process planning a composite part is developed to represent the range of manufacturing features present in a particular family, and a composite process plan is developed for that composite part. In simple terms, when a new part is identified as belonging to a particular family an appropriate subset of the composite process plan for that family is edited to create a process plan for the new part.

The variant approach is reasonably widely used in practice, although it suffers from some important disadvantages. Clearly, the parts to be planned are limited to variations of existing parts. Furthermore, experienced process planners are required to edit the composite process plan and also to add detail to it. The second approach, namely the generative process planning method, seeks to address some of these weaknesses.

The generative approach involves the creation of the process plan from information available in the manufacturing database. This approach requires a detailed description of the part to be planned, the various manufacturing operations available, and the capabilities of these operations in terms of process accuracy, tolerances, etc. Thus, for example, in the context of a machining application, the system looks at each surface to be machined and compares the surface tolerance with that achievable using an available process. If the tolerance can be achieved by the process, then that process may be selected to produce the surface. If not, it is eliminated from further consideration.

According to Chang (1990), a generative process planning system is composed of three main elements, namely part descriptions, manufacturing databases, and algorithms and decision logic. The manufacturing databases would typically provide data on process capability, machine selection, jig and tool availability, and selection, etc. The decision logic is frequently based around decision tables and decision trees, which define the conditions that result in appropriate process planning decisions or actions; for example, a certain size and tolerance of hole (conditions) in a part would result in a particular set of process planning decisions, say a particular combination of drilling and reaming operations (actions). Algorithms are used to calculate particular cutting conditions including, for example, tool speeds, number of passes of the tool, tool feed, depth of cut, tool life calculations, etc. For a fuller treatment of generative process planning the interested reader is referred to Chang (1990) and Wang and Li (1991). These references provide reasonably complete descriptions of generative process planning systems.

In recent times, researchers have begun to prototype CAPP systems using Artificial Intelligence (AI) techniques, for example the work of Descotte and Latombe (1981, 1985) and Bowden and Browne (1987). CAPP has many features that make it an appropriate application area for knowledge based systems. The process planner uses knowledge of the various manufacturing processes, machines and tools required to carry out particular operations, as well as knowledge in the form of experience gained from planning previous parts. AI tools provide the capability to represent such knowledge efficiently and control its application to the process planning problem. For example, knowledge representation techniques borrowed from AI technology and reasonably widely used in knowledge based CAPP systems include production rules (IF condition(s) – THEN action(s)) used to represent decision table type logic and procedural knowledge and semantic networks and frames used to represent objects and their associated attributes (milling cutter M01 has a length of 2 cm). AI techniques find particular application in generative process planning systems.

As we observed earlier, by and large computer based process planning systems have been developed mainly for machining applications. Few applications have been realized in assembly. Unlike machining and fabrication, where well-defined standardized operations have been in place for years, there is no widely accepted categorization of assembly operations. Assembly process planning relies heavily on the experience of the process planner and the industry in which the planner is working. Thus, expert systems designed to support assembly process planning tend to be intelligent decision support systems, with the process planner making the final selection of the operations. Browne *et al.* (1991) outline one example of such an approach. An alternative approach to assembly process planning seeks to develop a multistage system, which tries to determine the interfaces between components, evaluate the handleability of the assembly parts, analyze the accessibility of these parts, select the base parts, and finally determine the sequence of assembly operations. The procedure is made complex because of the difficulty of applying geometric reasoning to assembly tasks, the range of possible surface relationships between individual components and the range of possible assembly structures (see Wang and Li 1991).

Probably the most interesting problem in the area of CAPP is that of integrating CAPP systems with CAD and CAM systems. The integration problem is significant, and involves consideration of the transfer of data between design and manufacturing systems, as well as consideration of such issues as the role and positioning of Design for Manufacture (DFM) and Design for Assembly (DFA) analysis. From a functional point of view, the process planning system lies at the heart of the transition from the design to the manufacture of the product. Earlier, in Chapter 1, during our discussion on reduced product life cycles, we pointed to the competitive pressures for faster time to market for new products. Clearly, an integrated CAD, CAPP, and CAM system greatly facilitates time to market. In Chapter 4 this discussion is taken further when integrated manufacturing and the emergence of concepts such as time base competition and concurrent engineering are discussed.

Automatic storage and retrieval systems (AS/RS)

An AS/RS (sometimes referred to as an automated warehouse) is a system which stores and retrieves materials using automatic stacker cranes under computer control. The system identifies each arriving pallet, typically using bar code technology, selects an appropriate open location on the storage racks, and directs the stacker crane to route the pallet to that location. When a request is made to retrieve a stored pallet, the computer identifies the storage location, and directs the stacker crane to the specified location for retrieval. Rygh (1980) claimed the following benefits for an AS/RS over conventional warehousing methods:

- improved floor space utilization,
- reduced direct labor cost,
- virtually 100% accuracy in inventory measurement,
- reduced pilferage,
- lower energy consumption,
- reduced product damage,
- improved customer service.

Computer aided design (CAD)

CAD involves the use of computer hardware and software to assist the designer in the storage, manipulation, analysis, and reproduction of his/her design ideas. Modern engineering CAD systems allow designers to produce 3D (three dimensional) geometric models. These geometric models may be constructed using wireframe models, surface models or solid models.

Wireframe models represent the edges of products by lines. In fact, they are the simplest form of model from both the computational and user perspectives. They are useful when dealing with simple shapes and with the relative motion of reasonably simple shapes, but suffer from serious problems when used to model more complex products or components. Models can be difficult to interpret, and can even be ambiguous. Further, the wireframe model does not facilitate detailed analysis of the mechanical properties of the product or component, for example the calculation of mass and inertial properties or the analysis of stress or thermal flows using finite element analysis.

Surface models overcome many of the difficulties associated with wireframe models, and allow the faces of a component to be built up so that it can be represented by all of its faces in the form of a shell. The representation is based on a set of geometric entities including planes, cylinders, so-called swept surfaces, etc.

Solid models allow the true 3D geometry of a part to be represented, in the sense that the solid model is geometrically and mathematically complete. Complete means that the designer can calculate the mass of the design, determine its volume, check clearances and tolerances, determine the center of gravity of the part, calculate its moments of inertia, and even take sections through it. McMahon and Browne (1993) suggest that solid models are a natural extension from the use of essentially "one dimensional" entities (lines and curves) or "two dimensional" entities (surfaces) to the construction of models using 3D solids. The so-called Constructive Solid Geometry (CSG) approach to solid modeling illustrates this well. In the CSG approach, models are constructed using a combination of simple solid primitive shapes or primitives, such as cylinders, cubes, spheres, etc. Using simple Boolean operators, such as union, intersection and difference, quite complex products can be modeled by combining available primitives.

As might be expected with this rich functionality, solid modelers are very expensive and require significant computer resources. However, the representation that solid models provide is complete and unambiguous, and consequently allows the analysis necessary to, for example, check for interference between parts that are to be assembled together.

Another approach to modeling, which differs radically from the three approaches just discussed, is feature based modeling. A feature has been defined formally as "any perceived geometric or functional element or property of a object useful in understanding the function, behaviour or performance of that object" (see Browne *et al.* 1992). Thus, features are higher level entities than the geometric entities use in solid models.

Typically, feature based CAD systems offer the designer a library of features to choose from and also the possibly of adding user defined features to that library. In many cases the features are defined in terms that facilitate automated process planning. In fact the notion of feature based design seems to have arisen from consideration of process planning issues; one of the big advantages of a feature based design system is that it facilitates automated process planning and the integration of process planning with design, thus partially realizing concurrent engineering. Thus, for example, a system used to design machined parts might include in its library features such as hole, flat surface, boss, etc. For a more detailed treatment of this topic, see McMahon and Browne (1993). For a discussion on the integration of CAD, CAPP, and DFA see Molloy *et al.* (1993).

Robotics

A robot is a reprogrammable multifunctional manipulator, designed to move material, parts, tools or specialized devices through variable programmed motions, for the performance of a variety of tasks. The manipulator is the arm of the robot, and it might typically take one of perhaps six configurations; namely cartesian, polar, cylindrical, gantry, jointed arm, and SCARA (Selective Compliance Assembly Robot Arm). At the end of the arm or manipulator a device or **end effector** is fitted. The end effector takes different forms depending on the tasks that the robot is intended to undertake. It might be a simple gripper or a complex welding gun or spray paint dispenser. Clearly, the mechanical system (manipulator and end effector) must be controlled in order to accomplish particular tasks. The robot control system positions the manipulator and orients the end effector with defined speed and precision. The control system, normally using position and velocity based servomechanisms, drives the robot actuators and power transmission systems. Actuators include pneumatic, hydraulic, and – more frequently – electric motors. The power developed by these actuators is normally transmitted to the robot arm joints using gears or pulleys. So-called direct drive systems also exist.

Of course, the key point about the robot is that it is a programmable device. The robot program defines the motions which the robot arm and end effector must undertake in order to complete a defined task. Robots can be programmed in a number of ways. Leadthrough programming allows the programmer to take the robot through the required steps, automatically recording the steps (in terms of the positions and orientations of the individual robot joints) in the controller memory for subsequent playback. In this way, the robot can be taught "best practice" in tasks such as spray painting or spot welding of car bodies.

Robot programming languages have also been developed by robot manufacturers. These languages, frequently similar to English in basic syntax, allow the programmer to specify, for example, the moves made by individual axes of the robot to defined points in space, the speed and timing of these moves, the interpretation of data coming from external sensors which might influence the actions of the robot, etc. Off-line programming of robots is also possible; essentially, the robot program can be prepared off-line at a computer and then downloaded to the robot controller. Further, off-line systems are available which integrate with CAD/CAM systems and include software emulators which allow the robot programmer to test the program and to test for possible difficulties such as collisions between the robot arm and fixtures or components in the work area, prior to downloading it to the robot controller. For a detailed discussion on robot technology, see Malcolm (1988), Tzafestas (1991) or Rembold (1990).

Robot applications (see Williams 1988) can be found in virtually all branches of industry, particularly in the automotive, electrical, electronic, and mechanical engineering sectors. The major application areas across these industries are spot welding, arc welding, surface coating, including spray painting, and servicing machines which includes the loading and unloading of machine tools, die casting machines, forging presses, and plastic injection molding machines. An early survey (Sanderson *et al.* 1982) designed to determine the basis for installing robots in industry indicated the following reasons in decreasing order of importance:

- To reduce labor cost.
- To replace people working in dangerous or hazardous conditions.
- To provide a more flexible production system.
- To achieve more consistent control of quality.
- To increase output.
- To compensate for a local shortage of skilled labor.

It is fair to say that these reasons are still largely valid today. Although robot technology has advanced considerably in the past 10 years it is true to say that the present generation of robots is more or less restricted to working in highly structured environments. Essentially, the present generation of robots consists of programmable devices with limited external sensing capability, in the sense that they are largely unable to respond to unpredicted events in their environment. In fact, their flexibility is limited in that all but the most advanced robots are unable to deal with their environment in an intelligent way. For this reason, the vast majority are involved in relatively primitive, simple and repetitive manufacturing tasks. The emerging generation of robots is *intelligent* in that they have built-in sensor systems capable of detecting changes in their working environment and responding to them in an appropriate way. The use of intelligent sensors, such as vision or tactile sensors, means that robots, which up to now have been limited to performing structured, highly repetitive operations, will be better able to react to changes in their working environments. However, present-day industrial robot technology is still at a very early stage of development, and the robots portrayed in fiction with advanced levels of mobility and intelligence are still technologically and economically infeasible.

It seems that the research efforts in the area of robotics are moving in two directions. One clear direction of research is to develop robots capable of adapting to changes in their immediate work environment, through the use of sophisticated sensors and associated tools and grippers. A second important research direction is the integration of robots into manufacturing systems. Clearly, robots are important components of flexible automation systems and, therefore, of integrated manufacturing systems. Efforts are under way to create software tools which support the planning and development of robot based manufacturing and assembly systems and the programming of robotized systems. One such effort, directed at robotized assembly systems, is described by Bernhardt *et al.* (1992). The integrated procedure starts with the generation of an assembly sequence plan, which includes assembly sequence planning, precedence analysis, preselection of robots suitable for the different assembly steps, and selection of available feeders and grippers. A proposed workstation layout is then suggested based on the assembly sequence plan and this is evaluated. The proposed layout is considered using supporting tools which evaluate cycle times and consider material flow and capacity issues using simulation techniques. Once the overall layout has been determined a layout optimization procedure is used to consider component type variants and the precise location of robots, tools, and various peripheral devices. Finally, the data generated in the planning system is transformed into a structure suitable for an offline programming procedure.

2.6 Flexible manufacturing and assembly systems

Because of the special significance of Flexible Manufacturing Systems (FMS) and Flexible Assembly Systems (FAS) within manufacturing, FMS and FAS will be dealt with at some length in this section.

A flexible manufacturing system is an integrated computer controlled system of automated material handling devices and CNC machine tools, that can simultaneously process medium sized volumes of a variety of parts. An FMS, therefore, incorporates many different automation concepts into one system. These include:

- Numerical Control (NC) and Computer Numerical Control (CNC).
- Robotic process equipment.
- DNC control of the material handling system and the individual CNC machines.

- Automatic material handling.
- Automatic tool changing.
- Automatic machine loading and unloading.

Parts enter and leave the FMS at a central location and the material handling system automatically transports the parts to the machines identified by the process plan or routing. The routing for each part, and the operations required to produce it, differ across the range of products. This routing is finally determined within the FMS by a scheduler which has access to the product data and the requirements schedule. It can thus determine on which machines a part should be processed next. Knowing this, the scheduling algorithm or heuristic generates the required schedule.

The control of the FMS is exercised by a computer, or perhaps a hierarchy of computers. The control system is responsible for scheduling work within the FMS and coordinating the material handling system and the machines to meet this schedule. The programs required to produce the parts are downloaded to the individual CNC machines. Orders are transmitted to the materials handling system, detailing which part should be moved to each location. The computer also has the responsibility for producing reports on the operation of the FMS. Data is gathered from each of the machines and this is collated into system reports. Hierarchical scheduling systems for flexible manufacturing systems are described by Akella *et al.* (1984).

The development of FMS is important because, in a sense, an FMS can be considered a mini-CIM system. FMSs are designed to fill the gap between high volume hard automation transfer lines and CNC machines. On the one hand, transfer lines are very efficient at producing parts in large volumes at high output rates, with the important limitation that the parts be identical. These highly mechanized lines are very inflexible and will not tolerate variations in part design. The CNC machine, on the other hand, offers great inherent flexibility through its ability to be reprogrammed to machine parts of varying contours and sizes. The FMS lies somewhere between these two extremes, as indicated in Figure 2.3.

Furthermore, the term FMS covers a range of systems including single machine Flexible Manufacturing Cells (FMC) through to Flexible Transfer Lines (FTL) and the FMS itself, which consists of a group of FMCs and/or CNC machines connected through an automated materials handling system. (See Stecke and Browne (1985) for further details.) The definition of flexibility in the context of FMS is important. Browne *et al.* (1984) identified and defined eight types of flexibility in the context of FMS.

(1) Machine flexibility refers to the ease of making the changes required to produce a given set of part types.

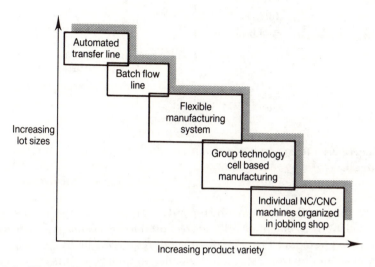

Figure 2.3 The applicability of FMS.

(2) Process flexibility refers to the ability to produce a mix of jobs.

(3) Product flexibility refers to the ability to change over to produce new products very economically and quickly.

(4) Routing flexibility refers to the ability to handle breakdowns and to continue producing a given set of part types.

(5) Volume flexibility refers to the ability to operate the FMS profitably at different production volumes.

(6) Expansion flexibility refers to the capability of expanding a given FMS, as needed, easily and in a modular fashion.

(7) Operation flexibility is the ability to interchange the ordering of several operations for each part type.

(8) Production flexibility refers to the universe of part types which the FMS can produce.

Clearly some of these types of flexibility are related (see Browne *et al.*, 1984). Figure 2.4 indicates the dependency relationship among the various flexibility types. The arrows in this figure signify the relationship *necessary for*.

Butcher (1986) describes an FMS for the production of aero-engine disc components, installed at Rolls-Royce in the UK. The objectives set for the FMS were to "cut work in progress by two thirds, compress production lead times from 20 to 6 weeks and increase manpower productivity by over 40%". The installation of the CNC machines for the FMS reduced the number of operations from 21 to 5. The machine tool population within the plant was halved from 62 to 31 machines and the scrap rate

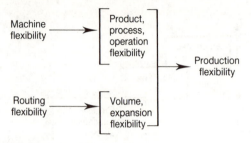

Figure 2.4 Relationship between flexibilities.

was reduced by 40%. Westkamper (1986) describes the results of FMS installations at one of MBB's aircraft production plants in Germany. Lead times were reduced by 25%, floor space requirements by 42%, the number of machines by over 50%, and personnel by over 50%. It is clear, even from these two examples, that the characteristics of FMS are somewhat similar to the likely characteristics of the *factory of the future*, namely, a small number of multifunction production machines, low WIP (work in progress), short lead times and very low labor content. These characteristics will be discussed in more detail in Chapter 3.

According to Owen (1984), the primary function of an FMS is the removal or shaping of metal to produce a component, while the primary function of an FAS is the processing of components and materials into a product. The emphasis in an FAS is on the compatibility of the components in order to achieve high assembly rates, and the automatic testing of components and assemblies. Owen defines an FAS as "a computer controlled automated assembly system for converting raw materials and components into products of a known and desirable functional quality." Owen claims that assembly is a major activity within industry, accounting for 53% of the time and 22% of the total labor incurred in the manufacture of a typical product. Hall and Stecke (1986) offer a definition of an FAS which is analogous to the definition of FMS: "An FAS is a computer-integrated manufacturing system consisting of automated materials handling devices and workstations that can simultaneously assemble a variety of part types." Each robotic workstation or cell in an FAS is flexible and performs a wide variety of operations, enabling the system to simultaneously assemble different low volume part types. For a discussion on the differences between FMS and FAS, the interested reader is referred to Kusiak (1990).

In the past, many people have underestimated the complexity of the assembly task. Williams (1988) provides an interesting perspective on this issue. To indicate the complexity of a typical assembly operation, he examines the skills which a human operator brings to the assembly of two simple objects:

"First the person will locate, using vision, the two objects, one at a time. Then he will move first one hand to grip one part and then the other hand to grip the other. Using vision once again (and his manual dexterity) the person will bring the two objects together. He will then begin to put them together, first monitoring their relative position with his eyes, correcting this relative position with his hands and then detecting when they contact by using force sensing in his hands."

Essentially, we are talking about skills of manual dexterity, vision, eye–hand coordination and sophisticated sensing capability in the hands and fingers, not to mention an overall ability to adapt readily to changes in the working environment, through, for example, misplaced or missing components, tools or fixtures, faulty components, etc. It is not surprising that the automation of relatively common manual assembly tasks has proved more difficult and expensive that might appear at first sight.

The application of FAS technology in industry is very sector dependent. In some sectors, such as high volume electronic assembly and the mass production of consumer goods, the technology is widely used. In other sectors, for example, medium volume assembly of electromechanical products, the technology is virtually unused. Many electronic assembly processes, e.g. the high volume assembly of Surface Mounted Technology (SMT) components in the computer and office equipment industries, would be impossible without FAS technology.

The design of FASs is a complex task; frequently more complex than the design of an FMS because of the nature of the workstations, assembly robots, parts presentation, and parts feeding subsystems required. Also, the cycle times in FASs tend in general to be much shorter than those of FMSs. Frequently, computer based workflow simulation models are used to configure FAS systems and to detail the design in terms of buffer sizes, workstation capacities, cycle times, etc. Graphic simulators are used to configure individual assembly workcells and to check for parts clearance and interference between the various elements of the cell. For a case study of the use of a workflow simulator in the design of an FAS, see Browne and Timon (1991).

2.7 Conclusion

In this chapter, we reviewed the various stages of the application of automation to manufacturing. On the way, it was pointed out that a holistic approach is necessary in the design of integrated systems. Brief descriptions were presented of some of the important islands of automation to be seen in manufacturing firms today, with particular emphasis on flexible manufacturing systems. This has all served to act as a foundation for the discussion of computer integrated manufacturing, which follows in Chapter 3.

Questions

(2.1) "Since the CIM problem is primarily about integration, it follows that a holistic approach using organic work structures may well be necessary to attain a workable solution." Discuss.

(2.2) Distinguish between point automation and islands of automation.

(2.3) "For many manufacturers, islands of automation represent the current state of manufacturing integration. The proliferation of such locally expanding islands of automation has given rise to the CIM problem." Discuss.

(2.4) Distinguish clearly between direct and indirect applications of the computer in manufacturing.

(2.5) "The major challenge now, and the major opportunity for improved productivity is in organizing, scheduling, and managing the total manufacturing enterprise, from product design to fabrication, distribution, and field service." Comment.

(2.6) What are the essential differences between the variant and the generative approaches to computer aided process planning?

(2.7) Why is assembly process planning (as distinct from process planning for machining) so complex and difficult to support with computer based tools?

(2.8) "Solid models are a natural extension from the use of essentially one dimensional entities (lines and curves) to two dimensional (surfaces) to the construction of models using three dimensional solids." Discuss.

(2.9) What do you understand by the term feature based modeling?

(2.10) "The present generation of robots is largely restricted to working in highly structured environments." Comment.

(2.11) What do you understand by the word *flexible* in the term *flexible manufacturing system*?

(2.12) "The design of an FAS is a complex task; frequently more complex than the design of an FMS." Why?

CHAPTER THREE

Computer integrated manufacturing

3.1 Introduction

Over the next two chapters we will look at advanced manufacturing systems. In particular we will discuss Computer Integrated Manufacturing (CIM) and Computer Integrated Business (CIB) and the **extended enterprise**. Further, we will try to focus in particular on the role of Production Management Systems (PMS) in CIM and future manufacturing systems. Our perspective is as follows. Manufacturing is a practised activity. Further, the term *manufacturing* represents a range of activities within a wide range of industrial sectors and across a wide variety of company sizes. It is difficult to characterize the state of the art in manufacturing in general. One must distinguish between the state of the art as understood in university and industry research laboratory pilot projects and the state of the art as practised in different industrial sectors. In addition, the state of the art in manufacturing is constantly changing. Our understanding of the very nature of manufacturing systems, and, in particular, our understanding of integrated manufacturing is, at the time of writing, incomplete and evolving. Our definition of integrated manufacturing is also evolving; indeed, whether the term CIM is still the best term to use is now an open question.

For the purposes of this book, and of Chapters 3 and 4 in particular, we will adopt the following approach. In this chapter we will talk about CIM and present some definitions and models of CIM systems. In Chapter 4 we will look beyond CIM systems and present some of the more recent and still evolving ideas of future manufacturing systems. Essentially, our view is as follows: CIM represents an attempt at integration inside the "four walls" of the factory. The emerging thinking, which we will call CIB and the extended enterprise, considers integration across the value chain;

integration, on the one hand, between the suppliers and the manufacturing plant, and on the other hand, between the manufacturing plant and its customers. In each case (CIM and CIB) we will concentrate on the PMS aspects of the integration problem.

3.2 What is CIM?

CIM represents the integrated application of computer technology to manufacturing in order to achieve the objectives of the firm. In this chapter, some of the characteristics of the CIM environment are identified. The goal is not to specify a CIM architecture, but instead to describe various viewpoints of CIM. In this manner a position will be approached from which the role of a PMS within CIM can be discussed. Readers interested in a more technical discussion of CIM from an architectural point of view are referred to such sources as the ESPRIT (European Strategic Programme for Research and Development in Information Technology) publications, for instance Yeomans *et al.* (1985), Harrington (1984), Sheer (1988) and the work done within the CIM OSA (CIM Open Systems Architecture) project of ESPRIT.

This section initially focuses on the nature of CIM by outlining some definitions of the term as offered by some leading authorities in the field. Some time is then devoted to discussing CIM from various functional perspectives, paying particular attention to the PMS function. We also examine some models of CIM, which received reasonably wide acceptance in the 1980s.

3.2.1 The nature of CIM

CIM seeks to achieve in discrete parts manufacturing the type of integration already achieved in many continuous process industries, such as steel making and oil refining. There are many reasons for the emergence of CIM. Ultimately it is driven by the desire to apply ever increasing levels of automation to the manufacturing system in order to attain improved productivity. Japanese competition has spurred on the western industrial nations to great efforts to achieve this. The ever decreasing cost of computer technology has accelerated this process.

In factories we can see that existing islands of automation are beginning to overlap and compete with each other for the right to perform certain tasks within the factory. For example, a manufacturing plant considering the implementation of a Manufacturing Resource Planning system (MRP II) and an Automated Storage and Retrieval System (AS/RS) will typically deal with two different vendors. Moreover, plant inventory status can be monitored by either or both of the two systems. The user of this technology is faced with the need for adequately defined communications between the systems, or else has to live with some degree of duplicate data entry and all of its consequences in terms of effort and possibility of error.

It is worth exploring for a moment the **islands of automation** concept, which was certainly very widely presented and use in the 1980s. The notion of an island of automation emerged from the development of a series of technical solutions to problems in manufacturing industry. Indeed, many of the types of computer based systems described in Chapter 2 – for example, CAD systems, computer aided process planning systems, robots, and AS/RS – could be described as islands of automation, in that they are solutions developed in isolation to solve specific and well-defined problems or to automate particular processes or procedures. Many people went on with this model to consider integration, and therefore CIM, in terms of interfacing between these existing islands of automation. Thus, for example, systems were developed to take the output (e.g. the component description in terms of geometry for a machined or formed part) from a CAD system and prepare the part programme for the appropriate Computer Numerically Controlled (CNC) machine directly from it.

Interfacing islands of automation which have been designed in isolation will always be problematic. The research programs into CIM are attempting to alleviate these problems by redesigning the modules of the manufacturing system with a view towards full integration. Authors such as Miller *et al.* (1986) identified three types of integration which are necessary, namely technical integration, procedural integration, and goal integration. Technical integration is concerned with the activity of establishing electronic communication between different functional areas – issues such as communication channels, communication protocols, and standards. The emergence of MAP (Manufacturing Application Protocol) and TOP (The Office Protocol) has greatly facilitated the technical integration of islands of automation (see Dwyer and Ioannou (1987) for a review of MAP and TOP). Procedural integration is achieved when the different functional groups which share data have a consistent view of how to interpret that data and thus are able to use appropriate shared procedures. The highest level of integration is referred to as goal integration, which is considered to have been achieved when different functional areas (or islands) use the shared data and information to achieve shared common goals.

Thus it seems that CIM, at least as conceived in the 1980s, seems to involve the integration of the various islands of automation into a coherent whole. Although a number of definitions have been put forward, no strong agreement has been reached on the scope of CIM. CIM is an industry driven technology, with each branch of industry conditioned by its own particular set of experiences, requirements, and circumstances. Furthermore, it is clear that an industrial company seeking to realize CIM, will have to take account of its own existing investment in *islands of automation,* often referred to as legacy systems, before planning an evolution towards CIM. Because of all these circumstances, descriptions of CIM tend to be highly dependent on the background and perspective of the individuals offering them. The following are some examples of statement describing CIM.

> "A closed loop feedback system whose prime inputs are product requirements and product concepts and whose prime outputs are finished products. It comprises a combination of software and hardware, product design, production planning, production control, production equipment and production processes."
>
> Merchant (1977)

> "The logical organization of individual engineering, production and marketing/support functions into a computer integrated system. Functional areas, such as design, inventory control, physical distribution, cost accounting, planning and purchasing, are integrated with direct materials management and shop floor data acquisition and control. Thus the loop is closed between the shop floor and its controlling activities. Shop floor machines serve as data acquisition devices for the control system and often its direct command . . ."
>
> Anon (1981)

> "Computer integrated system involving the overall and systematic computerization of the manufacturing process. Such systems will integrate computer aided design, computer aided manufacture and computer aided engineering, testing, repair and assembly by means of a common database."
>
> ESPRIT, Commission of the European Communities (1982)

> "The integrated application of computer based automation and decision support systems to manage the total operation of the manufacturing system, from product design through the manufacturing process itself, and finally on to distribution; and including production and inventory management, as well as financial resource management."
>
> Harhen and Browne (1984)

We indicated earlier that the understanding of the CIM problem depends on the background and perspective of the individual looking at the problem. In Figure 3.1 some of the differing perspectives offered on CIM are presented.

Consider a pure engineering perspective. Engineers tend to see CIM primarily in terms of CAD/CAM integration, as illustrated in Figure 3.2. CIM from this perspective is dominated by the Computer Aided Engineering (CAE) task.

CAE has a view of CIM that is a partial reality in some industries today, e.g. VLSI (Very Large Scale Integration) fabrication and, to a lesser extent, electronics assembly. There are greater difficulties in realizing CIM in the mechanical engineering industry, where the major difficulty is the interface between CAD, CAPP, and NC programming. Much research is under way to develop systems that overcome these problems, integrating, for example, CAD and robot programming systems.

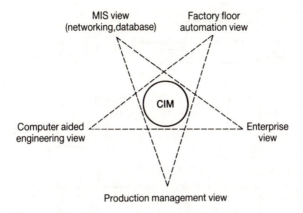

Figure 3.1   Different perspectives on CIM.

In the domain of CAE, there is increasing awareness of the need for *design for production and assembly*. There is a consequent necessity for the manufacturing function to influence the design process and to ensure that the designers are aware of the effects of various design features on the ease of manufacture of a part. A good description of the issues is contained in Boothroyd and Dewhurst (1983).

In the medium term, the benefit of an integrated CAD/CAM facility is the reduction in the lead time from initial design concept to the manufactured product. This greatly reduced design cycle provides industry with the facility to respond quickly and economically to changes in the marketplace.

If CIM is viewed from the point of view of the PMS, a very different picture is obtained, as illustrated in Figure 3.3. The system is

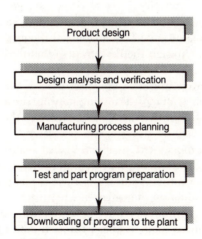

Figure 3.2   CAE view of CIM.

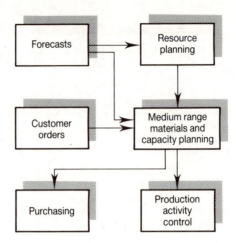

Figure 3.3   PMS view of CIM.

essentially seen as a hierarchy of scheduling systems. The resource planning system is concerned with setting long range aggregate production programs and resource needs. Medium range materials and capacity planning is typically an information systems function that converts the master schedule into a more detailed plan for the medium range, using appropriate batching techniques for planning both production and material acquisition. Material Requirements Planning (MRP) is a good example of such a system. The management of the satisfaction of actual customer orders is achieved at this level as well. The lowest level in the PMS involves the execution systems, such as the production activity control system and the purchasing system.

The Production Activity Control (PAC) system plays a particularly important role within the CIM system. The PAC system manages the flow of material and the associated flow of data through the plant (see Figure 3.4). Essentially, it is through the PAC system that the PMS is linked to the factory floor.

If CIM is viewed from the point of view of the material flow, then the CIM issue becomes one of designing appropriate material flows across the various stages of manufacturing. This involves the specification of the manufacturing process, as well as the provision of effective means to execute the material movement, as illustrated in Figure 3.5.

Figure 3.6 presents a unified view of CIM. The connection with sales and marketing occurs through the master planning and order entry functions within production management.

The lines of communication highlight the integration of these functions and the closed loop feedback through data collection to production management and other systems. In summary, computer integrated

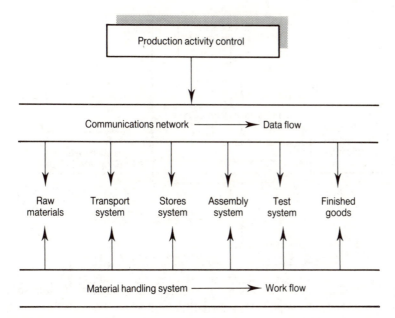

Figure 3.4 PAC and the factory floor.

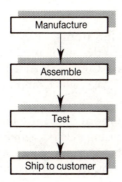

Figure 3.5 Material flow view.

manufacturing is the functional integration of the following functions, served by computer communications and data storage facilities:

- **Administration and financial systems** The administration and financial systems cover order invoicing, long range planning, and budgeting within the organization. These systems are concerned with the costing of production and materials, and control of administrative and financial aspects of the firm.

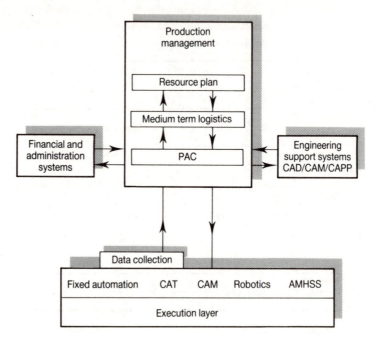

Figure 3.6 CIM and its constituent functions.

- **Engineering support systems** Engineering and support systems are concerned with the design of products and the development of processes. Included are Computer Aided Design (CAD), Computer Aided Engineering (CAE), and Computer Aided Process Planning (CAPP).

- **Production management** The production management function coordinates manufacturing related activities in order to achieve an appropriate balance between the goals of customer service, process efficiency, and minimum inventory investment.

- **Execution layer systems** The execution layer systems are those computer based applications which directly affect the execution of production. Examples are Computer Aided Test (CAT) and Automated Material Handling Systems (AMHS).

It is no coincidence that the PAC system is represented as the heart of the CIM system. This, in the authors' opinion, is the key function within CIM at the operational level. It represents the gateway between the planning functions of PMS and CIM, and the manufacturing process. Plans flow downward through this gateway and data detailing progress flows upward. Because of its central importance in the realization of CIM at the operational level, Section 3.5 devotes considerable effort to describing the PMS and, in particular, the role of the PAC system within the CIM environment. Before doing so, however, we consider it worth reviewing some of the more interesting "models" of CIM developed in the mid-1980s, and which reflect well the perception of CIM which was widely accepted at that time.

3.2.2   Models of CIM

Three CIM models developed in the 1980s, each of which achieved reasonably wide acceptance, are now reviewed briefly. We believe that these models reflect to varying degrees the notion of interfacing or integrating between islands of automation, and although they are a little out of date now (see Chapter 4) they represent important milestones in the development of our understanding of the nature of integrated manufacturing systems. The models reviewed are those of Harrington (1984), Yeomans et al. (1985), and Sheer (1988).

Harrington argued that the "structure of the science of manufacturing is the same, whether one is making aeroplanes, carpets, computers, canned soups, automobiles, paper clips, electric motors, washing machines, typewriters, lead pencils, newspapers, pianos, clocks, shoes or television sets. The same basic functions are performed, the same basic managerial controls must be exercised." Interestingly, although he identified the context within which manufacturing takes place in terms of four basic functions, namely managing the enterprise, manufacturing the products, marketing the products and supporting corporate activities, Harrington developed a model of the manufacturing function only. This "isolation" of the manufacturing function confirms the "four walls of the factory" view of CIM which was prevalent in the 1980s and which we referred to earlier.

Harrington went on to analyze the basic functions and to present his analysis using a modeling tool called IDEF0. IDEF0 is one tool within a family of tools which facilitate the creation of activity or functional models (IDEF0), data models (IDEF1), and dynamic – that is, time based – models (IDEF1x). IDEF0 is a graphical technique based on two principles; firstly, a hierarchical top-down decomposition from the general to the specific; and secondly, an identification of the activities which occur at each level and a specification of those activities in terms of their inputs, outputs, constraints, and the mechanisms available to carry out each activity. Harrington's model, which extended to four levels, offered a useful structuring of the generic functions found in a typical manufacturing facility. Jagdev (1981) developed a similar model, with the important difference that he concentrated on the production planning and control aspects of manufacturing and developed his model in much greater depth.

The approach of Yeomans et al. (1985) is a little different to that of Harrington. Their approach was the result of a European project, funded within the ESPRIT framework, involving a consortium of industrial and academic partners, whose objective was to develop "design rules" for CIM systems. Their thinking, which was deeply rooted in advanced industrial practice, can be summarized as follows. Although CIM comprises many separate modules or subsystems, there is no generally agreed subsystem structure. Thus different vendors or suppliers of subsystems package their products in different ways, and manufacturing companies experience great difficulty in incorporating products from different vendors into a single composite integrated manufacturing operation. The principle objective of the study which was the basis of the book by Yeomans *et al.* was to propose a European CIM systems structure. To achieve this the study addressed three separate but related goals:

(1) "To modularize the total CIM into functionally discrete subsystems.

(2) To describe the minimum functional specification of each subsystem.

(3) To identify the relationships that exist between any one CIM subsystem and all of the other subsystems."

Given the resources available to the project, it was necessary to restrict its scope. Clearly, it is virtually impossible to provide CIM structures which address all of the needs of all of the branches of manufacturing industry. Thus the model presented was restricted to activities directly related to the design and manufacture of machined products and components in the mechanical engineering sector. The functions addressed are those normally described as the "engineering" activities of a company and included CAD (Computer Aided Design), CAPE (Computer Aided Production Engineering), CAM (Computer Aided Manufacture), CAST (Computer Aided Storage and Transportation), and CAPP.

Yeomans *et al.* argued that the ordering and structuring of CIM systems requires the creation of two types of rules, namely **design rules** and **maxims**. Design rules relate to a particular subsystem and interface and are principally concerned with defining the functional scope of individual subsystems. Maxims are rules which have universal applicability across all subsystems and interfaces. Yeomans *et al.* developed maxims in three areas, namely processing, data, and communications.

In our view, the design rules and the approach used to derive them represent the most interesting element of this work. Initially, flowcharts were developed for each of the functions (CAD, CAM, etc.) identified above. These flowcharts presented in chronological sequence the various activities, procedures, and, ultimately, tasks which need to be carried out in order to take a product from the conceptual design stage through to final manufacture. The individual tasks were grouped into logical activities, which were considered to be CIM subsystems. The identification of activities as CIM subsystems took into account two important factors, namely

functionality and **processability**. Functionality refers to the identification of logical procedural breaks in activities, processability to the recognition of differing processing (essentially CPU and memory) requirements. Subsystem interfaces were then described for each of the subsystems, by identifying the various data inputs and outputs for each subsystem and also determining which subsystem has prime responsibility for each data element.

The model of Sheer (1988) differs from those of Harrington and Yeomans *et al.* in that it is more academic in nature and concentrates on integration of what are termed the "operational and technical tasks of an industrial enterprise." In fact, in the very first page of his book Sheer defines CIM as follows: "CIM refers to the integrated processing requirements for the technical and operational tasks of an industrial enterprise." The operational tasks, as seen by Sheer, relate to the production planning and control system, while the technical tasks are characterized by a series of subsystems including CAD, CAE, CAM including NC programming. process planning, etc. Again, we have the integration of islands of automation syndrome which we talked about earlier. Sheer also shares some of the ideas of Yeomans *et al.* when he talks about the challenge to "hardware and software producers to coordinate their separately developed systems for technical and business use."

3.3 The role of the production management system in CIM

The Production Management System (PMS) lies at the heart of the CIM system. It regulates the pulse of the manufacturing system at the operational level through its decisions of what and when to buy and make. This section is devoted to describing the role of the PMS within CIM. Initially, we shall look at the hierarchical nature of manufacturing planning. Secondly, we shall explore the role of the manufacturing process organization and its impact upon the nature of the production management system. Finally, as has been seen, the PAC system is the main gateway between the PMS and the rest of the CIM system. Consequently, the remainder of the chapter is devoted to discussing how PAC is interfaced with other islands of automation and thus facilitates the achievement of CIM.

3.3.1 Overview of production management systems

Manufacturing planning can be viewed as a hierarchical process. The hierarchy of planning and control functions in manufacturing extends from the corporate charter down to the real-time control aspects of PAC. This hierarchy is illustrated in Figure 3.7. The distinguishing features at each level are the time horizon employed and the level of detail used in representing planning information.

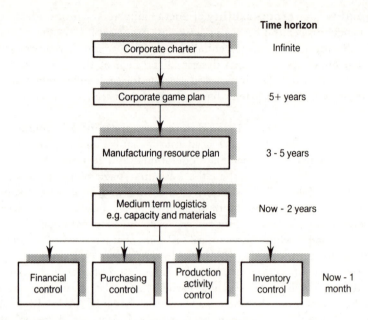

Figure 3.7 The hierarchy of manufacturing planning.

The corporate charter is a statement of the fundamental goals and policies of the organization and, as such, can be considered as having an infinite time horizon. This statement includes reference to the market in which the organization operates, its relationship with its employees, and its policy towards growth, profit, and quality.

The corporate game plan is a statement of the operating goals that will guide the organization for the next five years or more. It is corporate by nature. Included are quantitative statements about product strategy, manufacturing strategy, global investment strategy, growth of sales, and market share. This is developed with the aid of financial, manufacturing, and marketing macro-models.

The manufacturing resource plan is a quantitative statement of requirements, in terms of people, plant, inventory, and finance, for three to five years ahead. It can be plant focused or corporate focused. It is determined by the time phased explosion of a gross top level production plan. It allows for the design of hiring programs, plant construction programs, and the planning of the provision of long term finance. The production plan that drives the manufacturing resource planning system must be in tune with the market plan over the same time horizon. Collectively, the production plan and the market plan are known as the business plan.

The next level is the medium term logistics level, which includes setting the Master Production Schedule (MPS) as well as the determination of material and capacity requirements. Many of these functions are

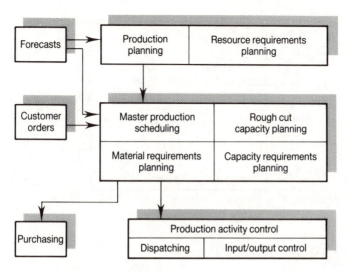

Figure 3.8   The hierarchy of PMS.

supported by MRP II (Manufacturing Resource Planning) systems. The MPS is a detailed statement of top level planned production over the short to medium term. The master production schedule seeks to balance incoming customer orders and forecast requirements with available material and capacity. The material plan is a detailed recommended schedule for both purchase and production order release. It can be calculated by applying the time phased explosion and netting off process of MRP to the MPS. The MPS and the material plan can look up to two years ahead, depending on the specific industry. The material plan feeds the various lower levels which execute the plan, making adjustments as necessary. These are financial control, inventory, purchasing and production activity control.

Not only does good planning at the higher levels facilitate control but good control can also facilitate planning, as indicated by French (1980). These various control functions are inextricably interrelated. For example, an inventory shortage caused by a purchasing problem affects production and eventually profits. The hierarchy can be further articulated for production activity control, and this is done later in Chapter 17.

At each level, the decision process has to maintain a balance between two opposing forces, i.e. between determining what has to be produced (priority) and whether the facilities are available to produce these (capacity). This opposing balance is clearly visible in Figure 3.8.

PMS and product structure

Clearly the more components a product contains and the more levels of manufacturing involved, then the greater the complexity in controlling the

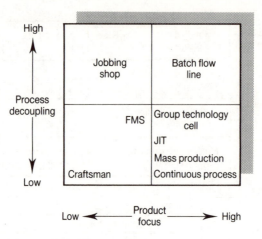

Figure 3.9 Types of process organization.

production of that product. Thus the PMS system tends to be simpler in the case of a one-piece fabricated product, such as a bushing or a casting, and more complex in the case of complex assembly products, such as automobiles or computer systems.

Manufacturing process organization and PMS

Manufacturing process organization has already been discussed in Chapter 1. There we identified mass production, batch production, and the jobbing shop as the dominant forms. In this subsection, we shall develop that discussion and seek to understand how the manufacturing process organization influences the nature of production management.

A manufacturing process organization may be viewed along two dimensions:

(1) **The degree of process decoupling** To what extent is the production process for a product divided into separate operations and decoupled by inventory buffers?

(2) **The degree of product focus** To what extent are production facilities devoted to specific products?

Using these dimensions to create a matrix, we can then position various forms of manufacturing process organization on this framework. This is illustrated in Figure 3.9.

An example of low process decoupling, low product focus is a solitary craftsman who makes a variety of products. So too is the automatic engineering cell known as a Flexible Manufacturing System (FMS). In

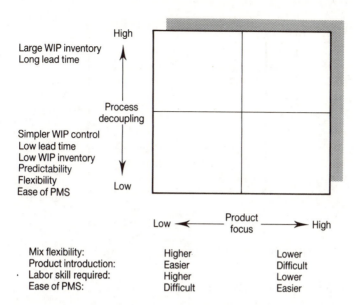

Figure 3.10   Benefits of differing types of process organization.

these cases there is product variety and little or no decoupling of the various stages of manufacturing.

The traditional jobbing shop involves high process decoupling and low product focus, whereas manufacturing systems developed using the group technology approach result in low process decoupling and high product focus, as do continuous process plants (e.g. oil refining). Mass production with a fully automated transfer line also has the same characteristics since, although there may be a fine division of the process into many process stages, each stage is finely balanced with the next and, in general, there are no intermediate buffers to decouple the process stages. The JIT system also emulates this by removing all buffers from the process and by organizing the material flow process and the master schedule so that continuous flow manufacturing can be approached. (See Chapter 13.)

Finally, the medium to large batch flow line with many process stages falls into the high process decoupling, high product focus category. The benefits of the various types of manufacturing process organization are illustrated in Figure 3.10.

A process which is not decoupled into many stages has a short manufacturing lead time and consequently a low Work in Progress (WIP) investment. WIP control is also facilitated. It also has the most predictable delivery performance and can support flexibility at the master schedule level in response to the mix or volume changes. In addition, low process decoupling tends to encourage ownership and responsibility by the

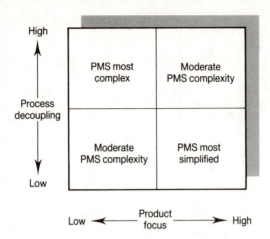

Figure 3.11 Effect of manufacturing process organization on PMS.

operator for good manufacturing performance as measured in product quality and delivery performance.

Where a manufacturing process is highly decoupled, high process efficiency, in terms of both labor and capital utilization, can, in theory, result. This is because the decoupling of the various stages of the process avoids problems, such as *waiting for work*, and enables set-up cost economies to be made by batch oriented production. In addition, the physical division of the process facilitates the application of automation to the manufacturing process. It is interesting to note that the automated transfer line type of mass production does not exploit all potential efficiency gains. This is because of the so-called balancing loss in a transfer line. Process efficiency has been marginally sacrificed in order to reduce lead time and WIP inventory.

Where a process is product focused then product quality also tends to improve. Less labor skill is required. In addition, set-up economies are possible because machines are permanently set-up, or at least there is high set-up commonality. However, flexibility tends to be impacted, since there is less flexibility in the system for dealing with product variety. As a result, new product introduction is more difficult.

The complexity of PMS in each of the four quadrants of the process organization framework is illustrated in Figure 3.11. The jobbing shop is the most difficult PMS environment. In batch line production, PMS is of medium difficulty. In FMS or in the case of a craftsman, the PMS problem has lower complexity. PMS is least complex in the case of JIT, group technology and transfer line type mass production.

The above sections have described the functionality of PMS and given an indication of the complexity of PMS in different manufacturing process organizations. We shall now proceed to focus on PAC and the role that it plays in CIM systems.

3.4 Production activity control

Production Activity Control (PAC) is the layer of the PMS that lies closest to the production process. As has been clearly indicated, it plays a very important role in linking the factory floor with the other elements of PMS. It transforms planning decisions reached at the higher levels of the PMS hierarchy into control commands for the production process. Complementary to this role, it also translates data from the shop floor into information which is used to aid the higher level planning functions in the PMS. The remainder of this chapter is devoted to expanding the description of PAC. PAC can be defined as follows.

"Production activity control describes the principles and techniques used by management to plan in the short term, control and evaluate the production activities of the manufacturing organization."
Harhen and Browne (1984) adapted from the APICS definition.

PAC is thus concerned with all activities from making firm the planned manufacturing order release of medium term production planning systems such as MRP, up to and including the analysis done after the order completion and at order level, to evaluate the effectiveness of manufacturing activities (see Harhen *et al.* 1983). PAC thus includes all of the following PMS functions:

- manufacturing order approval and release,
- operation scheduling and loading,
- material staging and issue,
- priority control in work in progress (WIP),
- capacity control in WIP,
- quality control in WIP,
- manufacturing order close,
- process evaluation with regard to labor, material, and equipment costs,
- facilitating the download of CAPP instructions.

Basically, PAC can be seen as the execution of the long term plans developed from the master production schedule and materials plan. It is a short term activity and, by nature, tends to be a *data intensive* activity.

The goals of PAC can be divided into four categories concerning the control of WIP, quality, labor, and equipment, respectively. These goals are as follows.

(1) Work in progress
- reduced WIP investment,
- balanced workload,

- improved delivery performance,
- reduced manufacturing lead time.

(2) Quality
- reduced incidence of defects and scrap,
- reduced appraisal costs.

(3) Labor
- improved efficiency,
- improved utilization,
- increased operator satisfaction.

(4) Equipment
- improved utilization,
- improved availability,
- reduced set-up costs.

All of these goals are inextricably interrelated and are in some cases conflicting. For example, both WIP investment and manufacturing lead time could be reduced by sacrificing labor and machine utilization.

3.5 The role of PAC in CIM

In the previous section we have placed PAC within the hierarchy of PMS and we shall now extend that description to cover the very important role of PAC in the CIM environment. This involves describing the PAC interfaces to some key islands of automation in the CIM environment. This is illustrated in Figure 3.12.

As we have already discussed the relationship between the PAC system and the rest of the PMS, we shall now describe the following interfaces:

- automated material handling and storage systems,
- automation of the fabrication/assembly process,
- computer aided testing,
- computer aided process planning

3.5.1 PAC and automated material handling and storage systems

The interface between PAC and Automated Material Handling and Storage Systems (AMHSS) is quite complex and information flows in both directions. PAC, as it were, supplies much of the intelligence to drive the material handling system. This intelligence is of three types:

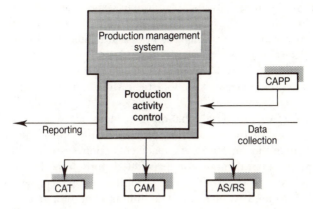

Figure 3.12   PAC interaction with CIM.

(1)   **Routing control**   To which locations is a part to be moved?

(2)   **Real-time material status**   What is the current location of each part being moved?

(3)   **Schedule control**   When is a part to be routed to a location?

AMHSS has two functions:

(1)   **Handling**, as evidenced by:
- Automatic Guided Vehicle Systems (AGVS),
- computer controlled conveyors,
- overhead delivery systems, and
- flexible transfer devices.

(2)   **Storage**, as evidenced by:
- Automatic Storage and Retrieval Systems (AS/RS),
- automatic carousels, and
- automatic small parts storage and kitting systems.

It is at the interface between storage and handling (i.e. order picking) that the relationship to PAC is at its most complex. The bill of materials required for the order is compared with the shop routing to identify which work center requires the material. Information on operation lead times is required to identify the lead time offset from order release until component/material delivery to the work center. Intelligent PAC systems may have the ability to consolidate component issue requirements across both schedules and planned orders in order to achieve picking efficiencies by using *optimal* issue quantities. Component issue schedules are presented in *optimal* location sequence so as to minimize retrieval times (this is a dynamic problem since storage locations are often random). Finally, the picked material can be transferred automatically from the storage systems to the transport system. Current technology in PMS is typically very weak in optimizing the material issue logistics. Most systems typically offer issue to order functionality only.

Because the materials handling system is in such close contact with each stage of the production process, it provides a good foundation on which to build an automatic data collection system. The technology of automatic identification of bar-coded tote bins by laser scanners is already well established. The problem is in communicating this information to the PAC system. The linking of automatic data collection to the physical control of materials leads to almost 100% accuracy of WIP status.

One of the key PAC objectives is to minimize manufacturing lead time and WIP inventory. Too often systems designers look to the automation of materials handling to deliver this lead time reduction. Design for automated materials handling does place constraints on queue sizes and, consequently, lead time. However, it is not often understood that manufacturing lead time is primarily a function of the manufacturing process organization and that it is through combination or elimination of separate stages of the manufacturing process that lead time is primarily reduced. Setting constraints on inter-operation buffers is also important but automating the movement of material, in itself, frequently has little effect.

3.5.2 PAC and automation of fabrication/assembly

The relationship between PAC and process automation is much discussed in the case of existing and proposed flexible manufacturing systems, for example see Akella *et al.* (1984). The PAC system must schedule and manage communication between all the subsystems of the FMS. In the future we will continue to see the proliferation of intelligent process equipment on the manufacturing floor. The PAC module will be the primary source of intelligence to drive this equipment and use will also be made of the local intelligence of this equipment to gather information from the factory floor. The principal examples of intelligent process equipment in the CIM environment will be as follows:

- robots,
- CNC/DNC systems and FMS cells,
- computer controlled processes,
- automatic and semiautomatic assembly equipment.

One principal role of the PAC system is to download process instructions, typically generated by Computer Aided Process Planning (CAPP) using DNC technology. Production schedules may be communicated to robots and FMS cells. The PAC system automatically tracks tooling usage and controls automatic tool changes. The intelligent equipment relays information on operation completions and tool wear; it may also function as an automatic test equipment and report quality problems.

3.5.3 PAC and computer aided testing (CAT)

The nature of the link between CAT and PAC is similar to the link between PAC and the automation of fabrication and assembly. PAC downloads test diagnostics to the CAT stations. PAC, as part of its routing control, manages the test and rework procedures for each part going through the process. Intelligent PAC systems can dynamically calculate *optimal* test and rework tactics based on analysis of historical information. The PAC system also feeds back corrective action requests from the CAT station to fabrication and assembly stations. In return for this, the CAT system can act as an automated data collection system, feeding information on quality events back to the PAC system in real time. The PAC system can direct exception messages to management when quality performance is unacceptable. The integration of PAC and CAT will most likely require the bar-coded identification of each individual unit, as opposed to each tote bin as would suffice in the case of stand-alone PAC. The principal examples of CAT systems include:

- testing of physical dimensions after fabrication (perhaps by systems with vision capability or through the use of coordinate measuring machines),
- component verification as part of the assembly process,
- in-circuit testing after assembly,
- system functional testing after system configuration.

3.5.4 PAC and computer aided process planning

We have already discussed computer aided process planning briefly (see Chapter 2). The problem of interfacing CAPP to a PAC system consists of communicating the routings, operation descriptions, and process instructions (including NC part programs, tooling instructions and time standards) to the PAC database. The PAC system, because of its access to demonstrated historical performance on the factory floor, can relay and generate revisions to the parameters used in the CAPP process. Further, if alternative routings are available in the process plan, the PAC system can select such an alternative process routing if unexpected bottlenecks occur at particular workstations.

3.6 Interaction between PAC and other levels in PMS

The interaction of PAC to the higher levels in the PMS has been outlined earlier. The problem is that current PAC modules in production management systems lack the functionality to control and communicate with the factory floor. The key factors include:

- Absence of *off the shelf* interfaces to automatic data collection devices.
- Absence of quality management functionality.
- The routing control functionality of PAC modules in PMS is extremely naive. Only straight line flows are typically allowed and there is no support of multilevel tracking, i.e. tracking both the top level product and key subassemblies and components through parallel routings. In addition, tracking is primarily by manufacturing order and support is rarely given for individual identification of units within a batch.
- Tooling control is rarely adequately provided for.
- Preventative maintenance and equipment tracking is rarely available.
- Finally, in systems such as MRP II (see Chapter 7), relatively few systems provide for real-time schedule regeneration by bucketless net change MRP.

It is clear that there must be major enhancements to the PAC functionality of PMS before they can operate fully in the CIM environment. The need is for the development of PMS with control and communications capability sufficient for the CIM environment. These conclusions are supported by the CAM-I Factory Management Project (Computer Aided Manufacturing International 1983) comment on MRP II systems:

> "Although a large number of manufacturing control systems are currently on the market, the greatest emphasis is on bill of material processing and material requirements planning. A distributed system oriented for separate levels of factory management and which implements closed-loop communication and control, including the coordination of all shop service functions as well as material flow control, was not found."

These comments remain largely valid today, over 10 years later.

3.7 Conclusion

In this chapter we have described CIM and the various levels of planning and control in manufacturing systems. In so doing, the different approaches to CIM, some models of CIM, and the different levels within the production management system hierarchy were briefly outlined. We then proceeded to discuss how the PMS is affected by different forms of manufacturing process organization and we noted that the production management problem may be more or less complex, depending on the manufacturing process organization within which it resides. We concentrated our discussion on production activity control, since PAC is the gateway between the execution layer on the factory floor and the remainder of the manufacturing and production management system. We noted that, at the operational level, PAC is the module which integrates the various operational elements of the manufacturing system and ultimately leads to CIM on the shop floor. We went on to study the linkages of PAC to various other islands of automation within the CIM environment.

Later, we will go on in Parts II, III, and IV to examine the underlying philosophies of the various approaches to production management, in order to understand the environment within which PAC exists, from a production management point of view. We shall see that it is important to design a manufacturing system which facilitates PAC. This in turn helps us along the road to manufacturing integration.

We also indicated that the discussion on CIM in this chapter is, in some ways, a little dated. Researchers and advanced manufacturing practioneers are now looking beyond CIM and thinking in terms of Computer Integrated Business and the integrated enterprise. This will be the subject of Chapter 4.

Questions

(3.1) "CIM represents an attempt at integration inside the four walls of the factory. The emerging thinking represents integration across the value chain." Discuss.

(3.2) "Interfacing islands of automation which have been designed in isolation represents a problematic approach to CIM." Discuss.

(3.3) Differentiate clearly between technical integration, procedural integration, and goal integration.

(3.4) "Understanding of the CIM problem depends to a significant degree on the technical background and perspective of the individual reviewing the problem." Do you agree? Why?

(3.5) "It is no coincidence that the PAC system is represented as the heart of the CIM system. It is the key function within CIM at the operational level." Discuss.

(3.6) Harrington (1984) argued "that the science of manufacturing is the same" whatever product one is making. Do you agree? Can this view be reconciled with the discussion on manufacturing typology of Chapter 1?

(3.7) How does the manufacturing process organization influence the production management system?

CHAPTER FOUR

Beyond CIM toward the factory of the future

4.1   Introduction

We have already indicated that the concept of CIM which predominated in the 1980s, and which was described in detail in Chapter 3, was primarily concerned with integration within the four walls of the manufacturing plant. We will now go on to look at Computer Integrated Business (CIB), which seeks to integrate the total business of the manufacturing firm, in order, for example, to tie in marketing and sales with production planning, Work in Progress (WIP) monitoring (within the Production Management System – PMS) with cost accounting. Later we will see that this concept of integration is now being extended further to take into account the activities of key suppliers and customers. This we will term the **extended enterprise.**

4.2   Computer integrated business

CIM is regarded as a system which represents the highest level of integration between the various manufacturing functions inside the manufacturing plant. However, implicit in this discussion of CIM, has been the idea that CIM is a *four walls* activity. This focused view of CIM does not directly consider integration with outside systems such as customers, sales or suppliers. For example, sales personnel must know what products are being produced by manufacturing and must also have an accurate estimate of the length of time it takes to procure products. In larger enterprises, a more complex situation exists in which interaction between the several different levels of manufacturing plants must also be managed.

A system can therefore be visualized wherein functions such as sales, marketing, and vendors are all integrated with the factory CIM system by means of an appropriate set of applications. This view of CIM as the integration of all these external systems with the factory CIM system, we call **Computer Integrated Business** (CIB). The achievement of CIB depends to a large extent on the development of protocols and applications to support Electronic Data Interchange (EDI). Figure 4.1 represents a single plant CIB system.

CIB is concerned with reducing the cost and time taken to transfer information between the factory and the external systems with which it must interface. For example, at the front end of the business, it can take a significant amount of time to process the order from the customer, and later to manage the shipment of the order. At the back end of the business, the transaction processing time in acquiring the raw material from the vendors is also often significant.

In some industries, the lead time and cost of manufacturing is less significant than the transaction cycle times and costs associated with processing customer orders, acquiring raw material and distributing finished product. This is so for a number of reasons, primarily because of the problems associated with product diversity and customized products. For example, in the purchase of complex products such as mainframe computers or telecommunications systems, the technical verification of an order as a valid configuration is quite a complex task. Knowledge based approaches have been shown to solve this problem successfully. The pioneering work in this area was the XCON project of Digital Equipment Corporation, described by McDermott (1981) and Bachant and McDermott (1984). An extreme example of the relative complexity of transaction processing as opposed to manufacturing, is met in the case of volume manufacturing of complex software and documentation.

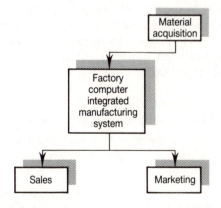

Figure 4.1 Computer integrated business.

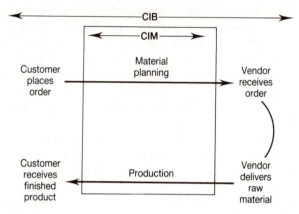

Figure 4.2   The scope of CIB.

CIB can thus be seen as taking a wider view than CIM in its management of the various cycle times associated with manufacturing. This is depicted in Figure 4.2. As the diagram suggests, CIM is concerned with activities in the manufacturing phase of an order, whereas CIB is concerned with all aspects of the relationship with the customer from receipt of initial order to dispatch of product and in certain cases with the post-order relationship with the customer to cover maintenance and product update.

In the discussion thus far, CIB is considered in the context of the single plant company. In many large manufacturing companies, systems of multiple plants must be coordinated to produce finished products. CIB systems, therefore, need to be able to manage the global nature of modern manufacturing enterprises. This of course makes the CIB problem much more complicated.

In such a situation, a plant may either be a feeder plant or a header plant, which links directly with the customer. There are thus supplier/customer relationships between many of the plants in the manufacturing system. However, not all of the manufacturing functions discussed previously as part of CIM exist separately in each plant. The following are some of the situations that may arise.

- The total knowledge of a product is not solely owned by a single plant, but is shared with other supplier or customer plants.

- A product cannot be designed with consideration for just one plant, as the needs of alternate manufacturing plants must be taken into consideration.

- Certain functions such as master planning and order entry, are not local independent activities, but must be connected with related functions within all other plants in the corporation.

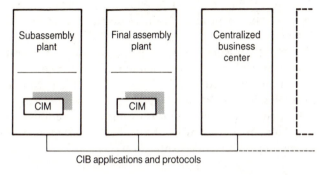

Figure 4.3   Corporate-wide CIB.

- Alternatively, such functions may be centralized in one location and so not necessarily reside in any of the plants. There still remains a problem of how this centralized function should communicate with the plants.

From these observations we can see that four walls CIM in these plants would not be as functionally rich as in a single plant company. However, the integration with the business functions in the rest of the firm will be a much more complex activity. Figure 4.3 represents the multiplant case of CIB.

To summarize, CIB represents the integration of the factory CIM subsystems with those business functions outside the plant, with which the factory must interface.

4.3 The emergence of the extended enterprise

In Chapter 1 we talked about the pressures now being brought to bear on the management of manufacturing systems. We made reference to rising customer expectations in terms of price, quality, customization, and Just in Time delivery of quasi-customized products. We talked also about the increasing environmental concerns of consumers and, indeed, society in general. A further important issue is the fact of global competition, which arises from the removal of trade barriers, the emergence of the newly industrialized nations of the Pacific Rim area, the free flow of information around the world which means that consumers are aware of high quality products available elsewhere, developments in manufacturing technology such as miniaturization, and developments in transportation systems. For many of today's most sophisticated products, near state of the art manufacturing technology is increasingly available in many parts of the world. For many manufactured products, direct labor costs are less than 10% of total costs, so products can be manufactured anywhere and sold everywhere (Sackett 1994).

All of these pressures require the management of manufacturing systems to take a much broader view than in the past and to reach back into the supply chain and forward to the customer to achieve competitive advantage. An interesting model, now widely used to understand the roles and linkages between suppliers, manufacturing and assembly firms, distributors, and customers is the **value chain**. We will use this model to support our discussion of the extended enterprise.

4.3.1   What is the extended enterprise?

The ability to network the activities of a number of entities to produce and sell manufactured products profitably depends on the relationship of these entities and the communication that passes between them. We are accustomed to thinking about this in the context of a single enterprise with different departments: sales, design, engineering, manufacturing, distribution, etc. However, within a global marketplace, entities from many different enterprises, or entities which in themselves are nominally independent enterprises, relate via a single product to produce a designed result. An example might be a merchandising entity recognizng a business opportunity and requesting:

- a design entity to design it,
- a manufacturing entity to build it,
- a distribution entity to distribute it,
- a marketing entity to sell it.

The implication of such an example is that all of the entities can be considered as "flexible" or "programmable" within their expertise envelope (Sackett 1994).

One view of the extended enterprise is represented in Figures 4.4 and 4.5. In the past the emphasis was on integration inside the four walls of the manufacturing plant (see Figure 4.4). CAD/CAM integration, integration of production planning and control systems, the development of sophisticated manufacturing processes, and their control through sophisticated shop floor control systems, formed the agenda. Today, the emphasis has changed to include supply chain management (integration of the supply chain through EDI and JIT), and customer driven manufacturing, including, for example, the integration of manufacturing and distribution planning and control systems. In fact, this issue of the integration of manufacturing and distribution is a good example. In the past, the two systems were seen to be quite separate and decoupled by warehouses and storage

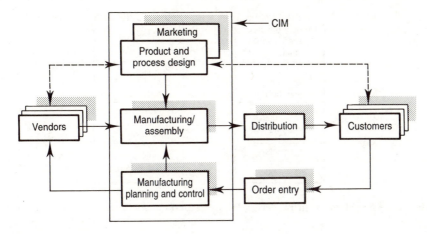

Figure 4.4 CIM.

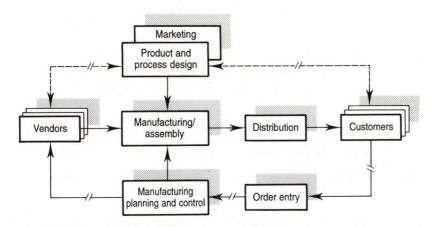

Figure 4.5 The extended enterprise.

points of various descriptions (see Figure 4.6). Today, with the need to support customization and to realize shorter product delivery lead times, we need to develop integrated manufacturing and distribution control systems (see Figure 4.7).

The emergence of the extended or networked enterprise is of course facilitated by today's emerging computing and telecommunications technologies. EDI is one such technology, as indicated in Figure 4.5. We will discuss this issue in more detail in Section 4.5.

A key element of the extended enterprise, which is perhaps not well developed in Figure 4.5, is the notion of interfirm or inter-enterprise cooperation. In a major study of 21st century manufacturing, Nagel and Dove

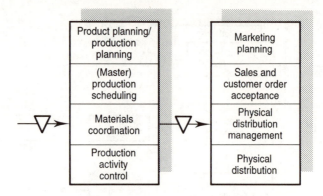

Figure 4.6 Manufacturing decoupled from marketing and physical distribution.

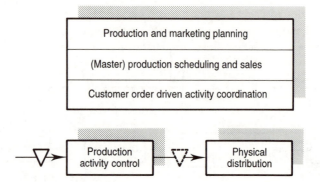

Figure 4.7 Manufacturing and physical distribution driven by customer orders.

(1991) placed particular emphasis on this issue. They suggested that successful future manufacturing systems will be agile, capable of responding rapidly to demand for high quality and highly customized products, and "with flexible management structures that stimulate cooperative initiatives within and *between* firms" (our emphasis).

Nagel and Dove talk about the formation of "virtual companies, enabled by information exchangeability" and "modular plug compatible organizational structures and production facilities." In their words, "the quickest route to the introduction of a new product is selecting organizational resources from different companies and then synthesizing them into a single, electronic business entity: a virtual company." The virtual company then behaves as if it were a single company dedicated to one product line, in effect one project. Virtual companies form, reform, and dissolve over time. They dissolve as their people turn to new products/projects, and new virtual companies form.

4.3.2   The value chain and the extended enterprise

The value chain is a tool introduced by Porter (1980) in order to examine and articulate all of the activities a firm performs and, therefore, to identify sources of competitive advantage. In Porter's words, "value chain analysis helps a manager to separate the underlying activities a firm performs in designing, producing, marketing and distributing its product or service." According to Porter, there are two fundamental categories of competitive advantage that a firm may possess, namely low cost and differentiation. Differentiation is a strategy by which a firm seeks to be unique in its industrial sector and market. The firm identifies one or more attributes that buyers in the industry perceive to be important, and seeks to position itself to produce products or services which score highly on those attributes. In theory the firm should be rewarded for its uniqueness with a premium price.

Value chain analysis identifies the strategically important activities of the firm in order to clearly understand the structure and behavior of costs and the actual and potential sources of differentiation. According to Porter, a firm then gains a competitive edge by performing those strategically important activities more cost effectively and more efficiently than its competitors.

Although value adding activities are the building blocks of competitive advantage, the value chain is not simply a collection of independent activities, but is a system of interdependent activities. Individual value adding activities are related by linkages within the value chain. Linkages are relationships between the way one value activity is performed and the cost or performance of another activity.

Linkages may lead to competitive advantage by optimization and coordination. Linkages often reflect tradeoffs among a group of activities to achieve the same overall result. For example, a more costly product design, more stringent materials specifications, or greater in-process inspection may reduce service costs.

A firm's value chain is embedded in a larger stream of activities, which Porter terms the **value stream**. Suppliers have value chains which create and deliver the purchased items used by the firm's value chain. Clearly, suppliers not only deliver a product but also influence a firm's business performance in many other ways. Furthermore, many products pass through channel value chains on their way to the customer. These channels perform activities such as advertising, promotion, and sales, which should be designed to complement the activities and products of the firm. Clearly, the firm must coordinate and indeed optimize its own activities and those of its supply, distribution, and sales channels in order to attain lower cost and, where possible, enhance differentiation.

Linkages exist not only within a firm's value chain but also between a firm's chain and the value chains of suppliers and distribution channels. These linkages in the value stream, which Porter terms vertical linkages, are similar to the linkages within the value chain – the way supplier or channel activities are performed affects the cost or performance of a firm's activities (and vice versa). For example, suppliers produce a product or service that a firm employs in its value chain and which influences the cost and quality of the firm's products.

Exploiting linkages usually requires information, or information flows, that allow optimization or coordination to take place. Thus, information systems are often vital to gaining competitive advantages from linkages. Indeed, recent developments in information systems technology are encouraging new linkages and increasing our ability to make better use of old ones.

In fact, the notion of the extended enterprise arises partly from the attempts of manufacturers to gain competitive advantage from the linkages within their supplier chain and their distribution chain. Furthermore, the availability of sophisticated computer and telecommunications based networks, and the emergence of data exchange standards, including STEP, PDES, etc., facilitate the creation of competitive advantage by creating enduring and mutually beneficial linkages with suppliers, distributors, etc.

The extended enterprise concept is also in tune with the concept of core competence and the **focused factory.** The focused factory is based on the idea that a plant which concentrates on a narrow range of products for a particular market segment is likely to outperform a more traditional plant with a wider range of activities, products, and markets. By focusing on particular products, markets, skills, activities, and technologies, the firm's objectives are more likely to be achieved without the compromises which are often required to be made in less focused environments. Core competences are those competences which are central to the achievement of the firm's business objectives and which deliver low cost and/or product differentiation. In a world of increasing specialization, the development of focus and core competence is necessary to achieve world class performance. But world class product delivery and service frequently require an amalgam of multiple world class capabilities. The extended enterprise allows a firm to take advantage of external competences and resources without owing them. The extended enterprise thus marks a shift in our traditional thinking about the structure and ownership of value adding activities in the value stream. We are accustomed to thinking about a single enterprise with many functional departments, performing functions such as sales, marketing, design, engineering, manufacturing, assembly, distribution, etc. However, within today's global markeplace, entities from different enterprises, or indeed entities which are in themselves nominally independent enterprises, may come together to produce a particular product or service. This "networking" of enterprises we term the **extended enterprise,** and it is facilitated by today's information and telecommunications technologies.

4.4   Toward the extended enterprise

For the past 10 years or so manufacturing systems specialists have evolved a series of approaches to the design and operation of manufacturing systems. In our view, the extended enterprise represents an extension and a synthesis of many of these approaches. Approaches – listed here in order of their development – such as MRP, JIT, EDI, World Class Manufacturing (WCM), concurrent engineering, lean production, benchmarking and business process redesign essentially synthesize to the extended enterprise model. In this section these approaches are outlined briefly and it is shown how they lead to the extended enterprise.

The ideas of MRP, which we will discuss in greater detail in Part II, were originally developed by Orlicky at IBM in the 1960s. They are valuable because they emphasize the importance of hierarchical planning and the active involvement of many departments and functions within the manufacturing plant to solve materials planning and control problems. During the late 1970s and early 1980s, JIT, which will be discussed in detail in Part III, was developed in the Japanese automotive industry, particularly in companies such as Toyota. Among other things, JIT emphasized customer involvement in the final scheduling of production systems and close cooperation with suppliers to ensure high quality components and timely delivery. Thus, already in the early 1980s JIT began to focus the view of manufacturing systems specialists on issues outside the four walls of the manufacturing plant, namely customer and supplier involvement.

4.4.1   World class manufacturing

In many ways, the ideas of the WCM school (see, for example, Schonberger (1987)) developed from the experience of JIT implementations in factories in the USA. Issues of continuous improvement, training and cross-training of personnel, and integration of product design and process design to facilitate efficient manufacturing were also emphasized. Hayes *et al.* (1988), for example, identified the key characteristics of a world class manufacturing plant as follows:

(1)   Becoming the best competitor. Being better than almost every company in the industrial sector in at least one aspect of manufacturing.

(2)   Growing more rapidly and being more profitable than competitors. World class companies are able to measure their superior performance by observing how their products are accepted in the marketplace.

(3)   Hiring and retaining the best people. Having operators and managers who are so skilled and effective that other companies are continually seeking to attract them away from the organization.

(4)   Developing engineering staff. Being so expert in the design and manufacture of production equipment that equipment suppliers are
continually seeking advice about possible modifications to their
equipment, suggestions for new equipment, and agreement to be a
test site for pilot models.

(5)   Being able to respond quickly and decisively to changing market
conditions. Being more nimble and flexible than competitors in
responding to market shifts or pricing changes, and in getting new
products into the market faster than they can.

(6)   Adopting a product and process engineering approach which maxi-
mizes the performance of both. Intertwining the design of a new
product so closely with the design of the required manufacturing
process that when competitors reverse engineer the product they find
that they cannot produce a comparable one in their own factories
without major retooling and redesign expenses.

(7)   Continually improving. Continually improving facilities, support
systems and skills that were considered to be near optimal or state of
the art when first introduced, so that they increasingly surpass their
initial capabilities.

Hayes *et al.* go on to say that the emphasis on continuous improvement is the ultimate test of a world class organization.

4.4.2   Concurrent engineering

Meanwhile, the proponents of Concurrent Engineering (CE) began to
emphasize the issue of product design time and to research business, technological, and organizational themes in order to reduce the time to market
for new products and product variants. The motivation for concurrent or
simultaneous engineering is clear. Today, the successful design of products
requires the input of specialists in many different areas, including, for
example, manufacturing, quality, health and safety, environment, purchasing, etc. Furthermore, as we indicated earlier, time to market is important
in today's very competitive business environment. The design lead time
may be short if the specialist input occurs throughout the design phase,
thus avoiding costly design and redesign activity. Further, realistic and
cost effective tradeoff between, say, design and manufacturing parameters
can be made to ensure near optimal design of product and manufacturing
process. Frequently, particularly in sectors such as the automobile, aerospace and electronics industries, specialist design expertise may reside in
particular suppliers or subcontractors. Product and, in particular, component design may therefore become a shared activity; it is interesting that
one of the important themes in CE is the development of standards to support the exchange of product data between the CAD systems of suppliers

and those of their customers. Indeed, much of today's work on CE is concerned with the issue of joint and shared design between specialist suppliers and their customers.

4.4.3 Electronic data interchange (EDI)

EDI emerged as a reasonably mature technology in the mid- to late 1980s. EDI (also known as paperless trading) may be defined as the electronic transfer from computer to computer (or from application to application) of commercial or administrative transactions using an agreed standard to structure the transaction or message data. Properly installed EDI offers benefits in terms of reduced data errors through the avoidance of double entry of data, reduced costs through improved business process, reduced lead time, and better service and customer support through faster and better business process. EDI can be used across the value chain to improve the administrative systems and linkages between suppliers and the manufacturing plant and those between the manufacturing plant and its distributors and customers. Initially, EDI was used to support business transactions (invoicing, purchase orders, purchase order acknowledgements, dispatch notifications, stock reports, etc.) between suppliers and their customers. EDI also facilitates JIT ordering and Kanban supply. (See Part III for a detailed discussion on JIT and Kanban.)

EDI is now beginning to be used to exchange technological product data. In fact, some analysts use the global term **Electronic Data Exchange** (EDE) to incorporate EDI and CDI (CAD/CAM Data Interchange). CDI is extremely important in an era of joint product and component development between, say, suppliers and a final assembler, and clearly promotes the concept of CE. CDI is facilitated by the development of product data exchange and product modeling systems such as PDES/STEP.

Clearly, EDI is more than the automation of the transfer of data between business partners. EDI affects the way companies and enterprises interact with each other and the way they do business. For example, in many applications it fundamentally redefines the role of the purchasing organization and radically impacts the business processes used therein by, for example, automating simple but time consuming activities, and freeing up resources for other, more value adding activities. In other words, EDI is not simply the automation of current methods; it makes newer and better methods possible. Over time EDI brings trading partners closer together, and supports the creation of the extended enterprise. In fact, many of today's most advanced manufacturing companies use EDI to exchange production and purchasing information and to support joint (with suppliers and/or customers) engineering development teams.

4.4.4 Lean production

The term **lean production** was coined by the research team involved in the IMVP (International Motor Vehicle Programme) research program. Womack *et al.* (1990) defined lean production as the successor to mass production. Like mass production, the ideas of lean production were developed initially in the auto industry. Mass production arose in the USA in the early 20th century in the Ford Motor Company; lean production developed initially in the Toyota plants in Japan at the end of the 20th century. Clearly, our ideas on lean production are still under development.

Womack *et al.* claim that the origins of lean production go back to the early 1950s, when Toyota concluded that mass production was inappropriate to Japan and set about developing an alternative. This alternative approach sought to make a greater variety of vehicles, as demanded by the Japanese market, focused on reducing set-up and changeover times at individual processes, developing new human resources ideas and quality ideas, and developing sophisticated supply chains to supply components and subassemblies to the plants. Further, these sophisticated supply chains were duplicated at the distribution and customer end, where a network of distributors and dealers was established. The dealer became part of the production system as Toyota gradually stopped building cars in advance for unknown buyers and slowly converted to a build to order or customer driven system, in which the dealer was the first step in the Kanban system, actually sending orders for presold cars to the factory for delivery to specific customers in two to three weeks.

According to Jones (1992) the essential characteristics of lean production can be summarized as follows:

(1) Production is customer driven, not driven by the needs of manufacturing.

(2) All activities are organized and focused on a product line basis led by a product champion, with functional departments playing a secondary, servicing role.

(3) All activities are team based and the organization is horizontally rather than vertically oriented.

(4) The whole system involves fewer actors, all of whom are integrated with each other. For example, in an automotive environment, according to Jones, 330 engineers in the product development team versus 1400 previously, 340 suppliers versus 1500, about 300 dealer principals versus 3600 (to sell 2 million vehicles) and 2000 assembly employees versus between 3000 and 5500 (for a plant assembling 250 000 units a year).

(5) There is a high level of information exchanged between all of the actors and a transparent and realistic cost structure.

(6)   The activities are coordinated and evaluated by the flow of work through the team or the plant, rather than by each department meeting its plan targets in isolation.

(7)   The discipline necessary for the system to function and expose problems is provided by JIT and total quality in the plant, and supplier and dealer performance evaluation.

(8)   Wherever possible, responsibility is devolved to the lowest level possible, in the plant or to suppliers.

(9)   The manufacturing system is based on stable production volumes but with a great deal of flexibility, particularly in terms of product mix.

(10) Relations with employees, suppliers, and dealers are based on reciprocal obligations that are the result of treating them as fixed costs.

Womack *et al.* (1990) see the lean producer as embodying a synthesis of the characteristics of the mass producer and the craftsman:

> "The craft producer uses highly skilled workers and simple but flexible tools to make exactly what the consumer asks for – one item at a time. Custom furniture, works of decorative art, and a few exotic sports cars provide current-day examples. We all love the idea of craft production, but the problem with it is obvious: goods produced by the craft method – as automobiles once were exclusively – cost too much for most of us to afford. So mass production was developed at the beginning of the twentieth century as an alternative.
>
> The mass-producer uses narrowly skilled professionals to design products made by unskilled or semi-skilled workers tending expensive, single-purpose machines. These churn out standardized products in very high volume. Because the machinery costs so much and is so intolerant of disruption, the mass-producer adds many buffers – extra supplies, extra workers, and extra space – to assure smooth production. Because changing over to a new product costs even more, the mass-producer keeps standard designs in production for as long as possible. The result: the consumer gets lower costs but at the expense of variety and by means of work methods that most employees find boring and dispiriting. The lean producer by contrast, combines the advantages of craft and mass production, while avoiding the high cost of the former and the rigidity of the latter. Toward this end, lean producers employ teams of multiskilled workers at all levels of the organization and use highly flexible, increasingly automated machines to produce volumes of products in enormous variety."

The elements in lean production, according to Womack *et al.*, are lean manufacturing, lean design, coordination of the supply chain, dealing with customers, and lean management.

Lean supply chains

The Japanese supply chain is based on a small number of key suppliers, sometimes called first-tier suppliers, who in turn have a team of so-called second-tier suppliers. These second-tier suppliers in turn engage subcontractors in what becomes a supply pyramid. There are very close relationships between the links in the chain and its lower level suppliers design engineers are engaged early in the design process of the customer company. In the auto industry, for example, the first-tier suppliers have full responsibility for component systems and subassemblies that perform to an agreed performance specification in the finished car. The supplier's development team, with support from resident design engineers from the auto manufacturer and the second-tier suppliers, conducts detailed development and engineering (see Womack *et al.* (1990) p.147). Clearly, the supply chains and "supplier pyramids" require substantial sharing of proprietary information on costing, volumes, and production techniques. The relationships between the auto producer and the various tiers of suppliers are managed through regional supplier associations. Through these associations new techniques, including statistical process control, CAD, etc., are disseminated. The extent of these supply chains can be gauged from the following figures. According to Womack *et al.* Toyota Motor Company accounts for 27% of the total cost of the materials, tools, and finished parts required to make a car. The equivalent figure for General Motors in the US is 70%.

It is clear that lean supply chains completely redefine the role of the purchasing organization in the manufacturing firm. Whereas the traditional role of purchasing was to define alternative suppliers, negotiate lower prices and expedite delivery to meet demand, lean manufacture refocuses and greatly extends its role. The new purchasing function must work to develop an extended organization or enterprise based on close collaboration within the supply chain. Essentially, the purchasing function must seek to develop partnership relationships with a smaller number of suppliers, who themselves form the first tier in a supply pyramid. In the context of the extended enterprise the purchasing department must move towards a role which is essentially that of external resource (i.e. supplier chain) management. This external resource management role supports the early involvement of suppliers in new product development and design, very close customer–supplier relationships in terms of the sharing of cost and technical information previously considered proprietary, the sharing of specialists, etc.

Lean customer chains

According to Womack *et al.*, the lean approach to dealing with customers is significantly different in concept from the mass producer's concept. Specifically:

> "First, the Japanese selling system is active, not passive; indeed the Japanese call it 'aggressive selling.' Rather than waiting at the dealership for customers attracted by advertising and publicly announced price cuts, such as factory rebates, the dealer's personnel periodically visit all households in the dealer's

service area. When sales lag, the sales force puts in more hours; when sales lag to the point that the factory no longer has enough orders to sustain full output, production personnel can be transferred into the sales system. [Womack *et al.* claim that this type of transfer occurred during Mazda's crisis in 1974.] Second, the lean producer treats the buyer – or owner – as an integral part of the production process. The elaborate data collection on owner preferences for new vehicles is fed systematically to development teams for new products, and the company goes to extraordinary lengths never to lose an owner once he or she is in the fold. Third, the system is lean. The whole distribution system contains three weeks' supply of finished units, most of which are already sold. The system that delivers this high level of service is also very different from a mass-production dealer system. The industry is very much more concentrated – there are only a total of 1621 dealer firms in Japan, compared with some 16 300 dealer principals in the United States, a market two and a half times larger than Japan. Almost all Japanese dealers have multiple outlets and some of the largest easily match the very large dealers found in the United States.

In the same way as lean manufacturers only have a limited number of suppliers, they only work with a limited number of dealers, who all form an integrated part of their lean-manufacturing system."

Thus, lean production addresses a whole series of issues, including product strategy, product development, the supply chain, manufacturing, and product distribution. Essentially, it addresses many issues in the value chain, resulting in a networking of customers, assemblers, and suppliers.

4.4.5 Customer driven manufacturing

According to Stendel and Desruelle (1992), a true customer driven manufacturing system:

- Has a clearly articulated business and manufacturing strategy which defines the product set of the company and the market at which it is directed, as well as the organization, technology, knowledge, and skills required to meet the needs of that market.

- Is managed by a management team which seeks to achieve continuous improvement.

- Has defined a set of performance measures which serve to direct behavior in accordance with the manufacturing strategy and customer needs, as well as to measure performance.

- Has developed a reward system which is appropriate in terms of the performance measures defined earlier.

- Has developed excellent communications systems with customers and vendors. These external communications systems serve to develop partnership relations with customers and vendors.

- Has developed excellent internal communications systems in terms of product and customer based teams with clearly defined roles and responsibilities. The emphasis on customer/product based teams is important in terms of defining customer and product responsibility rather than functional or process responsibility.

- Has developed flow based manufacturing systems which are customer demand driven rather than capacity driven.

- Has developed internal systems which capture learning and experience for reuse in subsequent orders.

- Recognizes that well trained, motivated people are critical to success and has developed policies to continuously retrain, reskill, and motivate people.

- Has developed a manufacturing process which supports flexibility and responsiveness through very low levels of inventory, very low reject and scrap notes, high on-time deliveries, very low set-up times and very low lead times.

- Has developed a responsive organization in terms of its ability to reconfigure itself to meet external and internal demands.

4.4.6 Business process redesign

In more recent years, benchmarking and business process redesign have emerged as techniques to support companies seeking to gain competitive advantage in manufacturing. The central idea of benchmarking is to decompose a business into its essential processes, identify examples of best practice for each of these processes, and then define an approach to achieve best practice. Thus, benchmarking seeks to improve existing processes. Business process redesign (sometimes termed business process reengineering) offers a more radical approach. It seeks to identify each business process, question its relevance to the achievement of business objectives, and redesign the overall business to incorporate only appropriate processes. In fact, benchmarking may well be used following business process redesign to identify and achieve best practice for each individual process. For a detailed discussion on business process redesign and benchmarking, see Hammer and Champy (1992). It is worth noting also that most of the work on benchmarking and business process redesign was done in the USA. Also, the software tools for business process redesign come primarily from North America. In Section 4.5, when we come to look at the impact of Information Technology (IT) on business and manufacturing systems, we will suggest that business process reengineering is necessary as we expand the reach and range of IT applications.

4.5 Information technology and the extended enterprise

Inter-enterprise networking encompasses the compression of "concept to customer" lead time, working with JIT supply chains and logistic support throughout the product life. Against a background of accelerating specialization and the visual disintegration of previously integrated businesses, these trends drive the requirements for elements of integration such as EDI to new levels of complexity. The extended enterprise, where core product functionalities are provided separately by different companies, who come together for the purpose of providing a customer defined product/service, is made possible and viable through information technology (Sackett 1994).

Referring to EDI and to the emerging integration of computing and telecommunications technologies, Keen (1991) uses the terms "reach" and "range". *Reach* is the extent to which one can interact with other communication nodes – in the limit it becomes anyone, anywhere. *Range* defines the information types that can be supported, from simple messaging between identical platforms to any computer generated data between any operating platforms (Figure 4.8). Electronic mail available to all members of a single department offers the lowest level of technology integration.

Until recently, extending reach across other parts of the company and, particularly, beyond the company has been both technologically difficult and expensive. Extending range requires a good definition of business processes. Tools and organizational attitudes are now becoming available that make range extension viable. The driver to both reach and range

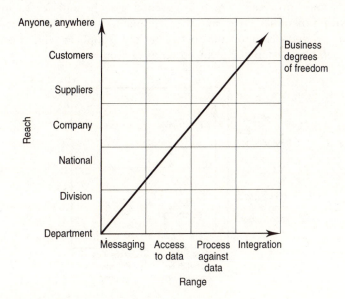

Figure 4.8 Business and technology integration.

increases is the enhancement of business degrees of freedom to respond to the volatile marketplace. The level of change in the marketplace requires that we have flexibility not only in product but in business structure and business processes. A high level of reach and range provides the business freedom to operate in the extended enterprise. The mapping of a company onto the range/reach chart gives a good indication of its scope for innovative business improvement through the use of integration technologies (Figure 4.9). In the extended enterprise the bringing together of core competencies from many different organizations to provide a short manufactured life product, means regular enterprise business process restructuring. The pressure on time scales means interactive decision support is required. Companies without appropriate reach and range will not be able to participate in this extended enterprise business system. Technology integration price/performance improvements will greatly reduce price entry barriers to all companies worldwide. In the past, high reach/range has been recognized as valuable but has been only available in specialist applications.

Today the emergence of a communications infrastructure such as the Internet is changing the business environment more rapidly than even the most optimistic thought possible. Work done within the US-led CALS (Computer Aided Acquisition and Logistics Support) program is also very important to this discussion. This, together with initiatives such as PDES (Product Data Exchange Standard), will certainly influence the standards and the pace of inter-organization technical communication.

In summary, we can say that the emerging business and technical communications infrastructure will facilitate:

- Business processes which cross-enterprise boundaries to interface with functional areas in other companies; for example co-design of products/components between key suppliers and their final assembler customers in the automotive sector.

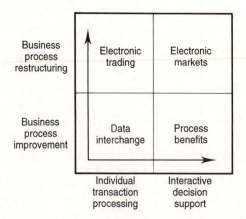

Figure 4.9 Scope for business improvement through integration.

- Supplier/customer integration through interchange of commercial and technical data.

- The ability for business entities to function effectively as links for information and product in relatively unbuffered supply and distribution chains.

In this way, the emerging telecomputing environment allows a number of business entities to network together to design, produce, and sell product efficiently.

4.6   The emerging environmental imperative

Every product has a life cycle, and the product may impact on the environment at many points in its life cycle. In this context we are referring to the physical life cycle of the product, as distinct from its business life cycle, which we referred to earlier. At the raw materials stage nonrenewable material such as crude oil is used in relatively high quantities. Of course metals, plastics, and, increasingly, composite materials are also used. At every process stage, material, energy, and labor are consumed; waste material may be produced to be disposed of in the air, in water or on land. At some process stages, recycled material may well be used. Following production, products are made available to the market and ultimately to consumers and users. But what happens at the end of life? In the past, for the majority of products, the answer was relatively straightforward. Products by and large were disposed of through the use of landfill with minimal attempts at recovery of components or product reuse.

However, the situation is changing. For the more densely populated regions of Europe and the United States, landfill capacity is greatly constrained. Disposal of waste through landfill is becoming increasingly expensive and even difficult. Societal awareness of pollution and the impact of uncontrolled waste on the natural environment is resulting in legislative pressure to minimize waste and maximize reuse where possible. Consumers are aware of the depletion of nonrenewable natural resources.

The end result of all of this is increasing pressure on manufacturers to take responsibility for products "beyond the factory gate." The scope of the manufacturer's responsibility is gradually being expanded. In the past, manufacturers were concerned with four steps (see Figure 4.10), namely raw material acquisition, manufacturing itself, distribution and transport, and service and maintenance. Today the focus is changing and, increasingly, the manufacturer is taking more responsibility for products.

Legislation now under discussion in Europe is likely to require manufacturers of electronic and automotive products to take responsibility for their products throughout the life cycle. In this context it is clearly desirable to maximize the possibility for reuse of components/subassemblies

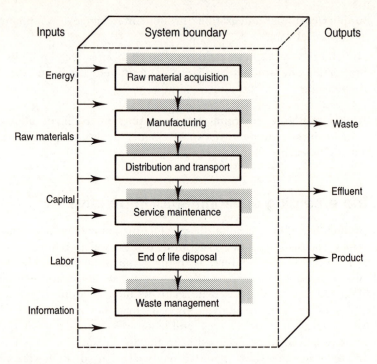

Figure 4.10 The scope of the manufacturer's responsibility.

and, indeed, products at the "end of life" stage. Today, the balance between "reuse" and "waste disposal" is heavily geared towards disposal. In the future this is likely to change (see Figure 4.11).

Of course, the aspiration depicted in Figure 4.11 will require tremendous changes. The design of products will have to change. Indeed, the whole nature of the design process will change. Today the emphasis is on design for manufacture and assembly; in the future it is likely that designers will focus on design for disassembly/reuse and long life. There are also likely to be interesting problems in developing logistics and information systems to support the takeback of products from customers and the resource sustainment process of disassembling, refurbishing, recycling, and reusing those products.

The important point from our view here is that the emerging interest in product takeback enlarges the system boundary (see Figure 4.11). Manufacturers will be required to put in place systems and, indeed, resource sustainment plants to deal with end of life products. Such plants are already in place in the computer and telecommunications industry, where manufacturers such as Digital Equipment Corporation, Sun Microsystems, Alcatel and Hewlett-Packard have established recycling plants. In fact, the electronics industry seems to be leading the way in this

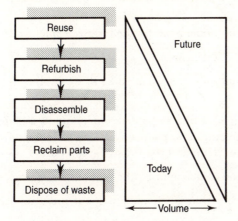

Figure 4.11   The changing balance between reuse and waste disposal.

area, possibly because of the physical volume associated with electronics products and the hazardous nature of some of their contents. Within the European Union (EU) it is estimated that there are 6 million tons of end of life electronic products disposed of per year. British Telecom claims to recycle over 3 million telephones per year through specialist recycling companies. Over 85% of the material from telephones is recovered and some components are extracted for resale in new product and for spares.

Looking at the experience of electronics and telecommunications companies, it seems that the use of specialist recyclers is the way forward for manufacturers seeking to support product takeback and recycling. Such specialist recyclers will need to cooperate closely with the original manufacturers, to share product structure and engineering data and, of course, to advise manufacturers of good design practice to facilitate recycling and reuse where possible. This necessary cooperation and close relationship is another manifestation of the extended enterprise model.

4.7 Conclusion

In this chapter we have tried to look beyond CIM and forward to future manufacturing systems. We believe that manufacturing companies must now begin to analyze themselves in terms of their position on the value chain, and seek cooperation with upstream and downstream entities. This cooperation is necessary in a world of increasing specialization where *core competence* and *focused factories* are the watchwords and where the emerging telecomputing infrastructure will facilitate electronic cooperation. Furthermore, the requirement to take responsibility for the end of life disposal of products requires manufacturers to expand their system boundaries.

Questions

(4.1) What do you understand by the term *computer integrated business?*

(4.2) What is a 'value chain'?

(4.3) How can linkages in a value chain or in a value stream create competitive advantage?

(4.4) "The notion of the extended enterprise arises partly from the attempts of manufacturers to gain competitive advantage from the linkages within their supply chain and their distribution chain." Discuss.

(4.5) What do you understand by the term *core competence?*

(4.6) What are the essential characteristics of the extended enterprise?

(4.7) How would you characterize a world class manufacturing plant?

(4.8) "EDI is not simply the automation of current methods. It makes newer and better methods possible." Discuss.

(4.9) Womack *et al.* (1990) see the lean producer as embodying a synthesis of the characteristics of the mass producer and the craftsman. Do you agree? Why?

(4.10) How do lean supply chains redefine the role of the purchasing function?

(4.11) "The emergence of the extended networked enterprise is facilitated by today's emerging computing and telecommunications technologies." Discuss.

(4.12) What do you inderstand by the terms *reach* and *range* as used by Keen in his discussion on business and information technology integration?

(4.13) Business process re-engineering is necessary as we expand the reach and range of information technology applications. Do you agree? Why?

(4.14) "In the future, manufacturers are likely to be required to take responsibility for their products throughout the products' total life cycle." Explain.

References to Part I

Akella, R., Choong, Y. and Gershwin, S. 1984. "Performance of hierarchical production scheduling policy," *IEEE Transactions on Computers, Hybrids and Manufacturing Technology* **CHMT-7** (3), September.

Anonymous 1981. "Implementing CIM," *American Machinist*, August, 152–174.

APICS. 1987. *APICS Dictionary*, 6th Edition. Falls Church, VA: American Production and Inventory Control Society, 18.

Bachant, J. and McDermott, J. 1984. "Rl revisited, four years in the trenches," *AI Magazine*, Fall, 21–32.

Baumol, W. and Braunstein, Y. 1977. "Empirical study of scale economics and production complementarity; the case of journal productions," *Journal of Political Economy*, **85**(5), 1037–1048.

Bernhardt, R., Diliman, R., Hormann, K. and Tiemey, K., editors, 1992. *Integration of Robots into CIM*. London: Chapman & Hall.

Bonsack, R. 1986. "Cost accounting in the factory of the future," *CIM Review*, **2**(3) 2832.

Boothroyd, G. and Dewhurst, P. 1983. *Design for Assembly: A Designer's Handbook*. Amherst, MA: University of Massachusetts.

Bowden, R. and Browne, J. 1987. "ROBEX – an artificial intelligence based process planning system for robotic assembly," in *Proceedings of the IXth ICPR*, edited by A. Mital. Cincinnati, OH: University of Cincinnati, College of Engineering.

Brown, K.M., Sims Williams, J.H. and McMahon, C.A. 1992. "Grammars of features in design," in *Artificial Intelligence in Design, Proceedings of the Conference on AI in Design*, edited by J. Gero. New York: Kluwer Academic.

Browne, J. and Timon, F.J. 1991. "Design of flexible assembly systems using simulation modelling," in *Handbook of Flexible Manufacturtng Systems*, edited by N.K. Jha. San Diego, CA: Academic Press, 217–274.

Browne, J., Dubois, D., Rathmill, K., Sethi, S. and Stecke, K. 1984. "Classification of flexible manufacturing systems," *The FMS Magazine*, April, 114–117.

Browne, J., Tierney, K. and Walsh, M. 1991. "A two-stage assembly process planning tool for robot-based flexible assembly systems," *International Journal of Production Research*, **29**(2), 247–266.

Bullinger, H.J. and Ammer, E.D. 1984. "Work structuring provides basis for improving organization of production systems," *Industrial Engineering*, **16**(10), 74–82.

Burbidge, J. 1986. "Production planning and control: a personal philosophy," paper presented to IFIP Working Group 5.7 meeting in Munich, Germany, March.

Butcher, M. 1986. "Advanced manufacturing system (AIMS) for aero engine turbine and compressor discs," in *Proceedings of the FMS5 Conference*, edited by K. Rathmill. UK: IFS Publications, 93–104.

Chang, T.C. 1990. *Expert Process Planning for Manufacturing*. Reading, MA: Addison-Wesley Publishing Co.

Commission of the European Communities. 1982. *ESPRIT – The Pilot Phase*, COM (82) 486 Final 1/2, CEC. Brussels: Commission of the European Communities.

Computer Aided Manufacturing International. 1983. *CAM-I Factory Management Project, PR-82-ASPP-01.6*. USA: Computer Aided Manufacturing International Inc.

Conway, R., Maxwell, W. and Miller L. 1967. *Theory of Scheduling*. Reading, MA: Addison-Wesley Publishing Co.

Cross, K.F. 1984. "Production modules; a flexible approach to high tech manufacturing," *Industrial Engineering*, **16**(10), 64–72.

Descotte, Y. and Latombe, J.C. 1981. "GARI: a problem solver that plans how to machine mechanical parts," *IJCAI*, 766–772.

Descotte, Y. and Latombe, J.C. 1985. "Making compromises among antagonistic constraints in a planner," *Artificial Intelligence*, 27, 183–217.

Dwyer, J. and Ioannou, A. 1987. *MAP and TOP Advanced Manufacturing Communications*. London: Kogan Page.

Forrester, J. 1961. *Industrial Dynamics*. Cambridge, MA: MIT Press.

French, R. 1980. "Accurate work in process inventory: a critical MRP system requirement," *Production and Inventory Management*, First Quarter, 17–22.

Gerwin, D. 1982. "Do's and don'ts of computerized manufacturing," *Harvard Business Review*, 60(2), 107–116.

Gerwin, D. and Tarondeau, J.C. 1986. "Consequences of programmable automation for French and American automobile factories: an international case study," in *Production Management: Methods and Studies*, edited by B. Lev. Amsterdam: Elsevier Science Publishers, 85–98.

Gold, B. 1986. "CIM dictates change in management practice," *CIM Review*, 2(3), 3–6.

Goldhar, J. 1983. "Plan for economies of scope," *Harvard Business Review*, 61(6), 141–148.

Goldhar, J. and Jelinek, M. 1985. "Computer integrated flexible manufacturing: organizational, economic and strategic implications," *Interfaces*, 15(3) 94–105.

Goldratt, E.M. 1983. "Cost accounting is enemy number one of productivity," in *APICS 1983 Conference Proceedings*. Falls Church, VA: American Production and Inventory Control Society.

Gould, L. 1985. "Computers run the factory," *Electronics Week*, March 25.

Groover, M. 1980. *Automation, Production Systems, and Computer Aided Manufacturing*," Englewood Cliffs, NJ: Prentice-Hall Inc.

Gunn, T. 1982. "The mechanization of design and manufacturing," *Scientific American*, 247(3), 87–110.

Hall, D.N. and Stecke, K.E. 1986. in *Flexible Manufacturing Systems: OR Models and Applications,* edited by K.E. Stecke and F. Suri. Amsterdam: Elsevier, 145–156.

Hammer, M. and Champy, J. 1992. *Reengineering the Corporation – A Manifesto for Business Revolution*. New York: Harper Business Press.

Harhen, J. and Browne, J. 1984. "Production activity control; a key node in CIM", in *Strategies for Design and Economic Analysis of Computer Supported Production Management Systems*, edited by H. Hubner. Amsterdam: North Holland.

Harhen, J., Browne, J. and O'Kelly M. 1983. "Production activity control and the new way of life," *Production and Inventory Management,* Fourth Quarter, 73–85.

Harhen, J., Cohen, P., Graves, R. and Ketcham, M. 1987. "Using multiple perspectives in manufacturing macro-planning," in CIM Europe 1987 Conference Proceedings. UK: IFS Publications.

Harrington, J. 1984. *Understanding the Manufacturing Process Key to Successful CAD/CAM Implementation*. New York: Marcel Dekker.

Hayes, R. and Wheelright, S. 1984. *Restoring our Competitive Edge: Competing through Manufacturing*. New York: John Wiley and Sons.

Hayes, R., Wheelwright, S. and Clark, K. 1988. *Dynamic Manufacturing: Creating the Learning Organization*. New York: Free Press.

Hitomi, K. 1979. *Manufacturing Systems Engineering*. London: Taylor and Francis.

King, J. 1976. "The theory practice gap in job shop scheduling," *The Production Engineer*. March, 137–143.

Jackson, S. 1991. *Qualitative Modelling of Unstructured Knowledge to Support Strategy Determination*, Ph.D. thesis, University College Galway, Ireland.

Jackson, S. and Browne, J. 1992. "AI-based decision support tool for strategic decision making in the factory of the future," *Computer Integrated Manufacturing Systems*, **5**(2), 83–90.

Jagdev, H.S. 1981. *A Minicomputer Based Job Shop Control System*, Ph.D. thesis, University of Manchester Institute of Science and Technology (UMIST), UK.

Jones, D.T. 1992. "Beyond the Toyota production system: the era of lean productivity," in *Manufacturing Strategy Process and Content*, edited by C. Voss. London: Chapman & Hall.

Kaplan, R.S. 1984. "Yesterday's accounting undermines production," *Harvard Business Review*, July/August, 95–101.

Kerr, R. 1991. *Knowledge-Based Manufacturing Management*. Wokingham: Addison-Wesley Publishing Co.

Keen, P.G.W. 1991. *Shaping the Future: Business Design through Information Technology*. Harvard Business School Press.

King, J. 1976. "The theory practice gap in job shop scheduling," *The Production Engineer*. March, 137–143.

Kusiak, A. 1990. *Intelligent Manufacturing Systems*. Englewood Cliffs, NJ: Prentice Hall.

Little, J.D.C. 1974. "Models and managers: the concept of a decision calculus," *Management Science*, **16**(7), 466–485.

Lyneis, J. 1980. *Corporate Planning and Policy Design: A Systems Dynamics Approach*. Cambridge, MA: MIT Press.

Malcolm, D.R. 1988. *Robotics: An Introduction*. Boston, MA: PWS-Kent Publishing Co.

McDermott, J. 1981. "Rl: the formative years," *AI Magazine*, Summer, 21–29.

McMahon, C. and Browne, J. 1993. *CADCAM: From Principles to Practice*. Wokingham: Addison-Wesley Publishing Co.

Merchant, M. 1977. "The inexorable push for automated production," *Production Engineering*, January, 4–49.

Meredith, J. and Suresh, N. 1986. "Justification techniques for advanced manufacturing technologies," *International Journal of Production Research*, **24**(5), 1043–1057.

Miller, J.G., Rosenthal, S.R. and Vollman, T.E. 1986. *Taking Stock of CIM*, Manufacturing Roundtable Research Report Series.

Molloy, E., Yang, H. and Browne, J. 1993. "Feature-based modelling in design for assembly," *International Journal of Computer Integrated Manufacturing*, **6**(1/2), 119–125.

Nagel, R. and Dove, R. 1991. *21st Century Manufacturing Enterprise Strategy – An Industry-Led View*. Lehigh University, USA: Iacocca Institute.

Nanda, R. 1986. "Redesigning work systems – a new role for IE," in *Proceedings of the 1986 Fall Industrial Engineering Conference*, AIIE, 222–229.

Nicholls, B. 1992. "ABC in the UK – a status report," *Management Accounting*, May, 22–23.

Owen, A.E. 1984. *Flexible Assembly Systems – Assembly by Robots and Computerized Integrated Systems.* New York: Plenum Press

Porter, M.E. 1980. *Competitive Strategy: Techniques for Analysing Industries and Competitors,* New York: Free Press.

Primrose, P. and Leonard, R. 1986. "Conditions under which flexible manufacturing is financially viable," in *Flexible Manufacturing Systems: Methods and Studies,* edited by A. Kusiak. Amsterdam: North-Holland.

Rembold, U., editor, 1990. *Robot Technology and Applications.* New York: Marcel Dekker.

Roberts, E. 1978. *Managerial Applications of Systems Dynamics.* Cambridge, MA: MIT Press.

Rolstadas, A. 1986. "Trends in production management systems," in *Advances in Production Management Systems '85,* edited by E. Szelke and J. Browne. Amsterdam: North Holland.

Rosenthal, S. and Ward, P. 1986. "Key managerial roles in controlling progress towards CIM," in *Manufacturing Research: Organizational and Institutional Issues,* edited by A. Gerstenfeld, H. Bullinger, and H. Warnecke. Amsterdam: Elsevier Science Publishers.

Rygh, O. 1980. "Succeeding with AS/RS technology in the 80s," *Industrial Engineering,* September, 56–63.

Sackett, P. 1994. (Private communication.)

Sanderson, R.J., Campbell, J.A. and Meyer, J.D. 1982. *Industrial Robots, A Summary and Forecast for Manufacturing Managers.* Tech Tran Corporation, USA.

Sheer, A.W. 1988. *CIM Computer Steered Industry.* Berlin: Springer-Verlag.

Schonberger, R. 1987. *World Class Manufacturing Casebook Implementing JIT and TQC.* New York: Free Press.

Shingo, S. 1981. *Study of Toyota Production System from Industrial Engineering Viewpoint.* Japanese Management Association, 352.

Skinner, W. 1969. "Manufacturing – the missing link in corporate strategy," *Harvard Business Review,* May/June, 156.

Skinner, W. 1985. *Manufacturing: The Formidable Competitive Weapon.* New York: John Wiley and Sons.

Solberg, J.J. 1989. "Production planning and scheduling in CIM," in *Information Processing '89,* edited by O.X. Rifler. Amsterdam: North Holland.

Stecke, K. and Browne, J. 1985. "Variations in flexible manufacturing systems according to the relevant types of automated materials handling," *Material Flow,* **2**, 179–185.

Stendel, M.J. and Desruelle, P. 1992. *Manufacturing in the Nineties.* New York: Van Nostrand-Reinhold.

Towill, D.R. 1991. "Supply Chain Dynamics," *International Journal of Computer Integrated Manufacturing,* **4**, 197–208.

Tzafestas, S.G., ed., 1991. *Intelligent Robotic Systems.* New York: Marcel Dekker.

Umble, M. and Srikanth, M. 1990. *Synchronous Manufacturing Principles for World Class Excellence.* Cincinnati, OH: South-Western Publishing Co.

Van Veen, E. 1992. *Modelling Product Structures by Generic Bills of Material.* Amsterdam: Elsevier.

Wang, H.S. and Li, J.K. 1991. *Computer-Aided Process Planning.* Amsterdam: Elsevier.

Warnecke, H.J. 1993. *The Fractal Factory: A Revolution in Corporate Culture*. Berlin: Springer-Verlag.

Wemmerlov, U. 1984. "Assemble to order manufacturing: implications for materials managment," *Journal of Operations Management*, **4**(4), 78–99.

Westkamper, E. 1986. "Increase in flexibility and productivity with computer integrated and automated manufacturing," in *Proceedings of FMS5*, edited by K. Rathmill. UK: IFS Publications, 121–126.

Wild, R. 1971. *The Techniques of Production Management*. London: Holt, Rinehart and Winston.

Williams, D.J. 1988. *Manufacturing Systems: An Introduction to the Technologies*. Milton Keynes: Open University Press.

Womach, J.P., Jones, D.T. and Roos, D. 1990. *The Machine that Changed the World*. New York: Rawson Macmillan.

Wortmann, J.C. 1984. "Factory of the future: towards an integrated theory for one-of-a-kind production," in *One-of-a-Kind Production: New Approaches*, edited by B.E. Hirsch and K.D. Thoben. Amsterdam: North-Holland, 37–74.

Yeomans, R.W., Choudry, A. and Ten Hagen, P.J.W. 1985. *Design Rules for a CIM System*. Amsterdam: North-Holland.

PART II

The requirements planning approach: MRP and MRP II

Overview

Material Requirements Planning (MRP) and Manufacturing Resource Planning (MRP II) have, almost certainly, been the most widely implemented large scale production management systems since the early 1970s. Several thousand systems of this style are in use in industry around the world. The aim in Part II of this book is to describe and review the MRP approach. This discussion addresses both material requirements planning, which generates a schedule of manufacturing and purchase orders to meet a given demand, and manufacturing resource planning, which is an extension of MRP to support the integrated management of many of the functions of the manufacturing enterprise. An attempt will be made to give the reader an insight into the assumptions and techniques of the material requirements planning and manufacturing resource planning approach. Part II is organized in the following manner.

Chapter 5 serves as an introduction to MRP. It provides some insight into the history of MRP and identifies the important assumptions and attributes of the MRP approach. The approach is illuminated by the presentation of an MRP example.

In Chapter 6, the use of the more important techniques within the MRP system is discussed. This discussion covers such topics as bottom-up replanning using pegged requirements and the firm planned order. The net change versus regenerative planning approaches to requirements planning is discussed, as are bucketed and bucketless systems.

In Chapter 7, *closed loop* MRP is described, together with its evolution to the extended version of MRP known as MRP II. Master production schedule development, resource and capacity planning, forecasting techniques, and finally production activity control including a review of scheduling techniques are discussed.

Chapter 8 describes the manufacturing database while Chapter 9 presents a review of lot sizing approaches used within MRP.

In Chapter 10 the status of MRP/MRP II as a paradigm for production management is discussed. In so doing, the effectiveness for MRP II implementations and practice is covered. Various criticisms of the MRP approach are reviewed and some of the current trends in MRP research are described. Finally, some of the philosophical debate that surrounds MRP is examined. This chapter serves as the basis for a comparative review of alternative approaches presented in Part V.

It will be seen that MRP/MRP II is certainly a viable approach to production management with a proven track record. Although MRP II will continue to be widely applied in its present form, it will likely be subject to radical modularization in the future in order to reemerge, in new hybrid production management environments that complement the other production management paradigms described in Parts III and IV.

CHAPTER FIVE

Introduction to requirements planning (MRP and MRP II)

5.1   Introduction

Material Requirements Planning (MRP) has been the most widely implemented large scale production management system since the early 1970s, with several thousand MRP type systems implemented in industry around the world. The aim in this chapter is to describe what requirements planning is. The history of requirements planning and the assumptions that underlie its application are discussed. The key attributes of the approach are described and its operation is illustrated by an example.

5.2   History of requirements planning

MRP originated in the early 1960s in the USA as a computerized approach for the planning of materials acquisition and production. The definitive textbook on the technique is by Orlicky (1975a). The technique had undoubtedly been manually practised in aggregate form prior to the second world war in several locations in Europe. However, what Orlicky realized was that a computer enabled the detailed application of the technique, which would make it effective in managing manufacturing inventories.

These early computerized applications of MRP were built around a Bill of Material Processor (BOMP) which converted a discrete plan of production for a parent item into a discrete plan of production or purchasing for component items. This was done by exploding the requirements for the top level product, through the Bill of Material (BOM), to generate component demand. The projected gross demand was then compared with available inventory and open orders over the planning time horizon and at each level in the BOM. These systems were implemented on large mainframe computers and run in centralized material departments for large companies.

As time passed, the installations of the technique became more widespread and various operational functions were added to extend the range of tasks that these software systems supported. In particular, these extensions included Master Production Scheduling (MPS), Production Activity Control (PAC), Rough Cut Capacity Planning (RCCP), Capacity Requirements Planning (CRP), and Purchasing.

The combination of the planning (MPS, MRP, CRP) and execution modules (PAC and purchasing), with the potential for feedback from the execution cycle to the planning cycle, was termed **closed loop MRP**. With the addition of certain financial modules, as well as the extension of master production scheduling to deal with the full range of tasks in master planning and the support of business planning in financial terms, it was realized that the resultant system offered an integrated approach to the management of manufacturing resources. This extended MRP was labeled **manufacturing resource planning** or **MRP II**. Since 1980, the number of MRP installations has continued to increase as MRP applications became available at lower cost on minicomputers and microcomputers.

MRP's popularity stems back to the *MRP crusade* launched by the American Production and Inventory Control Society (APICS) in the early 1970s. The focus of this was to convince people that MRP was the solution, since it represented an integrated communication and decision support system that supports the management of the total manufacturing business. It was emphasized that in order to succeed, MRP implementation programs required management commitment and total work force education. The role of optimizing techniques drawn from operations research and management science was frowned upon. The real problems, it was declared, were problems of discipline, education, understanding, and communication. This message was promoted by APICS and a stream of almost evangelical consultants, and finally echoed by a computer industry eager to expand the range of applications it could offer.

One of the significant reasons MRP was adopted so readily as the production management technique was that it made use of the computer's ability to store centrally and provide access to the large body of information that seemed necessary to run a company. It helped to coordinate the activities of various functions in the manufacturing firm such as engineering, production, and materials. Thus the attraction of MRP II lay not only in its role as decision making support, but, more importantly, in its integrative role within the manufacturing organization.

Today there is some concern as to how systems of the style of MRP can be integrated into a Computer Integrated Manufacturing (CIM) environment and the adequacy of such systems compared with alternate philosophies such as Kanban/Just in Time (JIT) and proprietary techniques such as Optimized Production Technology (Fox 1985). Questions are being raised regarding the effectiveness of MRP, as managers see the extent of the effort required to implement such systems and the all too frequent failure to realize the promised benefits.

5.3 The attributes of material requirements planning

Prior to the widespread use of material requirements planning, the planning of manufacturing inventory and production was generally handled through inventory control approaches, for example:

- The **two bin policy** under which inventory availability is continuously reviewed and a predetermined quantity (fixed batch size) of items is ordered each time stocks fall below a predetermined level (reorder point).

- The **periodic order cycle policy** under which inventory is reviewed on a fixed periodic basis and sufficient items (a variable quantity) are ordered to bring the stock level up to a predefined level (target inventory).

The implicit assumption of these inventory control approaches is that the replenishment of inventory items can be planned independently of each other. The planning philosophy is that the inventory availability of each component should be maintained. Orlicky offered several important insights, which revolutionized manufacturing inventory management practice.

- Manufacturing inventory, unlike finished goods or service parts inventory, cannot usefully be treated as independent items. The demand for component items is dependent on the demand for the assemblies of which they are part.

- Once a time phased schedule of requirements for top level assemblies is put in place (master schedule), it follows that the dependent time phased requirements for all components can be calculated. Consequently, it makes little sense to forecast them.

- The assumptions underlying inventory control models usually involve a uniform or at least a well defined demand pattern. However, the dependency of component demand on the demand for their parents gives rise to a phenomenon of discontinuous demand at the component level. Orlicky termed this *lumpy* demand. Lumpy demand occurs even if the master scheduled parts face uniform demand because of the effects of lot sizing and the fact that demand for an

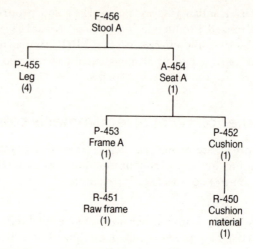

Figure 5.1   Product structure for Stool A.

item often arises from a number of product sources. The implication of the lumpy demand phenomenon is that order point techniques are inappropriate for managing manufacturing inventories.

- A computer provides the data processing capability to perform the necessary calculations efficiently.

The shift from the stock control approach to the MRP approach can be viewed as a shift from control of the level of stock to discrete control of the flow of material. MRP is a flow control system in the sense that it orders only those components that are required to maintain manufacturing flow. Moreover, such orders can either be for purchased parts or manufactured parts. Therefore a requirements planning system lays the basis for both production scheduling and raw materials purchasing.

MRP is to be seen as a priority planning system in that it determines requirements, but it does not acknowledge all constraints that exist in the planning problem, particularly capacity. In the case of material constraints it points out the constraint violation but leaves the replanning to the user. In this way, MRP tells the users what must be done in order to meet the master schedule, as opposed to what can be done.

Thus the starting point for MRP is the recognition that products to be manufactured or assembled can be represented by a bill of material. A bill of material describes the parent/child relationship between an assembly and its component parts or raw material. This is illustrated for an example stool in Figure 5.1 and shown in tabular form in Table 5.1. As can be seen,

Table 5.1 BOM for Stool A, Seat A, Frame A, and Cushion.

STOOL A Part number	Description	Quantity per	Make or buy
P-455	Leg	4	B
A-454	Seat A	1	M

SEAT A Part number	Description	Quantity per	Make or buy
P-453	Frame A	1	M
P-452	Cushion	1	M

FRAME A Part number	Description	Quantity per	Make or buy
R-451	Raw frame	1	B

CUSHION Part number	Description	Quantity per	Make or buy
R-450	Cushion material	1	B

the bills of material may have an arbitrary number of levels and will typically have purchased items at the bottom level of each branch in the hierarchy. An implicit assumption is that there is an adequate part numbering system in the company to differentiate all parts and components at various stages of manufacturing where planning intervention may be required. The MRP system is based very simply on the fact that the BOM relationship allows one to derive the demand for component material based on the demand for the parent item. MRP was thus proposed as a technique for managing dependent component demand by transmitting the independent demand for top level products and spares through the component hierarchy, as represented by the BOM.

An MRP system is driven by the master production schedule, which records the independent demand for top level items. It is derived from evaluating forecasts, customer orders, and distribution center requirements. MRP uses this requirements information, together with information on product structure from the bill of materials file, current inventory status from the inventory file, and component lead times data from the master parts file. MRP produces a time phased schedule of planned order

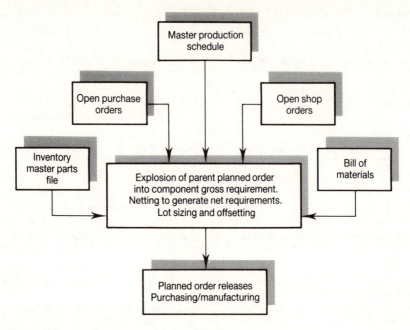

Figure 5.2   Basic structure of an MRP system.

releases on lower level items for purchasing and manufacturing. This time phased schedule is known as the materials requirements plan. This flow of information is illustrated in Figure 5.2.

Some of the main characteristics of MRP, which are apparent from the discussion above, include:

- MRP is *product oriented* in that it operates on a bill of materials to calculate the component and assembly requirements to manufacture and assemble a final product.

- MRP is *future oriented* in that it uses planning information from the master production schedule to calculate future component requirements instead of forecasts based on historical data.

- MRP involves *time phased requirements* in that during MRP processing, the requirements for individual components are calculated and offset by their expected lead time to determine the correct requirement date.

- MRP involves *priority planning* in that it establishes what needs to be done to meet the master schedule, as opposed to what can be done, given capacity and material constraints.

Table 5.2 Netting off MRP calculation.

Gross requirements
+ Allocations
− Projected inventory
− Scheduled receipts
= Net requirements

- MRP promotes control by *focusing on orders*, whether purchase orders or orders for the manufacturing plant.

5.4 How does MRP work?

In MRP, time is assumed to be discrete. Time is typically represented as a series of one week intervals, though systems which operate on daily planning periods are readily available. Demand for a component can derive from any of the products in which it is used, as well as independent spares parts orders.

A materials requirements planning system starts with the master production schedule as input and applies a set of procedures to generate a schedule of net requirements (and planned coverage of such requirements) for each component needed to implement the master production schedule. The system works down the BOM, level by level and component by component, until all parts are planned. It applies the following procedure for each component:

- Netting off the gross requirement against projected inventory and taking into account any open orders scheduled for receipt, as well as material already allocated from current inventory, thus yielding net requirements. The calculation is carried out as illustrated in Table 5.2.
- Conversion of the net requirement to a planned order quantity using a lot size.
- Placing a planned order in the appropriate period by backward scheduling from the required date by the lead time to fulfill the order for that component.
- Generating appropriate action and exception messages to guide the user's attention.

- Explosion of parent item planned production to gross requirements for all components, using the bill of materials relationships.

As is apparent, the prerequisites to operate an MRP system include:

- A master production schedule must exist. This master production schedule is a clear statement of the requirements in terms of quantities and due dates for top level items.
- For every parent item there must be a corresponding bill of materials, which gives an accurate and complete statement of the structure of that item.
- For every planned part there must be a set of inventory status information available. Inventory status is a statement of physical stock on hand, material allocated to released orders but not yet drawn from physical stock, and scheduled receipts for the item in question.
- For each planned part, either purchased or manufactured, a planning lead time must be set.

In order to explain these concepts more fully, the MRP technique will now be illustrated by a very simple example.

5.5 A simple MRP example

Consider the following example. Gizmo-Stools Inc. manufactures a simple four-legged stool. The company has an order for 100 stools to be delivered four weeks from now. There are no stools or stool legs in stock. There are four legs per stool and the lead time to assemble the stools, once the legs are available, is one week. Consequently, 400 legs must be available three weeks from now. If we know that it takes approximately two weeks to manufacture the stool legs (i.e. the planning lead time for the stool legs is two weeks), then we must issue the order to manufacture the legs by the end of this week. The MRP calculations for the stool are illustrated in Table 5.3 and for the legs in Table 5.4.

Let us now extend this example to explore more fully the basic procedures of the MRP system. We will assume that Gizmo-Stools Inc. manufactures two types of stool, namely a four-legged stool and a three-legged stool. The product structures, in the form of product family tree diagrams, are shown in Figure 5.3.

Within the diagram we have indicated the quantity of each item per parent. Thus, for example, there are three legs per Stool B and four legs per Stool A. We also indicate the part number. Furthermore, we note that the

Table 5.3 Analysis for stool.

Item: Stool

Week number	1	2	3	4	5	6	7	8	9	10
Gross requirements				100						
Scheduled receipts										
Projected inventory	0			−100						
Net requirements				100						
Planned orders			100							

Table 5.4 Analysis of stool leg.

Item: Stool leg

Week number	1	2	3	4	5	6	7	8	9	10
Gross requirements			400							
Scheduled receipts										
Projected inventory	0		− 400							
Net requirements			400							
Planned orders	400									

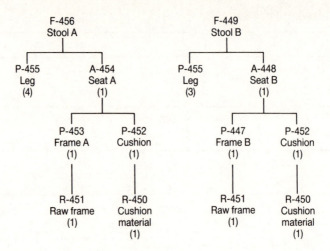

Figure 5.3 Two product structures.

two products have common components. Both stool types have the same legs, the same raw frames, and the same cushion material. This situation is typical of the type of situation that MRP handles very well, i.e. where production covers a range of products with common components and subassemblies.

In Table 5.5, the master parts information needed for the example is presented. The information is presented in part number order. The level code refers to the lowest level of any bill of material on which the component is to be found. Lead time is in weeks. The make/buy code refers to whether a part is manufactured or purchased. The lot sizing policy is **lot for lot** (L), by which the net requirement quantity is scheduled as the batch size for the replenishment order.

Within an MRP system, the **planning horizon** refers to the span of time the master production schedule covers, while the **time bucket** refers to the units of time into which the planning horizon is divided.

In this example a planning horizon of ten weeks and a time bucket of one week are used. In real MRP systems, time horizons should extend beyond the longest cumulative lead time for a product. The data structures used to represent time can be bucketed or non-bucketed. In the bucketed approach, a predetermined number of data cells are reserved to accumulate quantity information by period. In the non-bucketed approach, each part-quantity information pair has associated with it a time label. The bucketless approach is more flexible. The current week is beginning of week 1 and the master production schedule is shown in Table 5.6.

The relevant inventory data on each component are listed in Table 5.7. The **current inventory** represents the amount of material physically

Table 5.5 Master parts data.

Level	Part number	Lot size	Lead time	Description	Make/Buy
0	F-449	L	2	Stool B	M
0	F-456	L	2	Stool A	M
1	A-448	L	1	Seat B	M
1	A-454	L	1	Seat A	M
1	P-455	L	2	Leg	B
2	P-447	L	1	Frame B	M
2	P-452	L	1	Cushion	M
2	P-453	L	1	Frame A	M
3	R-450	L	3	Cushion Material	B
3	R-451	L	2	Raw frame	B

Table 5.6 Master production schedule.

Week number	1	2	3	4	5	6	7	8	9	10
Stool A							50			80
Stool B						40			70	

Table 5.7 Inventory data.

Part number	Current inventory	Allocated
A-448	10	0
A-454	0	0
F-449	30	0
F-456	10	0
P.447	10	0
P-452	60	20
P-453	50	10
P-455	40	0
R-451	0	0
R-4S0	0	0

Table 5.8 Open orders data.

Part number	Scheduled receipts	Due date
A-454	40	2
P-455	20	3
R-450	100	1

in stock. The **allocated** represents that quantity of physical stock already committed for released orders but not yet issued.

Table 5.8 lists those orders which are open, i.e. due as scheduled receipts. The concept of allocated material is best explained by an example. For example, we see that there is a manufacturing order for Seat A (part number A-454) due for completion by the end of week 2. At this stage not all of the raw material to build this order has been drawn from the stock-room. There are quantities of the components of Seat A, i.e. Frame A (part number P-453) and the cushion (part number P-452), allocated to the released order for Seat A, and so this allocated material cannot be considered available to satisfy other material requirements.

There is now sufficient data on which to illustrate a simple MRP calculation. The analysis begins with the top level items in the bill of materials. We will start with Stool A (see Table 5.9). We take as our **gross requirements** for Stool A the requirements identified in the master production schedule. We are also aware that according to the inventory data there are 10 of Stool A in stock. There are no scheduled receipts for this item and hence the **net requirement** is as shown in Table 5.9. The **order release** date is calculated simply by offsetting the net requirement due date by the lead time. The analysis for the other item in the master production schedule, i.e. Stool B, is similar and is presented in Table 5.10.

The next item in the bill of materials is the leg, which is common to both types of stool. Initially we must generate the gross requirements for legs based on the planned orders for Stool A and Stool B. From our bill of materials data, we know that there are three legs per Stool B and four legs per Stool A. Hence the gross requirement for legs is as indicated in Table 5.11. There are also scheduled receipts for legs to be delivered in week 3 and these must be taken into account in our calculation of net requirements as in Table 5.11.

The calculation for Seat A, based on the planned orders for Stool A, is shown in Table 5.12. The calculation of the net requirements for Seat B, based on the planned orders for Stool B, is shown in Table 5.13.

Table 5.9 Analysis of Stool A.

Item: Stool A	Part number: F-456									
Week number	1	2	3	4	5	6	7	8	9	10
Gross requirements							50			80
Scheduled receipts										
Projected inventory	10						−40			−120
Net requirements							40			80
Planned orders					40			80		

Table 5.10 Analysis of Stool B.

Item: Stool B	Part number: F-449									
Week number	1	2	3	4	5	6	7	8	9	10
Gross requirements						40			70	
Scheduled receipts										
Projected inventory	30					−10			−80	
Net requirements						10			70	
Planned orders				10			70			

Table 5.11   Analysis of legs (common part).

Item: Leg	Part number: P-455									
Week number	1	2	3	4	5	6	7	8	9	10
Gross requirements				30	160		210	320		
Scheduled receipts			20							
Projected inventory	40		60	30	−130		−340	−660		
Net requirements					130		210	320		
Planned orders			130		210	320				

Table 5.12   Analysis of Seat A.

Item: Leg	Part number: A-454									
Week number	1	2	3	4	5	6	7	8	9	10
Gross requirements					40			80		
Scheduled receipts		40								
Projected inventory	0	40			0			−80		
Net requirements								80		
Planned orders							80			

Table 5.13   Analysis of Seat B.

Item: Seat B	Part number: F-4448									
Week number	*1*	*2*	*3*	*4*	*5*	*6*	*7*	*8*	*9*	*10*
Gross requirements				10			70			
Scheduled receipts										
Projected inventory	10			0			−70			
Net requirements							70			
Planned orders						70				

We now go on to consider the requirements for Frame A (see Table 5.14), which are based on the planned orders for Seat A calculated previously. Next, the requirements for Frame B (Table 5.15) are reviewed, based on the results of the analysis of the needs of Seat B analyzed earlier. The requirements for the cushion, given that it is common to both types of stool, is based on the net requirements for Seat A and Seat B. The calculation is shown in Table 5.16.

Similarly the requirement for the raw frame is based on both types of frame and is shown in Table 5.17. The requirement for the cushion material is based on the net requirement for the cushion itself and is calculated in Table 5.18.

Thus we have managed to make our way down through the two relevant BOMs. For each component we have taken into account the gross requirements and calculated an appropriate schedule of planned orders based on inventory data and planning lead times. Finally, we exploded the planned orders to gross requirements for all component parts. This concludes our treatment of the introductory MRP example.

Table 5.14   Analysis of Frame A.

Item: Frame A	Part number: P-453									
Week number	*1*	*2*	*3*	*4*	*5*	*6*	*7*	*8*	*9*	*10*
Gross requirements						80				
Scheduled receipts										
Projected inventory	40						−40			
Net requirements							40			
Planned orders						40				

Table 5.15   Analysis of Frame B.

Item: Frame B	Part number: P-447									
Week number	*1*	*2*	*3*	*4*	*5*	*6*	*7*	*8*	*9*	*10*
Gross requirements						70				
Scheduled receipts										
Projected inventory	10					−60				
Net requirements						60				
Planned orders					60					

Table 5.16   Analysis of cushion.

Item: Cushion	Part number: P-452									
Week number	*1*	*2*	*3*	*4*	*5*	*6*	*7*	*8*	*9*	*10*
Gross requirements						70	80			
Scheduled receipts										
Projected inventory	40					−30	−110			
Net requirements						30	80			
Planned orders					30	80				

Table 5.17   Analysis of raw frame.

Item: Raw frame	Part number: R-451									
Week number	*1*	*2*	*3*	*4*	*5*	*6*	*7*	*8*	*9*	*10*
Gross requirements					60	40				
Scheduled receipts										
Projected inventory	0				−60	−100				
Net requirements					60	40				
Planned orders			60	40						

Table 5.18 Analysis of cushion material.

Item: Cushion material					Part number: R-450					
Week number	1	2	3	4	5	6	7	8	9	10
Gross requirements					30	80				
Scheduled receipts	100									
Projected inventory	100				70	−10				
Net requirements						10				
Planned orders			10							

5.6 Conclusion

In this chapter the MRP approach was introduced. Its assumptions were described and its operation illustrated by means of a simple example. Much of what remains to be known about the mechanics of the technique of MRP is really implementation detail, which is important from the perspective of operating an MRP system. Some factors fall within the domain of software engineering, some within the domain of decision science. None really changes the fundamental procedure. In any MRP system, the decision making procedures are no more complex than the basic arithmetic illustrated in this chapter. These implementation factors are discussed mainly in Chapter 6. Extensions of MRP are described in Chapter 7. Discussion of the manufacturing database is left until Chapter 8 and lot sizing techniques until Chapter 9.

Questions

(5.1) Distinguish clearly between MRP and closed loop MRP.

(5.2) "MRP is a flow control system in the sense that it orders only those components required to maintain manufacturing flow." Comment.

(5.3) What is lumpy demand?

(5.4) What do you understand by the term *time phased dependent demand*?

(5.5) Distinguish clearly between dependent and independent demand items.

(5.6) "The MRP system is based very simply on the fact that the BOM relationship allows one to derive the demand for component material based on the demand for the parent." Discuss.

(5.7) What are the main characteristics of MRP?

(5.8) Identify the four prerequisites of an MRP system.

(5.9) What do you understand by the term *planning horizon*?

(5.10) Distinguish clearly between current inventory, projected inventory, and allocated inventory.

The use of the MRP system

6.1 Introduction

An overview of the MRP approach to production planning was presented in Chapter 5 through a simple example. In this chapter, several important aspects of the operation of an MRP system are presented. The issues covered include such concerns as:

- Top-down planning in MRP.
- Bottom-up replanning.
- Time representation in MRP systems.
- The role of safety stocks in an MRP system.

Each of these issues will now be discussed in turn.

6.2 Top-down planning with MRP

Change is continuous within the manufacturing environment. The master schedule changes. The inventory status changes. Engineering activity modifies BOMs. Orders are released to the shop floor or purchasing. Orders are completed. Some of these events are planned. Some are unplanned. For example, if an order is completed on time then this is a planned event. In this case the original material plan should still be valid. If, however, an order is completed ahead of time or is late, then this usually means that the material plan is no longer valid. In either case, the MRP system must accommodate such changes. There are two basic approaches to replanning within MRP systems. These are top-down planning and bottom-up replanning. Section 6.2 discusses top-down planning, and bottom-up replanning is covered in Section 6.3.

We will discuss four important aspects of top-down planning:

(1)   Regenerative planning and net change.

(2)   The frequency of top-down planning.

(3)   The use of low level coding.

(4)   Rescheduling in top-down planning.

6.2.1   Regenerative and net change MRP

There are two basic styles to top-down planning. These are termed the **regenerative** approach and the **net change** approach. These involve alternative approaches to the system driven recalculation of an existing material plan based on changes in the input to that plan.

Regenerative MRP starts with the master production schedule and totally re-explodes it down through all the bills of materials to generate valid priorities. Net requirements and planned orders are completely *regenerated* at that time. The regenerative approach thus involves a complete re-analysis of each and every item identified in the master schedule, the explosion of all relevant BOMs and the calculation of gross and net requirements for planned items. The entire process is carried out in a batch processing mode on the computer and, for all but the simplest of master schedules, involves extensive data processing. Because of this, regenerative systems are typically operated in weekly and occasionally monthly replanning cycles.

In the net change MRP approach, the materials requirements plan is continuously stored in the computer. Whenever there is an unplanned event, such as a new order in the master schedule, an order being completed late or early, scrap or loss of inventory, or engineering changes to the BOMs, a partial explosion is initiated only for those parts affected by the change. If an event is planned, for example when an order is completed on time, then the original material plan should still be valid. The system is updated to reflect the new status but replanning is not initiated. Net change MRP can operate in two ways. One mode is to have an on-line net change system by which the system reacts instantaneously to unplanned changes as they occur. In most cases, however, change transactions are batched (typically by day) and replanning happens overnight.

In the regenerative approach there is a vulnerability because of the need to maintain the validity of the requirements plan between system driven replanning runs. The role of user driven bottom-up replanning is discussed in Section 6.3. The MRP system also supports transactions that modify the status of the various planning inputs, such as inventory status, the MPS or the BOMs. However, in a regenerative system, these changes are only reflected in a new requirements plan after a new planning run. Net change systems typically operate with many frequent partial replanning

Table 6.1 Original master production schedule.

Week number	1	2	3	4	5	6	7	8	9	10
Stool A							50			80
Stool B						40			70	

Table 6.2 Revised master production schedule.

Week number	1	2	3	4	5	6	7	8	9	10
Stool A							50	10		80
Stool B						40			70	

runs and, as a result, are not subject to the same degree of vulnerability in plan validity between runs.

The difference between regenerative and net change can be illustrated by considering how each system treats the master schedule in replanning. Regenerative systems view the master schedule as a document, new editions of which are released on a periodic basis. Net change systems, on the other hand, see the master schedule as a document in a state of continuous change. The master schedule is processed in terms of the changes which have taken place since the last run. If we recall our simple MRP example from Chapter 5, we can illustrate this difference. The original master schedule is as shown in Table 6.1.

In our example in Chapter 5, we calculated the net requirements and planned order releases to meet this master schedule. Now consider what happens if, at the beginning of week 2, a new order comes in from a customer for 10 of Stool A to be delivered in week 8. This order is placed on the master schedule which now appears as illustrated in Table 6.2.

In a regenerative MRP approach, this new master schedule would be the basis for a *complete rerun* of the MRP analysis at the next replanning cycle. The analysis would proceed in the same manner adopted in Chapter 5. In a net change approach, it is the *change* to the master schedule that forms the basis of replanning, as in Table 6.3.

Table 6.3 Net change in the master production schedule.

Week number	1	2	3	4	5	6	7	8	9	10
Stool A								+10		
Stool B										

Under net change, it is only necessary to replan the requirements for Stool A. This replanning is executed by exploding the change in the master schedule through the bill of materials for Stool A and modifying all requirements information from the previous analysis. Parts unique to Stool B, such as Frame B (part number P-447) would not be replanned, whereas in a regenerative mode they would have been. We note that a net change system must store all the requirements analysis on an ongoing basis, whereas in a regenerative system this is not necessary, but may be done.

One potential difficulty with net change systems is that there is a reduced self-purging capability. Errors may creep into the requirements plan, perhaps because of planner actions in bottom-up replanning. Since the master schedule is not completely re-exploded, as in the regenerative approach, any errors in the old plan tend to remain. As a result, errors in the material plan may accumulate over time. In order to counteract this problem, firms using net change MRP tend occasionally to do a complete regeneration so as to purge the system of these errors.

The net change approach offers the advantages of reactiveness. The pressures for competitiveness will tend to encourage the migration towards net change style systems. The disadvantage of a net change system is its *nervousness*. A badly run net change system, as it reacts to many unplanned events, will flood the materials planners with exception messages.

6.2.2 Frequency of replanning

As we have seen, regenerative systems are typically replanned on a weekly or monthly basis. Net change systems support more frequent replanning, either on-line or batched in daily or weekly increments. There is a tradeoff between data processing costs and the maintenance of valid priorities on manufacturing and purchase orders. The consensus view seems to be that the replanning cycle should be no longer than a week.

6.2.3 Low level codes

Low level codes determine the sequence in which the processing of part requirements is carried out. Components may be common to many bills of materials. In regenerative systems, if MRP processing were simply to follow a path through the bill of material hierarchies in its replanning, it would, as a result, replan common components several times over. Low level coding is a data processing mechanism which serves to overcome this inefficiency. The procedure is to assign to each component a code which designates the lowest level in any bill of material on which it is found. MRP processing then can proceed level by level and a component will not be planned until the level currently being processed is that of its low level code. Low level codes are also a useful feature in net change systems when these systems are operated on a batch basis.

6.2.4   Rescheduling in top-down planning

Ho *et al.* (1986) describe rescheduling as one of the difficult problems to resolve in production scheduling, within an MRP context. When an MRP system is replanning in a top-down fashion, it typically will adjust either the due date or the quantity of any planned order. If it identifies the need to make a change to an open order (a scheduled receipt), it typically sends an exception message for the materials planner to execute the change.

Consider the following situation. The requirements for Stool A, as determined from calculation based on the master schedule at week 1, are shown in Table 6.4. A fixed lot size of 200 is being used. (Lot sizing techniques will be discussed in more detail in Chapter 9.) Analysis based on this master schedule results in the planned release of an order for 200 of Stool A in week 5.

At the beginning of week 2 a new master schedule is made available, which results in new gross requirements for Stool A. The new master schedule involves an extra requirement for 70 of Stool A in week 4. If we analyze the effects of this change we see that we can meet the overall requirement, including the new requirement for 70 in week 4, by rescheduling the original planned order for 200 from week 5 into week 2. (See Table 6.5.)

The type of situation just described occurs frequently in manufacturing. We may need to reschedule existing planned orders because of modifications to the master schedule, or because of failure of a vendor or shop to deliver in the planned lead time or, indeed, any unplanned event. Rescheduling may involve the retiming of a planned order, as in the example above, or it may require the modification of the order size or perhaps both.

The example above was a trivial one and the solution presented itself readily. However, how would we have coped if the new item in the master schedule could not be delivered within the available lead time? Let us review Table 6.6.

Table 6.4 Analysis of Stool A.

Item: Stool A	Part number: F-456									
Week number	1	2	3	4	5	6	7	8	9	10
Gross requirements							50			80
Scheduled receipts										
Projected inventory	10						−40			−120
Net requirements							40			80
Order coverage							200			
Planned orders					200					

Table 6.5 Analysis of Stool A based on a revised master schedule.

Item: Stool A	Part number: F-456									
Week number	2	3	4	5	6	7	8	9	10	11
Gross requirements			70			50			80	
Scheduled receipts										
Projected inventory	10		−60			−110			−190	
Net requirements			60			50			80	
Order coverage			200							
Planned orders	200 ◀───────────									

This revision of the gross requirements for Stool A shows a requirement for 70 of Stool A during week 3. This produces a net requirement of 60 in week 3. However the lead time for this item is 2 weeks, which implies that the order should be scheduled for week 1 and we are presently in week 2.

Orlicky (1976) suggested the use of a **minimum lead time** to deliver such an order (purchasing or manufactured). This minimum lead time is the time required to complete an order under the highest priority and in the case of a manufactured item might be little greater than the sum of the processing time and the transportation times. The result of this is that we could define two lead times and use the *minimum lead time* for automatic rescheduling in the event of a problem such as that in Table 6.6.

MRP practice did not follow Orlicky's suggestion in this case. If faced with a situation like the above, the system will send an exception message to the planner and leave it to him/her to resolve the problem by the use of bottom-up replanning.

6.3 Bottom-up replanning

As pointed out earlier, an MRP system must react to change. In top-down planning, the system itself does the planning. An alternative is for the planner to manage the replanning process. This is termed bottom-up replanning and makes use of two tools – the pegged requirements report and the firm planned order – both of which are described in this section.

6.3.1 Pegged requirements

Pegging allows the user to identify the sources of demand for a particular component's gross requirements. These gross requirements typically originate either from its parent assemblies or from independent demand in the MPS, or from the demand for spare parts. This process is again illustrated by recourse to our simple MRP example.

Within the BOMs for the two types of stool in our master schedule the leg is a common part. The gross requirements for the leg shown in Table 6.7 arise from a number of sources, as illustrated in Table 6.8.

A report, such as Table 6.8, allows the materials planner to *retrace* the steps of the MRP analysis and to understand the sources of the total gross requirements for the item in question. The procedure of identifying each gross requirement with its source at the next immediate higher level in the BOM is termed **single level pegging**. Through a series of single level pegging reports, we can eventually trace a set of requirements back to their sources in the master schedule.

Table 6.6 Analysis of Stool A based on a further revised master schedule.

Item: Stool A   Part number: F-456

Week number	2	3	4	5	6	7	8	9	10	11
Gross requirements		70				50			80	
Scheduled receipts										
Projected inventory	10	−60				−110			−190	
Net requirements		60				50			80	
Order coverage						200				
Planned orders	???			200						

Table 6.7 Analysis of legs (common part).

Item: Leg   Part number: P-455

Week number	1	2	3	4	5	6	7	8	9	10
Gross requirements				30	160		210	320		
Scheduled receipts			20							
Projected inventory	40		60	30	−130		−340	−660		
Net requirements					130		210	320		
Planned orders			130		210	320				

Table 6.8   Pegged requirements for the leg.

Requirement		Source	
Component quantity	*Week number*	*Parent*	*Parent quantity*
30	4	Stool B	10
160	5	Stool A	40
210	7	Stool B	70
320	8	Stool A	80

An alternative facility is **full pegging** where each individual requirement for a planned item is identified against a master production scheduled item and/or a customer order. This, however, is quite rare in practice for a number of reasons. As is clear even from our simple example, requirements tend to arise from a number of sources in the master schedule. If a lot sizing technique is used, it becomes practically impossible to associate individual batches or lots with particular customer orders. Other factors, such as safety stocks, shrinkage, and scrap allowances, further complicate the situation. As a result, the single level pegging facility is standard practice and full pegging is rarely used.

The technique of pegging is useful in that it allows the user to retrace the MRP systems planning steps in the event of an unexpected event, such as a supplier being unable to deliver in the planning lead time. By retracing the original calculations the user can detect what orders are likely to be affected and perhaps identify appropriate remedial action. The remedial action often involves overriding the normal planning procedures of MRP. This is done by using the **firm planned order** technique.

6.3.2   Firm planned orders

The firm planned order allows the materials planner to force the MRP system to plan in a particular way, thus overriding lot size or lead time rules. A firm planned order differs from an ordinary planned order in that the MRP explosion procedure will not change it in any way. This technique can aid planners working with MRP systems to respond to specific material and capacity problems.

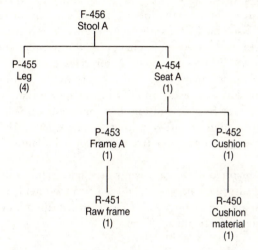

Figure 6.1 Product structure for Stool A.

A typical problem might be the failure of a vendor or the manufacturing plant to deliver an order within the allocated lead time. Consider the BOM for Stool A in Figure 6.1 drawn from our earlier example.

It is clear from this BOM that Stool A cannot be produced unless Seat A and the legs are available. The lead time for the legs is two weeks, while that for Seat A is one week. The lead time for Stool A, assuming that Seat A and the legs are available, is two weeks. The lead time for Frame A and the cushion is one week.

Assume we have a master schedule requirement for 100 of Stool A in week 10. This leads us to plan the availability of 100 of Seat A by the end of week 8, and 100 each of Frame A and the cushion by the end of week 7. We also plan the availability of 400 of the legs at the end of week 8. The unexpected occurs! We are informed by the factory department responsible for the manufacture of Seat A that it cannot deliver the required amount of Seat A until week 9 – one week late.

What are the consequences of this?

- The delivery of the 100 items of Stool A is now in danger unless the lead time for assembling the stool can be reduced from two weeks to the one week available.

- If a **rush job** on the stool assembly is possible, then it is clear that there is now no necessity to have 400 of the legs available at the end of week 8. They can wait until the end of week 9 when Seat A will also become available.

In this type of situation, we need a capability to override the normal *logic* of MRP in order to cater for the unexpected event. Assuming that Stool A can be assembled by a *rush job* in one week, rather than the normal two weeks, there is no need for a change in the master schedule. We can create a *firm planned order* for Stool A for release by the end of week 9, rather than week 8, and mark it due for delivery by the end of week 10. The MRP explosion will, as a result, modify in the appropriate manner the due dates for the legs, for Seat A, and for all components of Seat A. The significance of the firm planned order is that a subsequent MRP run will not attempt to *correct* the deviation from the normal planned lead times on Stool A.

The firm planned order can also override lot sizing rules (see Chapter 9). The availability of a *pegging* facility, combined with the use of firm planned orders, are the planner's chief tools in handling inevitable, unforeseen events in manufacturing.

6.4 Time representation

In this section **bucketed** and **bucketless** MRP systems will be discussed. Bucketed systems limit the time horizon that may be considered and the granularity of timing that may be ascribed to an order. Bucketless systems enable daily visibility to an order's date of requirement. The length of the planning horizon necessary to make an MRP system effective will also be discussed.

6.4.1 Bucketed and bucketless MRP systems

The data structures used to represent time in an MRP system can be bucketed or non-bucketed.

In the bucketed approach, a predetermined number of data cells are reserved to accumulate quantity information by period. This is illustrated by the matrix structure used in our calculations of requirements. These data cells are known as time buckets. A weekly time bucket contains all of the relevant planning data for an entire week. Since the number of buckets is predetermined, this means that there is a bound on the planning horizon, depending on what time divisions the buckets represent.

Weekly time buckets are considered to be the granularity necessary for near and medium term planning by MRP, whereas monthly buckets are considered too coarse. However, the normal bucket of one week may itself be too coarse to facilitate detailed short term planning. Further out in the planning horizon, monthly or perhaps quarterly time buckets are acceptable. There is no reason why the MRP system cannot accommodate a variable time bucket size over the span of the planning horizon.

Table 6.9 Planned orders for legs.

Item: Leg	Part number: P-455									
Week number	1	2	3	4	5	6	7	8	9	10
.			.		.	.				
.			.		.	.				
.			.		.	.				
Planned orders			130		210	320				

There is, however, a complication arising from the notion of time buckets which is best illustrated by means of an example. Recall the MRP example, in which we generated requirements for the stool leg (part number P-455). These were in the form of planned orders and are reproduced in Table 6.9.

These orders are scheduled for release in weeks 3, 5, and 6. But what do we mean by an order scheduled for release in week 3? Do we intend that the order be released at the beginning of the week, in the middle of the week or at the end of the week? In effect, each of these orders is an event which must be scheduled for a point in time. Our time bucket represents a span of time. The problem is resolved by the MRP system designer and users adopting a convention. One may choose to adopt the last day within the time bucket as the order receipt date. The important point is to adhere to the convention once it has been adopted.

In the non-bucketed approach, each element of time phased data has a specific time label associated with it and is not accumulated into buckets. What this means is that there is provision for daily visibility on requirements timing. Moreover, the bucketless approach has no limit on the extent of the planning horizon. Consequently, the bucketless approach is more flexible.

6.4.2 The planning horizon

The planning horizon refers to the span of time from the current date out to some future date, over which material plans are generated. The chief factor in determining the planning horizon is the longest cumulative manufacturing and procurement time for a master scheduled item. If our horizon does not extend this far, then a new order at the end of the planning horizon may require a release of a purchase order last week, and the master schedule will be infeasible before we start!

A planning horizon longer than the cumulative product lead time will avoid this problem and will give sufficient visibility to facilitate material procurement. The planning horizon is often extended further than the longest cumulative lead time for the purpose of gaining visibility of manufacturing capacity needs in the future.

The upper limit on the range of the planning horizon is determined by our ability to make meaningful statements about the nature and contents of the master production schedule. The longer the planning horizon, the more difficult it is to make useful forecasts about the marketplace and the likely demand for products and end level items. The need to put in place a master schedule over this planning horizon is the chief vulnerability of MRP systems. As Burbidge (1985b) says, "it is not given to man to tell the future." A naïve reliance on a dubious MPS is a recipe for failure. In general, firms have not recognized the critical need for reducing procurement and manufacturing lead times as a means of improving MPS accuracy.

6.5 The use of safety stocks

Safety stocks are a quantity of stock planned to be maintained in inventory, to protect against unexpected fluctuations in demand and/or supply. In this sense, safety stocks can be considered as a type of insurance policy to cover unexpected events, whether such events be the failure of a vendor to meet a promised delivery date or an unexpected increase in demand for the product. However, given the high cost of tying up capital in inventory, the use of safety stocks can be expensive.

Safety stocks can be incorporated into the MRP analysis. In the master parts database there is normally a field within each record which can indicate the safety stock of each part. Going back to our planning example of stool legs, let us assume that there is a safety stock requirement of 20. This implies that we should have at least 20 legs available at all times. The effect of this on the planned orders is illustrated in Table 6.10.

We could present Table 6.10 in an alternative manner by subtracting the safety stocks from the initial inventory and then calculating the item net requirements in the usual way. This is illustrated in Table 6.11. In the **projected inventory** row, we note that the value for week 1 has been reduced from 40 to 20. In this situation the meaning of the term projected inventory has, in effect, changed. Whereas in previous tables of this type the projected inventory referred to the quantity of material projected to be physically in stock less any allocations against open orders, it now refers to the projected physical stock less allocations, less safety stock.

Table 6.10 Analysis with safety stock of legs (method A).

Item: Leg	Part number: P-455				Safety stock: 20					
Week number	*1*	*2*	*3*	*4*	*5*	*6*	*7*	*8*	*9*	*10*
Gross requirements				30	160		210	320		
Scheduled receipts			20							
Projected inventory	40	40	60	30	−130		−340	−660		
Net requirements					150		210	320		
Planned orders			150		210	320				

Table 6.11 Analysis with safety stock (method B).

Item: Leg	Part number: P-455				Safety stock: 0					
Week number	*1*	*2*	*3*	*4*	*5*	*6*	*7*	*8*	*9*	*10*
Gross requirements				30	160		210	320		
Scheduled receipts			20							
Projected inventory	20		40	10	−150		−360	−680		
Net requirements					150		210	320		
Planned orders			150		210	320				

6.5.1   Should safety stocks be used?

It is clear that if we insert a safety stock requirement for a high level item then we will automatically generate additional requirements for lower level dependent items. This distortion of demand may more than outweigh the benefit of safety stocks. Orlicky agreed that safety stocks should be used for independent demand items as protection primarily against forecast errors. He also granted that in the case of an unreliable supplier, safety stock (or safety lead time) could be used for the component in question.

DeBodt and Van Wassenhove (1983) in a case study, commented as follows:

> "From our analysis . . . we concluded that, no matter what forecasting technique is being used, forecast errors are considerable . . . it follows that, in order to maintain a good customer service level, it will be necessary to have some safety provision on the finished product level. However, it is also necessary to protect the production departments against stockouts. Therefore, it may also be necessary to have safety stocks on (some) component levels . . ."

Besides the inventory cost, safety stocks have an additional disadvantage in the case of dependent demand items, since their use tends to cover up and make it easy to live with problems. The safety stocks may encourage the ongoing acceptance of a poor quality manufacturing process or poor delivery service by a supplier. As such, no one will be motivated to eliminate the problem. This discussion will be taken further when we consider the JIT (Just in Time) approach to production management in Part III. In any case, the use of safety stock across the board is unjustified.

6.5.2   How is the level of safety stock calculated?

The setting of safety stock quantities for dependent demand items in MRP tends, in practice, to be done on an ad hoc basis. For a particular item, it may simply reflect the *best guess* of the materials planner having regard to local knowledge of a particular supplier's past performance or even, perhaps, a whole industrial sector's characteristics.

The level of safety stock may alternately be calculated by reviewing the historical average demand for the item in question and then deciding to have safety stock to cover a given percentage of the likely demand over the lead time of the item. Let us illustrate this point from our ongoing example. Demand for legs (part number P-455) is 720 over a 10-week period, which averages 72 per week. The lead time for this item is 2 weeks. One policy might be to cover 25% of the lead time, i.e. maintain one half of a week's demand in stock as a reserve or safety stock. This suggests a safety stock of 36. A more conservative and, of course, expensive policy might be to cover 50% of the lead time and hold one week's stock or 72 items as safety stock. A similar margin of safety could also be achieved by the use of a safety lead time, whereby an additional safety lead time is added to the planning lead time to allow for unexpected events.

An open area of manufacturing research concerns the use of safety stocks for long lead time items. This can have the effect of improving a firm's ability to react quickly to unexpected demand. It is a matter of debate as to whether this is better handled by a floating MPS **hedge** or by using safety stock on a few key long lead time items.

6.6 Conclusion

In this chapter the operation of the MRP system was covered. Approaches for top-down and bottom-up replanning were described. The use of bucketless and bucketed systems, the length of the planning horizon and the use of safety stocks were also discussed. In Chapter 7 the extended version of MRP, known as manufacturing resource planning or MRP II, will be reviewed.

Questions

(6.1) Identify the types of changes with which an MRP system must deal.

(6.2) Distinguish clearly between regenerative and net change MRP systems.

(6.3) "Net Change MRP systems see the master schedule as a document in a state of continuous change." Discuss.

(6.4) What are low level codes? How and when are they used?

(6.5) When should minimum lead time be used?

(6.6) How are pegging and firm planned orders used to support bottom-up replanning?

(6.7) Distinguish clearly between single level pegging and full pegging.

(6.8) When might a planner use a firm planned order to override the normal MRP logic?

(6.9) Distinguish clearly between bucketed and bucketless MRP systems.

(6.10) What are safety stocks? Why are they used?

(6.11) Should safety stocks be used for top level (in the BOM) items? Why?

(6.12) How is the level of safety stock calculated?

CHAPTER SEVEN

Manufacturing resource planning (MRP II)

7.1 Introduction

This chapter describes Manufacturing Resource Planning (MRP II). Manufacturing resource planning represents an extension of the features of the MRP system to support many other manufacturing functions beyond material planning, inventory control, and BOM control. We shall review how the evolution from MRP to MRP II took place and examine the notion of *closed loop* MRP. Some of the major MRP II modules will also be outlined. Furthermore, we will review some of the quantitative techniques widely used in MRP II systems, including various forecasting and scheduling algorithms.

7.2 The evolution from MRP to MRP II

Manufacturing resource planning evolved from MRP by a gradual series of extensions to MRP system functionality. These extensions were natural and not very complicated as, for example, in the addition of transaction processing software to support the purchasing, inventory, and financial functions of the firm. In supporting the extension of decision support, similar and quite reasonable assumptions are made and similar procedures to those of MRP are applied. In this way, MRP was extended to support Master Planning, Rough Cut Capacity Planning (RCCP), Capacity Requirements Planning (CRP), and Production Activity Control (PAC). Production activity control is the term favored by the American Production and Inventory Control Society to cover activities traditionally described by shop floor control.

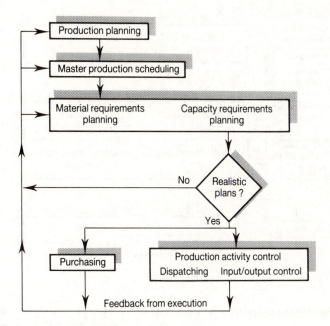

Figure 7.1   Closed route MRP.

The term *closed loop MRP* denotes a stage of MRP system development wherein the planning functions of master scheduling, MRP, and capacity requirements planning are linked with the execution functions of production activity control and purchasing. These execution modules include features for input/output measurement, detailed scheduling and dispatching on the shop floor, planned delay reports from both the shop floor and vendors, as well as purchasing follow-up and control functionality. Closed loop signifies that not only are the execution modules part of the overall system, but there is also feedback from the execution functions so that plans can be kept valid at all times. Figure 7.1 indicates the nature of closed loop MRP.

With the extension of master production scheduling to deal with all master planning and the support of business planning in financial terms, and through the addition of certain financial features to the closed loop system so that outputs, such as the purchase commitment report, shipping budget and inventory projection could be produced, it was realized that the resultant system offered an integrated approach to the management of all manufacturing resources. This extended MRP was labeled *manufacturing resource planning* or *MRP II*. The MRP II system is thus a closed loop MRP system with additional features to cover business and financial planning. MRP II nominally includes an extensive **what if** capability. However, several of the additional features included in MRP II software packages remain largely unused in practice. We shall see why in Chapter 10.

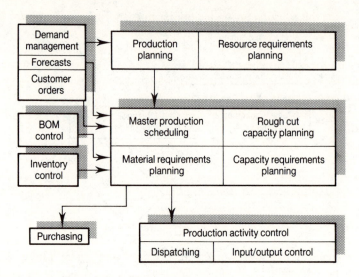

Figure 7.2 Manufacturing resource planning.

The modular structure of a typical MRP II system is shown in Figure 7.2.

In Chapter 3 it was seen that the production management system, as exemplified by an MRP II system, can be considered a significant island of automation in manufacturing. This is attested to by its integration of many diverse manufacturing functions, from financial systems down to the shop floor. However, as an island of automation, it has several inadequacies in terms of broader integration into CIM.

A brief description of the various modules is given in the following sections.

7.3 Master production scheduling

The MPS is a statement of what the company plans to manufacture. It is the planned build schedule, by quantity and date, for top level items, either finished products or high level configurations of material (either physical configurations or pseudo configurations used solely for planning purposes). The MPS module takes into account the sales forecast as well as considerations such as backlog, availability of material, availability of capacity, management policy, and company goals, etc. in determining the best manufacturing strategy.

The MPS *drives* MRP and is thus the key input into the MRP process. Any errors within it, such as poor forecasts, etc. cannot be compensated for by sophisticated MRP analysis as in lot sizing, calculation of safety stock or rescheduling. The MPS must be realistic in terms of the goals it sets for the manufacturing facility. It must not be merely a *wish list* of desirable production levels set by top management.

The accuracy of the MPS varies over the planning horizon. The planning data for the near term would tend to be more accurate since it is dominated by actual customer orders, distribution warehouse requirements, and spare parts requirements. Change to the short term MPS should be a rare occurrence and the short term MPS should be treated as a series of firm planned orders.

Further out in the planning horizon, the MPS is likely to be less accurate and to be dominated by forecasts rather than actual orders. Forecasts may be based on analysis of historical trends, consideration of the state of the economy and market, and the actions of competitors. It may reflect the *best guesses* of those close to the market or it may involve the use of analytic forecasting and trend analysis techniques. Techniques, such as moving average analysis, exponential smoothing, and regression analysis, may well be used to analyze past data in order to predict future data. These techniques will be presented in detail in Section 7.3.1. The person or group responsible for the forecast must be aware of where each product in the company's portfolio of products sits in terms of the product life cycle and take this into account when preparing a forecast. This latter is particularly important today in industries such as electronics and telecommunications, where product life cycles tend to be relatively short.

A typical MPS might look like Table 7.1. Typically, the master schedule module software allows for a system generated forecast, a manually entered forecast, a schedule of actual customer orders received, and a very simple procedure to combine the above into a working estimate of demand. The user may specify a master production schedule. Each order is treated as a firm planned manufacturing order. There is a netting process very similar to MRP as the forecast demand is netted with the MPS and current inventory to generate a projection of inventory on-hand and **available to promise**. Projected inventory is based on initial inventory plus the firm planned orders less total demand. Available to promise is based on initial inventory plus firm planned orders less actual orders.

The difference between the MPS module and the MRP procedure is that demand will only propagate from the scheduled MPS and not from the projected requirements. This means that the MPS will not influence manufacturing or purchasing orders without the intervention of the master planner.

In Table 7.2 the full MPS planning analysis for Stool B is illustrated. The aggregating procedure for demand in this instance is as follows: in the first 2 weeks the actual orders dominate while beyond this time, manual forecasts dominate. In the case where there is no manual forecast the system generated forecast dominates.

It is important that there be a check on the feasibility of the proposed MPS before it is frozen and released to the manufacturing system for

Table 7.1   The first 13 weeks of the MPS.

	Month 1			Month 2				Month 3				
	1	*2*	*3*	*4*	*5*	*6*	*7*	*8*	*9*	*10*	*11*	*12*	*13*
Stool A	70	70	70	70	70	70	70	70	70	70	70	70	70
Stool B	80	80	80	80	80	60	60	60	60	60	0	0	0
Stool C	100	100	120	120	120	120	140	140	140	140	160	160	160
Stool D	10	15	15	10	10	10	15	15	10	10	10	10	10
Stool E	40	40	35	35	30	30	30	20	20	20	20	20	20

Table 7.2 MPS analysis of Stool B.

Item: Stool B						Part number: F-449							
Week number	1	2	3	4	5	6	7	8	9	10	11	12	13
System forecast	60	60	60	60	60	60	60	60	60	60	60	60	60
Manual forecast	50	60	40	50	70	80	80	70	70				
Actual orders	55	60	30	20	25	5		10					
Total demand	55	60	40	50	70	80	80	70	70	60	60	60	60
Firm planned orders	80	80	80	80	80	60	60	60	60	60			
Net requirements													55
Starting inventory	60												
Projected inventory	85	105	145	175	185	165	145	135	125	125	65	5	−55
Cumulative available to promise	85	105	155	215	270	325	385	435	495	555	555	555	555

implementation. This feasibility check may be carried out through rough cut capacity planning. Master planning and rough cut capacity planning are thus two techniques that are employed in parallel. Actual MRP II systems vary somewhat in the support they give to these functions. Master planning systems often allow for planning at multiple levels, and similar techniques to MPS and RCCP can be applied at the more aggregate business planning and production planning levels. The whole area of master planning is well treated by Berry *et al.* (1979) and also by Vollman *et al.* (1984). We will also return to the topic of the master schedule in more detail in Chapter 17.

7.3.1   Forecasting and the master production schedule

As indicated earlier, the planning data used in the master production schedule, particularly the data used further out in the planning horizon, is based on forecasts of customer orders and requirements. In this section we will offer a short overview of the type of forecasting algorithms which might find application in MPS development.

It is worth while to offer some definitions of forecasting initially (see Makridakis and Wheelwright (1985) for a comprehensive review of forecasting techniques and methods for industrial and management use):

> "To calculate or predict some future event or condition, usually as a result of rational study and analysis of available pertinent data."
>
> (Webster's dictionary)

> "A forecast is the extrapolation of the past into the future. It is an objective computation involving data as opposed to a prediction which is a subjective estimate incorporating management's anticipation of changes."
>
> (APICS dictionary)

> "A procedure which enables a company to predict future events upon which decisions controlling the allocation and use of resources can be based."
>
> Friessnig (1979)

Webster's definition suggests an explanatory or extrinsic approach where outside factors are used to make a forecast. The APICS definition reflects the time series approach, where statistical analysis of prior experience is used in order to help predict the future. We will now look at some of the more common time series and explanatory forecasting techniques that are currently in use.

There are three basic types of forecasting technique: **qualitative, quantitative** and **causal**. The first uses qualitative data (expert opinion, for example) and information about special events. It may or may not take the past into consideration. The second, on the other hand, focuses entirely on pattern changes, and thus relies entirely on historical data. The third uses highly refined and specific information about relationships between

Table 7.3 Quantitative forecasting techniques (adapted from Makridakis and Wheelwright 1985).

Important groups of forecasting methods	Major forecasting methods	Description
Time series (history repeats itself; thus the future will be some kind of continuation of the past)	Naïve	Simple rules, such as: forecast equals most recent actual value or equals last year's same month + 5%
	Decomposition	A data stream is broken down into trend, seasonal, cyclical, and random parts
	Simple time series	Forecasts are obtained by averaging (smoothing) past actual values
	Advanced time series	Forecasts are obtained as combinations of past actual values and/or past errors
Explanatory (future can be predicted by understanding the factors that explain why some variable of interest varies)	Simple regression	Variations in the variable to be forecast are explained by variations in another variable
	Multiple regression	Variations in the variable to be forecast are explained by variations among more than one other variable
	Econometric models	Systems of simultaneous equations where the interdependence among variables is taken into account
	Multivariate methods	Statistical approaches allowing predictions through analysis of multivariate time series data
	Monitoring	Non-random fluctuations are identified so that a warning signal can be given

system elements, and is sufficiently powerful to take special events into account (Chambers *et al.* 1971).

Here we will concentrate on the quantitative forecasting techniques frequently used by planners in master scheduling analysis and decisions. The two most important groups of forecasting methods in this context are those defined in the **time series** and **explanatory** categories of Table 7.3, which has been adapted from Makridakis and Wheelwright (1985). We will now review some of the more widely used methods from these two categories.

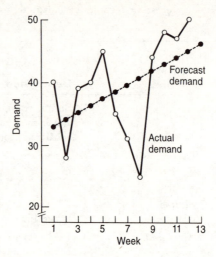

Figure 7.3   Actual values with least squares regression line.

Simple regression

Simple regression enables the forecaster to predict the value of a particular variable (the dependent variable) based on its relationship to another variable (the independent variable). This relationship is assumed to be linear, that is:

$$\hat{Y} = \alpha + \beta X \tag{7.1}$$

where X is the independent variable, α and β are constants, and $\hat{Y}$ represents the forecast value for Y, which is the actual or observed value.

For example, a manufacturer may use the simple regression technique to predict the future demand for his products based on historical demand data. In this case the independent variable is time and the dependent variable is the demand for the products. The objective of least squares regression is to draw a line though a set of points that minimizes the distance between the actual observations and the corresponding points on the line. A graphical representation of the regression forecasts in comparison with the observed demand values is shown in Figure 7.3, which illustrates forecast and actual demand for the manufacturer's product for each of 13 weeks.

The values of the regression forecasts are tabulated in Table 7.4. In this, each of the deviations (errors) can be computed as $e_i = Y_i - \hat{Y}_i$, and each of the values on the regression line can be computed as $Y_i = \alpha + \beta X_i$. The method of least squares determines the values of α and β in such a way that the sum of the squared deviations $\Sigma e_i^2 = \Sigma (Y_i - \hat{Y}_i)^2$ is minimized. The forecast equation is calculated as follows:

$$\beta = \frac{\Sigma XY - n(\bar{X}\bar{Y})}{\Sigma X^2 - n(\bar{X}^2)}$$

Table 7.4 Regression.

X	Observed demand Y	XY	Forecast $\hat{Y} = \alpha + \beta X$	Absolute error e_i	Squared error e_i^2
1	40	40	33	7	49
2	27	54	34	7	49
3	39	117	35	4	16
4	40	160	36	4	16
5	45	225	38	7	49
6	35	210	39	4	16
7	31	217	40	9	81
8	25	200	41	16	256
9	44	396	42	2	4
10	48	480	43	5	25
11	47	517	44	3	9
12	50	600	45	5	25

$\Sigma X = 78$ $\Sigma Y = 471$ $\Sigma XY = 3216$ $\Sigma e_i = 73$ $\Sigma e_i^2 = 595$

$\Sigma X^2 = 650$ $\Sigma Y^2 = 19\,235$ MAD = 6.08   MSE = 49.58

$\bar{X} = 6.5$ $\bar{Y} = 39.25$

$$= \frac{3216 - 12(6.5)\,(39.25)}{650 - 12(6.5)^2} = 1.08 \tag{7.2}$$

$$\alpha = \bar{Y} - (\beta \times \bar{X})$$
$$= 39.25 - (1.08 \times 6.5) = 32.23 \tag{7.3}$$

Substituting these values into Equation 7.1, we obtain:

$$\hat{Y} = 32.23 + 1.08\,(X) \tag{7.4}$$

In this calculation, $\bar{Y} = \Sigma Y/n$, $\bar{X} = \Sigma X/n$ and n is the number of observations upon which the regression analysis is based. A continuation of the line $\hat{Y}\alpha + \beta X$ will give forecast values which are dependent on the X variable. The manufacturer can predict the demand for week 13 using the forecast equation:

$$F_{13} = 32.23 + 1.08\,(13) = 46 \tag{7.5}$$

The mean of the absolute errors, known as the Mean Absolute Deviation (MAD), and the Mean Squared Error (MSE) are calculated for all forecasts. The relatively low values of the MAD and the MSE indicate that the simple regression technique provides a reasonably accurate forecast in this case.

Simple moving average

Simple moving average provides a means whereby randomness is eliminated from a forecast by taking the average of a number of observed values and using this as the forecast for the following period. The term *moving average* is used because as each new observation becomes available, a new average can be computed and used as a forecast. It can be mathematically represented by the following equation:

$$F_{t+1} = S_t = \frac{X_t + X_{t-1} + \dots + X_{t-N+1}}{N} \tag{7.6}$$

where F_{t+1} is the forecast for time $t + 1$, S_t is the smoothed value at time t, X_t is the actual value at time t, and N is the number of values included in the average.

For the manufacturer, Table 7.5 compares the moving average forecast with the actual demand. The three-week moving average forecast is equivalent to the average demand for the three previous weeks. Thus, for example, the forecast of 48 for week 13 is the average demand for weeks 10, 11 and 12. The five-week moving average forecast is calculated similarly.

Clearly, the observed demand values for at least n periods must be available before an n-period moving average forecast can be made. From Table 7.5 it is clear that the observed demand values for the first three weeks are required before the first three-week moving average forecast can be made. Similarly, the five-week moving average forecast is first available for week 6.

For the three-week moving average forecasts, the smallest value is 30 and the largest value is 48, representing a range of 18. For the five-week moving average forecasts the range is 8 (43 − 35). Clearly, the greater the number of observations used in the moving average calculation, the greater the smoothing effect on the resulting forecasts.

The MAD and the MSE are calculated for both forecasts. In this instance the five-week moving average forecast is slightly more accurate. In general a larger number of periods should be used to compute the forecast if the historical observations contain a large degree of randomness, or if little change is expected in the underlying pattern. However, if the underlying pattern is changing, or if there is little randomness in the observed values, a small number of periods should be used to calculate the forecast value.

Single exponential smoothing

Single exponential smoothing uses three pieces of data to calculate a one-period-ahead forecast. The data in question is the most recent

Table 7.5   Simple moving average.

		Three-week moving average			Five-week moving average		
Week	Observed demand	Forecast demand	Absolute error (e_i)	Squared error (e_i^2)	Forecast demand	Absolute error (e_i)	Squared error (e_i^2)
1	40	–	–	–	–	–	–
2	27	–	–	–	–	–	–
3	39	–	–	–	–	–	–
4	40	35	5	25	–	–	–
5	45	35	10	100	–	–	–
6	35	41	6	36	38	3	9
7	31	40	9	81	37	6	36
8	25	37	12	144	38	13	169
9	44	30	14	196	35	9	81
10	48	33	15	225	36	12	144
11	47	39	8	64	37	10	100
12	50	46	4	16	39	11	121
13	–	48	–	–	43	–	–
		$\Sigma(e_i) = 83$	$\Sigma(e_i^2) = 887$		$\Sigma(e_i) = 64$	$\Sigma(e_i^2) = 660$	
		MAD = 9.2	MSE = 98.5		MAD = 9.14	MSE = 94.28	

observation, the most recent forecast and a value for α, where α is the parameter that gives weight to the more recent values. The equation is as follows

$$F_{t+1} = F_t + \alpha\,(X_t - F_t) \quad \text{or} \quad F_{t+1} = F_t + \alpha e_t \qquad (7.7)$$

where F_{t+1} is the forecast for time $t + 1$, F_t is the forecast for time t, X_t is the actual value at time t, e_t is the error in the forecast at time $t = X_t - F_t$, and α is the smoothing constant ($0 \leqslant \alpha \leqslant 1$).

Therefore, in fact, the new forecast is the old forecast plus α times the error in the old forecast. For values of α that are close to 1, the new forecast will contain a large adjustment for any error in the previous forecast. For values close to 0, the new forecast will show little adjustment for the error in the previous forecast.

Table 7.6 demonstrates the single exponential forecast with values for α of 0.2 and 0.8. The demand for week 1 is used as the initial forecast for

Table 7.6   Single exponential smoothing.

		Forecast with $\alpha = 0.2$			Forecast with $\alpha = 0.8$		
Week	Observed demand	Forecast demand	Absolute error (e_i)	Squared error (e_i^2)	Forecast demand	Absolute error (e_i)	Squared error (e_i^2)
1	40	–	–	–	–	–	–
2	27	40	13	169	40	13	169
3	39	37	2	4	30	9	81
4	40	38	2	4	37	3	9
5	45	38	7	49	39	6	36
6	35	40	5	25	44	9	81
7	31	39	8	64	37	6	36
8	25	37	12	144	32	7	49
9	44	35	9	81	26	18	324
10	48	37	11	121	40	8	64
11	47	39	8	64	46	1	1
12	50	41	9	81	47	3	9
13	–	44	–	–	48	–	–
			$\Sigma(e_i) = 86$	$\Sigma(e_i^2) = 806$		$\Sigma(e_i) = 83$	$\Sigma(e_i^2) = 859$
			MAD = 7.8	MSE = 73.27		MAD = 7.5	MSE = 78.1

week 2. The remainder of the forecasts are then calculated using the above equation. The smoothing effect on the forecast is more apparent with small values of α.

Seasonal exponential smoothing

Seasonal exponential smoothing was developed by Winter in the 1960s and can handle seasonal data (i.e. a situation where the size of data value depends on the period or season of the year), as well as the existence of an underlying trend in the data values. There are four equations involved in Winter's method, three of which smooth a factor associated with one of the three components of the pattern – randomness, trend, and seasonality:

$$S_t = \alpha \, \frac{X_t}{I_{t-L}} + (1 - \alpha)\,(S_{t-1} + T_{t-1}) \tag{7.8}$$

Table 7.7 Seasonal exponential smoothing.

Period (quarter)	Actual value X_t	Smoothed deseasonalized value S_t	Smoothed seasonal factor I_t	Smoothed trend value T_t	Forecast when $m = 1$
1	338	–	0.89	–	–
2	378	–	0.99	–	–
3	447	–	1.17	–	–
4	339	–	0.89	–	–
5	409	409.00	0.90	19.92	–
6	447	433.44	0.99	20.37	425
7	546	456.38	1.17	20.63	531
8	422	476.44	0.89	20.57	425
9	493	507.16	0.90	21.59	447
10	572	538.55	0.99	22.57	523
11	638	577.96	1.17	22.25	656
12	457	566.86	0.89	20.92	516
13	–	–	–	–	529

$$T_t = \beta (S_t - S_{t-1}) + (1 - \beta)T_{t-1} \tag{7.9}$$

$$I_t = \gamma \frac{X_t}{S_t} + (1 - \gamma) I_{t-L} \tag{7.10}$$

$$F_{t+m} = (S_t + T_t m)I_{t-L+m} \tag{7.11}$$

where S is the smoothed value of the deseasonalized series, T is the smoothed value of the trend, I is the smoothed value of the seasonal factor, X is the actual value, L is the length of seasonality (e.g. number of quarters in a year), F_{t+m} is forecast m periods (quarters) after time t, and α, β, and γ are constants used to smooth *seasonal data*.

X_t is the actual data value which contains seasonality, while S_t is smoothed and does not. However, seasonality at each period is not perfect, as it contains randomness. Thus, it must be smoothed or averaged to remove such randomness. To smooth this seasonality, the equation for I weights the newly computed seasonal factor (X_t) with γ and the most recent seasonal number corresponding to the same season I_{t-L} with $(1 - \gamma)$.

The equation for T_t smooths the *trend* since it weights the incremental trend $(S_t - S_{t-1})$ with β and the previous trend value T_{t-1} with $(1 - \beta)$. In the equation for S_t, the first term is divided by the seasonal factor I_{t-L}. This is done to deseasonalize (eliminate seasonal fluctuations) from X_t.

Table 7.7 demonstrates Winter's method using values of $\alpha = 0.2$, $\beta = 0.1$, and $\gamma = 0.05$. In this example the given data extends over twelve quarters. Over the three years, demand tended to increase from one quarter to the next. However, there is a large reduction in demand for the final quarter of each year (seasonality factor); see Figure 7.4.

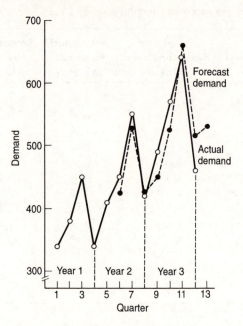

Figure 7.4   Graph of actual and forecast figures.

Initial values must be determined before any forecast can be made. Thus:

$$S_{L+1} = X_{L+1} \tag{7.12}$$

gives $S_{4+1} = X_{4+1} = 409.00$,

$$I_{1 \leqslant i \leqslant L} = \frac{X_i}{\bar{X}} \tag{7.13}$$

where:

$$\bar{X} = \sum_{i=1}^{L+1} X_i / (L + 1) \tag{7.14}$$

gives

$$I_1 = \frac{338}{(338 + 378 + 447 + 339 + 409)/5} = 0.89$$

and

$$T_{L+1} = [(X_{L+1} - X_1) + (X_{L+2} - X_2) + (X_{L+3} - X_3)]/3L \tag{7.15}$$

gives

$$T_{4+1} = [(409 - 338) + (447 - 378) + (546 - 447)]/12 = 19.92$$

The other values of S_t, T_t, I_t, and F_t are calculated using the formulae given above.

For example, the calculations for period 12 are as follows:

$$F_{12} = [S_{11} + T_{11}(1)]I_8$$
$$= (557.96 + 22.25)0.89 = 516.39 \tag{7.16}$$

$$S_{12} = (0.2)(X_{12}/I_8) + 0.8(S_{11} + T_{11})$$
$$= 0.2(457/0.89) + 0.8(557.96 + 22.25) = 566.86 \tag{7.17}$$

$$T_{12} = 0.1(S_{12} - S_{11}) + 0.9(T_{11})$$
$$= 0.1(566.86 - 557.96) + 0.9(22.25) = 20.91 \tag{7.18}$$

$$I_{12} = 0.05(X_{12}/S_{12}) + 0.95(I_8)$$
$$= 0.05(457/566.86) + 0.95(0.89) = 0.89 \tag{7.19}$$

Forecasts for periods 13, 14, 15, and 16 (year 4) can be obtained by varying the value of m and the seasonal factor I_t:

$$F_{12+m} = [566.86 + 20.92(m)]I_{12-4+m} \tag{7.20}$$
$$F_{13} = [566.86 + 20.92(1)](0.90) = 529.00 \tag{7.21}$$
$$F_{14} = [566.86 + 20.92(2)](0.99) = 602.13 \tag{7.22}$$
$$F_{15} = [566.86 + 20.92(3)](1.17) = 736.65 \tag{7.23}$$
$$F_{16} = [566.86 + 20.92(4)](0.89) = 578.98 \tag{7.24}$$

The major difficulty associated with Winter's method lies in the determination of the values for α, β, and γ that will minimize MSE or MAD. However, computer based systems have dramatically reduced the burden of this task.

Forecasts provide an important input to the production planning and control system. In this section we have looked at some of the techniques in use in recent years. Many people argue that we need to apply properly the existing techniques rather than seeking out new forecasting techniques. Later, in Chapter 17, we will look at the information contained in a typical master production scheduling record where forecasts are combined with other information, typically actual customer orders and inventory data, to develop the complete MPS record (Higgins and Browne 1992).

7.4 Rough cut capacity planning

Rough cut capacity planning involves a relatively quick check on a few key resources required to implement the master schedule, in order to ensure that the MPS is feasible from a capacity point of view. The MPS and the rough cut capacity requirements plan are developed interactively.

In rough cut capacity planning, a bill of resource is attached to each of the master scheduled items. This bill of resource describes the capacity of various key facilities and/or people required to produce one unit of the item. Provision is made for using lead time offsets. No consideration is given to component inventories and the capacity requirements plan is driven solely by exploding the MPS against the bill of resource. The technique thus determines the impact of the master production schedule or the production plan on key or aggregate resources, such as man hours, machine hours, storage, standard cost dollars, shipping dollars, inventory levels, etc.

If the rough cut capacity planning exercise reveals that the MPS, as proposed, is infeasible then either the master production schedule must be revised or, alternatively, more resources must be acquired. Long term planning of overtime or subcontract is thus possible with the procedure.

Here again, the concept will be illustrated by an example. We are checking total man hours required to produce the master production schedule. Returning to the MPS example of Table 7.1, let us assume each stool requires 1 man hour of resource. A bill of resource for Stool A through E is illustrated in Table 7.8. We are ignoring any lead time offset. Each week there are a total of 300 man hours available in the factory. The rough cut capacity plan is illustrated in Table 7.9. The source of capacity requirements is illustrated in Table 7.10.

Table 7.8 Bill of resource for Stools A through E.

STOOL A

Part number	Part description	Resource description	Resource quantity
F-456	Stool A	Man hours	1.0

STOOL B

Part number	Part description	Resource description	Resource quantity
F-449	Stool B	Man hours	1.0

STOOL C

Part number	Part description	Resource description	Resource quantity
F-431	Stool C	Man hours	1.0

STOOL D

Part number	Part description	Resource description	Resource quantity
F-426	Stool D	Man hours	1.0

STOOL E

Part number	Part description	Resource description	Resource quantity
F-412	Stool B	Man hours	1.0

Table 7.9 Rough cut analysis.

Resource: Total man hours

Week	1	2	3	4	5	6	7	8	9	10	11	12	13
Required std. hours	300	305	320	315	310	290	315	305	300	300	260	260	260
Available std. hours	300	300	300	300	300	300	300	300	300	300	300	300	300
– Deviation		–5	–20	–15	–10		–15	–5					
+ Deviation						+10					+40	+40	+40

Table 7.10 Source of resource requirements.

Item: Total man hours

Week	1	2	3	4	5	6	7	8	9	10	11	12	13
Stool A	70	70	70	70	70	70	70	70	70	70	70	70	70
Stool B	80	80	80	80	80	60	60	60	60	60	0	0	0
Stool C	100	100	120	120	120	120	140	140	140	140	160	160	160
Stool D	10	15	15	10	10	10	15	15	10	10	10	10	10
Stool E	40	40	35	35	30	30	30	20	20	20	20	20	20

7.5 Capacity requirements planning

The MRP system produces a set of planned orders for both manufactured and purchased items to meet the requirements of the master schedule. The MRP system has generated this material plan based on planned lead times for manufactured and purchased items. In so doing, the system has ignored any capacity constraints in the manufacturing facility.

MRP output can, however, be used for capacity requirements planning. This is done by exploding the manufacturing orders (planned and actual) through the routing specified in the production activity control system. This generates a detailed profile of what capacity is required in each work center. Required capacity is then compared with available capacity and overload/underload conditions are identified.

Capacity requirements planning generates a more detailed capacity profile than that generated by RCCP. However, CRP is only performed after each MRP run and these runs are typically performed only once a week. Therefore CRP does not facilitate interactive planning and is used primarily as a verification tool. In the days when the notion of closed loop MRP was popular, the CRP module was emphasized but, since then, its role seems to have diminished in importance when compared with RCCP.

There are two common capacity planning methods, namely capacity planning based on **forward scheduling** and capacity planning based on **backward scheduling**. The principle of forward scheduling is illustrated in Figure 7.5. We identify the earliest start time for the operation in question through consideration of the planned order release date generated by MRP. We then use the lead time to calculate the completion date. If the completion time is prior to the due date then we have slack time available. If the completion time is after the due date then we have a delay.

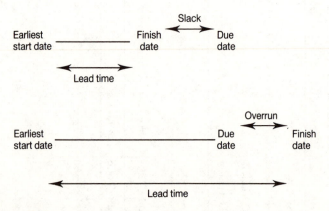

Figure 7.5 Forward scheduling.

In backward scheduling we identify the due date for the operation in question and use the operation lead time to calculate the latest operation start date. If the latest start time is after the earliest start date then we have slack time available. If the operation start time is prior to the earliest start date then we have negative slack. This is illustrated in Figure 7.6.

From the production activity control system we have available the planned operation time for each operation in the manufacturing routing, as well as the details of the work center at which the work will be carried out. What CRP does is to develop a load profile for each work center which describes what capacity is required over the planning horizon and what capacity is available. Some CRP systems ignore operation lead times and use only the planning lead time for the order from MRP. In any case, the principle is the same. In our CRP example we are using operation detail from the PAC system to drive CRP.

The **operation lead time** referred to here is to be distinguished from the **planning lead time** used by MRP. The planned lead time, as used by MRP, is the average lead time for the completed component. In manufacturing a component or subassembly, several operations may be required, for example assembly, painting, and inspection, to complete the item. Each of these operations has associated with it, in the PAC system, an operation lead time. These operation lead times when added together make up the planning lead time for the component, as used by MRP.

We will use the example of the stool, which we discussed earlier, to illustrate this. Consider again the assembly of Stool A, assuming that the requisite components – the legs and the seats – are available. Table 7.11 presents the routing information for assembling Stool A while Table 7.12 presents the work center information.

If we assume a batch size of 20 then the calculation of the operation lead times is as illustrated in Table 7.13.

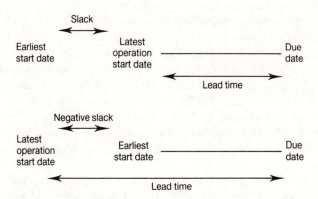

Figure 7.6   Backward scheduling.

Table 7.11   Routing information for stool A.

Operation number	10
Description	Assemble legs to seat
Set-up time	0.5 hours
Processing time	0.25 hours
Operator time	0.25 hours
Transport time	1.00 hours
Work center	Assembly shop
Next operation	20
Operation number	20
Description	Paint the stool
Set-up time	0.75 hours
Processing time	0.35 hours
Operator time	0.35 hours
Transport time	1.00 hours
Work center	Paint shop
Next operation	30
Operation number	30
Description	Inspect the stool
Set-up time	0.05 hours
Processing time	0.20 hours
Operator time	0.20 hours
Transport time	1.00 hours
Work center	Inspection laboratory
Next operation	Stock room

The item lead time for Stool A is the sum of these three operation times, namely 76.3 hours or approximately two weeks, assuming a 40-hour working week. Hence the figure of two weeks lead time attributed to Stool A and stored with the master parts information.

We note that the estimated lead time is a function of the batch size. If we doubled the batch size, i.e. increased it to 40, there would not be a significant increase in the estimated lead time, since only the process time component of lead time increases. In fact, a simple calculation will show that doubling the batch size increases the component lead time to 92.3. Thus, although the lead time is a function of the batch size, the fact that, in conventional manufacturing systems, queue time typically occupies the lion's share of manufacturing lead times allows MRP analysts to assume that the lead time is, for all practical purposes, independent of the batch size in use.

Given the importance of lead times within MRP let us now review the lead time issue in some detail. The APICS dictionary (Wallace 1980) defines lead time as follows:

Table 7.12 Work center information.

Work center	Assembly shop
Queue time	8.0 hours
Available capacity	40.0 hours

Work center	Paint shop
Queue time	16.0 hours
Available capacity	40.0 hours

Work center	Inspection laboratory
Queue time	32.0 hours
Available capacity	40.0 hours

Table 7.13 Calculation of operation lead times.

Operation number: 10 Assembly

Queue time	8.00 hours
Set-up time	0.50 hours
Processing time × Batch size	
(0.25 hours × 20)	5.00 hours
Transport time	1.00 hours
Total operation time	14.50 hours

Operation number: 20 Painting

Queue time	16.00 hours
Set-up time	0.75 hours
Processing time × Batch size	
(0.35 hours × 20)	7.00 hours
Transport time	1.00 hours
Total operation time	24.75 hours

Operation number: 30 Inspection

Queue time	32.00 hours
Set-up time	0.05 hours
Processing time × Batch size	
(0.20 hours × 20)	4.00 hours
Transport time	1.00 hours
Total operation time	37.05 hours

Set-up time	Process time	Transport time	Queue time

Figure 7.7 Breakdown of the lead time in a batch production system.

"A span of time required to perform an activity. In a production and inventory context, the activity in question is normally the procurement of materials and/or products either from an outside supplier or from one's own manufacturing facility. The individual components of any given lead time can include some or all of the following: order preparation time, queue time, move or transportation time, receiving and inspection time."

The manufacturing lead time is "the total time required to manufacture an item. Included here are order preparation time, queue time, set-up time, run time, move time, inspection and put away time."

The purchasing lead time is "the total time required to obtain a purchased item. Included here are procurement lead time, vendor lead time, transportation time, receiving, inspection, and put away time."

Lead times must then be determined for both purchased and manufactured items. Lead times for purchased items are determined following discussions and negotiation between the purchasing people within a company and suppliers. Lead times for manufactured items, on the other hand, must be estimated based on past experience and through consideration of the various elements which together make up total lead time.

Within batch production systems, the lead time or throughput time for a batch through the shop floor is typically much greater than the processing time for the batch, as shown in Figure 7.7. It is not unusual for the actual processing (including set-up time) to represent less than 5% of the total throughput time. The throughput time or lead time is made up mainly of four major components – the set-up time, the process time including inspection process time, the transport time, and the queuing time. In real life this latter component is the largest, often representing in excess of 80% of total throughput time.

In estimating lead times we must therefore pay particular attention to the calculation of the queuing element of the lead time. It is clear that this queuing time depends greatly on the load in front of a work center at a given point in time. Thus, if the machine is idle with no work queued in front of it, the queue time for an arriving job will be almost zero. If the machine is busy with a large queue of work then, depending on the priority of the job in question, the queue time could be quite large. It is clear that the actual queuing time is variable and, consequently, the lead time is variable also. For capacity planning purposes we use an average lead time based on our experience of the flow of work through the shop floor. Hoyt

(1983) suggests that the lead times should be determined dynamically and offers a simple method for their determination. The suggestion was that the lead time for a given work center is "the most recent production period's average queue divided by its average output." Thus, if the average queue of work in front of a work center is 600 hours and the work center's average output per week is 200 hours then the lead time, based on this method, is three working weeks or 15 days. As we shall see in Chapter 10 and Part IV of this book, this attitude to lead times is seen by many people as a fundamental weakness in the MRP approach.

Returning to our example, the planned orders for Stool A for our example MRP output are as in Table 7.14.

The load on the three departments arising from the planned order release of 40 of Stool A at the end of week 5 can now be calculated as in Table 7.15.

Table 7.14 Planned orders for Stool A.

Release date	Due date	Planned orders	Number of batches of 20
Week 5	Week 7	40	2
Week 8	Week 10	80	4

Table 7.15 Calculation of department loads.

Assembly department

Load from Stool A
  (Batch size × Processing time) + Set-up
     40   ×   0.25   +   0.5   = 10.5 hours

Painting department

Load from Stool A
  (Batch size × Processing time) + Set-up
     40   ×   0.35   +   0.75   = 14.75 hours

Inspection department

Load from Stool A
  (Batch size × Processing time) + Set-up
     40   ×   0.20   +   0.05   = 8.05 hours

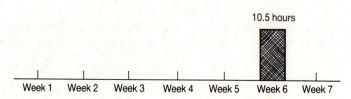

Figure 7.8 Load projection for assembly work center.

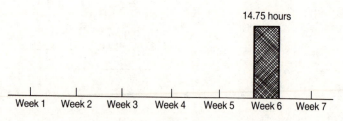

Figure 7.9 Load projection for the painting work center.

Based on the planned orders defined above, the load projection for each department is given in Figures 7.8 through 7.10.

Note that both the assembly and painting operations have been scheduled for week 6 due to lead time considerations, while the inspection was loaded in week 7. This is the effect of the operation scheduling procedure.

Assume we are using backward scheduling. (If we use forward scheduling we get more or less the same result.) The backward scheduling

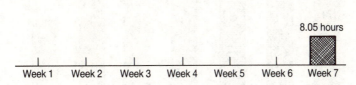

Inspection department   40.0 hours

8.05 hours

Week 1   Week 2   Week 3   Week 4   Week 5   Week 6   Week 7

Figure 7.10 Load projection for the inspection work center.

procedure works as follows. The finish of the last operation (inspection) is scheduled for the due date, i.e. end of week 7. The operation lead time for the inspection operation is 41.05 hours for a batch of 40. Therefore, the previous operation (painting) is scheduled for the previous week (week 6). The operation lead time for the painting operation is 31.75 hours for a batch of 40, which means that the assembly operation can be scheduled for completion in week 6 also.

The above example illustrates the build-up of load projections using the set-up and processing times to determine the machine or department hours and, secondly, the operation times to understand the lead times between operations.

In a similar manner to the above, we can calculate the capacity requirements arising from all planned orders for all products and thus build up a comprehensive picture of the load on the production departments arising from the MRP planned output. In this way, the feasibility of the schedule from the point of view of capacity can be studied, bottlenecks can be identified, and overtime or subcontract planned, if necessary.

A typical load projection arising from CRP appears in Figure 7.11. This shows a projected overload in the assembly department in week 2 and a low load or underload in week 7.

7.6 Production activity control

At the production activity control level, functions have been added to the basic MRP system which describe the process routing for fulfilling a

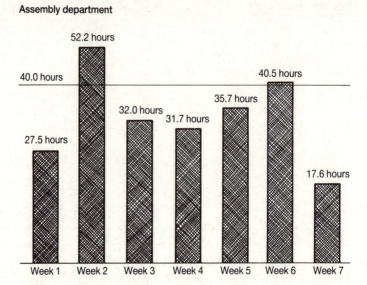

Figure 7.11 Load projection for the assembly work center.

manufacturing order (i.e. the sequence of steps a part goes through in its manufacturing process), as well as work center and standard time information. The routing information and work center information of the PAC system have already been described in Section 7.5.

The same operation scheduling procedures, which we saw in the CRP system, are used to set planned operation start times on dispatch lists. Work in progress tracking facilitates the prioritizing of manufacturing orders on the dispatch list. There are a variety of techniques, including the use of critical ratio techniques, available for generating this priority. The critical ratio is calculated as the ratio of the time remaining until the due date, as compared with the sum of operation times remaining.

Capacity control, in the form of input-output control, is provided in some systems. This reports on the planned workload that should flow into and out of each work center by week, as well as the actual workload inflow and outflow and, finally, the cumulative deviation between plan and actual. This is useful in determining if a problem in a work center's output is caused by a capacity problem at that work center or, alternatively, by late input from upstream work centers.

Some of the inadequacies of PAC modules in MRP II systems were described in Chapter 3. Some of these weaknesses are again listed:

- Absence of *off the shelf* interfaces to automatic data collection devices.
- Absence of quality management functionality.

- The routing control functionality of PAC modules in MRP II systems is typically rather naïve. Only straight line flows are typically allowed and there is no support of multilevel tracking, i.e. tracking both the top level product and key subassemblies and components through parallel routings. In addition, tracking is primarily by manufacturing order and support is rarely given for individual identification of units within a batch.
- Tooling control is rarely adequately provided for.
- Preventative maintenance and equipment tracking is rarely available.

7.7 Scheduling techniques

Clearly scheduling is an important aspect of PAC. It is worth reviewing the various approaches to the scheduling problem which have been proposed over the past fifty years or so. In our experience few of them have found widespread application in manufacturing systems. However, they do offer interesting insights into scheduling problems, which can be used, however informally, by manufacturing planners.

7.7.1 Performance measures

The scheduling problem is one of timetabling the processing of jobs or batches on to machines or workstations so that a given measure of performance achieves its optimal value. The performance measures or objectives, which vary from manufacturer to manufacturer and sometimes from day to day, are numerous, complex, and often conflicting. For example, it might be desirable to ensure a uniform rate of activity throughout the scheduling period so that demands for labor and power are stable. Conversely, it might be necessary to concentrate activity into periods when labor is available. At given times, senior management may focus strongly on reducing cost through reduced overtime and work in progress. At other times the emphasis may be on meeting the due dates of particular rush orders.

The following is a list of key terms that are used to define performance measures in mathematical terms:

r_i is the **ready time** of job $\mathcal{J}_i$, i.e. the time at which $\mathcal{J}_i$ becomes available for processing.

d_i is the **due date** for job $\mathcal{J}_i$, i.e. the time at which processing of $\mathcal{J}_i$ is required to be completed.

a_i is the **period allowed for processing** of job $\mathcal{J}_i$:

$$a_i = d_i - r_i \tag{7.25}$$

P_{ij} is the **processing time** of job $\mathcal{J}_j$ on machine $M_{j.}$

W_{ik} is the **waiting time** of job $\mathcal{J}_i$ preceding its kth operation.

W_i is the **total waiting time** of job $\mathcal{J}_i$.

C_i is the **completion time** of job $\mathcal{J}_i$.

F_i is the **flow time** of job $\mathcal{J}_i$. This is the time that the job $\mathcal{J}_i$ spends in the workshop:

$$F_i = C_i - r_i \tag{7.26}$$

L_i is the **lateness** of job $\mathcal{J}_i$. $L_i = C_i - d_i$. Clearly when a job is completed before its due date, L_i is negative.

T_i is the **tardiness** of $\mathcal{J}_i$. $T_i = \mathrm{MAX}(L_i, 0)$

E_i is the **earliness** of $\mathcal{J}_i$. $E_i = \mathrm{MAX}(-L_i, 0)$

I_j is the **idle time** on machine M_j.

N_u is the number of **unfinished jobs**.

N_w is the number of **jobs waiting between machines**.

N_p is the number of **jobs actually being processed**.

Depending on the individual measure of performance in question the maximum or the minimum or the mean of one or more of these variables may have to be considered. So, for example, if X_i is a variable relating to $\mathcal{J}_i$, then $\bar{X} = (1/n) \sum_{i=1}^{n} x_i$ is the average over all the jobs and $X_{\max} = \mathrm{MAX}(X_1, X_2, ..., X_n)$, the maximum over all the jobs.

Equivalence of performance measures

When two performance measures are termed **equivalent** this implies that if a schedule is optimal with respect to one, it is also optimal with respect to the other, and vice versa. The usefulness of equivalent performance measures is that while it may not be practical to study a schedule on a particular criterion, a solution to the problem may be found by using another performance measure which is equivalent to it. Some equivalent performances are (French 1982):

(1) $\bar{C}, \bar{F}, \bar{W}, \bar{L}$

(2) $C_{\max}, \bar{N}_p, \bar{I}$

(3)   A schedule which is optimal with respect to $L_{\max}$ is also optimal with respect to $T_{\max}$. The opposite does not hold, which means that these two measures are only partially equivalent.

(4)   For single machine problems the following performance measures are equivalent: $\bar{C}, \bar{F}, \bar{W}, \bar{L}, \bar{N}_u, \bar{N}_w$.

7.7.2   A classification of scheduling problems

A simple notation is used to represent the various types of scheduling problem. Problems can be classified according to four parameters: $n/m/A/B$, where:

n is the number of jobs, and m is the number of machines. A describes the flow pattern or discipline within the manufacturing system, and may take one of the following forms:

- F for the flow shop case, i.e. all of the jobs follow the same route through the manufacturing system.
- P for the permutation flow shop case. Here the search for a schedule is restricted to the case where the job order is the same for each machine.
- G for the general job shop case.

B describes the performance measure by which the schedule is to be evaluated.

For example: $3/2/F/\bar{F}$ describes a 3 job, 2 machine, flow shop problem where the objective is to minimize the mean flow time, i.e. mean flow time is the measure of performance.

Now that we have defined the essential terminology, we will go on to discuss some of the more widely known and used scheduling techniques. Specifically, we will review the following approaches:

- Operations research approaches to scheduling.
- Scheduling algorithms.
- Heuristic approaches to scheduling.
- The Gantt chart.

Other approaches, for example PERT/CPM, which are frequently used to schedule projects, will not be considered.

7.7.3 Operations research approaches to scheduling

There are two reasonably well-known methods of scheduling which fall into the category of operations research approaches, namely:

- Dynamic programming
- Branch and bound

We shall now examine the branch and bound method of scheduling in some detail. We consider that the dynamic programming approach is beyond the scope of this book.

Branch and bound

Branch and bound is a form of implicit enumeration. It involves the formation of an elimination tree, which lists possible permutations. Branches in this tree are eliminated if it is evident that their solution will not approach

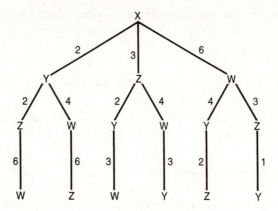

Figure 7.12 Possible sequence of four jobs X, Y, Z, and W.

the optimal. In theory, as with the dynamic programming approach, an optimal solution is found, but this can be costly in terms of computation time (Cunningham and Browne 1986).

The branch and bound method uses a **search tree** to check for feasible solutions to a problem and then compares these solutions to find the optimum. The process involves implicit enumeration of all the possible solutions, which means that it checks along the various paths for the optimum solution. To illustrate the application of the branch and bound approach, consider the following example. The tree for the possible sequences of four jobs X, Y, Z, and W is shown in Figure 7.12 (for the purposes of simplicity in the example we will assume for technological reasons that job X must be completed first). The numbers represent the cost of scheduling the jobs in that order. For example, the number 2 on the YZ branch indicates that it costs 2 units to set up job Z having completed job Y. The objective is to select the schedule for the four jobs which minimizes the total set-up time.

The partial schedules are examined as follows. The values in the brackets indicate the length of the branch.

(1) First we branch on XY(2) producing XYZ(4) and XYW(6).

(2) These are more costly than XZ(3).

(3) So we branch on XZ producing XZY(5) and XZW(7).

(4) The "cheapest" is now XYZ(4) so we continue and get XYZW(10).

(5) XYWZ(12) is eliminated as it is more expensive than XYZW(10).

(6) XZYW(8) displaces XYZW(10).

(7) Finally, XZWY(10), XWY(10), and XWZ(9) are eliminated as too expensive.

(8) Therefore XZYW(8) is the optimal schedule, in this case the schedule with minimum set-up time.

The branch and bound approach, in general, has the following advantages over other methods:

- Many different objective functions may be employed, although the most frequently encountered is minimum flow time. This criterion is generally adopted if no other criterion or performance measure is set.
- The first pass solutions of branch and bound algorithms are frequently better than the solution obtained by heuristic methods.
- The "quality" of the current solution is known, since it is possible to compare the value of the current solution with the lowest free bound in the branch and bound tree.
- Pre-loading and due dates are readily incorporated into the solution.

The major disadvantage with the branch and bound scheduling method is that the number of operations, and hence the time required to solve a particular problem, is unpredictable whatever search strategy is used. It might happen that the procedure has to explore fully virtually every node, in which case it would take almost as long as complete enumeration. In fact, it might take longer because branch and bound involves more computation per node than complete renumeration. Nevertheless, in general, branch and bound does perform a great deal better than complete enumeration.

7.7.4 Scheduling algorithms

An algorithm consists of a set of conditions and rules. If all of the conditions for a particular algorithm are met and if the rules are applied properly an optimal schedule will be generated. The problem with using these algorithms is that they apply only to specific cases under very well defined and restrictive conditions.

For example, there are several algorithms which deal with so-called one machine problems. They generally involve the manipulation of due dates or processing times. Rules such as Shortest Processing Time (SPT) and Earliest Due Date (EDD) can be used as algorithms in the one machine environment. However, they are usually associated with multiple machine environments, where they are used as heuristics. The SPT and EDD rules will be discussed in more detail in Section 7.7.5.

A number of optimizing algorithms are available for one machine problems, a smaller number for two machine problems, and one for a specific three machine problem. Table 7.16 lists some of those algorithms (Cunningham and Browne 1986), which we will now present in some detail.

While there may be very few systems in which there is only one machine to schedule, the methods available for one machine scheduling are often useful when certain conditions arise in the multi-machine

Table 7.16 Some algorithms and the performance measures or criteria they satisfy.

Criteria	Algorithm	Problem
$\bar{C}, \bar{F}, \bar{W}, \bar{L}, \bar{N}_u, \bar{N}_{tc}$	SPT	One machine
L_{max}, T_{max}	EDD	One machine
N_T (number of tardy jobs)	Moore's algorithm	One machine
$\bar{F}$ subject to $T_{max} = 0$	SPT subject to $T_{max} = 0$ (Smith 1956)	One machine
$\bar{F}$ subject to $T_{max} \leqslant r$	SPT subject to $T_{max} \leqslant r$ ($r = 0, 1, 2, ..., r$)	One machine
F_{max}	Johnson's algorithm	Two machines
F_{max}	Johnson's algorithm	Three machines

environment. An example might be where a bottleneck occurs in the system, i.e. an individual machine holding up production and keeping machines further down the production line idle. In this case an appropriate algorithm is used to develop an optimal sequence for the bottleneck machine. This sequence is then used as the basis on which the remainder of the schedule is constructed, i.e. a schedule is generated forward and backward of the bottleneck machine. An approach similar to this is used in OPT scheduling, which will be discussed in Chapter 14.

We shall now review some of the algorithms presented in Table 7.16. The SPT and the EDD methods will be looked at later when we come to consider heuristic approaches.

Moore's algorithm

In some cases it makes sense to penalize all late or tardy jobs equally, no matter how late they are. Essentially we are suggesting here that it may cost as much to miss a due date by a day as to miss it by a month. Moore's approach to the scheduling task is to minimize the number of tardy jobs (N_T), i.e. an $n/1/N_T$ problem. The algorithm proceeds as follows:

- **Step 1:** Sequence the jobs in the order of the earliest due date to find the current sequence ($\mathcal{J}_{i(1)}, \mathcal{J}_{i(2)}, ..., \mathcal{J}_{i(n)}$) such that $d_{i(k)} \leqslant d_{i(k+1)}$ for $k = 1, 2, ..., n-1$.
- **Step 2:** Find the first tardy job, say $J_{i(l)}$, in the current sequence. If no such job is found, go to Step 4.
- **Step 3:** Find the job in the sequence ($\mathcal{J}_{i(1)}, ..., \mathcal{J}_{i(l)}$) with the largest processing time and reject this from the current sequence. Return to Step 2 with a current sequence one shorter than before.

- **Step 4:** Form an optimal schedule by taking the current sequence and appending to it the rejected jobs, which may be sequenced in any order.

The rejected jobs which are placed at the end of the schedule will be tardy jobs.

Example: The $8/1/N_T$ problem shown in Table 7.17

First, the EDD sequence is formed (Step 1). The first cycle of the algorithm consists of computing the completion times until a tardy job is found (Steps 1 and 2). The first "Completion time" row in Table 7.18 represents this first cycle. Job 4 is the first tardy job in the sequence. In this sequence (2, 3, 1, 4), job 1 has the largest processing time and hence is rejected (Step 3). Job 1 is ignored in further cycles of the algorithm, by blanking its completion time with an asterisk.

The second cycle of the algorithm is represented by the second "Completion time" row in Table 7.18. Job 8 is the first tardy job in the next sequence. In the new sequence (2, 3, 4, 5, 8) it has the largest processing time. Thus job 8 is rejected for the moment. For the third cycle of the algorithm, jobs 1 and 8 are ignored. No tardy jobs are found. Moving on to Step 4, jobs 1 and 8 are now brought back into consideration and the optimal sequence (2, 3, 4, 5, 7, 6, 1, 8) is formed.

Table 7.17 $8/1/N_T$ problem.

Job number	1	2	3	4	5	6	7	8
Due date	14	5	9	16	18	25	20	19
Processing time	6	3	5	3	4	5	4	5

Table 7.18   Completion time calculations.

EDD sequence	2	3	1	4	5	8	7	6
Due date	5	9	14	16	18	19	20	25
Processing time	3	5	6	3	4	5	4	5
Completion time (1)	3	8	14	17				
Completion time (2)	3	8	*	11	15	20		
Completion time (3)	3	8	*	11	15	*	19	24

Johnson's algorithm for the n/2/F/F$_{max}$ problem

Johnson's algorithm constructs a schedule which minimizes the maximum flow time for a two machine flow shop. The algorithm tries to push products with the shortest processing times on to the first machine (machine one) as near to the beginning of a sequence as possible, so that the first job will be available as soon as possible for machine two to start work. Likewise, it tries to push jobs with the shortest processing times on to machine two as near to the end of the schedule as possible. This is to reduce the time that machine one is left idle having completed its schedule, compared to the time that machine two takes to complete its schedule. The algorithm solves both the $n/2/P/F_{max}$ problem and the $n/2/F/F_{max}$ problem.

Thus the algorithm generates the processing sequence by working from both ends of the schedule towards the middle. The following example of a $6/2/F/F_{max}$ problem shows how the algorithm works. Table 7.19 shows the processing times on each of two machines for six jobs (French, 1982).

Applying the algorithm, the schedule builds up as follows:

- Job 3 scheduled: 3   –   –   –   –   –
- Job 1 scheduled: 3   –   –   –   –   1
- Job 4 scheduled: 3   4   –   –   –   1
- Job 5 scheduled: 3   4   –   –   5   1
- Job 2 scheduled: 3   4   2   –   5   1
- Job 6 scheduled: 3   4   2   6   5   1

Thus the jobs should be sequenced in the order (3,4,2,6,5,1).

This algorithm can only be used in situations where there are two machines involved. Sometimes machines can be grouped together because of their operation or because of the product routings. In this way a

Table 7.19 Processing times for six jobs on two machines.

Job number	Processing time (min)	
	Machine 1	*Machine 2*
1	8	2
2	3	11
3	1	9
4	2	8
5	5	4
6	7	5

"factory" or cell can be considered as a two-machine situation and Johnson's algorithm used to create a schedule. Therefore, this algorithm potentially has wider application then one might initially suspect.

Johnson's algorithm for the $n/3/F/F_{max}$ problem

Johnson's algorithm for the $n/2/F/F_{max}$ problem may be extended to a special case of the $n/3/F/F_{max}$ problem. This case arises when all of the processing times for all the jobs on machine two are either:

(1) all less than the minimum processing time of all times on machine one; or

(2) all less than the minimum processing times of machine three.

In other words the maximum processing time on the second machine cannot be greater than the minimum processing time on either the first or the third machine.

In effect, a special two-machine problem is constructed from the data. The processing times on machines one and two are added for each job to give the times for the first machine of our constructed problem. Likewise, the times on the second and third machines are added to give the times for the second machine. Then the problem is treated as an $n/2/F/F_{max}$ problem, and a sequence of jobs is generated which is common to all three machines.

7.7.5 Heuristic approaches to scheduling

A heuristic is a "rule of thumb". In other words, these methods are justified purely because, based on experience, they seem to work reasonably well. It is extremely unlikely that optimal solutions to realistic and large scheduling problems will ever be possible, except by partial enumerative methods such as branch and bound (Spachis and King 1979). If an optimal schedule cannot be found within a reasonable time, knowledge and experience of the system can be used to find a schedule which, if not optimal, may at least be expected to perform better than average. Here we consider heuristics which do just that. The major drawback of the heuristic methods is that they may take a lot of computer time for large problems.

The shortest processing time heuristic

As was indicated earlier in Table 7.16 for the single machine environment, the SPT rule is optimal with respect to certain measures of performance. The jobs are queued in order of ascending processing times, i.e. the job with the shortest processing time is queued first. The schedule developed using this rule minimizes the mean flow time through the system, for a one machine problem. The SPT heuristic also develops optimal schedules for one machine systems with respect to the following criteria:

- $n/1//\bar{C}$ (minimizes the mean completion time)
- $n/1//\bar{W}$ (minimizes the mean job waiting time)
- $n/1//\bar{L}$ (minimizes the mean job lateness)
- $n/1//\bar{N}_u$ (minimizes the mean number of unfinished jobs)
- $n/1//\bar{N}_w$ (minimizes the mean number of jobs waiting between machines.

Conway and Maxwell (1962) explored the performance of the SPT rule in an m machine environment. They found that in a multi-machine system the SPT rule retained the advantages of throughput maximization it had shown in the single machine situation, and that even imperfect data on the processing times had little effect on the operation of the SPT rule.

When using the SPT rule to schedule production in a multi-machine environment, the process time for a job is generally taken as the sum of the process times for that job through all the machines. Under this system, each machine has the same schedule. However, jobs can also be scheduled at a machine according to the process time for each job at that particular machine.

Example: SPT heuristic

Assume four jobs A, B, C, and D are ready for processing at machine J (M_j) in an m machine environment. Take the data in Table 7.20; the SPT schedule using the total process time is (B,C,D,A), i.e. perform job B first, then job C and so on. Each machine has the same schedule. The SPT schedule for M_j using the process time for M_j is (C,B,D,A). However, the SPT schedule for M_j using the total process time is (B,C,D,A).

A problem with the SPT rule is that a job $\mathcal{J}_x$ which has a longer processing time than the other jobs being processed will remain at the bottom of the schedule list. The jobs ahead of $\mathcal{J}_x$ on the schedule list are replaced on the list by other jobs as they become available for processing. To overcome this, the SPT rule can be modified by placing jobs which have been at the bottom of the schedule list for a defined period of time to the top of the schedule list, in effect overriding the processing time priority. This procedure is known as a modified SPT rule.

Table 7.20 SPT example.

Job	A	B	C	D
Process time for M_j	8	4	3	6
Total process time	33	25	27	31

The EDD heuristic

With this rule jobs are processed so that the job processed first has the earliest due date, the job processed second the next earliest due date, and so on. For a single machine problem the maximum job lateness is minimized by sequencing such that

$$d_{i(1)} \leqslant d_{i(2)} \leqslant d_{i(3)} \leqslant \ldots \leqslant d_{i(n)}$$

where $d_{i(k)}$ is the due date of the job that is processed kth in the sequence. Using this rule also minimizes T_{max}, i.e. maximum tardiness. The EDD rule can be applied to the data in Table 7.21, to obtain the schedule (C,B,A,D).

Another due date based rule is the critical ratio rule, which can take one of several forms. In its most general form the critical ratio is computed as follows:

$$\text{critical ratio} = \frac{\text{due date} - \text{date now}}{\text{lead time remaining}} \tag{7.28}$$

Thus, using the critical ratio rule requires an estimate of the lead time or queue time remaining for a job. The jobs are scheduled in descending order of their critical ratios. The principal advantage of due date based rules over processing time based rules (such as simple SPT) is a smaller variance of job lateness, and often a smaller number of tardy jobs.

Heuristic rules involving neither processing times nor due dates

The most commonly used rule in this category is First In First Out (FIFO). A number of researchers have found that the FIFO rule performs substantially the same as a random selection with respect to mean flow time or mean lateness (Blackstone *et al.* 1982). In fact, in general FIFO performs practically the same as random selection with respect to many measurement criteria. However, FIFO is an attractive alternative because of its simplicity of definition and usage. In general, FIFO has been found to perform worse than SPT and EDD with respect to both the mean and variance of most measurement criteria.

There are a large number of other rules that have been developed, such as Number In Next Queue (NINQ), which selects the job going next to the queue having the smallest number of jobs, or Work In Next Queue (WINQ), which selects the job going next to the queue containing the least total work. However, they have greater mean flow time than SPT, and generally perform worse than the other rules.

Table 7.21 Earliest due date example.

Job	A	B	C	D
Due date	18	15	12	25

7.7.6 The Gantt chart

A Gantt chart is a manual means of scheduling. It works by placing a time scale on one axis of a graph (usually the horizontal axis) and machines or work centers on the other (normally the vertical) axis. A simple chart is shown in Figure 7.13 with three machines and a time period of 4 hours (Duggan *et al.* 1987). Three different jobs have been scheduled.

Each job has a process route through some or all of the machines. The user simply places a block on the correct machine axis for the particular job being scheduled at the time he wishes it to be processed. The length of the block corresponds to the process time of the operation. The process route for each job is worked through in this fashion, using a different colored block for each job, until the chart is full. The number of blocks corresponds to the total number of operations carried out on the various jobs. Once this first attempt has been made at scheduling the different jobs, there will be gaps between the blocks on the various machine axes. These correspond to time intervals when the machines are not being utilized. It usually becomes apparent at this stage that some of these gaps can be filled by rearranging the blocks. This is done and the chart is reexamined to determine if any further improvements can be made. The process is continued until it is felt that an acceptable result has been achieved. At this point the schedule can be released, with the option of further modification at any time in the future. This may become necessary because of unforeseen events, such as machine breakdown, absent operators, etc.

While a Gantt chart has its limitations, since the placing of the blocks (i.e. the scheduling of the different jobs) lies with the user, it can be very useful in certain situations. If the number of jobs to be processed is small,

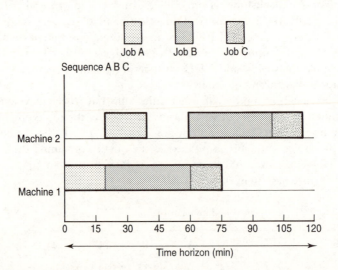

Figure 7.13 Simple Gantt chart.

then a realistic schedule can be worked out intuitively. Because the whole area of scheduling is so complex, often an intuitive approach is the only feasible method of achieving a realistic schedule. The value of a Gantt chart lies in its ability to present the scheduling problem in a graphical form which allows the user to see exactly where and how it is possible to achieve the best schedule.

The Gantt chart is usually used in batch type operations, where the number of products is small. In this case each block of processing time on the chart is taken as the processing time for the batch as a whole. This may or may not include the set-up time for the machine. However, it may also be used in certain types of job shop if the number of products is not too high, since the more jobs involved the more unlikely it is that they can be scheduled intuitively. In this case, each block of processing time corresponds to an individual job. Once again this may or may not include set-up time.

7.8 Conclusion

This chapter has focused on MRP II systems, highlighting closed loop MRP, as well as several of the important modules that make up an MRP II system. Some of the data needed to operate an MRP II system will be discussed in Chapter 8.

Questions

(7.1) Distinguish clearly between MRP, closed loop MRP and MRP II.

(7.2) How do we calculate the Available To Promise (ATP) line in the Master Production Schedule (MPS) tableau?

(7.3) What is rough cut capacity planning? How does it support MPS planning?

(7.4) What is the bill of resource?

(7.5) How does capacity requirements planning (CRP) support MRP?

(7.6) How does CRP differ from RCCP? Why is CRP less widely used today?

(7.7) Distinguish clearly between forward scheduling and backward scheduling.

(7.8) What is meant by the term *operation lead time*?

(7.9) How does the operation lead time differ from the planning lead time?

(7.10) What are the elements of lead time in a batch production system?

CHAPTER EIGHT

The production database

8.1 The production database

It is clear from our discussion thus far that an MRP II, or indeed an MRP, system relies on a great deal of data. The intention in this section is to look in more detail at this data. We call it the production database. The intention is not to give an exhaustive list but merely to discuss, in general terms, the more important sources of data used and maintained by an MRP II system. The implementation of the database will not be discussed. MRP II systems are gradually migrating from file oriented data storage to database management systems and in particular relational database systems. Suffice it to say that data should be stored in a manner that avoids redundant storage, with links between related fields being system maintained, and which facilitates the ease of access in any desired manner (either for inquiry or reporting purposes) or by applications external to the MRP II system.

A typical production database contains several related major sources of information including:

- The master parts information.
- Full inventory information.
- Bill of materials information.
- The manufacturing routing.
- Work center information.
- Tooling information.

We have already touched upon nearly all of these information sources. We will now review each source in turn and indicate the type of data it contains.

170

Table 8.1   Typical master parts information on each item.

• Part number	– a unique identifier for each item
• Part description	
• Unit of measurement	
• Lot size policy	
• Lot size quantity	
• Safety stock	– if relevant
• Shrinkage factor	– if relevant
• Lead time	
• Safety lead time	
• Make or buy code	
• Supplier code	
• Stores location	– if relevant
• MPS code	– indicates whether this is a master planned part
• Low level code	– indicates the lowest level on any BOM that the part is to be found
• Standard cost	– if relevant
• Material cost	– if relevant
• Labor overhead	– if relevant
• Overhead cost	– if relevant

8.2 The master parts information

Master parts information contains detailed data on each planned item in the MRP II system. Each part is typically described in the terms given in Table 8.1.

The data in Table 8.1 is what might loosely be termed **static data**, in the sense that the individual data values do not change very frequently. Furthermore, changes to any of these data values are typically initiated by the user, as distinct from being derived from calculations within the MRP explosion procedure. The user has software support in lot size determination and in low level code maintenance.

The majority of the data fields listed are self-explanatory. Lot sizing procedures will be discussed in Chapter 9. The lead times are predetermined and used to offset the purchasing and manufacturing orders, and hence generate a schedule. In many systems the possibility exists to capture data directly from the shop floor or from the purchasing system on actual lead times. This facility supports the user in maintaining up-to-date lead times. The shrinkage factor allows the system to account for likely stock wastage, scrap or obsolescence.

Table 8.2 Full inventory information.

- Current inventory (by location)
- Allocations
- Open orders per period/time bucket over the planning horizon

- Gross requirements per period/time bucket over the planning horizon
- Net requirements per period/time bucket over the planning horizon
- Planned order releases per period/time bucket over the planning horizon

Table 8.3 Bill of materials information.

- Parent part number

- For each component:
  - the component part number
  - the quantity required

8.3 Full inventory status

The second data source (Table 8.2) can be termed **dynamic**, in that the values stored within the data fields change very frequently and many are generated as a consequence of MRP calculations. This data describes the full inventory status for the part, including requirements, allocations, open orders, and planned orders. As noted in Chapter 6, it is necessary for a net change system to store full requirements information. In a minimal regenerative MRP system, it is possible merely to retain inventory data in the narrow sense of stock, allocations, and open orders data.

The full inventory information may also include data to support master scheduling, as described in Tables 7.1 and 7.2 of Chapter 7.

8.4 Bill of materials information

The bill of materials (see Table 8.3) defines the structure of a product. Data is stored in a manner that supports the BOM inquiry options normally available in a bill of materials system. Such options include the ability to generate single level assembly BOMs, indented bills of materials, summary bills of materials, and *where used* tables for individual assemblies and components.

Table 8.4   Routing information.

- Parent part number
- For each component:
  - the operation number
  - a description of the operation in question
  - the work center at which the operation should be performed
  - an alternative operation to do the same task
  - a reference to the manufacturing documentation associated with the operation
  - the tools required for operation
  - the set-up time of the job on the machine/work center
  - the processing time of the job on the machine/work center
  - the operator time for the job in question
  - the time to transport the batch or job to the work center
  - the operation lead time

8.5   Routing information

Routing information defines the manufacturing and/or assembly operations which must be performed on a manufactured component. Its use has
already been discussed in Chapter 7. The data is primarily of an engineering nature. Typical data maintained on a manufactured parts routing is
shown in Table 8.4.

8.6   Work center information

Work center information is used primarily for capacity planning purposes.
It contains data on each work center in the production facility. In this
context a *work center* is a set of resources. Thus, it may refer to a group of
machines and/or operators with identical functionality and ability to
discharge that functionality or it may refer to a single resource. A typical
work center description is outlined in Table 8.5.

8.7   Tooling information

Tooling information provides detailed data on tools which are available
and are associated with particular operations and work centers. For a company engaged in substantial metal cutting or metal forming operations, one
would certainly expect to find great emphasis on such information. Less
emphasis would be placed on the same information by a firm engaged
primarily in, say, electronics assembly. Table 8.6 shows what a typical
description might include.

Table 8.5 Work center information.

- Work center number
- Work center description

- Available capacity
- Units of capacity

- Normal queue time at the work center

- Work center costs
  - labor cost per unit time
  - machine cost per unit time
  - overhead cost per unit time

Table 8.6 Tool information.

- Tool number
- Tool name
- Tool description
- Tool drawing number if relevant
- Tool location in stores
- Tool status
- Alternative tool if available
- Tool life
- Accumulated tool life worked
- Unit for tool life calculations

8.8 Conclusion

An attempt has been made, in very general terms, to describe some of the information required to support the operation of an MRP II system. The implementation of this production database was not discussed. Lot sizing techniques in MRP systems will be discussed in Chapter 9. Readers may, if they so desire, skip directly to Chapter 10 without loss of understanding.

Question

(8.1) Distinguish clearly between static and dynamic data in the production database.

CHAPTER NINE

Lot sizing in MRP systems

9.1 Introduction

Most of the examples on MRP that have been presented in this book have simply taken the offset net requirements to constitute the planned order schedule. However, there are many situations where constraints on the order lot size make this an unsuitable procedure. For purchased items, vendors may supply only in multiples of a given number and the net requirements may have to be batched so as to accommodate this. Similarly for manufacturing, a process involving high set-up costs may dictate the use of a definite lot size policy.

An MRP system must, therefore, accommodate a procedure which facilitates the calculation of lot sizes on some basis other than simple acceptance of the values that fall out from the net requirements calculation. Furthermore, this procedure must be embedded within the MRP explosion procedure since the order size for a parent item determines the gross requirements for its components. Lot sizing decisions made high up the BOM structure will have ripple effects right down through the planning of all components in the bill of materials.

A number of procedures are available to help determine the appropriate lot size. These range from relatively simple procedures to very complicated algorithms. A representative selection of the procedures will be reviewed here including:

- The lot for lot method.
- The fixed order quantity method.

Table 9.1   Analysis of Stool A using lot for lot technique.

Item: Stool A	Part number: F-456									
Week number	*1*	*2*	*3*	*4*	*5*	*6*	*7*	*8*	*9*	*10*
Gross requirements							50			80
Scheduled receipts										
Projected inventory	10						−40			−120
Net requirements							40			80
Planned orders					40			80		

- The economic order quantity method.
- The method of fixed order periods.
- The periodic order quantity method.
- The method of part period balancing.
- The Wagner Whitin algorithm.

The Wagner Whitin algorithm is discussed since it results in an *optimum* ordering policy, provided the relevant assumptions hold. The other procedures listed here are more in the form of heuristics which give good or poor results depending on the set of data in question. Other lot sizing methods, such as the Gaither method (1981), the modified Gaither method (1983), the Silver Meal technique (1973), or the method proposed by Groff (1979) will not be covered. The interested reader may pursue the references at the end of Part II.

9.2   The lot for lot method

Lot for lot is the simplest of the lot sizing methods and involves the direct translation of net requirements into order quantities. It is, in effect, the method used in almost all of the MRP examples thus far. For each net requirement in each period there is an order offset by the appropriate lead time as in Table 9.1.

Table 9.2 Analysis of Stool A using fixed lot size.

Item: Stool A	Part number: F-456									
Week number	*1*	*2*	*3*	*4*	*5*	*6*	*7*	*8*	*9*	*10*
Gross requirements							50			80
Scheduled receipts										
Projected inventory	10						−40			−120
Net requirements							40			80
Planned order receipt							200			
Planned orders					200					

9.3 The fixed order quantity method

This method is quite frequently used in practice. The net requirements are checked against the assigned fixed lot size. If the net requirements were less than or equal to the lot size, then the amount specified in the lot size is ordered. Otherwise the order size is equal to the net requirements. Taking the example of Stool A and assuming that the fixed order quantity for this item is 200, we arrive at the situation depicted in Table 9.2.

Note that another line has been added to the planning sheet, which indicates the receipt of planned orders. This is done in order to see the effect of lot sizing independently of the application of the lead time offset.

The fixed lot size quantity may be set for an item based on local constraints around packaging, material handling or, alternatively, may be calculated by the economic order quantity analysis described in Section 9.4.

9.4 The economic order quantity method

Large batch sizes result in high inventory levels which are, of course, expensive in terms of the cost of capital tied up in inventory. Small batches imply a proportionately lower inventory cost. However, there is a set-up cost incurred with the placing of an order or the start-up of a batch on a machine.

Table 9.3 Calculation of EOQ.

Let S = set-up cost per batch
Let C = inventory carrying cost per item per unit time
Let Q = the batch size
Let D = the demand for the item per unit time
Let TC = the total cost of inventory and set-up

Average inventory level	$= Q/2$
inventory cost per unit time	$= CQ/2$
Set.up cost per unit time	$= SD/Q$
Therefore TC	$= (CQ/2 + SD/Q)$

To minimize the total cost (TC) with respect to Q we simply differentiate with respect to Q:

$$\frac{dTC}{dQ} = (C/2 - SD/Q^{**}2)$$

Equating this first derivative to zero gives us a point of inflection, in this case the minimum cost batch size:

$$
\begin{aligned}
(C/2 - SD/Q^{**}2) &= 0 \\
\Rightarrow \qquad Q^{**}2 &= 2SD/C \\
\Rightarrow \qquad Q &= \sqrt{2SD/C}
\end{aligned}
$$

This set-up cost (for manufactured items) or ordering cost (for purchased items) must be amortized over the batch or order size. If set-up or ordering costs are high then we may need to resort to larger batches to reduce the per unit cost of set-up and thereby incur larger inventory costs. It is clear, therefore, that there is a tradeoff between order (or set-up costs) and inventory costs. The Economic Order Quantity (EOQ) formula is simply a mathematical expression of this tradeoff and reflects the minimum total cost of carrying stock and set-up. The EOQ is also known as the EBQ (Economic Batch Quantity).

The derivation of the simple EOQ model is illustrated in Table 9.3. There are some important assumptions underlying this calculation, namely:

(1)   Demand for the item in question is known and constant.

(2)   The set-up cost and the inventory carrying cost are known.

Thus we have a value of Q, the order size that is optimum and reflects the most effective tradeoff between set-up and inventory costs.

This type of analysis can be used for lot sizing in MRP systems, provided we understand the basic assumptions inherent in the calculation and use the result with care. For example, the assumption of constant

Table 9.4 Numerical example of EOQ calculation.

$$EOQ = \sqrt{\frac{2 \times 150 \times 676}{10}}$$

$$\Rightarrow EOQ = \quad 142$$

Table 9.5 Analysis of Stool A using EOQ.

Item: Stool A	Part number: F-456									
Week number	1	2	3	4	5	6	7	8	9	10
Gross requirements							50			80
Scheduled receipts										
Projected inventory	10						−40			−120
Net requirements							40			80
Planned order receipt							142			
Planned orders					142					

demand for an item is clearly not true in most MRP installations. Demand in MRP type situations tends to be non-uniform, in fact, lumpy. Furthermore, it is often difficult to calculate accurately the cost of set-up and carrying inventory. However, the greatest difficulty in applying EOQ in manufacturing situations stems from the fact that the majority of parts in a BOM are dependent parts and cannot be considered in isolation. The EOQ formulation implicitly assumes that demand for an item is independent and that its batch size need not take into account the demand for or the batch sizes of other items.

As an example, consider Stool A once more. The demand for this item is 130 over a ten-week period which represents an annual demand of 676. Let us assume that the set-up cost is $150 and that the inventory carrying cost is $10 per unit per year. The EOQ is calculated as in Table 9.4.

The revised planned order schedule is as in Table 9.5.

Table 9.6   Relationship between set-up cost and EOQ.

Set-up cost = $150	=> EOQ = 142
Set-up cost = $15	=> EOQ = 45
Set-up cost = $1.5	=> EOQ = 14

Perhaps the most important point about the EOQ formula is not whether it can be used directly within an MRP environment, but rather the insights it offers. In particular, this formula illustrates how the batch size increases with higher set-up cost.

Taking the example of Stool A referred to above we can see how a reduction in the set-up cost reduces the economic batch quantity in Table 9.6.

Clearly, in a situation where flexibility is of key importance, we must seek to achieve small batches and ultimately a batch size of one. A *liability* of MRP is that, as an *island of automation*, it seeks to generate a schedule for purchased and manufactured parts and takes data, such as set-up time/cost, as *given*. It does not focus our attention on extremely important issues, such as the possibility of *reducing* set-up cost.

9.5 The fixed order period method

This method is somewhat similar to the fixed quantity approach in that it sets a fixed time between orders (as distinct from a fixed order size) and orders the amount required to meet the demand in that period. In effect, the ordering policy is saying *order X weeks supply* where *X* is determined for the part being planned. Weeks with no net requirement are passed over and not counted as part of the ordering interval.

Continuing our example using Stool A, if we set a fixed order period of 4 weeks our planned orders would be as in Table 9.7.

The order period can be set on an ad hoc basis or, perhaps, calculated on a similar basis to the EOQ described above. This latter option is termed the periodic order quantity (POQ).

9.6 Periodic order quantity

Periodic Order Quantity (POQ) is a variation of the fixed order period method discussed above, where the ideas from EOQ are used to calculate the time between orders. EOQ leads to a fixed order quantity and a variable interval between orders, while the periodic order quantity approach leads to variable order sizes with a fixed and constant time interval between orders.

Table 9.7 Analysis of Stool A using fixed order period.

Item: Stool A	Part number: F-456									
Week number	*1*	*2*	*3*	*4*	*5*	*6*	*7*	*8*	*9*	*10*
Gross requirements							50			80
Scheduled receipts										
Projected inventory	10						−40			−120
Net requirements							40			80
Planned order receipt							120			
Planned orders					120					

As discussed earlier, EOQ gives the *optimum* order quantity for a given independent item based on a known set-up cost, known cost of carrying inventory, and a known demand level. In the case of the periodic order quantity, the time between orders is calculated by dividing the demand per period by the EOQ. In the case of our example of Stool A, the demand per year is 676 and the EOQ is 142, which suggests approximately 5 orders per year and a time interval between orders of 11 weeks.

In our ongoing example, POQ leads to the situation depicted in Table 9.8.

9.7 Part period balancing

This method also stems from the thinking behind the EOQ formula. The technique, as described by Berry (1972) and DeMatteis and Mendoza (1968), is probably best explained through an example. It seeks to equate the cost of set-up/order placement with the cost of inventory. It is based on the observation that the sum of the set-up/ordering costs and the inventory costs in the EOQ formula are minimized at the point at which the two costs are equal.

Table 9.8 Analysis of Stool A using POQ.

Item: Stool A	Part number: F-456									
Week number	*1*	*2*	*3*	*4*	*5*	*6*	*7*	*8*	*9*	*10*
Gross requirements							50			80
Scheduled receipts										
Projected inventory	10						−40			−120
Net requirements							40			80
Planned order receipt							120			
Planned orders					120					

Table 9.9 Weekly requirements.

Week number	*1*	*2*	*3*	*4*	*5*	*6*	*7*	*8*	*9*	*10*
Net requirements	30	50	20	40	50	20	30	40	60	20

This *equality condition* is applied as meaning *more or less equal*. We say more or less equal for two reasons. Firstly, we will have to use estimates for our values of set-up and inventory costs and, secondly, it is unlikely that we will have a ordering option available from our requirements profile which will give set-up costs equal to inventory costs.

The example which follows (Tables 9.9, 9.10, and 9.11) is based on the particular version of this procedure used by Berry (1972).

Let us assume set-up costs of $200 and inventory costs of $1 per unit per week. For the sake of the calculation we need to assume that the inventory is used up at a uniform rate over the period of the week. Thus, if 30 items are held in stock at the beginning of a week the inventory carrying cost will be $(30 \times {}^1\!/_2 \times 1)$ or $15.

Table 9.10 Part period balancing example.

Option 1 Order for week 1 only
Option 2 Order for weeks 1 and 2 only
Option 3 Order for weeks 1, 2, and 3 only
Option 4 Order for weeks 1, 2, 3, and 4 only

Option 1
Order policy   : Order 30 units
Set-up cost   = $200
Inventory costs = $(30 \times \tfrac{1}{2} \times 1) = \$15$

Option 2
Order policy   : Order 80 units
Set-up cost   = $200
Inventory costs = $(30 \times \tfrac{1}{2} \times 1) + (50 \times \tfrac{3}{2}))$
                = $90

Option 3
Order policy   : Order 100 units
Set-up cost   = $200
Inventory costs = $((30 \times \tfrac{1}{2} \times 1) + (50 \times \tfrac{3}{2}) + (20 \times \tfrac{5}{2}))$
                = $140

Option 4
Order policy   : Order 140 units
Set-up cost   = $200
Inventory costs = $((30 \times \tfrac{1}{2} \times 1) + (50 \times \tfrac{3}{2}) + (20 \times \tfrac{5}{2}) + (40 \times \tfrac{7}{2}))$
                = $280

Table 9.11 Planned receipts using part period balancing.

Week number	1	2	3	4	5	6	7	8	9	10
Net requirements	30	50	20	40	50	20	30	40	60	20
Planned receipts	100	–	–	140	–	–	–	120	–	–

Taking the position at the start of week 1, the various options and resulting analysis are illustrated in Table 9.10.

With option 4 the inventory costs exceed the set-up costs. Thus, somewhere between option 3 and option 4 there exists the crossover point where set-up and inventory costs are equal. It is clear that option 3 is where the set-up costs most closely approximate to the inventory cost. Thus our decision is to avail of option 3. We then start a similar exercise with week 4 as our starting point. If we continue this exercise over the ten weeks of the planning horizon we will end up with the ordering strategy presented in Table 9.11.

9.8 The Wagner Whitin approach

This algorithm uses a dynamic programming approach to determine the optimum order quantities, given that the level of demand for a defined planning horizon is known and can be broken down into the discrete time periods and that the set-up and inventory carrying costs are known. The title of the original paper (Wagner and Whitin 1958) describes the approach as a dynamic version of the EOQ model. It is dynamic in the sense that it deals with demand that varies over a discrete horizon and generates variable lot sizes economically to satisfy that demand.

It is not normally used in practice because it is considered computationally too demanding from a data processing point of view and overly complex to be used in a manufacturing situation. With the increasing cost performance ratio of computer technology, the first argument is less true each passing year. The argument of complexity is valid although Fordyce and Webster (1984) have presented a useful tutorial paper which explains the thinking behind the method very well. Probably the greatest objection to Wagner Whitin is its claim to be optimal. While this is certainly true in a case of known demand, it is not so true when the set-up and inventory carrying costs are, at best, estimates, and the statements of demand per time bucket in the planning horizon are less and less accurate the further out the planning horizon one looks.

9.9 How to choose the lot sizing policy

Berry (1972), in a study of lot sizing techniques, identified two sets of criteria for comparing lot sizing techniques. One set of criteria related to how easy the technique is to use in practice, how easy it is for production people to understand, and how efficient it is in terms of computing time. The second set of criteria relates to its performance as a lot sizing technique in terms of the inventory and set-up costs it generates.

Unfortunately, it is difficult to make a strong statement about the results of comparison studies. They tend to be based on specific sets of data used in simulation models and are, therefore, only true in so far as the data used is representative of real life situations. For example, the study of De Bodt and Van Wassenhove (1983), which used one set of actual company data, reported that the EOQ rule performed well. Berry's work found that the performance of EOQ depended very much on the data set under analysis, while the work of Silver and Meal (1973) indicates that EOQ is significantly worse than other techniques.

The lot sizing *problem* is the source of considerable divergence between those who practice MRP and many of those who are involved in research into production and inventory management systems. St. John (1984) puts it quite succinctly when he says

> ". . . the marginal value of one more lot sizing comparison study is virtually worthless to the P&IC (Production and Inventory Control) practitioner, . . . plead with authors, researchers, software companies and practitioners alike to direct their attention to subjects that really need attention. There are some significant payoffs to be achieved in other areas that are going unexplored while some of the most brilliant minds in our profession continue to pollute the literature with more and more lot sizings studies."

Mather (1985) offers a similar viewpoint and points out that a company is unlikely to be able to identify its set-up and work in progress costs accurately in order to plug them into the various lot sizing formulae. Mather also makes an interesting observation, which is particularly appropriate in the context of a manufacturing integration, namely:

> ". . . the question is, Why do we need to lot size? If we could remove the causes, then lot sizes could be small. Eliminating the causes completely would allow us to use the most economical lot size of all, one. The primary reasons for creating lot sizes are the cost of placing orders and the capacity lost during set-up. If these could both be reduced then lot sizes would reduce accordingly . . .".

This observation is very pertinent and is in line with a discussion in Chapter 1 about the difference between a holistic and a reductionist approach to manufacturing problems and opportunities. The massive research effort directed towards generating better lot sizing algorithms and heuristics over the past number of years is the result of a reductionist fixation with this portion of the overall production and inventory management problem, and a belief that by focusing on the consequences of the tradeoff between set-up and carrying costs, significant savings could be achieved. Few researchers have considered why set-up costs are high. They have simply accepted that they are high and gone on from that assumption. A holistic approach would have questioned the high set-up costs which presumably would have led to a drive to reduce them. This is the approach that seems to have been adapted in Japan and it will be discussed in more detail when we look at the JIT (Just in Time) approach in Part III.

9.10 Conclusion

In this chapter, lot sizing techniques for use in MRP systems were reviewed. Practice seems to support the use of simple and ad hoc techniques. The last word is left to Burbidge (1985b) who said: "In many ways perhaps the simplest argument against the EBQ is that it solves the wrong problem. The EBQ theory states that if set-up times are long one should make it in large batches too spread the set-up costs. A better argument is that if set-up times are long they should be reduced."

This chapter concludes the explanation of MRP technology. In Chapter 10, various criticisms of the approach and the status of MRP II as a production management paradigm will be discussed.

Questions

(9.1) Distinguish clearly between the economic order quantity and the periodic order quantity methods of lot sizing.

(9.2) "The EOQ formula is simply a mathematical expression of the tradeoff between order or set-up costs and inventory carrying costs." Discuss.

(9.3) How does the demand pattern assumption in the EOQ formula affect its application in MRP style systems?

(9.4) What criteria should be used to select an appropriate lot sizing technique?

CHAPTER TEN

The status of MRP/MRP II as a paradigm for PMS

10.1   Introduction

In this chapter, the status of MRP as a production management paradigm is discussed (see Harhen 1988). Five perspectives will be adopted in this review.

(1)   The practice of MRP/MRP II.

(2)   The reasons for failure of MRP systems.

(3)   Current research and development related to MRP/MRP II.

(4)   Criticisms of MRP.

(5)   The state of the philosophical debate underlying MRP/MRP II.

10.2   The state of practice of MRP/MRP II

There is a significant divergence between what is available in MRP software packages and what has turned out to be useful. Therefore, to assess MRP/MRP II and to understand what is the state of the art in practice, is not a question of understanding the range of functions embedded in MRP II software. If that was the question, then the answer would be that state-of-the-art MRP is represented by a bucketless and net change MRP II system, which puts appropriate emphasis on master planning and supports the other functions (capacity, PAC, etc.) adequately.

The question of what is the state of the practice of MRP II, in our view, relates primarily to understanding the effectiveness of MRP systems for the companies that use them.

187

The pragmatics of operating an MRP system, although originally presented by Orlicky, find strong expression in the work of Wight (1981). Wight proposed a classification scheme that seeks to rate how well companies operate their MRP systems. The scheme is quite simple and involves a series of 25 questions which relate to the technical capability of the MRP software package, the accuracy of supporting data, the volume of education that has been provided to the employees, and the results achieved by using the system. MRP system use is rated between class A, which represents excellence, and class D, which represents a situation where the only people using the system are those in the MIS (Manufacturing Information Systems) department.

Among the criteria that measure effective use of MRP are the following:

- MRP should use planning buckets no larger than a week.
- The frequency of replanning should be weekly or more frequent.
- If people are effectively using the system to plan, then the shortage list should have been eliminated.
- Delivery performance is 95% or better for vendors, the manufacturing shop, and the MPS (Master Production Schedule).
- Performance in at least two of the following three business goals has improved:
  - inventory,
  - productivity,
  - customer service.

The various surveys taken through the years indicate several problems with MRP system implementations:

- Only a very small percentage of users of MRP consider themselves to be successfully operating their MRP systems. Many systems are *installed*, as opposed to *implemented*, i.e. the formal system is not the real system.
- Master production scheduling is not computerized by MRP users as often as might be expected.
- Capacity requirements planning has a relatively low utilization by MRP users.
- In relatively few cases is computerized production activity control implemented.

However, experience with MRP installation suggests that there are important performance improvements which can be expected from the installation of such systems. In general inventory levels should drop, or equivalently inventory "turns" should increase. Delivery lead times to customers should be reduced and the need to employ expediters or "progress chasers" should be greatly reduced.

10.3   Reasons for failure of MRP installations

Many authors have tried to understand the background to MRP success and, indeed, failure. It seems to be generally agreed that failure of an MRP installation can be traced to problems such as:

- Lack of top management commitment to the project.
- Lack of education in MRP for those who will have to use the system.
- Unrealistic master production schedules.
- Inaccurate data, particularly BOM data and inventory data.

10.3.1   Top management commitment

Commitment by top management is seen as *essential* to the success of any MRP installation. Undertaking the installation of an MRP system is a major decision for any manufacturing company. It has implications for many areas throughout the manufacturing organization, for engineering (in terms of the need for accurate and completely up-to-date bills of materials), for purchasing (in terms of generating accurate purchase lead times), and for the materials and production people (in terms of the discipline necessary to maintain accurate inventory data and working to the schedule).

Safizadeh and Raafat (1986), among others, point to the fact that there are formal and informal systems within a manufacturing environment – "At the time of MRP implementation, a well-established, *somewhat accurate*, informal system is confronted with the demands and requirements of a new formal system. The installation of MRP may foster improved operations or it may lead to resistance and disintegration." As the authors point out, MRP is inevitably about trying to use accurate and timely data and rigorous procedures in the production and inventory management function. This often involves a *culture* change for a group of people, in particular shop floor supervisors/managers and *progress chasers* who have evolved a relatively efficient and well-tried manual informal system of shortage lists and priority schemes.

Latham (1981) argues that MRP "touches, in some way, all the functionaries in an organization from the chief stock clerk to the chief executive officer, and that within most manufacturing organizations, MRP threatens long established habits and prerogatives which are born out of necessity and informal systems." Latham goes on to appeal to production and inventory management professionals to learn "additional skills, skills in dealing with the human aspects of systems."

It is clear that if the manufacturing organization is to gain all of the potential benefits of introducing MRP, management must accept the responsibility for creating the environment which is amenable to, indeed positive in its support for, the changes which MRP implementation involves. Clearly such a favorable environment cannot be created without the full and enthusiastic involvement of top management.

Perhaps successful installation is most likely to be achieved by allowing the formal MRP system and the relatively informal pre-MRP system to sit side by side over a short period. The thinking is that those who have worked the informal system have the opportunity to become involved gradually in the new MRP system, while not feeling overawed, or even threatened, by it. However, it requires capable, sensitive and well-informed management to ensure that all those involved gradually adopt the new formal MRP system and work together to achieve its full potential.

10.3.2 Education in MRP thinking and operation

A key element in any MRP installation is to ensure that all personnel in the company who are likely to come into contact with the MRP system should have some MRP education. Given the nature of MRP, many people in the manufacturing plant are impacted by its introduction. Therefore, a comprehensive MRP education program has to be initiated to ensure that the system is used to its full potential. This is not to say that each employee from the chief executive officer down has to be an MRP expert, rather each should have sufficient understanding of MRP principles and operation to work with the system as required.

Hinds (1982) argues that "it is during . . . the education process, . . . that the success of MRP is often determined . . . Education is the first key to successful MRP implementation." He concludes that "the MRP process begins with, and its success is determined by, the education process, the goals of which are to support corporate objectives, acquire technical MRP knowledge, and create an atmosphere of company-wide cooperation."

10.3.3 The need for accurate data

The MRP procedure is deceptively simple. After all, what is involved but the calculation of net requirements from gross requirements, taking the overall stock position into account, and then using some lot sizing technique to generate firm orders? Unfortunately life is not so simple. Earlier in this book we listed some prerequisites for MRP analysis, items such as availability of inventory data, BOMs, master schedule data, etc.

Perhaps the greatest requirement of all for successful MRP installation and operation is discipline. This includes the discipline to maintain accurate stock records, the discipline to report accurately and in good time the completion of jobs and orders, and the discipline to report every event that MRP should be aware of to the system. If stocks are withdrawn from stores, then this fact should be notified to the system and the inventory status in the production database updated accordingly. Many successful MRP installations have padlocks on the doors to the stockroom.

10.4 Current MRP research and development

The main thrust of current development of MRP is the continued application of software engineering techniques to improve the MRP II system in terms of its user interface, its interconnectivity with other systems, data management, and the provision of low cost delivery systems. None of these developments have changed the basic MRP procedure.

At the user interface level, recent developments have concerned user access to, and presentation of, information. Linking spreadsheets to MRP financial information is a developed capability in several MRP systems. The layering of decision support tools, such as fourth generation languages, on top of the MRP II database is also commonplace. This is facilitated by the fact that today many MRP systems implement their data storage in relational database management systems, as opposed to earlier, less sophisticated, file based systems. Some user interface research has explored the provision of significant graphical display in MRP system outputs, particularly where concerned with capacity management and WIP management.

The problem of interconnecting MRP II to other manufacturing information systems is currently attracting a great deal of research attention. It is part of the general CIM problem and today, at any manufacturing conference, one will find papers presenting case studies of how an MRP II system was linked to a CAD system, an automatic storage and retrieval system or a flexible manufacturing system. The appropriateness of various approaches to constructing these interconnections is not fully understood today, partly because the application of modular design in the large scale, multivendor environment that is CIM, is not itself understood. There are significant open questions as to how control systems that drive intelligent manufacturing systems, such as flexible manufacturing systems, will link with MRP II. Similar problems exist with bill of materials information, which appears in a company in many forms in both design engineering and manufacturing engineering systems.

Today MRP systems can be interconnected with such systems by customized interfaces, but this *interconnection* does not represent an *integration* in accordance with an understood and generally agreed architecture. Initial research in this direction is being focused on the developments of appropriate architectures and standards to cope with the problem of a large scale multivendor, multi-application environment. It seems that MRP II will have to become more modular than is currently the case. Certain existing modules, such as bills of materials and production activity control, may have a separate existence at MRP II's interface with other environments, such as computer aided process planning, equipment control and material handling control.

Another development related to the interconnection of MRP II systems is Electronic Data Interchange (EDI). Emerging standards activity in the area of EDI will play an important role in facilitating the interconnection of the MRP system of one company with those of its suppliers. This has two purposes: to shorten the purchasing cycle and to transfer appropriate information for longer range material and capacity planning back to suppliers. This is currently being practiced to a limited extent and the pressure to move to the extended enterprise will accelerate this process.

On the factory floor, automatic data collection systems have been linked with the material tracking systems of MRP II systems, thus providing real-time access to WIP information. The interfaces are available off the shelf from some MRP II system suppliers.

MRP II packages that run on low end minicomputers and microcomputers are available at relatively low cost. These may represent viable approaches for the small firm. Nevertheless, the dominant research and development effort in MRP II has been towards enhancing the functionality of systems to cope with the needs of large scale manufacturing enterprises. Little has been written about the suitability and acceptance of MRP as an appropriate approach for the very small firm.

10.5 Important criticisms of the MRP approach

Burbidge (1985a) identifies some of the key deficiencies within the MRP paradigm. In answer to a question put by one of the authors, Burbidge pointed to the long planning horizon normally associated with the master schedule activity in MRP and the consequent errors due to the inability of master schedulers to make accurate forecasts of demand towards the latter end of the planning horizon. The long planning horizon arises because of what Burbidge considers the inflated lead times associated with the MRP approach – "MRP systems break the bill of materials into main, sub, sub-sub, . . . etc. assembly and fabrication stages, estimate lead times for each stage and add them together to establish lead times for ordering. This inflates lead times and stocks."

As will be seen in Part IV, when the OPT approach is discussed, this determination of lead times is seen by many people as a fundamental weakness in the MRP approach to production and inventory management. From an integration point of view, the MRP philosophy seems to accept long lead times as fixed and given and does not seek to reduce them. This is not to say that MRP users are unaware of the consequences of long queue times and lead times. Rather, MRP II is concerned only with estimating and using lead times and not with reducing them *per se*.

In fact, the lead time used in MRP offsetting is the planned or expected lead time and this represents no more than an estimate of the time it takes for an individual batch to go through the system. The actual lead time will depend on the load on the manufacturing shop floor and the priority assigned to a given batch.

One of PAC's functions is to *close the loop* between the MRP planning system and the manufacturing shop floor. One element of this **closing the**

loop process is the feedback of actual lead times to the MRP system. This data can then be used to establish the validity of the lead times in use and to signal the need for a change if necessary.

Thus the concept of a **planned lead time** involves a major assumption. MRP assumes that the lead time is known in advance of the schedule and is, furthermore, independent of the batch size. This is *true* if the largest component of lead time is the queuing time. However, this large queuing time reflects an inefficient flow of work through the manufacturing shop and perhaps a process rather than a product based layout. Furthermore it is an *average* queuing time whose value for a particular batch or job will vary from week to week, reflecting the load on the manufacturing shop and, in particular, on the work center in question. This notion of scheduling based on *known* lead times makes MRP essentially capacity insensitive and is one of the fundamental criticisms of MRP which the OPT approach to production control (see Part IV) seeks to address.

Another difficulty of MRP is its treatment of batch or lot sizes. The APICS dictionary (Wallace 1980) defines a lot size as "the amount of a particular item that is ordered from the plant or vendor." However, there are many other possible interpretations of the term lot or batch. Burbidge (1985b) identifies four possible definitions of a batch or lot:

(1)   "Run Quantity (RQ) is the quantity of parts run off at a work center before changing to make some other part.

(2)   Transfer Quantity (TQ) is the quantity of parts transferred as a batch between the work centers for successive operations.

(3)   Set-up Quantity (SQ) is the quantity of parts, not necessarily all the same, which are produced at a work center between changes in the tooling set-up.

(4)   Order Quantity (OQ) is the quantity of parts authorized for manufacture or purchase, by the issue of a written order."

The batch or lot in MRP is clearly what Burbidge terms the order quantity. The notion of a transfer quantity is an important one and has important ramifications for the lead time calculation. In fact, as will be seen later, the transfer batch plays an important part in JIT and OPT thinking. Let us take a simple example to illustrate the importance of separating the order quantity from the transfer quantity.

Assume we have an order quantity of 50 for a component which requires two machining operations, each of which involves ten minutes' machine time per operation. Let us further assume that in this case there is no queuing time and that the transfer time between operations is zero.

- **Case 1**   Transfer quantity = Order quantity = 50
  We can only transfer the complete batch from machine 1 to machine 2. We cannot transfer any component from the first machine to the

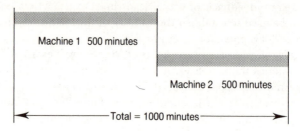

Figure 10.1   Transfer quantity equal to order quantity.

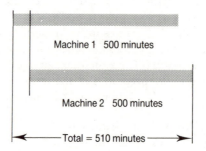

Figure 10.2   Transfer quantity equal to one.

second machine until all 50 have been machined. The time to complete the 50 items is (50 × 10 × 2) or 1000 minutes, or 16 hours and 40 minutes as in Figure 10.1.

- **Case 2**   Order quantity = 50. Transfer quantity = 1
  As soon as a component is finished on machine 1 it can be transferred to the second operation on machine 2. The time to complete 50 items is 510 minutes, or 8 hours and 30 minutes as in Figure 10.2.

This is, of course, an extreme case but, nevertheless, it illustrates the point. The only concession the MRP approach makes to this type of thinking is the **split lot**. The split lot is defined by the APICS Dictionary as "a manufacturing order quantity that has been divided into two or more smaller quantities usually after the order is in process. Lots are sometimes split so that a portion of the lot can be moved through manufacturing faster. This portion is called the send-ahead."

Batch splitting is not normally encouraged within MRP and it is seen as a facility which may be used only to progress a late and/or urgent job.

Why MRP assumes that there is only one batch is quite difficult to explain. Perhaps it goes back to the thinking behind batch production, that is, process based layouts, long lead times, and long set-up times.

10.6   The philosophical debate concerning MRP/MRP II

To understand what is the status of MRP/MRP II as a production management paradigm also requires some consideration of the state of the philosophy of MRP users. Two major influences have emerged to put pressure on the MRP II paradigm. There is the decision science concern of how MRP II compares with emerging popular alternative philosophies, such as Just in Time and OPT. There is also the software engineering concern of where the limits of an MRP II system should be and how MRP integrates with proliferating factory automation and the controllers that supervise it. As already stated, the road to CIM seems to involve some redefinition of what functions remain within or move outside the MRP II system, particularly in the areas of BOM management and PAC.

An essential and core proposal of the MRP paradigm is that the production management system should use a very simple technique, so that people may understand what decisions are being made by the system and what human interventions are appropriate. Once people understand and are motivated then they can be expected to assume responsibility for ensuring that the large amount of raw data processed by the system is accurate and that the recommendations made by the system are valid.

Therefore, since finite loading algorithms are necessarily heuristic and probably difficult for the layman to understand, they have been frowned upon by the MRP community. MRP II is seen in the role of an infinite loading/decision support tool, wherein the users develop the schedule particularly using the *what if* support provided by the MPS system. MRP II is also a hierarchical scheduling system since scheduling decisions are made at three levels of aggregation – the MPS level, the MRP level, and the PAC level. This prompts the question of whether decision support/infinite loading is the paradigm that is appropriate across each of the levels.

Hierarchical scheduling systems seem to be a way for the future. To the extent that manufacturing processes become more highly engineered, automated and predictable, and the people who operate these processes become more highly skilled, then it seems less reasonable to adopt an infinite loading/decision support strategy for scheduling manufacturing, particularly at PAC/MRP level, regardless of the *keep the responsibility with the people* argument. On the other hand, to the extent that manufacturing processes remain people intensive and less predictable, then finite loading becomes a very dubious proposition. Moreover, it is unlikely in any case that at the master planning level, any approach other than a decision support will ever be acceptable. The claim that MRP II would be made obsolete by OPT (Fox 1985) with its partitioned forward-finite/backward-infinite heuristic has not been fulfilled. Nevertheless, it seems likely that both finite and infinite paradigms will survive and in the future we will continue to see emerging hybrid approaches.

The debate around JIT seems to have reached some tentative understanding around some of the issues. MRP users can and have learned a great deal from Kanban about the evils of work in progress, for example. This has stimulated great attention to cycle times, throughout the whole manufacturing process. It seems that in repetitive manufacturing systems, MRP performance is inferior to a well engineered process using the JIT/Kanban approach. However, in non-repetitive situations, such as job shop and small batch production, full Kanban is difficult to implement and MRP remains a very workable solution. In between these situations there is probably much room for hybrid applications of both techniques.

In evaluating scheduling systems it is important to distinguish between the scheduling technique in itself and the technique as applied to a real system. The choice of technique may not be overly important compared with the need to improve the management and engineering process that supports the application of that technique. The point was well made by Galvin (1986) when he stated that:

> "Apparently the techniques employed are not such a dominant factor as we have been led to believe . . . The cohesive power of a successful system would appear to be due to the readiness and concerted efforts of all functional groups to achieve a common plan. If you haven't got a common plan, then you haven't got a system."

10.7 Conclusion

This chapter has attempted to discuss the status of MRP/MRP II as a production management paradigm. Practice, research, and philosophy have all been considered. In conclusion, MRP/MRP II is a viable approach to production management, with a proven track record. While MRP II will continue to be widely applied in its present form it may, nevertheless, be subject in the future to radical modularization in order to reemerge in new hybrid production management environments.

Questions

(10.1) "Many MRP systems are installed rather than implemented." Discuss.

(10.2) Discuss the main reasons for the failure of an MRP installation.

(10.3) "Perhaps the greatest requirement of all for successful installation and operation of MRP is discipline." Discuss.

(10.4) "The notion of scheduling based on known lead times makes MRP capacity insensitive." Discuss.

(10.5) Burbidge (1985b) identifies four possible deifintions of a batch or lot. What are they?

References to Part II

Actis-Dato, M., Erhet, O. and Barta, G. 1986. "Control systems for integrated manufacturing: the CAM solution," in *ESPRIT 86: Status Report of Ongoing Work*, edited by the Commission of the European Communities. Amsterdam: North-Holland.

APICS 1987. *APICS Dictionary*. Falls Church, VA: American Production and Inventory Control Society.

Berry, W. 1972. "Lot sizing techniques for requirements planning systems: a framework for analysis," *Production and Inventory Management*, **13**(2).

Berry, W., Vollman, T. and Whybark, D. 1979. "Master production scheduling, principles and practice," Washington DC: American Production and Inventory Control Society.

Blackstone, J.H., Phillips, D.T. and Hogg, D.L. 1982. "A state of the art survey of dispatching rules for manufacturing job shop operations," *International Journal of Production Research*, **20**(1), 27–45

Burbidge, J. 1985a. "Automated production control," in *Modelling Production Management Systems*, edited by P. Faister and R. Mazumber. Amsterdam: North-Holland.

Burbidge, J. 1985b. "Production planning and control: a personal philosophy," in *Proceedings of IFIP WG 5.7 Working Conference on Decentralized Production Management Systems*, Munich, Germany, March.

Chambers, J., Mullick, S. and Smith D. 1971. "How to choose the right forecasting technique," *Harvard Business Review*, July–August, 45–74.

Conway, R.W. and Maxwell, W.L. 1962. "Network dispatching by shortest operation discipline," *Operations Research*, 10, 51.

Cunningham, P. and Browne, J. 1986. "A LISP based heuristic scheduler for automatic insertion in electronics assembly," *International Journal of Production Research*, **24**(4), 1395–1408.

DeBodt, M. and Van Wassenhove, L. 1983. "Lot sizes and safety stocks in MRP," *Production and Inventory Management*, **24**(1).

DeMatteis, J. and Mendoza, A. 1968. "An economic lot sizing technique," *IBM Systems Journal*, **7**(1), 30–46.

Duggan, J. and Browne, J. 1988. "ESPNET: Expert system based simulator of Petri Nets", *IEE Proceedings – D Control Theory and Applications*, **135**(4), 239–247, July.

Fordyce, J. and Webster, F. 1984. "The Wagner-Whitin algorithm made simple," *Production and Inventory Management*, **25**(2).

Fox, R. 1985. "Build your own OPT," in *APICS 28th Annual International Conference Proceedings*. Falls Church, VA: American Production and Inventory Control Society, 568–572.

French, S. 1982. *Sequencing and Scheduling*. Chichester: Ellis Horwood.

Friessnig, R. 1979. "Building a simple and effective forecasting system," *APICS Conference Proceedings*, 156–158.

Gaither, N. 1981. "A near optimal lot sizing model for MRP systems," *Production and Inventory Management*, **22**(4).

Gaither, N. 1983. "An improved lot sizing model for MRP systems," *Production and Inventory Management*, **24**(3).

Galvin, P. 1986. "Visions and realities: MRP as system," *Production and Inventory Management*, **27**(3).

Groff, G. 1979. "A lot sizing rule for time phased component demand," *Production and Inventory Management*, **20**(1).

Harhen, J. 1988. 'The-state-of-the-art of MRP/MRP II', in *Computer Aided Production Management: The State-of-the-Art,* edited by A. Rolstadas. Germany: Springer-Verlag.

Higgins, P. and Browne, J. 1989. "The monitor in production activity control systems," *Production Planning and Control*, **1**(1), January–March, 1989.

Hinds, S. 1982. "The spirit of materials requirements planning," *Production and Inventory Management*, **23**(4), 35–50.

Ho, C., Carter, P., Melnyk, S. and Narasimhan, R. 1986. "Quantity versus timing change in open order: a critical evaluation," *Production and Inventory Management*, **27**(1), 122–138.

Hoyt, J. 1983. "Determining dynamic lead times for manufactured parts in a job shop," in *Computers in Manufacturing Execution and Control Systems*. New Jersey, USA: Auerbach Publishers.

Latham, D. 1981. "Are you among MRP's walking wounded?" *Production and Inventory Management*, **22**(3), 33–41.

Makridakis, S. and Wheelwright, S.C. 1985. *Forecasting Methods for Management*. New York: John Wiley.

Mather, H. 1985. "Dynamic lot sizing for MRP: help or hindrance?" *Production and Inventory Management*, **26**(2).

Orlicky, J. 1975. *Materials Requirements Planning: The New Way of Life in Production and Inventory Management*. New York: McGraw-Hill.

Orlicky, J. 1976. "Rescheduling with tomorrow's MRP system," *Production and Inventory Management*, **17**(2) 38–47.

Safizadeh, M. and Raafat, F. 1986. "Formal/informal systems and MRP implementation," *Production and Inventory Management*, **27**(1).

Schroeder, R., Anderson, J., Tupy, S. and White, E. 1981. "A study of MRP benefits and costs," *Journal of Operations Management*, **2**(1), 1–9.

Silver, E. and Meal, H. 1973. "A heuristic for selecting lot size quantities for the case of a deterministic time varying demand rate and discrete opportunities for replenishment," *Production and Inventory Management*, **14**(2).

Smith, W.E. 1956. "Various optimizers for single-state production," *Novel Research Logistics Quarterly*, **3**, 59–66.

Spachis A.S. and King, J.R. 1979. "Job shop scheduling heuristics for local neighbourhood search," *International Journal of Production Research*, **17**, 107–206.

St. John, R. 1984. "The evils of lot sizing in MRP," *Production and Inventory Management*, **25**(4).

Vollman, T., Berry, W. and Whybark, D. 1984. *Manufacturing Planning and Control Systems*. Homewood, IL: Dow Jones Irwin.

Wagner, H. and Whitin, T. 1958. "Dynamic version of the economic lot size model," *Management Science*, **5**(1), 89–96.

Wallace, T. 1980. *APICS Dictionary*, 4th Edition, Washington, DC: American Production and Inventory Control Society.

CASE STUDY I

Blue Bird Bus Company, Fort Valley, GA

by Michael S. Spencer

Identifying characteristics

Background

The Blue Bird Body Company is a manufacturer of school buses, transit buses, and motor lodges. The company was founded in 1927 by Albert Luce of Fort Valley, GA to make school buses with steel roofs on Ford truck chassis. Previously, school bus roofs were made from wood and, therefore, had a short life-span. In the 1950s the bus line was expanded to include a product called the All-American bus based on a European design observed by Luce on a trip. The All-American design has a flat front and gives drivers increased visibility. In the 1960s, the company opened additional factories to assemble buses closer to customers. Additional factories were located in Iowa and Ontario, Canada. In the 1970s, other factories were built in northern Georgia and Virginia. The company headquarters and research and development buildings are located in close proximity to the Fort Valley manufacturing facility.

The factory at Fort Valley manufactures all chassis and the majority of internal and external components for the product lines. (Figure 1 depicts the relationship between factories.) Components are shipped to the other factories for assembly as well as assembly operations at Fort Valley. Bus bodies are assembled at Fort Valley and at the four other factories. The Fort Valley factory assembles bus bodies for the truck-chassis (TC) line and the All-American (AA) line. Both the TC and AA products have front and rear engine designs. The Iowa plant assembles bus bodies for the TC line, micro-buses and conventionals. The micro-bus is a 9–12 passenger bus. The North Georgia factory assembles both the TC and conventional bodies. The Virginia factory assembles the TC bus body, conventionals, and the micro-bus. The Canadian factory assembles the TC, conventional, and micro-bus line. The motor lodges are assembled in the Fort Valley plant in a separate facility operated at Wonderlodge, a separate division.

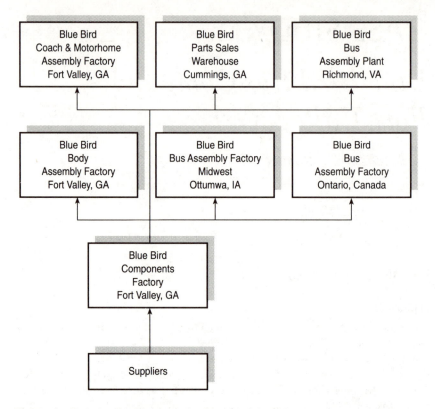

Figure 1 Relationship between the Blue Bird factories.

The Fort Valley factory operates on one shift throughout most of the year with a second shift added to meet peak production in the summer. Each shift is on a 10 hours per day, four days per week basis with no production scheduled on Fridays. Total plant employment is approximately 770 hourly employees and 60 salaried employees. Total plant annual sales are estimated to be approximately $100 million.

Production operations

The factory layout is the result of the manufacturing operations occurring in the same facility over the past 40 years. The fabrication areas have a functional layout throughout the facility. Manufacturing areas include weld operations, large press, punch press, and brake press operations, milling, metal drilling and sheet steel slitting and forming operations. There are also wood shaping operations for bus body flooring, seats, and inside siding. There are electrical subassemblies for components such as wiring harnesses and instrument panels. Other fabrication operations include fabric chair construction and cutting insulation. Manufacturing

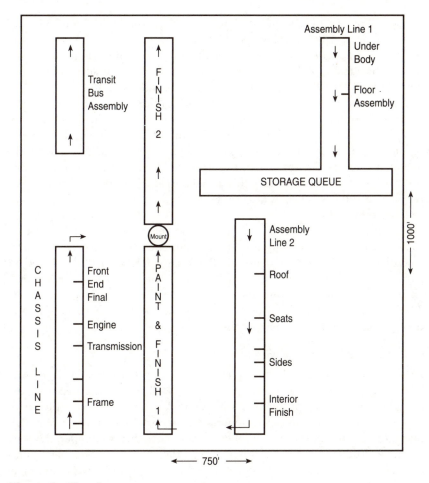

Figure 2 Shop layout.

cells have been created for the construction and cutting insulation. Manufacturing cells have been created for the door assembly, chair construction, and for the front end of the AA.

Assembly operations are located along six assembly lines. Five of the assembly lines feed one another to produce a finished bus. A separate assembly line is devoted to the production of the mini-bus chassis. (See Figure 2 for a shop layout diagram.) Along assembly line 1, the bus under-body and floor are constructed. The bus body rests on transport carts that look like small railroad flatcars, which transfer the body down the assembly line. After the underbody and floor have been constructed the bus transport cart is towed by a tractor to the second assembly line. The bus roof and sides are constructed and the internal components are assembled along this line. Insulation is cut and fitted into the inside panels, chairs installed, and the door assembly installed. The bus body is then towed into the third assembly area, called finished assembly line 1, for painting. At the end of the painting operation the bus body is mounted onto the chassis. The chassis is constructed in the chassis assembly line located parallel to the paint line. The painted bus and chassis assembly is towed to the final finished assembly line where external components and trim are attached, safety lights and equipment installed, and windows mounted. Finished buses are then driven into a finished goods lot to await a delivery driver. The assembly lines at Blue Bird are not conveyor linked, nor do units move down the line at pre-assigned rates. When the work has been completed at a station the work crews move the unit to the next area. Many operations are performed on the unit at each station rather than a more traditional machine paced assembly line.

There are approximately 500 machine centers operating at the Fort Valley plant. Employees are not on any individual incentive system, crew incentive or piece-work pay system. There are approximately 15 000 active part numbers used at the Fort Valley plant, including about 6000 purchased parts. Current production at the Fort Valley plant is approximately 20 chassis and 11 bodies per day. During the peak summer period production doubles for about three months.

Production planning environment

Production planning and control are divided into two areas at Blue Bird. The body assembly operations at the Fort Valley plant are decentralized except for the master production scheduling function. The assembly factories and Fort Valley assembly operations report to individual materials managers located at the facility. The component fabrication operations are centralized under a separate corporate materials manager. The master production scheduling function is centralized under the materials manager of the Fort Valley assembly plant, who also has responsibility for all chassis production.

The vice-president of manufacturing is located at the Fort Valley headquarters and reports to the company president. The five plant managers report to the vice-president of manufacturing. The five plant managers each have a factory materials manager reporting to them. The Fort Valley plant manager's materials manager has master production scheduling responsibility for the Fort Valley factory.

The Fort Valley factory materials manager has six purchasing planners, two master production schedulers, a customer order coordinator, and supervisors of receiving, stockroom, and line service (production control) reporting to him. The factory materials manager is responsible for the scheduling and expediting of all purchased components necessary for the assembly of buses, including major components such as engines and transmissions as well as raw materials such as steel and wood. All sourcing and price negotiation decisions are made by a small corporate purchasing department. Key performance measurements for materials management are inventory level targets and parts shortages. Blue Bird, similar to other repetitive manufacturers of heavy equipment, has a culture that assumes on-time delivery for end items. There is no specific performance measurement that relates to delivery performance, since a failure to maintain 100% performance is catastrophic and memorable to survivors. Inventory goals for the current year are to have no more than 10 days of assembly work in process (WIP) inventory. The use of a day's worth of inventory is a better performance measure than a dollar amount since production varies throughout the year to meet the peak summer demand. The parts shortage performance measurement target for the current year is to have no more than 10 items on shortage per day.

Inventory management is an important area for materials management. The lead time quoted to a customer is for delivery in less than six months. Assembly lead time is approximately one week. Manufacturing lead times for components average about three weeks, with the longest purchased component, an engine, requiring 16 weeks of lead time. Overall inventory turns at the Port Valley factory are approximately 20 times per year. About 35% of the total inventory is raw and purchased finished components, about 15% is work in process, and about 50% is finished goods. A marketing policy allows a customer up to one month from the finished production date to pick up the bus before finance charges begin to be levied. Finished inventory is approximately $2.5 million.

Marketing and sales is a centralized function at Blue Bird. The company is the largest supplier of school buses in the United States and Canada. There are four other major competitors: Wayne, Carpenter, Ward, and Thomas. All companies, including Blue Bird, use an independent sales distributor network. About 60 dealers purchase buses from the company and sell them to end customers. Typically, a dealer prepares a bid to supply buses to a school district or other end customer. The bid is made by the dealer based on the price the dealer pays for the bus to Blue Bird. Blue Bird may be approached by a dealer asking for a discount to make a successful bid. Blue Bird may or may not give the dealer a discount, depending on factory production levels and cost criteria. A successful bid is faxed to the order entry section of the marketing department. A PC based system is being implemented by the company. Order entry consists of two people, who prepare and check the dealer order for proper option selection and enter the order into the marketing system. The average customer order is for two buses although 75% of all orders are for a single bus. Each bus tends to be a unique configuration depending on the variety and type of options ordered. (See Figure 3 for an example of a bill of material.) The factory does not currently use a planning bill of material for bus configurations, but uses the actual orders instead. A distributor may order a bus to be built that does not yet have a final customer. However, most orders are for final customer requirements. As part of the Blue Bird corporate culture,

```
FINAL                          PICKUP DATE  03/06/92        FO98835
FO98835 ***         SCHEDULE NO. 91-40   ITEM   0            PAGE 1
          CUST 1992   SALES MTG.  CNG  GAS

          -------------------------------- CHASSIS ----------------------------
          NUMBER = FO49145     MAKE = CUMN MODEL =
          BRAKE TYPE = A        WHEELBASE = 277        CCWL-AXLE =
          TIRESIZE = 1100   X     22.5  0        CHAS SCHEDULE NO. 92-0o
          AXLE RATIO =        *W* NOT FOUND  *W*
URS =    SED 06R   SED 09L
CHASSIS ----------------------------------------------------------------------
     04339         RESERVOIR.ADDTNL WET TANK CAPACITY
     04367         ALTERNATOR.160 AMP                     CB/TC
     04372         TAIL PIPE EXTENDED
     04455         TACHOMETER DIESEL ENGINE
     04461         AMMETER                                CB/TC
     04465         ENGINE HOUR METER
     04466         TEMPERATURE GUAGE ALLISON
     04467         ENGINE WARNING SYSTEM                  CB/TC
     04525         TILT & TELESCOPING STRG WHEEL          TC
     04532-02      SHOCK ABSORBERS.REAR (J-190-S AXLE)
     04667         MICHELIN 11R22.5H RADIAL PLY
     05310-04      TOW HOOKS. FRONT AND REAR              TCRE
     05348         DISC WHEELS 8.25 = 22.5 TUBELESS


BODY --------------------------------------------------------------------------
     01506         SOUND DEADENING SPRAY COAT 1/16 THK
     02448-14      ALUMINIZED INNER SIDE PANELS
     03250-02      ROOF VENT/HATCH.20X23.(2).DUAL PURP
                   4TH & 10TH SEC.
     03315         2 PC CURVED TINTED W/S                 TCFC
     03337-14      77 HEADROOM AND SPLIT SASH 12IN
     03475-18      BODY CONSTRUCTION FMVSS/CMVSS 221
     03499         CALIF CONST
     53774-01      PANELS 0/S S SMOOTH 25 3/4 SKIRT
     53774-02      HEADLINING PERF FULL LENGTH
```

Figure 3   Sample information from a bill of material.

a customer is able to change an order through the dealer up to the time of final assembly. Most customer order changes are adjustments to finished trim and equipment.

Design engineering is a centralized function at the Blue Bird headquarters. There is a separate facility for research and product development. New products are introduced after considerable market research and dealer network coordination. The corporate vice-president of design engineering is responsible for all new product development. The factory involvement tends to be limited to prototype builds and methods builds. Manufacturing and industrial engineering is also centralized at Blue Bird, and reports through another corporate vice-president.

Quality is a decentralized function at Blue Bird. There is no quality department at the factory and the company is implementing a total quality control program. About 25 inspectors are currently at the Fort Valley factory. The inspectors report to factory manufacturing supervision. All

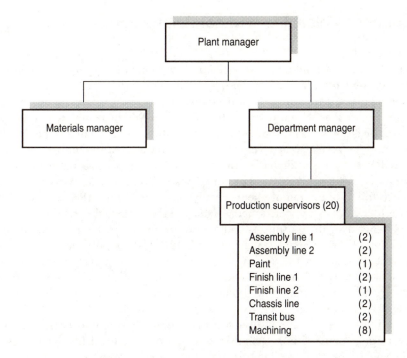

Figure 4 Manufacturing organization at Fort Valley.

wage employees have received quality orientation training and quality control charts are in evidence throughout the plant. Quality is viewed as a part of
each operator's responsibility, and the corporate culture reinforces quality
and safety for the final product. Each production supervisor and plant manager has quality goals and reports on quality performance on a monthly basis.

The accounting function is centralized at Blue Bird. There is a vice-
president for finance reporting to the president. Each plant has a finance
manager, who reports to the vice-president and who has a "dotted line"
reporting relationship to the plant manager. The company uses a
traditional cost roll-up system, and each factory has an operating budget
for control purposes. About 65% of total cost is material, about 15% is
labor, and about 20% is overhead.

The manufacturing organization at the Fort Valley plant is a traditional line relationship. There are about 20 manufacturing supervisors
throughout the factory, who supervise a functional area such as an assembly line or the chassis line. All manufacturing supervisors at the factory
report to a department manager who, in turn, reports to the plant manager.
The performance measurement system is based on budget performance,
overtime expense, quality and scrap goals, number of units in a repair
status, safety, and general housekeeping. (See Figure 4 for a diagram
depicting the manufacturing supervisors' assignments.)

Production planning and control methods

Background

Blue Bird Body Company developed and implemented an in-house material requirements planning system in 1976. The MRP system has undergone significant modifications throughout the past 20 years and continues to be modified as the need arises. In the mid-1970s, the company employed Oliver Wight as a consultant to facilitate the development of the MRP system. The system was developed in-house because of the limited amount of MRP software available at the time and the repetitive nature of bus production. The current system is regenerated on a weekly basis and uses weekly buckets for requirements. Daily net change for MPS changes and inventory netting are performed. Management is pleased with the system, reporting that the output is valid and useful in making management decisions. Further, management feels that the MRP reports are timely and accurate, and views the system as a key component to the success of the company. MRP education was extensive during the implementation process and throughout the 1980s. Education was conducted by Oliver Wight Associates and, later, by Garwood and Associates.

The MRP system is used by marketing for promise dates, and by accounting for determining figures to support the annual budget process. The shop floor uses MRP output for production planning and control, and engineering uses the system for coordinating engineering changes. Management describes the system as a closed-loop MRP II system.

Inventory accuracy is above 90% and a cycle counting system is in operation. The last physical inventory was taken in October 1991, since the results demonstrated to the outside auditors that the cycle counting system will allow them to omit the physical inventory unless accuracy declines. MRP ordering policies are based, in part, on the ABC classification scheme. For example, A items are allowed to have one day of safety stock in MRP calculation, B items may have a one-week safety stock, and C items may have up to a two-week safety stock, but each item's safety stock is monitored by materials management. Only about 500 parts (including both manufactured and purchased) are allowed to have safety stock as part of MRP calculations. Order policies are lot-for-lot throughout the plant. Lead times are established by part number and average two weeks for manufactured components and one week for assemblies. Routings are believed to be 99% accurate by materials management. Routings are seldom changed on existing components; major changes occur only when new products are introduced.

The bills of material are believed to be above 90% accurate. About 200 engineering changes are made to the bills of material each month. The majority of problems occur as the result of human errors in coding the customer order options from the order form into the MRP system. Bus orders have a variety of options from which the customers can choose. Some options require that other options must be selected at the same time, while some options require that others are not available for selection. There are about 150 option selections that can be made per order. Additionally, through an engineering change, a new or modified option can be requested and built. The factory allows changes to ordered options to be made up to the actual assembly of the bus. As a result, installed options on a bus may be different to options existing in the bill of material record.

Master production scheduling

The development of the master production schedule is a centralized function at Blue Bird and is the responsibility of the Fort Valley assembly materials manager. There are two master production schedulers who create the MPS. Orders are received from the dealer network and entered into an order file. The master schedulers are alerted to the new order or to changes by reviewing the order file. Orders are received with a requested due date set by the dealer. The master schedulers can accept the order or revision into the master production scheduling system, or they may adjust the due date and await a response from the dealers through the order entry file. Once an order is accepted, the system identifies the major components and options from the order and creates a unique configuration number for the order. The configuration number is then transmitted into the MRP system for requirements generation. The inventory is relieved once the end item is sent into the finished goods status. Depending on the geographic location of the dealer, the type of product ordered, and the current capacity of the assembly factory, the MPS is created for each factory. For example, an order from Chicago for one micro-bus and one AA school bus would be accepted by the master schedulers for a certain delivery date. The requirement for the AA body, the AA chassis, and the micro-bus chassis would be placed into the Fort Valley MPS. The order for the micro-bus body would be placed into the Iowa factory's MPS since the Iowa plant services the Midwest for micro-buses, and only the Fort Valley factory assembles the AA unit as well as all chassis.

The MPS has a 50-week horizon and uses weekly time buckets. The first eight weeks are viewed by management as firm although changes are permitted to the configured order within the eight-week horizon. Essentially, school districts are reserving capacity at the factory. The customers are free to make modifications to the bus configurations up to eight weeks prior to the build date. This can be allowed because there is a flow of material into the factory from suppliers based on the actual orders and the forecast in the MPS. At non-peak times during the year the company may not have a full eight weeks of actual dealer orders.

When actual orders are not enough to fill the eight-week horizon the forecast numbers remain in the MPS. Beyond the eight-week horizon forecast numbers are used to create the full 52-week MPS. As dealer orders are received the forecast quantity is reduced and replaced by actual orders.

The forecast is prepared annually and is based on a two-year historical pattern. The annual forecast is part of the budgeting process and has marketing, engineering, materials, and upper management involvement. The forecast is prepared for all chassis and body types available in the product line, regardless of the assembly factory involved in the actual production.

Once the MPS has been developed from the annual forecast, updates are made continuously as new orders and revisions are received. There is no formal monthly MPS meeting, nor is there a formal MPS approval process for changes or additions. The MPS reflects the anticipated peak and valley for production rates. Management attempts to "ramp up" to the peak schedule by using a higher production rate for assembly factories for the quarter before the peak, and "ramps down" using a lower rate for the quarter following the summer peak. There are no mathematical tools or simulations used to facilitate the MPS process. Management did use the MRP and MPS simulation capability to evaluate "what if" questions in the early 1980s but abandoned the approach as too time consuming. There is an in-house written system operating on a PC that converts the production rate of the various products into the workforce quantity required. There are 24 basic products used for the MPS and forecast. Major classifications are the length of the bus, the engine, the transmission, and the placement of the engine in the bus (front or rear).

Once the MPS has been established and actual customer orders accepted and configured, the MRP system explodes requirements for each factory. The components for the chassis and body are identified for the component manufacturing areas at Fort Valley. Components and assembly requirements for the assembly operations are identified by the final assembly schedule, which is prepared by the master schedulers from the MPS requirements. A typewritten final assembly schedule (FAS) schedule for each factory is produced by the master schedulers and faxed to the assembly factories.

The FAS is a more general management tool for manufacturing supervisors and materials management personnel. The actual assembly of a bus body and chassis for a specific order is executed by the assembly production order. The FAS lists only the general options that correspond to the MPS units and other major assemblies, while the assembly production order identifies all options.

Production for finished chassis, bodies, and buses is monitored on a daily basis using the FAS by manufacturing and materials supervision. The number of units produced per day is the basic unit of measurement used to determine the production status. As part of the Blue Bird corporate culture there is no backlog of scheduled build. Overtime is scheduled as required to maintain the rate of production. Information on production status is informally fed back from the assembly factories to the master schedulers. However, the assumption that all plants are on schedule is valid because of the underlying corporate culture.

Priority planning

Priority planning in the fabrication areas at the Fort Valley plant is based on material requirements planning. The MPS feeds base model and option requirements from the actual customer configuration. Each part number in the fabrication area has a lead time established by a manual review process at the time when MRP was implemented. New part numbers are reviewed by the materials management department and lead times established. Average lead time for manufactured components is three weeks, with 85% of all part numbers requiring less than four weeks of lead time. The longest manufactured lead time is six weeks for a few steel components.

MRP creates shop orders for all manufactured components. Material is released into the shop automatically for each production order. Manufacturing supervision schedules production based on the MRP due date and any informal grouping that minimizes lead times. The MRP system does not recognize family groupings or set-up times as part of its requirements calculation. Set-up times on machine centers throughout the factory have been studied and reduced during the past several years. Management feels that there is no need to use Kanban in the fabrication areas because the MRP shop order method provides satisfactory results.

The one bottleneck area that was identified by management was the metal parts final preparation area. All steel components go through this process prior to assembly. There is a wash operation followed by a spray treatment, then a drying operation. The space required for parts preparation is relatively large and drying times are set by engineering. The wash operation involves a conveyor based on two moving chains. There are concerns about environmental contamination as well as a high capital requirement to purchase additional equipment. There is a relatively large amount of inventory of many different components in front of the bottleneck.

Priority planning in the assembly area is based first on the FAS that is produced by the master schedulers, based on the MPS. This gives manufacturing management general guidance concerning the nature of the product required to be built during the day and week. There are some restrictions concerning the sequencing of products down the assembly lines, especially at the first finish area where the painting operations occur. An example of the restrictions is the number of buses sequenced on a single day that require a white roof rather than the standard yellow. Another example is the number of AA buses that can be assembled in a row since the front end of the bus goes through a special subassembly area because of the number of welded parts required. The line restrictions are known to the master schedulers, who adjust the FAS when the document is first prepared.

The main priority planning tool used for the assembly area is the assembly production order. Several copies of this document are produced by the computer system using the MRP bill of material. Each of the lines, except the micro-bus chassis assembly line, has a copy of the assembly production order for each specific bus to be assembled. The assembly production order has both body and chassis options listed, as well as major subassemblies. Operations along the assembly lines review the production order that accompanies each unit and produce the required subassembly and final assembly.

No use is made of a Kanban method of priority planning in the assembly area. An outside hardware item vendor uses a two-bin system and daily visual review and replenishment process. About 400 part numbers are planned using the two-bin method.

Priority planning for purchased components is accomplished through the MRP system. An in-house developed purchasing system is fed by the MRP requirements and purchase orders are created. The purchase orders are mailed to vendors on a weekly basis as the net changes from MRP require.

Capacity planning

Capacity is defined in terms of units produced per day for the chassis line and the body line at Fort Valley. Management has a policy of using only one shift for body assembly throughout the year at each plant. The policy also requires using only one shift for body assembly, except for the peak season in the summer when two shifts are scheduled. In order to level the peak season, the company uses temporary workers. Permanent workers are seldom reduced in order to adjust for different production levels. For example, there have been only two layoffs of permanent employees since 1974.

Long-term capacity planning occurs during the annual planning process, when the annual forecast is developed. The development of the long-term capacity plan is an integrated part of the MPS process. As the forecast is translated into the MPS, management develops an understanding of the capacity required for the daily production rate at each factory. No plant expansion or new factory acquisition is planned because the current production capacity is seen as adequate throughout the next several years. This view is reinforced by the policy of using only one shift on a four days per week basis, as mentioned earlier.

Short term capacity planning in the assembly areas is accomplished through the use of the final assembly schedule and the program that converts units into the workforce required. The master schedulers use the conversion numbers, production status expected in the next week, and their own knowledge of the assembly environment to judge the validity of a proposed final assembly schedule. Adjustments to the FAS are made as required by the master schedulers.

Capacity planning in the fabrication areas is accomplished through the use of capacity requirements planning. Planning orders for 12 weeks are used to calculate the amount of work hours required on each machine based on the standard hours developed by the industrial engineers at the time when the part was introduced. The MRP reports are reviewed by manufacturing supervision to identify new equipment requirements and adjustments needed in the work force. When requirements exceed capacity, overtime is planned. If requirements exceed capacity for more than three months, temporary workers may be hired in less skilled areas and skilled permanent employees trained to operate the equipment. The next step in increasing capacity is the use of Fridays as work days. If the requirements exceed capacity over the next six months, new equipment is considered. The six-month time frame is sufficient to view requirements through the next forecasted valley. If capacity exceeds the requirement over a three-month horizon the workforce is reassigned if temporary workers have been released. Capacity planning is viewed as the primary responsibility of manufacturing.

Priority control

In the assembly areas priority is controlled by the final assembly schedule. Once the assembly production order is released to the floor it cannot be withdrawn although some modifications to an order can be accepted. The FAS is adjusted by the master schedulers making a handwritten notation of the change in build sequence to the FAS for each supervisor. Changes to the FAS seldom occur in the current and next two days. Since the assembly area has ample component material on the line, changes to the build sequence do not cause adverse consequences in the assembly areas. The only area that would have to be reviewed by the master schedulers might be the sequencing of a chassis to the appropriate body on an order.

Priority control in the fabrication areas is the result of the daily MRP shop order schedule and the informal adjustments made by manufacturing supervision as the production environment changes. The corporate materials manager responsible for the fabrication area has production planners who review the daily net change MRP output and alert manufacturing supervisors to any changes in requirements. MRP produces a daily dispatch list for the planners and supervisors that highlights changes from the previous day. It is the responsibility of the five manufacturing supervisors in the fabrication area to adjust production priorities to ensure that due dates are met. When more than one production order is due on the same date at the same work center the manufacturing supervisor determines the sequence to be produced based on the supervisor's shop knowledge.

The MRP system is updated on an on-going basis to changes in the levels of inventory in stores and WIP. Each machine has a barcode that is scanned when a production order is finished. The scanning of the production order updates the MRP system as to the progress of the production material and the inventory quantity available for further processing. The daily dispatch list is updated over the evening for changes in the order's progress and inventory quantity.

Priority at the bottleneck parts preparation area is controlled informally by the manufacturing supervisor. No special MRP or other system reports are used to control priority at the bottleneck.

Capacity control

Capacity control in the assembly areas and in the fabrication areas is the responsibility of manufacturing supervision. All areas are routinely monitored and capacity adjustments made by the reassignment of employees, the scheduling of overtime, and the use of Friday as a scheduled work day. Manufacturing supervision requests overtime authorization from the plant manager. The materials management department has an informal interaction with manufacturing supervision concerning the scheduling of overtime. Overtime is reviewed by the plant manager each week through the budget process and he reports the amount of overtime required on a monthly basis to upper management. The major cause of short-run capacity problems in the assembly areas is parts availability although most parts are not required at the time of assembly and can be added later. The major cause of capacity problems in the fabrication area is machine breakdowns. No use is made of an input/output report at Fort Valley.

Summary

The Blue Bird Bus Company is the largest manufacturer of school buses in the United States and Canada. The company is profitable and has achieved a reputation for having the highest quality and best on-time delivery performance record in the industry. The company operates an MRP II system for planning and controlling production. The effective use of the MRP II system allows the Fort Valley Components factory to support vehicle assembly factories' production schedules and still maintain superior performance in a highly competitive industry.

PART III

Just in Time

Overview

Just in Time (JIT) production attracted the attention of management in the 1980s. Western industrial managers, aware of the success of their Japanese counterparts, understood that a commitment to achieving just in time in manufacturing was essential in order to compete on worldwide markets. In Part III, the JIT concept, its influence on production management, and the movement toward computer integrated manufacturing and the extended enterprise are discussed.

Our basic contention is that the Kanban card system is greatly overemphasized in the literature on JIT, at the expense of the JIT approach and JIT manufacturing techniques. In particular, we feel that JIT can be applied to good effect in all types of discrete parts manufacturing systems while Kanban can only be used in repetitive manufacturing systems.

The structure of Part III is very different to that of Part II. The discussion of the MRP approach in Part II started by looking at the mechanics of MRP and went on to discuss the MRP paradigm much later. In Part III the opposite approach is adopted, that is, Chapter 11 starts with the thinking underlying JIT and moves towards the mechanics, i.e. the techniques for reducing set-up times, Kanban, etc. in the later chapters. This is in line with the view expressed earlier, i.e. that up to now, not enough emphasis has been placed on the fundamental concepts of JIT.

Part III is structured as follows. In Chapter 11 the fundamental concepts behind Just in Time are introduced and the philosophy inherent in the approach is outlined. Chapter 12 describes how the manufacturing environment is designed and production planned in order to set up a context within which just in time production can be achieved. Finally, Chapter 13 attempts to outline how control of production is maintained in a just in time system using Kanban which, in our view, is simply a manual shop floor control system.

The just in time approach

11.1   Introduction

The success of Japanese firms in the international marketplace has generated interest among many Western companies as to how this success was achieved. Many claim that the keystone of the Japanese success in manufacturing is Just in Time (JIT). JIT is a manufacturing philosophy with a very simple goal, i.e. produce the required items, at the required quality, and in the required quantities, at the precise time they are required. JIT has been described by Schonberger (1984) as a production system which replaces "complexity with simplicity in manufacturing management."

The JIT system arose initially in the Toyota automotive plants in Japan in the early 1960s and is currently being used in a variety of industries including automotive, aerospace, machine tools, computer and telecommunications manufacturing.

Just in time can be viewed from three perspectives, all of which must be considered in order to achieve JIT. This is illustrated in Figure 11.1.

The shop floor control system for JIT is the most visible manifestation of the JIT approach because of its use of kanban cards. The Kanban technique controls the initiation of production and the flow of material with the aim of getting exactly the right quantity of items (components, subassemblies or purchased parts) at exactly the right place at precisely the right time. Its use is described in detail in Chapter 13.

Underlying the use of Kanban is the prior application of an array of techniques to the products and manufacturing processes, in order to ensure that the application of Kanban is feasible. The techniques involve the design of the manufacturing system in its broadest sense, addressing issues of marketing, sales, product design, process engineering, quality engineering, plant layout, and production management, in order to facilitate JIT production using the Kanban system.

The third and most fundamental level is the JIT philosophy of manufacturing on which JIT execution and the design and planning of the JIT manufacturing system are premised. This is frequently the least

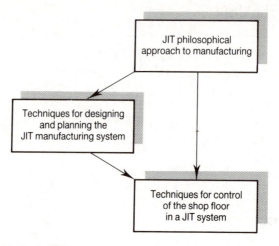

Figure 11.1   JIT approach.

understood aspect of JIT but in many ways it is the most important. The JIT philosophy is a set of fundamental manufacturing strategies which, when implemented, provide the basis for the JIT system and facilitate the use of the Kanban system.

This chapter will concentrate on reviewing the JIT philosophy, looking first at the goals of JIT and then discussing the key ideas making up the approach. Chapters 12 and 13 will examine the design and planning of the manufacturing system and finally the Kanban system.

11.2 The goals of the JIT approach

The JIT approach involves a continuous commitment to the pursuit of excellence in all phases of manufacturing systems design and operation.

JIT seeks to design a manufacturing system for efficient production of 100% good units. It seeks to produce only the required items, at the required time, and in the required quantities. This is probably the simplest statement of the JIT approach to manufacturing.

To be more specific, JIT seeks to achieve the following goals (Edwards 1983):

- zero defects
- zero set-up time
- zero inventories
- zero handling
- zero breakdowns

- zero lead time
- lot size of one.

There are two aspects of the set of goals listed above which are worth noting:

(1) In the minds of many manufacturing or industrial engineers trained in the traditional *Western* approach to manufacturing systems design and operation, these goals seem very ambitious, if not unattainable.

(2) The attempt to consider all of these goals simultaneously is unusual in the context of the traditional approach to manufacturing systems. As pointed out earlier in Chapter 2, the traditional approach to manufacturing has been reductionist, which involves consideration of well-defined aspects of the overall manufacturing problem – in fact, separate sub-problems – which are tackled and *solved* as separate problems. This approach has led to the proliferation of specialists in the various manufacturing functions, with a resulting absence of any generalist to consider the whole of the manufacturing system. The JIT approach can clearly be characterized as holistic, at least in terms of the range of goals it sets for itself.

11.2.1 Zero defects

In traditional manufacturing management the goal of *zero defects* is rarely considered. In fact, quality people have traditionally thought and planned in terms of LTPD (Lot Tolerance Percent Defective) and AQLs (Acceptable Quality Levels). The emphasis in these traditional systems is likely to be on inspection systems, control charts, and *acceptable* quality levels for the items produced. The underlying assumption seems to be the belief that a certain level of unacceptable product is unavoidable and that the emphasis should be on reaching an attainable or acceptable level of conformity to specification and to customer expectation. This contrasts with the JIT approach, which aims to eliminate once and for all the causes of defects, and so engenders an attitude of seeking to achieve excellence at all stages in the manufacturing process.

11.2.2 Zero inventories

In traditional manufacturing thinking, inventories, including Work in Progress (WIP) and the contents of finished goods stores, are seen as assets in the sense that they represent added value which has been accumulated in the system. From the perspective of the shop floor supervisor, inventories are also *good* in that they represent a build-up of work available in the supervisor's department. Furthermore, at the end of the week, the difference between the starting (i.e. beginning of the week) inventory and the inventory on hand represents a part of the *value added* during the week and tends to indicate increased efficiency for the department in question.

Inventories are seen, in many cases, as a buffer against uncertain suppliers in the case of raw materials and bought-in items. Outside suppliers are *distrusted* and the thinking is almost to assume that they may not deliver on time and hence the buffers – as *insurance* against uncertain availability of work by shop floor supervisors, and as a buffer against an unexpected customer order by the marketing and sales function.

Moreover, the quest for manufacturing efficiency, where efficiency is measured in terms of the utilization of equipment within shop floor departments, encourages shop floor supervisors and managers to keep individual machines and work centers busy continuously, producing items which are often not mandated by current orders and are perhaps required to meet future, as yet unannounced, demand. The expensive work centers, those with the highest cost or capital/overhead recovery per hour, tend to be singled out for special attention and a *good* supervisor works hard to keep such machines busy. Ironically, such expensive work centers are likely to be the most productive in the plant and therefore capable of generating huge amounts of inventory. One can see that the emphasis on *recovering* overhead by keeping machines busy stems from a reductionist approach to manufacturing since the overall cost of such behavior is ignored.

Clearly, the effect of this emphasis on recovering overhead is to build up inventories to levels higher than they might otherwise be. Occasionally pressure may be exerted by senior management to reduce the levels of stock in the plant, but this will be buried as part of an overall drive to increase productivity and manufacturing efficiency, and so we get bound again by the **utilization of equipment** goal. In addition, high inventories are traditionally seen as the responsibility of the materials management function in manufacturing organizations – particularly the production controllers – while efficiency/utilization are traditionally the responsibility of shop floor supervisors and management.

The accountants see inventory as an asset to be recorded on the balance sheet. Senior management may not have encouraged the build-up of large stocks but one feels that faced with a choice between low plant utilization with low stocks on the one hand and high plant utilization and high stocks on the other, they tend to choose the latter.

All of this contrasts with the JIT view that inventory is *evil* and that inventory is evidence of poor design, poor coordination, and poor operation of the manufacturing system.

11.2.3 Zero set-up time

The concepts of zero set-up time and a lot size of one are interrelated. If the set-up times are approaching zero, then this implies that there is no advantage to producing in batches. As seen earlier, the thinking behind the economic order quantity/economic batch quantity approach is to minimize the total cost of inventory by effecting a tradeoff between the costs of carrying stock and the cost of set-ups. Very large batches imply high inventory costs. Very small batches result in correspondingly lower inventory costs but involve a larger number of set-ups and, consequently, larger set-up costs. However, if set-up times and costs are zero, then the ultimate small batch, namely the batch of one, is economic. The consequences of a lot size of one are of enormous benefit from an inventory and overall manufacturing performance perspective.

11.2.4 Zero lead time

An equally important result of small lots is the effect they have on flexibility. Small lots combine with the resultant very short lead times to greatly increase the flexibility of the manufacturing system. It was seen in our discussion on the length of the planning horizon for master scheduling in MRP systems that the planning horizon must be at least as long as the longest cumulative product lead time. Long planning lead times force the manufacturing system to rely on forecasts and to commit to manufacturing product prior to, and in anticipation of, customer orders. Furthermore, if a batch of product has already progressed some way through a series of manufacturing processes, it is difficult, if not impossible, to modify the batch size to match short term fluctuations in market demand patterns. Small lot sizes, combined with short lead times, mean that the manufacturing system is not committed to a particular production program over a long period and can more readily adapt to short term fluctuations in market demand.

To approach zero lead time, the products, the manufacturing system, and the production processes must be so designed as to facilitate rapid throughput of orders. Traditional approaches tended to treat product and process design separately. The JIT philosophy takes a holistic approach and recognizes the interdependence between these activities.

The importance of the *zero lead time* goal cannot be overstated when considering the demands placed by the market on manufacturers to respond quickly to orders for a diversity of products (see Chapter 1). While zero lead time is impossible, a manufacturing system that pursues such an ideal objective and constantly strives to reduce the lead times for products to the absolute minimum will tend to operate with greater flexibility than its competitors.

11.2.5 Zero parts handling

Manufacturing and assembly operations frequently include a large number of non-value adding activities. Taking assembly operations as an example, many assembly tasks can be viewed as a combination of the following operations:

- component feeding,
- component handling,
- parts mating,
- parts inspection,
- special operations.

Operations such as *component feeding* and *component handling* are non-value adding operations. If components and assemblies could be designed to minimize feeding and if manufacturing systems could be designed to minimize handling, significant reductions in assembly problems and assembly times could be achieved. (See Boothroyd and Dewhurst (1982, 1983) and Browne *et al.* (1985) for some design guidelines on how to achieve this.)

As Boothroyd and Dewhurst (1983) stated, "design is the first stage of manufacturing. It is here that the manufacturing costs are largely determined. In addition, the assembly process is usually the single most important process contributing to both manufacturing costs and labour requirements."

As will be seen later, the product based manufacturing layout is preferred to the traditional process based layout. One reason for this is that product based layout results in much simpler patterns of material flow through the plant and, consequently, considerably reduces the planning and materials handling effort.

11.3 Key elements in the JIT approach

Given the goals discussed above the essential elements of the JIT philosophy for product and manufacturing system design can be determined. These important elements are:

- An intelligent match of the market demand with product design in an era of greatly reduced product life cycles and with the early consideration of manufacturing problems at the product design stage.
- The definition of product families based on a number of important manufacturing goals and the design of manufacturing systems to facilitate flow based production of these families where possible.
- The establishment of relationships with suppliers to achieve just in time deliveries of raw materials and purchased components.

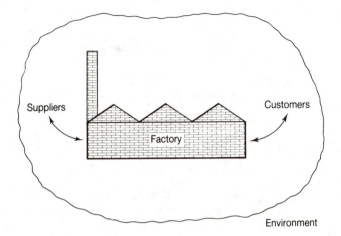

Figure 11.2 Plant environment from JIT perspective.

These three elements can be viewed as part of an overall approach to manufacturing which sees the factory sitting within an environment as shown in Figure 11.2. The front end involves the factory and its relationship with its customers in the marketplace and the back end is the relationship of the factory with its suppliers. The fact that the JIT approach considers the total manufacturing picture is not surprising in view of the wide range of goals that JIT seeks to address and which have been outlined above.

The importance of this approach to manufacturing, i.e. not restricting attention to the *internals* of the factory, cannot be overstressed. Let us return for a moment to our discussion in Chapter 4 on the distinction between computer integrated business and the extended enterprise and computer integrated manufacturing.

In Chapter 4 it was pointed out that manufacturing lead time is the time taken from receipt of the order in the plant to the completion of the order and its availability for delivery to the customer. CIM, it was noted, focuses on that part of the business organization whose goal is to reduce the manufacturing lead time, increase the quality and reduce the cost of the product. At the front end of the business it takes a certain time to process the order from the customer and to acquire the necessary raw material and purchased items from vendors. Similarly, it takes some time to assemble the finished products and to dispatch the completed order to the customer.

Figure 11.3, a replica of Figure 4.2, depicts this situation and suggests that, in many industries, the times for the processing of customer orders, the acquisition of the raw material, and the distribution of the finished product are larger than the manufacturing lead time. This is so for a number of reasons, partially because of problems associated with product diversity and semi-customized products. For example, actual understanding of

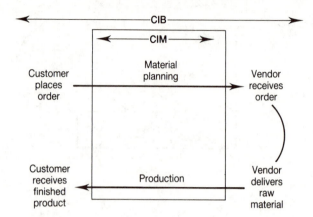

Figure 11.3 Time between when customer orders and receives product.

customer requirements and the conversion of this understanding into requirements for recognizable part numbers in the manufacturing database can take a long time and involve sales and technical sales support people.

As Figure 11.3 suggests, CIM is concerned primarily with activity during the manufacturing lead time, whereas computer integrated business and indeed the extended enterprise are concerned with all aspects of the relationship with the customer, from receipt of initial order to dispatch of product and, subsequently, to maintain a relationship with the customer for maintenance and product update purposes. Reducing the manufacturing lead time is a key goal of modern manufacturing. Through the use of computer technology, great opportunities exist to reduce the time taken from initial contact with the customer through receipt of the order, and onto the dispatch of the finished goods.

In our view, the JIT approach to manufacturing incorporates a business perspective, as distinct from a narrow or strictly manufacturing (i.e. inside the four walls of the plant) perspective. The three key elements of the JIT approach identified above are a result of this business perspective, and each of them will now be discussed in turn.

11.3.1 A match of product design to market demand

Chapter 1 reviewed the changed environment of manufacturing, focusing on greatly increased product diversity and greatly reduced product life cycles as important factors in this new environment. The heightened expectations of today's consumers, who demand considerable choice in the configuration of options, was also alluded to – the automotive market being an important example of this trend.

Of course, even with today's sophisticated and versatile manufacturing technology, companies cannot provide *customized* products at an economic price to the mass market. What is required is that industry interpret the wishes of the marketplace and, in a sense, direct the market in a manner that allows it (the industry) to respond to the market effectively. This involves designing a range of products which anticipate the market requirement and include sufficient variety to meet consumers' expectations, and which can be manufactured and delivered to the market at a price which the market is willing and able to pay.

To achieve this objective it is necessary to design products in a modular fashion. A large product range and a wide variety of product styles can result in high manufacturing and assembly costs due to the high cost of flexibility in manufacturing systems. In general terms, it is true that the greater the flexibility required, the more expensive will be the manufacturing system and, therefore, the products of that manufacturing system. (The effect of computer based manufacturing technology is simply to shift the cost curve in the sense that flexibility becomes relatively less expensive – however, it is still true that there is a cost premium associated with the provision of flexibility.) Thus, too broad a product range and variety of product styles will result in product which is too expensive for the market.

Modular product designs are achieved by rationalizing the product range, where possible, and by examining the commonality of components and subassemblies across the product range with a view to increasing it to the maximum level possible. Rationalization of the product range results in reduced production costs through fewer manufacturing set-ups, fewer items in stock, fewer component drawings, etc. These issues will be considered in more detail in Chapter 12 when the product design issue will be reviewed further.

The approach here is somewhat akin to that of Skinner (1974) and his concept of the **focused factory**. Skinner suggests that a new management approach is needed in industries where diverse products and markets require companies to manufacture a wide range of products in forms and quantities:

> ". . . One way to compete is to focus the entire manufacturing system on a limited task precisely defined by the company's competitive strategy and the realities of its technology and economics . . . Instead of permitting a whirling diversity of tasks and ingredients, top management applies a centripetal force, which constantly pulls inward towards one central focus – the one key manufacturing task. The result is greater simplicity, lower costs, and a manufacturing and support organization that is directed towards successful competition."

11.3.2 Product families and flow based manufacturing

A common approach to the identification of product families and the subsequent development of flow based manufacturing systems is Group

Technology (GT). In JIT systems, the use of GT to define product families is important for a number of reasons. Firstly, group technology is used to aid the design process and to reduce unnecessary variety and duplication in product design. Secondly, group technology is used to define families of products and components which can be manufactured in well-defined manufacturing cells. The effect of these manufacturing cells is to reorient production systems away from the process based layout and towards the product or flow based layout. As Hyer and Wemmerlov (1982) point out, group technology leads to cell based manufacturing which "promises shorter lead times, reduced work in progress and finished goods inventories, simplified production planning and control and increased job satisfaction." Group technology was not originally conceived by the Japanese but its philosophy was adopted by them and drawn into the JIT approach to manufacturing. Those readers interested in a short discussion on the historical background to group technology are referred to Gallagher and Knight (1973).

Group technology, in a sense, creates the conditions necessary for JIT because, as Lewis (1986) points out, it results in:

- "Control of the variety seen by the manufacturing system.
- Standardization of processing methods.
- Integration of processes."

In group technology, components are grouped into families on the basis of similarity of such features as part shapes, part finishes, materials, tolerances, and required manufacturing processes. Gallagher and Knight (1973) define group technology as "a technique for identifying and bringing together related or similar components in a production process in order to take advantage of their similarities by making use of, for example, the inherent economies of flow-production methods."

Group technology forms component families on the basis of the design or manufacturing attributes – sometimes both – of the components in question. A large number of classification systems have been developed, including the Brisch system in the UK and the Opitz system in Germany. These systems allow the manufacturing systems analyst to code the components manufactured in a plant and to identify families of components which have similar processing requirements and which, consequently, can be manufactured in a group technology cell. The effect of these cells is to generate simplified material flow patterns in a plant, to allow responsibility and *ownership* for a component or group of components to rest with one group of operators and their supervisor.

These effects are best understood by considering the differences between a traditional, functional (process based) plant layout and a group technology (product based) layout. In the functional or process layout, machines are organized into groups by function. Thus, in a metal cutting

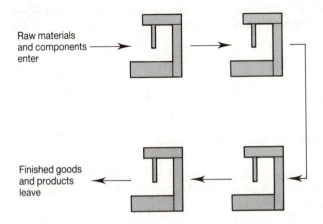

Raw materials
and components
enter

Finished goods
and products
leave

Figure 11.4   Cell layout.

machine shop the lathes would be grouped together, as would the milling machines, the grinders, the drilling machines, etc. A departmental foreman would be responsible for a particular function or group of functions. Individual components would *visit* some, or maybe all, departments and thus would pass through a number of different supervisors' areas of responsibility. Operators and their supervisors would be responsible for different operations on each component but not for the resulting component or assembly itself. Given the variety of components associated with batch type production systems, the actual route individual batches take through the various departments or functions in the plant varies and the material flow system is thus complex. Furthermore, given this complex and virtually *random* material flow system, it is not easy to say, at any point in time, what progress has been made on individual batches.

The product or cell based layout, as shown in Figure 11.4, is clearly considerably simpler than the process layout. In fact, this simplicity is a hallmark of JIT systems, and, for many writers and researchers on manufacturing systems, is a key characteristic of the system. (See, for example, Schonberger (1984)). As we shall see later, this simplicity facilitates the use of a manual production activity control system, namely Kanban, on the shop floor itself.

Burbidge (1975) suggests that the process based layout is a poor basis for manufacturing efficiency and argues that process layout results in very long throughput times and does not facilitate the delegation of product responsibility down to the shop floor level.

A technique used to plan the change from a process to a product based plant organization is Production Flow Analysis (PFA) (see Burbidge 1963). Production flow analysis is a technique based on the analysis of component route cards which specify the manufacturing processes for each component and, indeed, the manufacturing work centers which individual components must visit. PFA, according to Burbidge, is a progressive technique based on five sub-techniques, namely:

(1)   Company Flow Analysis (CFA).

(2)   Factory Flow Analysis (FFA).

(3)   Group Analysis (GA).

(4)   Line Analysis (LA).

(5)   Tooling Analysis (TA).

CFA is used in multiplant companies to plan the simplest and most efficient interplant material flow system.

FFA is used to identify the sub-products within a factory around which product based departments can be organized.

GA is used to divide the individual departments into groups of machines which deal with unique *product* families.

LA seeks to organize the individual machines within a line to reflect the flow of *products* between those machines.

TA looks at the individual machines in a cell or line and seeks to plan tooling so that groups of parts can be made with similar tooling set-up.

The important issue from our point of view is that flow based manufacturing is an important goal for manufacturing systems designers to aim towards and it is certainly central to the whole JIT approach.

11.3.3   The relationship with suppliers in a JIT environment

As indicated earlier, the ideas of JIT are not restricted to the narrow confines of the manufacturing plant but also reach out to the factory's customers and back to the vendor companies who supply the factory with raw materials and purchased items. The approach is to build strong and enduring relationships with a limited number of suppliers, to provide those suppliers with the detailed knowledge they need to be cost effective, to help them overcome problems they might encounter, and to encourage them to apply their detailed knowledge of their own manufacturing processes constantly to improve the quality of the components they supply. In many ways JIT predated today's thinking on supply chain management and the need for very close relations with suppliers/partners in the extended enterprise mode of operating.

This involves taking a long term view of the buyer/supplier relationship and also involves commitment to building an enduring cooperative relationship with individual suppliers where information is readily shared and both organizations work to meet shared goals. JIT execution (i.e. the Kanban system), applied to purchasing, gives rise to frequent orders and frequent deliveries. The ideal of single unit continuous delivery (delivery lot size of one) is impractical but it can be approached by having as small a lot size as possible, delivered from the supplier, as frequently as possible. The physical distance of suppliers from the buyer's manufacturing plant plays an important role in determining the delivery lot size.

The closer the supplier is to the buyer's plant, the easier it is to make more frequent deliveries of smaller lots. Ideally, this may allow the supplier to initiate JIT production in his/her own plant and so link up with the buyer's JIT production system. In the case of suppliers at a distance from the buyer's plant, various techniques may be used to reduce what might otherwise be a high cost per unit load.

> Consider for example the following situation. Four suppliers, A, B, C, and D, supply components to buyer E. The four suppliers are located in relatively close proximity to each other but all are at a distance from the buyer E. If they must all deliver four times each day then the possibility exists for them to cooperate in such a way that deliveries are made to the buyer four times each day, with each supplier responsible for only one delivery run per day. Supplier A might make the first delivery picking up product from B, C, and D *en route*. Supplier B could make the second delivery picking up the products of A, C, and D, etc.

On the one hand, the buyer places great demands on the supplier in terms of frequent or just in time deliveries of components. On the other hand, by providing the supplier with commitments for capacity over a long period and by ensuring that the supplier is aware of modifications to the company's master schedule as soon as is practicable, the company helps the supplier to meet the exacting demands of JIT. The ideal situation is where the supplier himself is able to focus a part of his/her plant to service each customer and the supplier starts to achieve a JIT environment in house.

The benefits from JIT purchasing include reduced purchased inventories, low rework, reduced inspection, and shortened production lead time. These all combine to increase adaptability to demand and hence achieve just in time production.

11.4 Conclusion

This chapter has laid out the goals of JIT and also indicated what are considered to be the key elements in the JIT approach to manufacturing. These have been listed as:

- An intelligent match of market demand with product design in an era of greatly reduced product life cycles, with early consideration of manufacturing problems at the product design stage.
- The definition of product families based on a number of important manufacturing goals and the design of manufacturing systems to facilitate flow based production of these families, where possible.

- The establishment of relationships with vendors and suppliers to achieve just in time deliveries of raw materials and purchased components.

Chapter 12 will go on to look at some JIT manufacturing systems design techniques which are focused on the above goals and which may be used in the context of the JIT approach to manufacturing.

Questions

(11.1) What are the goals of JIT?

(11.2) "Inventories are often seen as a buffer against uncertain suppliers and unexpected customers." Comment.

(11.3) "The emphasis on recovering overhead by keeping machines busy, stems from a reductionist approach to manufacturing." Discuss.

(11.4) What is the JIT view of inventory?

(11.5) "If set-up times and costs are zero, then the ultimate small batch, namely the batch size of one, is economic." Why?

(11.6) Why is "zero lead time" so important to modern manufacturers?

(11.7) What are the three key elements of the JIT approach or philosophy?

(11.8) "The JIT approach to manufacturing incorporates a business perspective, as distinct from a narrow or strictly manufacturing approach." Discuss.

(11.9) What do you understand by the term *focused factory*?

(11.10) What is group technology?

(11.11) Differentiate clearly between the *process* based plant layout and the *product* based plant layout?

(11.12) How is production flow analysis used to develop group technology layouts?

(11.13) How would you characterize the relationships of suppliers to the manufacturing plant in a JIT environment?

CHAPTER TWELVE

Manufacturing systems design and planning for JIT

12.1 Introduction

This chapter will focus on a set of manufacturing system design techniques that support the just in time approach. The design and planning of JIT manufacturing systems is applicable within the context of a just in time philosophy and is necessary to create the environment to allow Kanban, the shop floor control realization of JIT, to work as is illustrated in Figure 12.1.

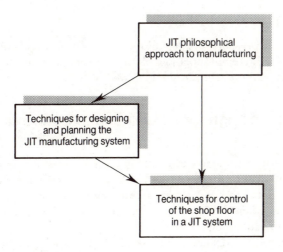

Figure 12.1   JIT approach.

The prime objective of this chapter is to review JIT techniques and to present the reader with an understanding of the role and importance of these techniques in JIT practice. These techniques relate primarily to manufacturing system design and production planning.

A primary focus of JIT is the reduction of the production lead time. Many advantages can be gained by reducing this lead time to a minimum. For example, a short lead time relative to competitors in the marketplace allows sales offices to quote shorter delivery times – an important competitive advantage in today's business environment. From the manufacturing planning perspective, short lead times reduce the manufacturing plant's dependence on forecasts and allow the plant to operate using a shorter planning horizon and, consequently, a more accurate master schedule. Reduced lead times also have important consequences for a plant's ability to respond to short term unexpected changes in the marketplace, as will be seen later.

There are many activities over the product life cycle and throughout the manufacturing enterprise which influence the product lead time, from product design right through to receipt of the completed order by the customer. Similarly, there are also approaches which improve manufacturing performance based on the reduced lead time. These approaches and techniques within JIT manufacturing can be grouped under five identifiable headings:

(1)   Product design for ease of manufacture and assembly.

(2)   Manufacturing planning techniques.

(3)   Techniques to facilitate the use of simple, but refined, manufacturing control systems, namely Kanban.

(4)   An approach to the use of manufacturing resources.

(5)   Quality control and quality assurance procedures.

Figure 12.2 presents the techniques that support the just in time approach and facilitate the creation of the environment needed for JIT execution. Each of these will now be reviewed in turn.

12.2 Product design for ease of manufacture and assembly

Chapter 11 identified some key elements in the JIT approach, one of which is an intelligent match of the product design with the perceived market demand. It was noted that this is important in an era of constantly changing market demands when a manufacturer must offer a diversity of products within a given product range to the market.

As suggested in Chapter 11, what is required of the product design team, among other things, is that it interprets the wishes of the

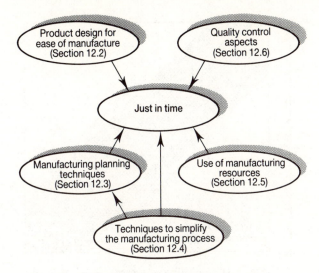

Figure 12.2   Manufacturing techniques which support JIT.

marketplace and, if possible, leads the market by introducing a product range that allows the production system to respond effectively to the market. This involves designing products that both anticipate the market requirement and include sufficient variety to meet consumers' expectations, while being manufactured at a price that the market is willing to pay. This can be achieved in many ways. One approach is to increase the variety of products offered without simultaneously increasing the required process variety, associated complexity and increased cost. Let us consider Figure 12.3.

At present, designers of manufacturing systems are required to move along a diagonal which is bounded by both economic and technological constraints as shown in Figure 12.3. The continuum of manufacturing mentioned in Chapter 1, which extends from mass production to jobbing shops, can be seen along this diagonal, with mass production in the bottom right corner and jobbing shop production in the upper left corner. However, given the new *environment* of manufacturing discussed in Chapter 1, we might surmise that designers are attempting to move in the direction of low process variety and high product variety (i.e. the bottom left corner of Figure 12.3). This effort is bounded by technological constraints, and the approach that seems to be prevalent in the West is often technologically driven, through the introduction of computer controlled and thus more flexible production facilities.

In our view, the just in time approach represents a more comprehensive attempt to move towards low process variety and high product variety. Not only concerned with technological improvements, JIT also utilizes

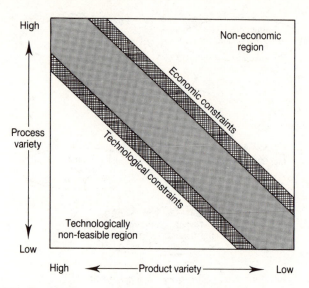

Figure 12.3 Tradeoff between product and process variety.

such techniques as product design for manufacture and assembly, flexible equipment, a flexible work force, and superior production engineering practice in areas such as the design of jigs and fixtures, to achieve simple and, therefore, fast and inexpensive set-ups and changeovers between products. The concepts behind the use of flexible equipment and a flexible work force will be brought out later in this chapter, as will the JIT approach to set-up reduction. For the moment, the effect of short set-up times will be illustrated using the following example.

A machine that manufactures two distinct products – A and B – can be considered, from the process viewpoint, to be producing one product if the set-up or changeover time between the two products is very small, in effect, approaching zero. To achieve this very desirable situation involves close collaboration between the product design, process engineering, and manufacturing people in the plant.

Traditional thinking about the interaction between product or process variety can be represented by Figure 12.4. From this perspective, a widening of the product range results in an increase in the process variety required to cope with the increased product options. If a manufacturing plant increases the options within its product range, this is normally expected to lead to increased process complexity because of increased process variety. Similarly, if the range of options in a product is reduced, this might be expected to lead to a reduction in the complexity of the

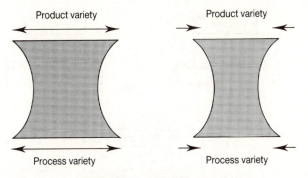

Figure 12.4 Product/process variety relationship (classical).

Figure 12.5 Product/process variety relationship under JIT.

production system. In fact, the classical distinction between mass production, batch production, and jobbing shop production is based, at least partially, on this notion – mass production uses specialized equipment to manufacture a narrow range of products in high volumes efficiently. However, where the product range is large and each product is required in relatively small volumes, more general purpose equipment is required and the resulting process variety is high. In effect economies of scale cannot be realized in batch based production systems. The impact of the introduction of computer based automation into plants has been to allow the manufacturer to deal with greater variety, but the basic underlying relationship has not changed. Increased product variety involves more process complexity and, therefore, increased cost.

However, the JIT approach tries, through intelligent product design and through consideration of process issues at the product design stage, to increase the variety of products within a manufacturing plant while maintaining, if not actually reducing, process variety (see Figure 12.5). (It should be pointed out that design for manufacture and design

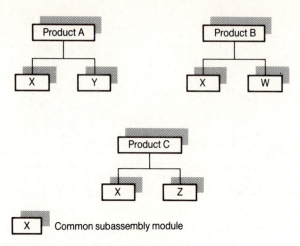

Figure 12.6 Common modules across BOMs.

for assembly are not unique to JIT. What is unique about JIT, in our view, is the emphasis it places on these issues and the fact that process and product design seem to have equal *status* and to work together effectively.)

This can be achieved using techniques such as modular design, design for simplification, and design for ease of manufacture and assembly. (See Treer (1979) for a more complete discussion on this important topic and its particular relevance when designing a product for automated manufacturing and assembly.)

12.2.1 Modular design

One of the consequences of good design is frequently a reduction in the number of components necessary to produce a given product and hence a reduction in the production lead time. Similarly, products may be designed in a modular fashion so that components and assemblies are common across a given product range and thus product variety is managed to good effect. With regard to the design process, it is possible to expand a basic model so as to increase the variety of products offered to the market. As illustrated in Figure 12.6, a common subassembly or module X is used across a number of products – A, B, and C. The effect of this is to increase the requirement for a single module X rather than having three different modules, each with a relatively low total requirement. Thus the use of standardized components and subassemblies results in increased production volumes of fewer different components and, consequently, reduced inventory levels.

This design philosophy is also reflected in the bill of materials through attempts to keep the differences between products as *high as possible* in the product structure and thus minimize the consequences of variability for manufacturing.

12.2.2   Design for simplification

Design for simplification seeks to design products which are relatively simple to manufacture and assemble. New product designs should, as far as possible, include **off the shelf** items, standard items or components that are possible to make with a minimum of experimental tooling. Product features, such as part tolerances, surface finish requirements, etc., should be determined while considering the consequences of unnecessary embellishment on the production process and thus on production costs. This approach can result in a major simplification of the manufacturing and assembly process.

12.2.3   Design for ease of automation

Design for ease of automation is concerned with the general concepts and design ideas which will, for example, in the case of assembled components, help to simplify the automatic parts feeding, orienting, and assembling processes. In the case of assembled components it is important to design products to be assembled from the top down and to avoid forcing machines to assemble from the side or particularly from the bottom. The ideal assembly procedure can be performed on one face of the part, with straight vertical motions and keeping the number of faces to be worked on to a minimum.

In fact, it is in the area of automated and, in particular, robot based assembly that the importance of the design for assembly approach can be most clearly seen. Until the early 1980s the application of robots in industry had been confined to relatively primitive tasks – machine loading and unloading, spot and arc welding, spray painting, etc. Relatively few applications in assembly were realized. Researchers and manufacturing systems designers adopted two main approaches: the development of sophisticated assembly robots and the redesign of products, components, etc. for robot based assembly. The first approach involves the development of *universal* grippers and *intelligent*, sensor-based robots with sufficient accuracy, speed, and repeatability, and which are capable of being programmed in task oriented languages. This approach seeks to mimic the flexibility and power of the human arm and hand. The second approach seems to be the more successful in practice. Laszcz (1985) points out that ". . . a product designed in this manner reduces assembly to a series of pick-and-place operations, thereby requiring a less sophisticated robot. This results in manufacturing cost savings and increases the likelihood of financially justifying robotic assembly."

12.3 Manufacturing planning techniques

An important purpose of JIT is clearly to reduce costs. This is achieved in many ways, the most notable being the elimination of all wastes, especially unnecessary inventories. For example, in sales, cost reduction is realized by supplying the market with first class products in the quantities required and at an affordable price. Stocks of finished goods are therefore minimized. To sell at a realistic price and in the quantities required, the production processes must be adaptable to changes in demand and be capable of getting the required products quickly through manufacturing and to the marketplace. Similarly, the warehouses must only stock materials in the quantities required. To help production to respond effectively to short term variations in market demand, Just in Time attempts to match the expected demand pattern to the capabilities of the manufacturing process and to organize the manufacturing system so that short term, relatively small, variations can be accommodated without major overhaul of the system. The technique used to help achieve this is known as production smoothing.

Through production smoothing, single lines can produce many product varieties, each day, in response to market demand. Production smoothing utilizes the short production lead times to *mold* market demand to match the capabilities of the production process. It involves two distinct phases as illustrated in Figure 12.7.

The first phase adapts to monthly market demand changes during the year, the second to daily demand changes within each month. The possibility of sudden large changes in market demand and seasonal changes is greatly reduced by detailed analysis of annual, or even longer term, projections and well thought out decisions on sales volumes, in so far as this is possible.

12.3.1 Monthly adaptation

Monthly adaptation is achieved though a monthly production planning process, i.e. the preparation of a Master Production Schedule (MPS), similar to the MRP process documented in Chapters 5 and 6. This MPS gives

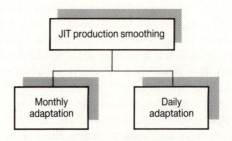

Figure 12.7 Components of production smoothing.

the averaged daily production level of each process and is typically based on an aggregate three month and a monthly demand forecast. The precise planning horizon depends very much on the industry in question – in the automotive industry where JIT originated, three months is typical. Thus the product mix and related product quantities are *suggested* two months in advance and a detailed plan is *fixed* one month in advance of the present month. This information is also transmitted to suppliers in order to make their task of providing raw materials as required somewhat easier. Daily schedules are then determined from the MPS.

In fact, the concept of production smoothing extends along two dimensions – firstly, by spreading the production of products evenly over each day within a month and, secondly, by spreading the quantities of each product evenly over each day within a month. Both of these are typically incorporated into the daily schedule as in the following example.

Consider a production line in, say Gizmo-Stools Inc., which produces six different stools – Stool A, Stool B, Stool C, Stool D, Stool E, and Stool F. These stools have different characteristics – some are three-legged stools, others are four-legged stools, some have round seats while others have square seats, etc. Let us also assume that the master production schedule calls for 4800 units to be produced in a month containing 20 working days. Then, by averaging the production of all stools over each day, 240 units must be produced per day. If the 4800 stools breaks down into the product quantities in Table 12.1(a) then, in the extreme case of traditional batch production, the floor schedule would produce 1200 of Stool A, followed by 400 of Stool B, 1600 of Stool C, 400 of Stool D, 600 of Stool E, and finally 600 of Stool F. However, by averaging the output of each product over all days within the month and assuming that there are 20 working days in the month the daily production schedule illustrated in Table 12.1(b) is calculated.

Therefore, the required 240 units must be produced within a shift (i.e. 8 hours or 480 minutes). Simple mathematics tells us that one unit must be produced every two minutes. This may be done in a batch of 60 of Stool A followed by a batch of 20 of Stool B, and so on. However, by carrying the second concept further and spreading the production of all products evenly within each day, we can develop a schedule for a small duration, e.g. 48 minutes, as in Table 12.2. This schedule is continuously repeated until the daily schedule is met.

12.3.2 Mixed model production

This concept of manufacturing and 'assembling a range of products *simultaneously* is known as **mixed model** production and it is widely used within what are termed repetitive manufacturing systems. Repetitive

Table 12.1 Monthly and daily product quantities.

Varieties	(a) Monthly demand	(b) Daily average output
Stool A	1200	60
Stool B	400	20
Stool C	1600	80
Stool D	400	20
Stool E	600	30
Stool F	600	30
Demand	4800 per month	240 per day

Table 12.2 Production schedule.

Varieties	Number of units
Stool A	6
Stool B	2
Stool C	8
Stool D	2
Stool E	3
Stool F	3
	24 every 48 minutes

manufacturing systems will be examined in more detail in Chapter 13. Mixed model production should be differentiated from **multi-model** production where a variety of models are produced but not simultaneously. Mixed model production is clearly not feasible unless the set-up times for individual models are extremely small so that there is no effective changeover in going from, say, Stool A to Stool B. This, in turn, can only be achieved if the designs of the products in question are such that they minimize *process variety* (see Section 12.2).

The benefits of mixed model assembly are potentially very great, particularly in an environment where customers expect rapid turnaround on orders and where the ability to respond at short notice is critical. Mixed model production offers a very high level of flexibility compared to traditional production methods.

Consider the following situation. Let us assume that Table 12.1 reflects the expectation of requirements for the six products – Stool A, Stool B, etc. at the start of the month. Based on this we have developed a basic production cycle as shown in Table 12.2. Now,

Table 12.3 Half-monthly and daily product quantities.

Varieties	Monthly demand	Daily average output
Stool A	600	60
Stool B	200	20
Stool C	800	80
Stool D	200	20
Stool E	300	30
Stool F	300	30
Demand	2400 per rest of month	240 per day

Table 12.4 Revised half-monthly product quantities.

Varieties	Monthly demand	Daily average output
Stool A	600	60
Stool B	600	60
Stool C	400	40
Stool D	200	20
Stool E	300	30
Stool F	300	30
Demand	2400 per rest of month	240 per day

further assume that in the middle of the month a major customer changes its order – for example, an important customer decides to change the order from 400 of Stool C to 400 of Stool B. How can this be accommodated? The expected requirement for the second half of the month has now been changed from that defined by Table 12.3 to that of Table 12.4.

Thus to meet this new situation, all that is required is that the planner modify the production cycle in line with the new mix within the daily output. In effect, all that is required is that the cycle represented by Table 12.2 is modified to that contained in Table 12.5.

This is clearly a trivial example but the point that it seeks to illustrate is nevertheless valid. Mixed model production results in a flexible production system and one which is very responsive to sudden market changes. What would the situation have been if the system described above had been operated in the traditional manner where, admittedly in an extreme case, all of Stool A might have been manufactured first followed by all of Stool B, etc.?

Table 12.5 Revised production schedule.

Varieties	Number of units
Stool A	6
Stool B	6
Stool C	4
Stool D	2
Stool E	3
Stool F	3
	24 every 48 minutes

12.3.3 Daily adaptation

After the development of a monthly production plan, the next step in the smoothing of production is the breakdown of this schedule into the sequence of production for each day. This sequence specifies the assembly order of the units to be produced. The sequence is arranged so that when the cycle time expires, one group of units has been produced. At every work center no new units are introduced until one is completed. This sequence schedule is *only* transmitted to the starting point of final assembly. Kanban (see Chapter 13) functions so that production instructions are simply and clearly transferred to all other assembly and manufacturing processes.

Referring back to Table 12.2, it can be seen that a mix of 24 units of the four stools must be produced within 48 minute intervals. The sequence of production for these 24 units might be as follows:

AAAAAA BB CCCCCCCC DD EEE FFF.

Or the sequence could be more varied, such as:

ACAECFBCACDAEFCBCADCFEAC.

Attaining the *optimal* sequence is difficult. Heuristic procedures have been developed (Monden 1983; Wild 1984) which produce a sequence that aims to achieve two plantwide goals:

(1) An even load at each stage of the manufacturing process.

(2) A constant depletion rate for each component.

In greatly simplified terms, the objective of the heuristic is to minimize the variations in consumed quantities of each component at final assembly and at all of the work centers. By this smoothing of production, large fluctuations in demand and the amplification of these fluctuations back through the production system are prevented.

Each day's schedule should resemble the previous day's schedule as closely as possible. Hence, uncertainties are eliminated and the need for dynamic scheduling and safety stocks is minimized.

The daily adaptation to the actual demand for varieties of a product during a month is the ideal of JIT production, which in turn requires the daily smoothed withdrawals of each part from the subassembly lines right back to the suppliers. Minor variations in demand are generally overcome by the Kanban system by increasing or decreasing the number of cards. This will be fully discussed in Chapter 13.

One might argue that the ideal of production smoothing is, in fact, very difficult to achieve in practice for many industries and individual companies. Nevertheless, it is clear that for all of manufacturing industry there are lessons to be learned from this approach. The key lesson is the fundamental importance of a firm master schedule from the point of view of control of the production system and the advantages, in terms of flexibility, to be gained from moving towards mixed model production and assembly. It was seen during the discussion on the master schedule (Chapter 7) that the longest cumulative lead time determines the length of the planning horizon. Section 12.4 will now go on to see how JIT seeks to reduce throughput times or lead times and hence reduce the planning horizon, which in turn lessens the dependence on forecasting in the master schedule development.

12.4 Techniques to simplify the manufacturing process and reduce lead times

As we discussed in Chapter 10, the lead time or throughput time for a batch through the shop floor is typically much greater than the actual processing time for the batch in question. It is not unusual in conventional batch manufacturing systems for the actual processing (including set-up time) to represent less than 5% of the total throughput time. Furthermore, of that 5%, only 30% may be spent in value adding operations. The throughput time or lead time for a product is composed of four major components – the actual process time including inspection time, the set-up time, the transport time, and the queuing time – as illustrated in Figure 12.8. In a typical batch manufacturing shop, this latter component is frequently the largest, often representing in excess of 80% of total throughput time.

Heard and Plossl (1984) describe the elements of lead time and their interrelationships. They recommend techniques to reduce these elements. JIT has long understood this and attempts to reduce each of these individual elements as much as possible.

Set-up time	Process time	Transport time	Queue time

Figure 12.8 Breakdown of the lead time.

The single largest element of throughput time in traditional batch manufacturing systems is the queuing and transport time between operations.

As discussed in Chapter 11, JIT encourages product based plant layouts which greatly reduce throughput times for individual batches by reducing queuing time. At a plant level, the product based layout reduces throughput time by facilitating easy flow of batches between operations and work centers. At a line or work center level, JIT reduces throughput time by using what are termed **U-shaped** layouts. In our view, the effort to reduce throughput time must be seen in the context of the product based layout at the macro-level and the U-shaped layout at the work center level.

How JIT addresses each of the elements of throughput time will be discussed later. Section 12.4.2 will focus on the JIT approach to the reduction of queuing time, Section 12.4.3 will consider transport time, Section 12.4.4 will consider set-up time reduction and, finally, Section 12.4.5 will look briefly at processing time. Before going on to this however, the U-shaped layout will be considered in some detail.

12.4.1 Layout of the production process

The major objectives in designing the production layout at the work center level are similar to the plant level objectives, and can be listed as follows:

- To provide flexibility in the number of operators assigned to individual work centers in order to be able to adapt to small changes in market demand and consequently in the schedule.
- To utilize the skills of the **multifunction** operators.
- To facilitate movement towards **single unit production and transport** between work centers.
- To allow for the re-evaluation and revision of the standard operations.

To meet these objectives, the U-shaped product based layout was developed as illustrated in Figure 12.9 (adapted from Monden 1983). This layout allows assignment of a multifunction operator to more than one machine due to the close proximity of the machines.

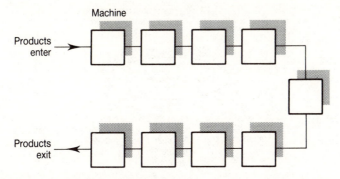

Figure 12.9 U-shaped work cell layout.

Using this layout the range of jobs that each operator performs may be increased or decreased, allowing flexibility to increase or decrease the number of operators. It allows *unit production and transport*, since machines are close together and may be connected with chutes or conveyers. Synchronization is achieved since one unit entering the layout means one unit leaving the layout and going on to the next work center.

The use of the U-shaped layout with its requirement for multiskilled operators clearly implies an increased need for operator training, as well as for very well defined and documented manufacturing instructions for operators. It is implicit in the JIT approach to manufacturing that no effort or expense be spared in training; where necessary, retraining operators in highly tested and refined work practices is considered.

12.4.2 Reduction of the queue time

Within the context of product based and U-shaped layouts, various techniques are used to reduce queue time. Figure 12.10 lists some of these techniques, which will now be considered briefly.

Small production and transport lots

In just in time manufacturing, one unit is produced within every cycle time and at the end of each cycle time a unit from each process in the line is simultaneously sent to the next process. This is already prevalent in the assembly line systems of virtually all companies engaged in mass production. However, processes supplying parts to the assembly lines are usually based on lot production. Just in time, however, seeks to extend the concept of **unit production and transport** to processes such as machining, welding, pressing, etc., which feed the final assembly lines. Therefore, as in an

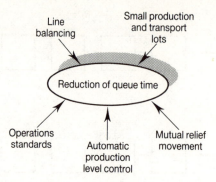

Figure 12.10   Methods of reducing queue time.

assembly line, operations must start and end at each process at exactly the same time. This is often called **synchronization**, i.e. continuous flow production.

In our discussion of the lead time and the MRP approach to production and inventory management, it was pointed out that MRP seems to consider only one batch or lot size, namely the production lot. The advantage of distinguishing between the production and conveyance lots was alluded to. For example, in situations where large production lots are necessary because of large and irreducible set-up times, smaller conveyance lots can be used to reduce overall throughput times. This notion is important to JIT manufacturing and worth restating.

Consider three operations with a cycle time of one minute each. One unit would take three minutes to go through all operations. If batch production is employed and the process lot is 200 then total throughput time is (200 + 200 + 200) minutes or 10 hours. In this case the transfer lot is equal to the process lot, as in Figure 12.11. In simple terms, a single lot size is used and lots are not normally split to facilitate early dispatch of partial lots to subsequent operations.

However, if the transfer lot (conveyance or transport lot) is less than the process lot, say, in the ultimate lot size one, then the total throughput time is greatly reduced as illustrated in Figure 12.12.

In fact, the total throughput time is 3 hours and 22 minutes. The total processing time is, of course, unaffected. In effect, the queue time has been greatly reduced.

JIT, in separating production lots from transport lots in situations where production lots are large, is seeking to move away from batch based production systems and towards flow based systems.

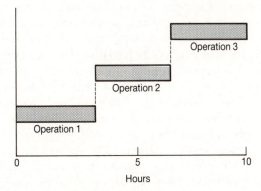

Figure 12.11   Transfer lot equals process lot.

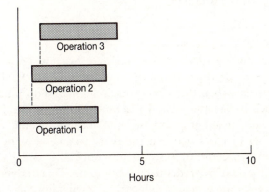

Figure 12.12   Transfer lot not equal to process lot.

Line balancing

Line balancing seeks to reduce the waiting time caused by unbalanced production times between individual work centers and ensures production is the same at all processes, both in quantities and timing. Variances in operators' skills and capabilities are minimized, by generating in advance well thought out and documented standard operations and by ensuring that all operators are trained in these *optimum* operation methods. What variances remain are smoothed through **mutual relief** (which will be discussed later). Line balancing is also promoted by the automatic control of production levels and *unit production and transport*. Synchronization also helps to balance the production timing between processes and facilitates line balancing.

It is interesting to compare briefly the notion of line balancing as seen from within a JIT perspective and the so-called *line balancing problem* well known to generations of students of industrial engineering. If we look at a typical Western textbook covering operations management and production systems design, we will, almost always, find a section on line balancing techniques. (See, for example, Wild (1984) and Groover (1980).) Line balancing is presented as a problem to be solved using algorithmic or heuristic procedures which seek to minimize what is termed the *balance loss* or some similar measure. The procedure is to take assumed elemental operations and operation precedence constraints and allocate the operations to assembly stations in order to divide the total work content of the job as evenly as possible between the assembly stations. The interesting point is that the emphasis is placed on allocating predefined operations to stations. The JIT approach places greater emphasis on the design of the operations and on ensuring that individual operators are skilled in carrying them out. Only then is the *analytical* approach to allocating the operations between stations brought to bear on the problem.

Automatic production level controls

In a particular work center, a situation may exist where two machines operate on the same product. If the machine performing the first operation has a greater capacity than the second machine, it would traditionally build up a safety stock before the second machine. However, the JIT approach would couple both machines, and the first machine would only produce when the number of parts between the two machines was below a predefined minimum. It continues producing until the queue between the machines has reached a predefined maximum. This reduces the safety stock between machines and also reduces the queue times of products. This concept and its relation to Kanban will be discussed in Chapter 13.

Operations standards

Standardizing the operations to be completed at work centers attempts to attain three goals:

(1)   minimum work in progress,
(2)   line balancing through synchronization within the cycle time,
(3)   high productivity.

Creating operations standards is a three-stage procedure – determination of the cycle time, specification of operations for each operator, and, finally, specification of a minimum quantity of WIP to allow smooth production.

The cycle time is determined, as illustrated in Table 12.6, with no allowance for defective units, downtime or idle time in the available daily production time.

Table 12.6 Determination of cycle time.

$$\text{Cycle time} = \frac{\text{Available daily production time}}{\text{Required daily output}}$$

For each component/subassembly at every work center, the completion time per unit is determined including manual and machine elements. By taking into account the number of components required for each finished product, the cycle time for the product and the completion times for each component, a list of operations for each operator is generated. This list of operations specifies the number and order of operations an operator must perform within the cycle time. This ensures production of the correct number of components/subassemblies to allow the production of one finished product within each cycle time.

Finally, the minimum quantity of WIP necessary to ensure production without material shortages is specified. This incorporates the minimum material between, and on, machines, that is required for continuous production.

Once the three phases (the cycle time, the order of operations, and the standard WIP levels) are completed, they are combined to give a standard operations sheet, which is then displayed where each operator can see it. With each new master planning schedule, gross estimates are presented to all processes of the demands likely to be made on them. At this point reevaluation of operations standards, through reassignment of tasks to operators, for example, may result in a reassignment of the work force to meet the projected requirement.

In this discussion on the U-shaped layout, the need for good manufacturing documentation and for constant training and retraining of operators in good work practices has been emphasized. This approach to generating operations standards clearly facilitates this documentation and training. In turn, well-trained operators ensure that operations standards are adhered to.

Mutual relief movement

As will be seen in Section 12.5.1, operators in a JIT environment tend to be very versatile and are trained to operate many different machines and carry out many operations within their particular work center, e.g. one operator may be able to operate a drilling machine, a lathe, and a milling machine. As the plant and equipment layout are product oriented, this means that advantage can be taken of the multiskilled operator. The multifunction operator also helps to reduce, if not eliminate, inventories between

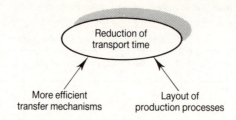

Figure 12.13 Reduction of the transport time.

processes since when he/she unloads a part from one machine he/she may load it directly onto the next machine.

Operators regularly help each other on the shop floor. The ANDON (see Section 12.6) allows an operator to call for help if he/she is in difficulty. Since the work centers are close together and the operators are multifunctional, this mutual support is feasible. Because an operator can go to the aid of a colleague who is temporarily overloaded, the queues in front of work centers can be reduced and the effect of what would otherwise constitute a bottleneck in the system is alleviated, thus reducing the overall queuing time.

12.4.3 Reduction of the transport time

Figure 12.13 depicts two techniques that help to reduce the transport time in the just in time approach, namely the layout of the production processes and faster methods of transport between production processes. We have already discussed the product oriented system of plant layout and the U-shaped layout of equipment which tend to minimize transport needs between individual operations on a component or assembly.

It should, of course, be remembered that approaching *unit production and transport* will most likely increase transport frequency, i.e. the number of transports of partially completed units between operations. To overcome this difficulty, quick transport methods must be adopted, together with improved plant and machine layout. Belt conveyors, chutes, and forklifts may be used. Generally, the close proximity of the subsequent process, as determined by plant layout, results in a minimum transport time between operations.

12.4.4 Reduction of set-up time

A major barrier to the reduction of the processing time and the ability to smooth production is the problem of large set-up times. The EOQ model has already been discussed (see Chapter 9) and it is graphically represented in Figure 12.14.

As noted earlier, the economic order quantity model seeks to determine a lot size which marks an optimum tradeoff between set-up and carrying costs in the case of manufactured items. EOQ calculations result

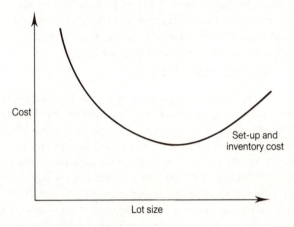

Figure 12.14 Economic order quantity model.

in large lot sizes when set-up times and costs are high. However, large lot sizes and the resulting buffer stocks are incompatible with the JIT approach and hence the concentration of effort on reduction of set-up times. This makes a smaller lot size feasible and is a step on the road to *unit production and transport*.

This JIT approach contrasts strongly with EOQ thinking and cultivates the idea that machine set-up time is a major source of waste that can, and should, be reduced. The influence of set-up time reduction is illustrated by the fact that if set-up time is reduced to $1/N$ of its initial value, the process lot can be reduced to $1/N$ of its initial value, without incurring extra costs.

The throughput time is therefore reduced, work in progress inventory is reduced, and the ability to produce many different varieties is enhanced. This makes for better response to demand. Likewise, the ratio of machine utilization to its full capacity will be increased without producing unnecessary inventory. In this way, productivity is enhanced. The techniques and concepts involved in reducing set-up are now briefly examined.

In order to shorten the set-up time, JIT offers four major approaches (Monden 1983):

(1) Separate the internal set-up from the external set-up. Internal set-up refers to that element of the set-up process which requires that the machine be inoperative in order to undertake it.

(2) Convert as much as possible of the internal set-up to the external set-up. This is probably the most important practical approach for the reduction of set-up in practice and helps to achieve the goal of **single set-up**. Single set-up means that the set-up time can be expressed in terms of a single digit number of minutes (i.e. less than 10 minutes).

(3) Eliminate the adjustment process within set-up. Adjustment typically accounts for a large percentage of the internal set-up time. The reduction of adjustment time is, therefore, very important in terms of reducing the total set-up time.

(4) Abolish the set-up where feasible.

In the JIT approach to reducing set-up, the first step is to carry out a detailed study on existing practices. Internal and external set-up invariably overlap and need to be rigorously separated. A written specification outlining the procedures involved in the set-up and giving any necessary information is drawn up. By converting as much as possible of the set-up time to external set-up, which can be carried out off-line, a significant improvement in internal or *at the machine* set-up time can be achieved.

The reader interested in a more detailed discussion on this topic of reducing set-up time is referred to Shingo (1985). He discusses the SMED system. SMED is an acronym for *Single Minute Exchange of Dies*, which denotes a group of techniques used to facilitate set-up operations of 10 minutes and under.

12.4.5 Processing time

The JIT approach to processing time is relatively straightforward. It sees *processing time* as the only time during a product's passage through the production system that real value is actually being added to it. Transport time, queue time, and set-up time are seen as non-value adding and to be reduced to the absolute minimum where they cannot be simply eliminated. Given that the processing time represents value added, JIT takes care to ensure that this time is used to the best advantage and to produce high quality product efficiently. Thus, as seen earlier in the discussion on the *U-shaped layout* and *operations standards*, great care is taken to ensure that the best manufacturing methods are refined to the highest degree, documented, and communicated to the operators concerned through training sessions, practice sessions, etc.

In fact, it is in the commitment to the best possible manufacturing methods practised by a skilled and trained work force that the pursuit of excellence in the JIT approach to manufacturing can be most clearly seen. So often in the conventional approach to manufacturing operations, manufacturing analysts and engineers forget the importance of good practice at the sharp end of manufacturing, namely the shop floor, and come to accept unnecessary deviation in operator performance as natural.

12.4.6 Concluding remarks on manufacturing process simplification

All the above ideas and techniques combine to reduce the overall throughput time and lead time for products. This results in order oriented production, a shorter master schedule planning horizon (remember that the master schedule planning horizon depends on the item in the master schedule with the longest cumulative lead time) and, consequently, a greatly reduced dependence on forecasts. Production smoothing is simplified if the production lead time is short. The ability to adapt to short term changes in market demand is enhanced and smooth withdrawals through the plant are easier to achieve.

12.5 The use of manufacturing resources

The JIT approach to the resources available in a manufacturing plant is interesting. The approach could be summarized in a single dictum – *do not confuse being busy with being productive*. This philosophy is particularly applied to the use of labor resource and is, as will be seen in Part IV, also fundamental in the OPT (Optimized Production Technique) approach to manufacturing.

The way which JIT seeks to use the major resources of labor and equipment efficiently and effectively will now be briefly reviewed.

12.5.1 Flexible labor

In JIT, those minor changes in demand which cannot be accommodated through the use of increased kanbans (see Chapter 13) are addressed through redeployment of the work force. Adaptation to increased market demand can ultimately be met through the use of overtime.

However, JIT has a more subtle and effective approach to meeting relatively small short term demand changes. As mentioned in Chapter 11, the basic tenet of the just in time philosophy is the production of only those products that are required and at the precise time they are required. Under the principle of multifunction operators and multiprocess handling, one operator tends to a number of different machines simultaneously to meet this demand. Such a situation invariably results in the possibility of increasing output through introducing more operators into the system.

Therefore, if market demand increases beyond a level where increased kanban utilization is able to cope, temporary operators may be hired. Each operator may then be required to tend fewer machines, thus taking up the equipment capacity slack. This approach presumes an economic and cultural environment where temporary operators of the required skill level are available and are willing to work in such a manner.

Adapting to *decreases* in demand is understandably more difficult, especially when one considers that many large Japanese companies offer lifetime employment. However, the major approaches are to decrease overtime, release temporary operators and increase the number of machines handled by one operator. This will cause an increase in the cycle time, thus reducing the number of units produced. Operators are encouraged to *idle* rather than produce unnecessary stock. They may be redeployed to practice set-ups, maintain and/or modify machines, or to attend quality circle meetings.

The work force is therefore flexible in two ways. It can be increased or decreased through temporary operators. It can also be relocated to different work centers. This latter flexibility demands a versatile, well-trained multifunction operator as well as good design of machine layout.

The most important objective is to have a manufacturing system which is able to meet demand and to accommodate small, short term fluctuations in demand with the minimum level of labor. This does not imply the minimum number of machines. Companies operating JIT usually have some extra capacity in equipment, allowing for temporary operators when increased production is required.

It is interesting to note that few manufacturing facilities have used the JIT approach at the manufacturing system design stage, i.e. have been designed according to JIT principles. A manufacturing facility designed for the continuous production of as many components and/or assemblies and/or products as possible, and not of the required amount of product at the right time as in JIT, frequently has some excess of capacity when examined from a JIT perspective.

12.5.2 Flexible equipment

Just in time requires production of different product varieties on the same assembly line each day (see the discussion on mixed model assembly in Section 12.3.1). This can involve a conflict between the market variety demanded by the customer and the production process available to service this market requirement since, in traditional manufacturing systems, it is normally desirable to reduce the variety of product going through the system. As has been seen, the JIT approach seeks to overcome these difficulties. Through consideration of process requirements at the product design stage, multifunction equipment is developed to help resolve this conflict by providing the production process with the ability to meet the variety demanded by the market. The specialized machines developed for mass production (as described in Chapter 2) are not suitable for repetitive manufacturing. By modifying these machines and adding minimum apparatus and tools they are transformed into multifunction machines capable of producing a product range that meets the marketplace demand. Such machines support just in time manufacturing and also facilitate production smoothing. Of course, the ultimate realization of this notion is the FMS (Flexible Manufacturing System) discussed in Section 2.6.

This approach contrasts greatly with MRP manufacturing thinking where the capacity of resources is generally considered as fixed, at least in the short term. Hence in MRP, to meet demand variations, extra capacity is sought rather than attempting to modify the existing machines.

12.6 Quality control aspects of JIT

In more conventional production systems, work in progress inventories are often used to smooth out problems of defective products and/or machines. Batch production and the concept of Acceptable Quality Levels (AQL) could be seen to promote this attitude. This approach is criticized by the promoters of JIT thinking on the basis that it is treating the symptoms while not attempting to understand and resolve the underlying fundamental problems. In JIT manufacturing, the emphasis is on the notion of Total Quality Control (TQC) where the objective of eliminating all possible sources of defects from the manufacturing process, and thereby from the products of that process, is seen to be both reasonable and achievable.

It has been pointed out that JIT seeks *zero defects*. The zero defects approach involves a continuous commitment to totally eliminate all waste including, in this context, yield losses and rework due to product or process defects. The methods used to achieve zero defects are those of continuous steady improvement of the production process. Schneidermann (1986) offers an interesting analysis of the process of continuous improvement towards zero defects and suggests that it should be contrasted with an alternative improvement process – the innovation process. On the one hand, the continuous improvement route involves groups seeking small steps forward on a broad range of issues, using the available know-how within the group. The innovation process, on the other hand, seeks to achieve great leaps forward in narrowly defined areas through the use of science and technology by well-qualified individuals. Here again there is evidence of the JIT approach being a systems approach with clear emphasis on involvement by all of those directly concerned.

Inspection is carried out to *prevent* defects rather than simply *detect* them. Machines, in so far as possible, are designed with an in-built capability to check all of the parts they produce as they are produced. The term **autonomation** was coined to describe this condition. This can be considered as one step on the road to total systems automation (i.e. a machine finds a problem, finds a solution, implements it itself, and carries on).

Autonomation suggests automatic control of defects. It implies the incorporation of two new pieces of functionality into a machine:

(1)   a mechanism to detect abnormalities or defects, and

(2)   a mechanism to stop the machine or line when defects or abnormalities occur.

When a defect occurs the machine stops, forcing immediate attention to the problem. An investigation into the cause(s) of the problem is initiated and corrective action is taken to prevent the problem from recurring.

Since, through autonomation, machines stop when they have produced enough parts and also only *good* parts, excess inventory is eliminated, thus making JIT production possible.

The concept of autonomation is not limited to machine processes, and *autonomous* checks for abnormal or faulty product can be extended to manual processes, such as an assembly line, using the following approach. Each assembly line is equipped with a call light and an ANDON board. The call light has different colors signifying the different types of assistance and support which might be required. It is located where anybody who might be called on to support the process (e.g. supervisor, maintenance, nearby operators, etc.) can easily see it.

The ANDON is a board which shows which operator on the line, if any, is having difficulties. Each operator has a switch which enables him/her to stop the line in case of breakdown, delay, or problems with defective product. In many cases there are different colors to indicate the condition of the station on the assembly line which is having problems. The following are some color signals that might be used and their respective meanings:

- red – machine trouble,
- white – end of a production run,
- green – no work due to shortage of materials,
- blue – defective unit,
- yellow – set-up required.

When an ANDON lights up, nearby operators quickly move to assist and solve the problem, and the supervisor takes the necessary steps to prevent it recurring. The ANDON also helps to ensure that completed products exiting the assembly line do not need rework, i.e. that they are right first time. Individual operators have *line stop* authority to ensure compliance with standards. Hence, the overall quality level is increased since each individual operator is encouraged to accept responsibility for the quality of the parts which he/she is involved with.

There are numerous other factors which assist in attaining extremely high quality levels. Small lot sizes, for example, will highlight quality problems very quickly as individual items are rapidly passed to the next process and any defects are quickly detected. Similarly, a good approach to *housekeeping* is encouraged and is considered important since a clean, well maintained working area leads to better working practices, better productivity, and better personnel safety. Preventive maintenance is an important concept of the JIT approach. Using the *checklist technique*, machines are checked on a regular basis and repairs/replacements are scheduled to take place outside working time. This, in turn, helps to increase machine availability.

As a result of autonomation only 100% good units are produced. Hence, the need for rework and buffer or *insurance* stocks is eliminated. This lends itself to adaptability to demand and JIT production.

12.7 Conclusion

This chapter has presented an overview of the ideas and techniques used to create the manufacturing environment within which JIT execution can be achieved. Clearly, within the JIT approach to manufacturing, great emphasis is placed and enormous planning and engineering effort is expended to ensure that the manufacturing environment is such that excellence can be achieved. The JIT approach to manufacturing systems design and operation has been considered in terms of a number of specific issues:

- product design for ease of manufacture and assembly,
- manufacturing planning techniques,
- techniques to facilitate the use of simple manufacturing control systems,
- an approach to the use of manufacturing resources,
- quality control and quality assurance procedures.

The JIT approach recognizes the importance of process and manufacturing system design. Perhaps, in the West, this work as been neglected and the organization of our manufacturing facilities reflects this neglect. The following chapter will describe the Kanban card system.

Questions

(12.1) Why is the reduction of production lead time so important to the achievement of JIT?

(12.2) "The JIT approach represents a move towards low process variety and high product variety." Discuss.

(12.3) What do you understand by the term *modular design*?

(12.4) Distinguish clearly between mixed model production and multi-model production.

(12.5) "Each day's schedule should resemble the previous day's schedule as much as possible. Hence uncertainties are eliminated and the need for dynamic scheduling and safety stocks is minimized." How is this state of affairs achieved through monthly and daily adoption?

(12.6)   What are the main objectives in designing a production layout to achieve JIT?

(12.7)   What techniques are available to reduce queue time?

(12.8)   "The JIT approach contrasts strongly with EOQ thinking and cultivates the idea that machine set-up is a major source of waste." Discuss.

(12.9)   Why is it so important to separate internal set-up from external set-up?

(12.10)   What do you understand by the term *autonomation*?

CHAPTER THIRTEEN

The Kanban system

13.1 Introduction

This chapter focuses attention on the shop floor implementation of just in time. The techniques used at this level have been well documented (APICS 1984; Monden 1981; Schonberger 1982; Monden 1983) as interest in Japanese manufacturing techniques has increased. The system that executes JIT delivery on the shop floor level is known as Kanban and the cards that are used in this system are called kanban cards. Therefore, to distinguish between the system and the cards, in this chapter we will use "Kanban" for the system and "kanban" for the cards. The discussion will concentrate on JIT execution on the shop floor and will not cover JIT execution from outside suppliers in any detail.

Before analyzing the operation of the kanban cards, the difference between **push** and **pull** systems of production control will be discussed, together with the notion of a repetitive manufacturing system, within which the kanbans can be used to greatest effect.

13.2 Kanban

Kanban was developed at the Toyota car plants in Japan as a program to smooth the flow of products throughout the production process. Its aim is to improve system productivity and to secure *operator involvement* and participation in achieving this high productivity by providing a *highly visible* means to observe the flow of products through the production system and the build-up of inventory levels within the system. Later it was further developed as a means of production activity control to achieve the goals of JIT and to manage the operation of just in time production. Kanban also serves as an information system to monitor and help control the production quantities at every stage of the manufacturing and assembly process.

Kanban is seen as a *pull* system, as distinct from the production activity control systems in MRP, which are regarded as *push* systems. Before discussing Kanban in detail, the differences between pull and push systems of production control will be explored briefly.

13.2.1 Pull system of manufacturing management

As stated above, the operation of MRP at the shop floor level is best described in terms of a *push* system, as distinct from Kanban, which is considered to be a *pull* system. Considering the difference between the two approaches may help bring out some of the essential characteristics of Kanban.

Both systems are driven by a master schedule which defines the requirement for individual products, i.e. top level items in the bill of materials. This master schedule, in turn, is broken down into a detailed plan for items to be manufactured, assembled, and purchased.

A push system operates as indicated in Figure 13.1 (Menga 1987). Let us consider, for a moment, a component which must be processed through a series of work centers, namely M through to 1, where work center M processes the item first, followed by work center M-1, etc. In a *push* system, work center M is given the due date (DD) for the item and the item is released for production at the release time (RT). The completion time for work center M becomes the release time for work center M-1, etc. Thus, a product is pushed through the production system starting at the release of raw material to the first processing work center and leading onto completion at the final work center. MRP is considered to be the classical example of a push system.

A *pull* system, on the other hand, looks at the manufacturing process from the other end, i.e. from the perspective of the finished item. The production controller works on the basis that his/her orders represent firm customer requirements. The time horizon is understandably short. The orders are broken down from the highest level and the controller checks whether sufficient component parts are available to produce the finished product. If the components are available, the product is produced. However, if they are not, components are *pulled* from the preceding work center. A similar procedure is followed right back through each production stage and extending all the way back to include outside vendors. Such a system places great demands on the production system and vendors. These

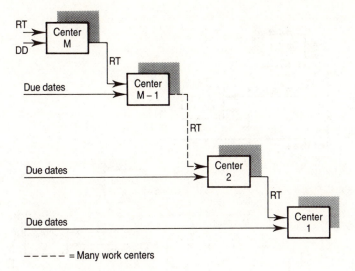

Figure 13.1 MRP "push" strategy.

demands can be met either by having all component parts in inventory or, alternately, having the capability to respond and make them available in a very short time (i.e. short lead time). A pull system is illustrated in Figure 13.2.

It should be noted, and this will become more obvious as the operation of Kanban is reviewed in more detail, that this type of control mechanism is only applicable in plants involved in what is termed by many manufacturing systems analysts as repetitive manufacturing. Let us quickly define **repetitive manufacturing** and then go on to look at how the kanban cards are used.

13.3 Repetitive manufacturing

Repetitive manufacturing is

> "the fabrication, machining, assembly and testing of discrete, standard units produced in volume, or of products assembled in volume from standard options . . . [it] is characterized by long runs or flows of parts. The ideal is a direct transfer of parts from one work center to another."
>
> Hall (1983)

Referring back to the discussion on the various categories of discrete parts manufacturing system in Chapter 1, repetitive manufacturing can be positioned in the modified version of Figure 1.5 shown in Figure 13.3.

One could argue that the end result of rigorously applying the JIT approach and of using JIT manufacturing techniques as described in

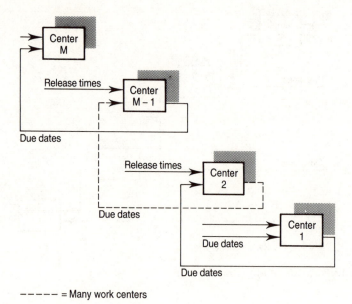

Figure 13.2 JIT "pull" strategy.

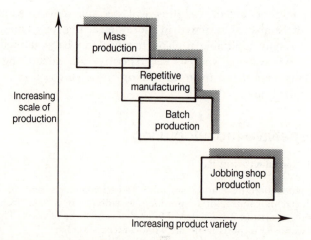

Figure 13.3 Classification of discrete production.

Chapters 11 and 12 is to move a manufacturing system away from jobbing shop or batch production towards repetitive manufacturing. The greater the degree to which the manufacturing system approaches repetitive manufacturing, the more relevant the Kanban technique.

13.4 Production activity control with Kanban

The Kanban system has been described as a *pull* system. We will now explore how this system works by taking the example of a very simple manufacturing and assembly system and illustrating the flow of kanban cards through it. The example is based on the two products, namely Stool A and Stool B, which were used to illustrate the logic of MRP in earlier chapters.

Under Kanban, only the final assembly line knows the requirements for the end product and, with this knowledge, it controls what is produced in the total manufacturing system using the following procedure:

> The final assembly line, having received the schedule, proceeds to withdraw the components necessary, at the times they are required and in the quantities they are required, from the feeding work centers or subassembly lines. These work centers or subassembly lines produce in lots just sufficient to replace the lots that have been removed. However, to do this, they also have to withdraw parts from their respective feeder stations in the quantities necessary. Thus, a chain reaction is initiated *upstream*, with work centers only withdrawing the components that are required at the correct time and in the quantities required.

In this way, the flow of all material is synchronized to the rate at which material is used on the final assembly line. Amounts of inventory will be very small if a regular pattern exists in the schedule and if the deliveries are made in small quantities. Thus, Just in Time can be achieved without the use of controlling work orders for parts at each work center.

13.5 The kanban card types

Kanban is the Japanese word for card. Kanbans usually are rectangular paper cards placed in transparent covers. There are two main types of card in use:

(1) **Withdrawal kanbans** Withdrawal kanbans define the quantity that the subsequent process should withdraw from the preceding work center. Each card circulates between two work centers only – the user work center for the part in question and the work center which produces it.

(2) **Production kanbans** Production kanbans define the quantity of the specific part that the producing work center should manufacture in order to replace those which have been removed.

Each standard container is assigned one of each card type. Examples of each card type are shown in Figure 13.4 (based on Monden 1983).

The withdrawal kanban, for example, details both the name of the consuming work center and the work center which supplies the part described by the item name and number on the card. The precise location

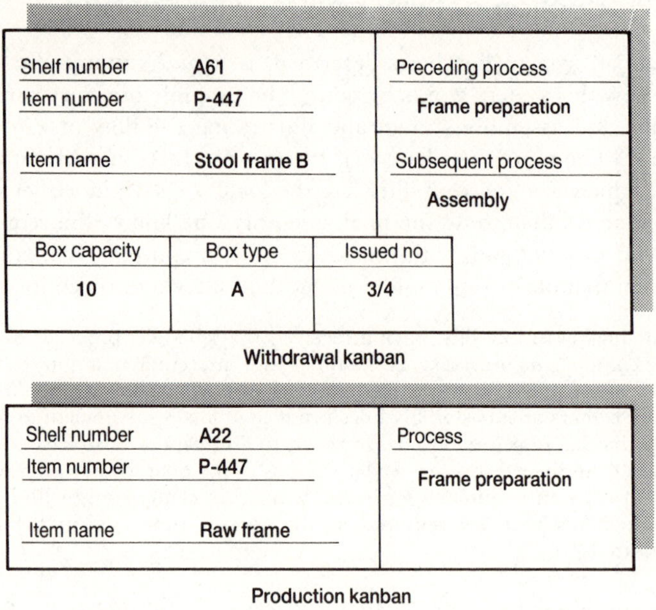

Shelf number	A61		Preceding process
Item number	P-447		**Frame preparation**
Item name	**Stool frame B**		Subsequent process
			Assembly

Box capacity	Box type	Issued no
10	A	3/4

Withdrawal kanban

Shelf number	A22		Process
Item number	P-447		**Frame preparation**
Item name	**Raw frame**		

Production kanban

Figure 13.4   Kanban card types.

in the inventory buffer is detailed, as well as the type of standard container used and its capacity. The issue number in the case shown in Figure 13.4 reveals that it is the third kanban issued out of four.

The production kanban details the producing work center name, the part to be produced, and where, precisely, in the buffer store it should be located.

There are other types of kanban differentiated by color, shape or format, such as subcontract, emergency, special, and signal cards. However the two cards just described are the basic types used in the Kanban system.

13.6 The flow of kanban cards

To explain the flow of these cards through the production process, some examples will be taken from a simulation model of a Kanban controlled production and assembly system in whose development the authors were involved. This system consists of a main assembly line of five assembly stations. The line is a mixed model line which simulates the assembly of two different products. Each product passes through the assembly line where components are assembled to it at each assembly station, as illustrated in Figure 13.5. Each of these stations, in turn, is fed components by a feeder line which can include up to four work centers.

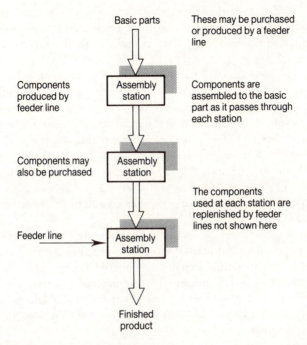

Figure 13.5   The production assembly line.

This model of the assembly line with its feeder lines will be used to show how production and withdrawal kanbans flow through the production system. The production process represented above highlights two different modes of material movement, namely:

(1)   the flow of parts along an assembly line,
(2)   the flow of parts along the feeder lines.

Section 13.7 will describe the flow of parts along the assembly line, while Section 13.8 will be concerned with the flow of parts along the feeder lines.

13.7   The flow of parts along the assembly line

The most important aspect of the flow of material within the assembly line is that it is controlled *without* the aid of kanban cards. The material which forms the base product and onto which all components will be assembled arrives at the first station of the line. These parts may be produced by another feeder line or, alternately, may be purchased parts. The order in which these parts arrive is determined by the final assembly schedule. From the assembly schedule a cycle time is determined, within which all stations must have completed their respective operations on the part.

The flow of material is dictated by the cycle time of individual operations. The partially completed products progress to the following assembly station when the operation at the present station has been completed at the end of the cycle. However, if a problem arises at an assembly station and the operation has not been completed within the allowed cycle time, the whole assembly line stops production. This is signalled by the use of ANDON lights (see Chapter 12), which use colors to indicate the condition of the line. For example, a red light may mean that an assembly station has been unable to complete its work or an orange light might mean that there is not enough material available.

When such a situation arises, every operator in the vicinity will help to solve the problem and start the line moving again. This may involve a short term solution, such as expediting material to the station, and a longer term approach which determines why the material was not at the assembly station in the first place and which ensures that the problem does not occur again. Once the problem has been solved the light changes to green and production resumes.

Material is consumed at each station from an incoming material stock point which is fed by the appropriate feeder line (or storage point in the case of purchased items) and which has standard containers and associated withdrawal kanbans. Once the parts are removed from a container, the kanban is released to the feeder line and brought with an empty container to the work center which feeds the assembly station. A full container is then brought back and placed in the incoming material store.

We now go on to look at the various types of manufacturing operations carried out at the feeder lines and how the material flow between these operations is controlled using the kanban cards.

13.8 Material movement in the feeder line

Before describing the flow of kanbans along the feeder lines, we will briefly examine the various classes of manufacturing operations which are carried out in a system, such as those illustrated in Figure 13.5.

Feeder lines are basically sequential processes in which a set of discrete functions are carried out on raw materials and semi-processed items. These different functions can be categorized into two main groups, namely materials handling functions and material processing operations. In materials handling, the material is simply moved from one location to another.

The material processing operations, in turn, can be subdivided into four distinct categories (see De *et al.* (1985)), namely:

(1)   Disjunctive processing operations.

(2)   Locational processing operations.

(3)   Sequential processing operations

(4)   Combinative processing operations.

We will now briefly review each of these types of processing operation in turn.

(1)   Disjunctive operations transform a single piece of raw material into many components. A punch press set-up to punch out a number of components from a single sheet of raw material is an example of a disjunctive processing operation. Another example is an automatic chucking lathe, designed to produce a number of components from a single piece of bar stock. The essential feature of a disjunctive operation is that a single piece of raw material results in a number of items produced – a one to many relationship.

(2)   Locational operations involve the storage of material in a location for a period of time. Warehousing is an example of a locational operation.

(3)   Sequential operations occur where a raw material or a partially finished component is modified at a work center and emerges intact as a single identifiable component. An example of a sequential operation is simple turning on a conventional lathe where, perhaps, the outside diameter of a component is turned to a specified value. The difference between a sequential operation and a disjunctive operation is that many items emerge from a single item input in a disjunctive operation, whereas an item is merely transformed or modified in a sequential operation.

(4)   Combinative operations occur when a number of components or subassemblies are assembled, or joined together, to produce a single assembly or product. All assembly operations, by definition, are combinative. Consider, for example, the stuffing of a PCB (Printed Circuit Board) in the electronics assembly business. A series of components are assembled onto a bare PCB to produce a stuffed PCB.

The distinction between disjunctive, sequential, and combinative processing operations is further developed in Figure 13.6.

Differing combinations of these four categories represent all possible types of discrete parts manufacturing. These four classes of manufacturing operation will be used to illustrate the use of kanban cards in controlling the flow of production on a feeder line in a JIT system. A pure assembly line consists totally of combinative processing operations, where components are added to the assembly as it progresses along the various assembly stations on the line.

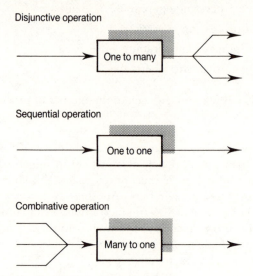

Figure 13.6   Types of manufacturing operations.

A typical feeder line can be composed of a number of work centers. Each work center has two *stores* – one for incoming components and a second for components that have completed processing at that work center. These stores could be considered locational processing operations. Some work centers are involved in combinative processing operations while others have sequential operations. At the beginning of the feeder line, the work centers are frequently disjunctive in nature since a single piece of raw material is processed to produce a number of components.

As an illustrative example of the nature of the work centers in the feeder lines, let us return to a *modified version* of the product that was used as an example to explain the workings of MRP in Chapter 5. A word of caution is in order here. This example is set up to facilitate the explanation of the operation of the kanban cards and, as such, is very simplistic.

Let us assume that Gizmo-Stools Inc. manufactures two types of stool, namely a four-legged stool and a three-legged stool. The original product structures are shown again in Figure 13.7.

In this case, let us further assume that Gizmo-Stools Inc. manufactures, as opposed to purchases, the legs of the stools. Let us also assume that the production system which manufactures and assembles the stools consists of a feeder line which produces the frame, another feeder line which produces the legs from tubular steel, and an assembly line. The frame is the basic item that enters the first assembly station, where the legs are assembled to the frame to form the bare stool. The next assembly station produces the complete stool by adding a cushion to the bare stool.

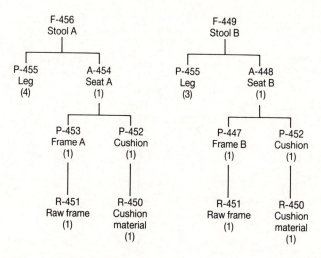

Figure 13.7   Two product structures.

For the purpose of illustrating the flow of material within a feeder line, we shall examine the line that produces the legs for the stools, where the legs are produced from lengths of tubular steel. Let us assume that there are three work centers in this line. The first cuts the tubular steel to length and produces the legs in groups of either three or four. The next work center forms the tops of these legs to facilitate their joining to the stool frame. At the final work center on this feeder line, rubber feet are attached to the bottom of the legs. Let us call these work centers, cutting, forming, and finishing, respectively.

The legs are produced therefore by the work centers in the feeder line according to the product/process structure diagram in Figure 13.8. This product/process structure shows that, at different work centers, each of the four basic categories of material processing operations (locational aside) identified above are carried out in the feeder line.

13.8.1   The flow of cards along the feeder line

This section reviews the movement of material between work centers and indicates how the kanbans are used to control it. The above example will be used to show the movement between the forming and cutting work centers on the feeder line. These operations are mainly of a material handling nature where newly cut legs are moved from the cutting work center to the forming work center. Figure 13.9 will be used as a basis for this description.

Let us assume that the forming work center has a requirement for material, i.e. preformed legs. These are the outgoing components from the

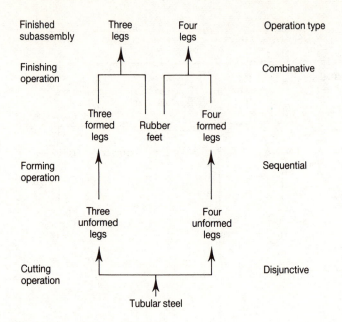

Figure 13.8 Manufacture of legs.

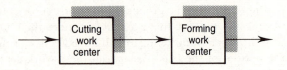

Figure 13.9 Flow of material between work centers.

cutting work center. Both work centers have two stockpoints – one for incoming material and a second for outgoing material. Stocks of parts are stored in standard containers which are located at these stockpoints. There are two types of standard container – one for batches of three legs and a second for batches of four legs.

Each standard container has a corresponding kanban card which details the type of material in the container and the quantity of that material. Those containers in the incoming material stockpoint are associated with withdrawal kanbans while those in the outgoing material stockpoint are linked to production kanbans.

For the forming work center to require material, there must be an empty standard container and a corresponding withdrawal kanban. The flow chart in Figure 13.10 depicts the various steps in the movement of

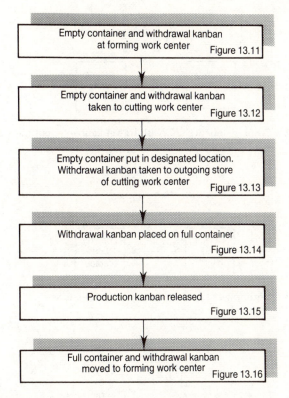

Figure 13.10   Events in moving materials between work centers.

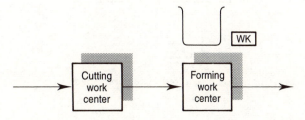

Figure 13.11   Empty container and withdrawal kanban at forming work center.

material and kanbans. Each step is depicted by a corresponding figure described later.

The empty container and the withdrawal kanban signal the requirement for materials at the forming work center, as shown in Figure 13.11.

Figure 13.12 shows this empty container and withdrawal kanban being taken to the outgoing material stockpoint of the cutting work center.

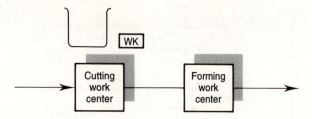

Figure 13.12 Empty container and withdrawal kanban at cutting work center.

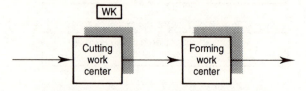

Figure 13.13 Withdrawal kanban taken to outgoing store.

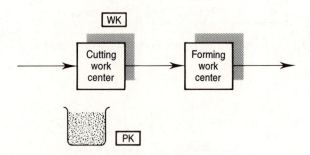

Figure 13.14 Container of required material selected.

At the cutting work center, the empty containers are placed in a designated location and the withdrawal kanbans are brought to the outgoing material stockpoint, as shown in Figure 13.13.

At the outgoing material stockpoint, a standard container which has the same parts as specified on the withdrawal kanban is removed, as shown in Figure 13.14. Remember that the outgoing material of the cutting work center is the same as the incoming material of the forming work center.

Attached to these containers are the production kanbans, and a quick check will verify that the parts are those that are required. The kanbans are

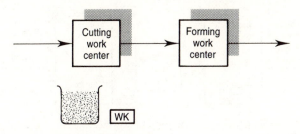

Figure 13.15   Production kanban released.

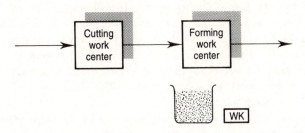

Figure 13.16   Full container and withdrawal kanban moved to forming work center.

then switched – the withdrawal kanban being attached to the container and the freed production kanban placed in a designated location as in Figure 13.15.

Figure 13.16 shows the full container with the attached withdrawal kanban brought to the incoming material stockpoint of the forming work center.

The flow of material between work centers has now been fully described, showing how it is controlled using withdrawal kanban cards. Section 13.8.2 will describe the flow of material and kanbans within an individual work center.

13.8.2 The flow of cards within a work center

Each work center has an inbound and an outbound stockpoint, as is illustrated in Figure 13.17. The material flows from the preceding work center into the inbound stockpoint, as discussed above for the case of the cutting and forming work centers. This is stored until the forming work center requires material. The outgoing product at this work center then proceeds to the outbound stockpoint. From here it flows to the next work center. These work centers can be any of the three material processing operations –

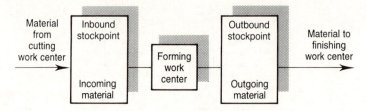

Figure 13.17 Schematic representation of work center.

disjunctive, sequential, or combinative. For illustrative purposes let us use, as an example, the forming work center. It represents a sequential processing operation where incoming material is simply modified. The other work centers in the line represent both of the other processing operations. The cutting work center performs a disjunctive operation where tubular steel is cut to form legs. On the other hand, the finishing work center represents a combinative operation, where the rubber feet and legs are assembled to produce the finished legs.

Figure 13.18 is a flow chart representing all the steps associated with the flow of kanbans within this work center. Each step is depicted by a corresponding figure described later.

The empty container with the withdrawal kanban is brought from the incoming material store of the finishing work center to the outgoing material store of this, the forming work center. As shown in Figure 13.19, the empty container is left in a designated location.

A full container of the parts described (i.e. three or four formed legs) on the withdrawal kanban is located in the outgoing material store. This has a production kanban attached, which contains similar information to that on the withdrawal kanban. The production kanban is removed to a designated location and the withdrawal kanban attached to the full container as in Figure 13.20.

This full container and the withdrawal kanban are then brought to the incoming material store of the finishing work center, as illustrated in Figure 13.21. As production kanbans become available, they are moved to the incoming material store of the forming work center.

The production kanban also contains information about the materials required to produce the outgoing goods. This will specify whether three or four legs are required. Figure 13.22 shows a full container of these materials being removed from the store and the withdrawal kanban being released.

If the material processing operation is a combinative operation, as in the finishing work center, the production kanban details that a container of legs and rubber feet is required. However, for a disjunctive operation (as in the cutting work center), production kanbans for three and four legs will

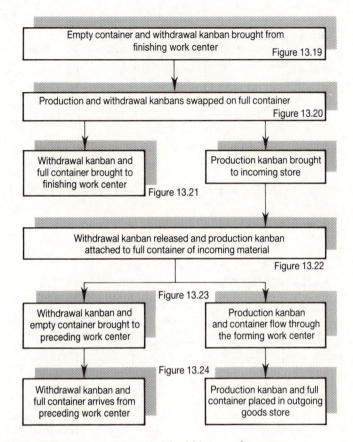

Figure 13.18 Events in moving material within a work center.

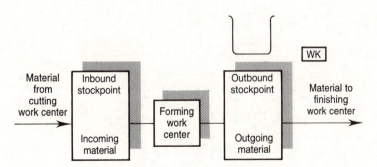

Figure 13.19 Empty container and withdrawal kanban brought from finishing work center.

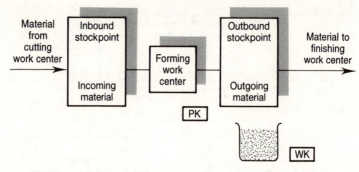

Figure 13.20 Production and withdrawal kanbans swapped on full container.

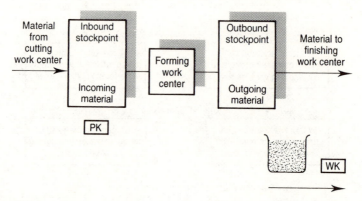

Figure 13.21 Withdrawal kanban and full container brought to finishing work center.

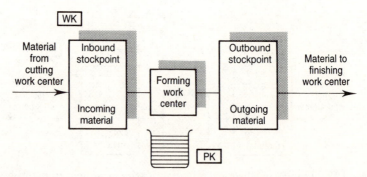

Figure 13.22 Withdrawal kanban released and production started.

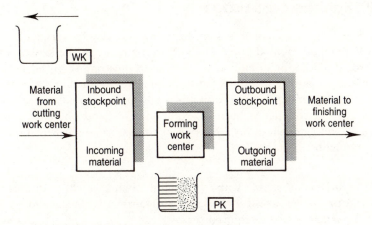

Figure 13.23 Processing partially complete.

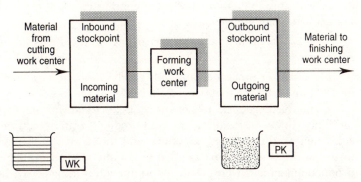

Figure 13.24 Full containers of incoming and outgoing material at stockpoints.

initiate the release of the same withdrawal kanban since both involve the same raw material, namely tubular steel.

Once an empty container is available, it and the withdrawal kanban are brought to the outgoing material store of the cutting work center to obtain a container of incoming material. Meanwhile, the production kanban stays with the container of material right through the production process at the forming work center, as shown in Figure 13.23.

When the preformed legs have been processed into formed legs, the container and the production kanban are placed in the outgoing material store. At some point during the processing of the legs, a full container of unformed legs is brought from the cutting work center outgoing store with an attached withdrawal kanban and placed in the incoming material store as in Figure 13.24.

13.9 Kanban card usage

It is clear that for a Kanban system to operate effectively, very strict discipline is required. This discipline relates to the usage of the kanban cards. This requirement for discipline also serves to illustrate the need for well-documented manufacturing procedures and a well-trained group of operators who are aware of the procedures and who are motivated to follow them rigorously – a confidence born of experience of good operator practice. There are five guidelines on the usage of the kanbans which help achieve JIT production:

(1) A work center should withdraw only the items which it requires from the preceding work center in the quantities required and, equally importantly, at the required time.

There are a number of operating principles which support this:

- No removal of material is allowed without an available withdrawal kanban and an available empty container.

- A withdrawal of more parts than indicated on the withdrawal kanban is not allowed.

- The kanban must be attached to one of the items within the container.

(2) A work center or process should only produce those items which have been removed by the following work center or process.

The freed production kanbans act as a *schedule* for the work center. The work center is not allowed to produce greater quantities than stipulated on the production kanban and the sequence of operations in the work center or process must follow the sequence in which the production kanbans were freed. As production is initiated by the final assembly schedule released to the assembly line, the schedule is passed back through the production system by the release of production kanbans.

Rigorously adhering to the above guidelines results in what is effectively an *invisible* conveyor line, constructed and controlled by the flow of kanbans through the production system.

(3) Defective or substandard items should never be passed to a following work center. This implies rigorous quality control at each work center or step in the production process. Allowing defective parts to stay within the production system will greatly upset the flow of parts at a later stage when the defective part is detected.

(4) The level of inventories in the production system is dictated by the number of kanbans since each kanban represents the contents of a standard container. The number of kanbans should therefore be

minimized. By reducing the number of kanbans and the size of each container the level of inventories is progressively reduced.

(5) The Kanban system is only suitable for dealing with relatively small fluctuations in the demand pattern in the final assembly line. The system is only relevant to a repetitive manufacturing situation and large changes in demand cannot be accommodated within it.

Sudden large changes in the demand for products should have been eliminated using the JIT techniques outlined in Chapter 12, i.e. by following the JIT approach to the market and design of products and by using a manufacturing system which facilitates flow based production. Clearly, if it is not possible to arrive at a stable master schedule for the end level items in the bill of materials, the Kanban system cannot be used. Small fluctuations in the demand can be handled by increasing the circulation frequency of the kanbans, by increasing overtime, or by hiring temporary operators.

The effort involved in making the Kanban system work well is tremendous. It requires extensive use of the JIT techniques outlined in Chapter 12 to establish the correct environment for Kanban and maintenance of the discipline of the kanban cards at all times.

13.10 The full work system – Kanban for automation

How can the Kanban system be used with automated manufacturing equipment? A variant of the system, known as the *full work system*, is used. With automated manufacturing processes, as with manual operations, it is necessary to match the number of items produced with those withdrawn. (See automatic production level controls in Chapter 12.) It is necessary to match the capacities and speeds of production of different machines, otherwise a build-up of inventory will arise between machines. Also, it is necessary for each machine to be sensitive to any problems on the following machine which might result in it being unable to process further parts. These problems are resolved by using the full work system. This system is illustrated for two machines in Figure 13.25 (adapted from Monden 1983).

The two machines are connected by a magazine or chute to store the items completed at machine A. The inventory level can be set to, say, 4 units. When machine A has processed 4 units, a limit switch (connected to the magazine) is activated and machine A stops processing. Machine B continues to withdraw the parts until there are, say, 2 units in the magazine, then another switch is activated and machine A starts processing again. In this way, only a fixed quantity of work in progress is allowed at

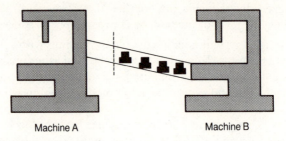

Machine A   Machine B

Figure 13.25 Full work system.

each process, and processes are linked, thus preventing unnecessary processing and build-up of inventory in the preceding processes.

The similarity between this system in its use of limit switches and a kanban card has resulted in the switch sometimes being referred to as an *electric kanban*.

13.11 The single card Kanban

So far, we have been discussing a Kanban system using two types of kanban cards, namely the withdrawal and production cards, i.e. a two-card Kanban system. However, there are other Kanban systems in existence that use only one type of kanban – the withdrawal kanban – i.e. a single-card system.

The single-card system is sometimes used as a first stage in the development of a full Kanban or two-card system. The operation of such a single card system will now be described briefly.

The procedures in a single-card Kanban system are relatively simple. Each production center produces parts according to a daily schedule, which is determined from the final assembly schedule along the lines of an MRP system. When the production centers require component parts, the withdrawal kanbans are used to acquire the required parts from other work centers.

The procedure is as follows:

- As each container of incoming parts is started at a work center, the associated withdrawal kanban is placed in a specific location. These incoming parts are then processed.

- At regular intervals, the withdrawal kanbans are collected. These kanbans contain information detailing the part type and work center which produces these parts. A full container is removed from the producing work center, the withdrawal kanban attached and the container is returned to the incoming parts store of the consuming work center.

Some points which differentiate this system from the two-card system are:

(1) The inbound stockpoint is not so important, given that deliveries of parts to the work center are controlled very tightly, so there is always a minimum number of containers available to be processed. This relieves space and prevents confusion around a stockpoint.

(2) Processed parts are allowed to build up at the outbound stockpoints. This may not be a serious problem if the production planners can readily associate the required quantities and timings of parts with the final assembly schedule. In such a system, the withdrawals of required component parts are controlled, while the production is driven by the daily parts schedule.

(3) It should be noted that this single-card kanban system is very similar to the *two bin* reorder point system. The difference relates primarily to the environment in which it is applied. The single-card Kanban system is used in an environment of standard container and flow based production systems, and all of the other attributes of a JIT environment. Also, only a small number of containers are allowed at work centers and, since the quantity per container is usually small, many replenishments are required per day.

The single-card system could be characterized as a *push* system for production control and a *pull* system for material delivery, since the cards are used only to pull materials between work centers.

13.12 Relationship to vendors

If the flow of kanban cards back through the production process is followed logically, it is clear that, ultimately, the incoming raw material and the purchased parts point is reached. This leads to the question of how the Kanban system might be extended to outside vendors. On the one hand, we can have large inventories of each part which are replenished by suppliers at weekly, or perhaps longer, intervals. However, this defeats one of the essential purposes of JIT which is to reduce inventories. On the other hand, we can carry the Kanban process right out and into the vendors' production systems. This procedure normally involves regular and frequent deliveries from the vendors and is achieved, as indicated in Chapter 11, through the establishment of close cooperation with suppliers and the sharing of as much information as necessary to help the suppliers' organizations achieve a JIT system. In effect, it involves establishing a true partnership with trusted suppliers.

13.13 Kanban as a productivity improvement technique

If the procedures of Kanban outlined earlier are followed rigorously, the level of work in progress inventory can be controlled by the number of cards issued for each component part into the system. This is because each card corresponds to one standard container and, knowing the size of the container and the number of cards on the floor, a simple calculation gives the inventory level.

Therefore, by reducing the number of cards issued for a particular part, the process inventory level for that part falls. Eventually, if the levels are reduced low enough, a work center will run out of material and stop processing. This stops the whole line and major efforts are made to get it running at the lower level of inventory, by either increasing the number of operators, reducing set-up times, or redesigning processes.

The thinking is as follows. Unnecessarily high inventory serves to disguise inherent problems and sources of inefficiency in the production process. Through gradual reduction of inventory levels, production problems are highlighted and are progressively eliminated.

13.14 Assumptions necessary for Kanban to work

As indicated above, strict rules must be followed to enable the Kanban system to work efficiently and effectively. Corresponding to these rules are some fundamental assumptions about the nature of the manufacturing system, within which the Kanban system operates. We will now briefly revisit these assumptions.

Since each daily assembly schedule must be very similar to all other daily schedules, it is essential that it is possible to *freeze* the master production schedule for a *fixed time period,* possibly of at least one month. The final assembly schedule must also be very level and stable. Any major deviations will cause a ripple effect through the production system causing upstream work centers to hold larger inventory stocks. What is required ultimately is that the manufacturing system conform as closely as possible to the *repetitive manufacturing* system model outlined earlier in this chapter.

To run a mixed model system effectively requires mixed model *capability* in *all stages* of the production process. Mixed model manufacturing and assembly, as seen in Chapter 12, involves frequent changes and set-up at the individual work centers. It follows that the set-up times in all work centers be as small as possible and that the set-up procedures be continuously reviewed to this end. A logical conclusion from this is the need for balancing between all operations in order to synchronize the starting and ending of work routines. This ensures that parts are fed to the assembly line at the same rate as they are consumed.

The plant configuration and layout must be *flow based* in order to link all operations to the final assembly line, thus reducing transport times and highlighting interdependencies between work centers. Each work center should have inbound and outbound stockpoints and there should be a fixed flow routing for each part through the work centers. The system should be designed to operate at somewhat less than full capacity in order to provide some flexibility if, and when, problems arise.

A *multiskilled* work force is a basic requirement for Kanban. Such a work force can be flexible in its work organization in that it can handle many different machines and operations. Moving people around allows supervisors to change the capacity of individual work centers. It is sometimes difficult to secure the level of operator commitment and involvement that is required for such activities and, in fact, many non-Japanese companies consider this a major obstacle to the installation of a strict Kanban system in their manufacturing plants.

13.15 Conclusion

This chapter has discussed the Kanban system and presented it in the context of JIT thinking.

There are clearly some limitations and disadvantages to the Kanban system. Kanban is intrinsically a system for repetitive manufacturing. It will not succeed without modification in a non-repetitive manufacturing environment.

As mentioned above, Kanban requires a leveled schedule, standard containers and very strict discipline. It could be considered inflexible in that it cannot easily respond to irregular changes or to large unexpected changes in market demand and it clearly requires great cooperation from outside suppliers.

From the perspective of the process, it places emphasis on process technologies, such as product based flow configurations, and may therefore require considerable investment in developing new methods, procedures, jigs and fixtures, etc., perhaps even new capital equipment.

If well implemented, there are many advantages to the Kanban system. The most important of these are that it stimulates productivity improvement, reduces inventory and production lead time, and, within the constraints of the product design and the manufacturing system design, allows the plant to respond to predictable small market variations. Kanban is a simple system of flow control with visible means of inventory control, which is simple to understand. It involves very little paperwork compared with other systems – such as the shop floor control modules of typical MRP systems – and is able to set valid priorities.

Improvements in operations are promoted through the development of a plant layout (which facilitates a smooth production flow and the redesign of equipment), jigs and tools for fast set-ups, and balanced production rates. Other benefits arise from the training of the work force to be multiskilled, greatly reduced scrap rates, higher quality levels, and saving on space due to lower inventory levels requiring less physical storage space.

Evolution towards more efficient repetitive manufacturing is ensured by promoting the reduction of set-up time and lot size, and the development of formal stockpoints within each work center.

To summarize, this chapter has described the shop floor control system, Kanban, which is an integral part of the realization of the just in time philosophy in repetitive manufacturing environments. Its operation has been described with particular emphasis on how the flow of material is controlled through production and withdrawal kanbans.

In our view, Kanban is the least important aspect of JIT. What is important is that, by implementing the ideas described in Chapters 11 and 12, it may be possible to streamline manufacturing systems, thereby realizing huge benefits in terms of productivity, efficiency, and flexibility. In some circumstances, the result of applying JIT may be such as to create the conditions for Kanban to be appropriate. Perhaps, in the majority of cases, this will not be so. Nevertheless, the benefits of implementing JIT are likely to be tremendous.

Questions

(13.1) "MRP is considered to be the classical example of a push system." Comment.

(13.2) Define "repetitive manufacturing".

(13.3) The Kanban system is sometimes referred to as a pull system. Explain.

(13.4) Is the flow of materials within a JIT final assembly line controlled by kanban cards? Why?

(13.5) Distinguish clearly between sequential and combinative processing operations.

(13.6) Explain the differing roles of the production and withdrawal kanbans.

(13.7) Discuss the guidelines and procedures for the use of kanban cards to achieve JIT production.

(13.8) Discuss the differences between the single-card Kanban and the two-card systems.

(13.9) "Unnecessarily high inventory serves to disguise inherent problems and sources of inefficiency in the product process." Discuss.

(13.10) Identify the assumptions necessary for Kanban to operate.

(13.11) "In our view, Kanban is the least important aspect of JIT. By implementing the JIT approach and using JIT manufacturing techniques, it is possible to streamline manufacturing systems, thereby realizing benefits in terms of productivity, efficiency, and flexibility." Discuss.

References to Part III

APICS. 1984. *JIT and MRPII Partners in Manufacturing Strategy*, Report on 27th Annual APICS Conference on Modern Materials Handling, December, 58–60.

Boothroyd, G. and Dewhurst, P. 1982. *Design for Assembly: A Designer's Handbook*. Amherst, MA: University of Massachusetts.

Boothroyd, G. and Dewhurst, P. 1983. "Design for assembly: choosing the right method," *Machine Design*, November, 94–98.

Browne, J., Furgac, I., Felsing, W., Deutschlaender, A. and O'Gorman, P. 1985. "Product design for small parts assembly," in *Robotic Assembly*, edited by K. Rathmill. UK: IFS Publications Ltd, 139–156.

Burbidge, J.L. 1975. *The Introduction of Group Technology*. New York: John Wiley and Sons.

De, S., Nof, S.Y. and Whinston, A.B. 1985. "Decision support in computer integrated manufacturing," *Decision Support Systems*, **1**, 35–56.

Edwards, J.N. 1983. "MRP and Kanban, American Style," in *APICS 26th Annual International Conference Proceedings*, 586–603.

Gallagher, C.C. and Knight, W.A. 1973. *Group Technology*. London: Butterworths.

Groover, M.P. 1980. *Automation, Production Systems and Computer-Aided Manufacturing*. Englewood Cliffs, NJ: Prentice-Hall Inc.

Hall, R.W. 1983. *Zero Inventories*. USA: Dow Jones-Irwin.

Heard, E. and Plossl, G. 1984. "Lead times revisited," *Production and Inventory Management*, third quarter, 32–47.

Hyer, N.L. and Wemmerlov, U. 1982. "MRP/GT: a framework for production planning and control of cellular manufacturing," *Decision Sciences*, **13**, 681–700.

Laszcz, J.Z. 1985. "Product design for robotic and automatic assembly," in *Robotic Assembly*, edited by K. Rathmill. UK: IFS Publications Ltd.

Lewis, F.A. 1986. "Statistics aid planning for JIT production," *Chartered Mechanical Engineer*, June, 27–30.

Menga, G. 1987. (Private communication.)

Monden, Y. 1981. "Adaptable Kanban system helps Toyota maintain Just in Time production," *Industrial Engineering*, May, 29–46.

Monden, Y. 1983. *Toyota Production System: Practical Approach to Production Management*. American Institute of Industrial Engineers.

Schneidermann, A.M. 1986. "Optimum quality costs and zero defects: are they contradictory concepts?" *Quality Progress*, November, 28–31.

Schonberger, R.J. 1982. *Japanese Manufacturing Techniques: Nine Hidden Lessons in Simplicity*. New York: The Free Press.

Schonberger, R.J. 1984. "Just in Time production systems: replacing complexity with simplicity in manufacturing management," *Industrial Engineering*, **16**(10), 52–63.

Shingo, S. 1985. *A Revolution in Manufacturing: The SMED System*. USA: The Productivity Press.

Skinner, W. 1974. "The focused factory," *Harvard Business Review*, May–June.

Treer, K.R. 1979. *Automated Assembly*. Dearborn, MI: Society of Manufacturing Engineers.

Wild, R. 1984. *Operations and Production Management Principles and Techniques*. London: Holt, Rinehart and Winston.

CASE STUDY 2

UDS Motorola, Inc., Huntsville, AL

by Michael S. Spencer

Identifying characteristics

Background

UDS Motorola is a producer of a line of computer modems for use in industry and by private customers. The company was founded as UDS, Inc. in 1972 by Mr Mark Smith in Huntsville, Alabama, to produce modems for personal computers. It was acquired by Motorola, Inc. in 1982 in a friendly purchase from Mr Smith. UDS Motorola is currently a wholly owned subsidiary of Motorola. The company has a single manufacturing facility located in Huntsville adjacent to the company headquarters. The factory was designed by UDS Motorola to produce modems and has undergone modifications to the basic layout as technology has changed over the past 20 years.

UDS Motorola manufactures about 25 families of modems, which are modified by customer specifications with options that include both hardware and software changes. As a result, the factory manufactures approximately 500 end items. The company employs approximately 1000 people, of whom less than 200 are direct labor employees. The factory operates on a five-day per week basis on one shift. There is a second shift consisting of one crew that shifts among the four product lines as required to maintain schedule performance.

Estimated annual sales are $140 million. The company markets its product lines on a worldwide basis. Recently, overseas sales have been increasing more rapidly than domestic sales. The overseas market is seen by management as the most significant growth area for the company's products.

Production operations

The factory was originally configured in a functional layout. This layout was rearranged during the past seven years to a product layout as part of a just in time (JIT) program. There are now five product flow areas with a total of about 30 workstations throughout the factory. One product line manufactures the basic board used to hold the electronic components that configure into a finished modem. Two product layout lines assemble the modems that are made using a through-hole process (THP) in the boards. The through-hole process is an older technology that requires the electronic components to be inserted through holes in the base board. The components have wire legs which are then folded and scaled onto the back of the board to hold the components in place. Two other product layout lines affix the components directly onto the board using surface mounting technology (SMT), a newer technology than THP. The company's older product lines were originally assembled using the through-hole method and continue to be assembled using that technology. The actual assembly of all modems uses a similar process but requires different types of equipment because of the through-hole and on-board technology used.

Approximately 300 electronic components are assembled onto the boards to produce a finished modem. The electronic components are selected from purchased finished stores in relatively large rolls that are used by the component suppliers for transport. The rolls of components are sent to the first station, where an operator selects the required roll of components and loads the roll into a fixture. The sequence of the components along the fixture determines which of the components is affixed to the board in a particular position. The operator loads the fixture in the sequence dictated by a computer-generated report depending on the modem to be manufactured. The computer program is generated from the engineering CAD-CAM system that will be discussed in a later section.

The fixture is then loaded into position along the product layout line and positioned to be used by the automatic insertion or placement machines that actually fix the electronic components onto the boards. The automatic insertion robots take the components from the rolls on the preloaded fixture and position the components into the correct position on the board based on the type of modem being assembled. The robots' programs are also defined by the engineering CAD-CAM system. There is a series of robotic stations along the four product layout lines that assemble the modem's main board. The type and positioning of the electronic components determine the type of modem and options produced. Some electronic modules comprise the software options while others comprise the basic modem. There is a total of about 4000 different electronic components used to make the entire product line.

The next station along the four product lines is the wave solder operation, which cements the components onto the board. The wave solder station then feeds the final assembly station, where the board is placed into a plastic outer shell. The outer shell differs by the type of modem produced and the customer specifications desired. Some customers, for example, have their names on the outer shell along with the identification of various user information buttons.

The next station consists of the testing benches. Operators test all modems to ensure proper operation and assembly. The testing stations are separated from the product layout lines so that each station can be operated independently by an employee. The test process is viewed by management as the bottleneck operation in each of the four assembly lines.

The final station in the product layout lines is packaging. At this station the tested modem is inserted into a cardboard package and then placed into a cardboard shipping box. Instruction sheets are included as required by the customer specification. The box is sealed at the station and transported to the loading dock.

Production planning environment

Production planning is primarily the responsibility of the master scheduler. The master scheduler reports to the vice-president of manufacturing, who reports to the company's president. The master scheduler has five shop schedulers reporting to her, who are responsible for the production planning and scheduling activities for each of the five product areas. There is also an inventory analysis function that is currently being formed, reporting to the master sheduler. The inventory analysis section will be responsible for cycle counting, inventory corrections, and auditing inventory activities. There is no production control manager employed at UDS Motorola.

The purchasing manager also reports to the vice-president of manufacturing. Reporting to the purchasing manager are two purchasing supervisors, and supervisors of receiving and stockroom. The purchasing supervisors have 10 buyers and about 10 buyer-associates reporting to them. Purchasing is responsible for vendor selection, price negotiation, and scheduling activities. The key performance measurements for vendors are quality and on-time delivery. The quality measure is based on attaining a sigma level determined by the manufacturing engineering department, based on product design and vendor capability. The measurement for on-time delivery is the percentage of parts delivered to the factory on the day scheduled. Currently, on-time delivery is about 75% and is seen as an area of concern. There are over 300 vendors used by UDS Motorola, many of which are located overseas. The longest lead time for purchased components is about 20 weeks for customized chips, with an average lead time for common components of about 12 weeks. By using purchased-finished inventory in a stores area the lead time quoted to customers is three weeks.

No formal inventory management targets are established for the master scheduler or for the purchasing department. Inventory is seen as the result of attaining other company goals rather than an end in itself. Actual manufacturing lead time for modems is four days. Customer lead time for distributors is quoted at three weeks. About 50% of the total inventory is in purchased finished material, about 30% is held in work in process (WIP) inventory, and about 20% is in finished goods. WIP inventory turnover is approximately 50 times per year, raw material turns approximately 20 times per year, and finished inventory turns approximately 80 times per year.

Marketing is a worldwide function for UDS Motorola, directed by the vice-president of sales and marketing. There are about 50 sales people operating out of field offices worldwide. These sales people are UDS Motorola employees engaged in finding new customers for the product lines. An internal sales force of approximately 20 people is used for order entry and customer relations with the existing customer base, and an additional 15 people are employed to encourage the overseas expansion. Current international sales are about 20% of the total. The average customer order size is 50 units.

There are three other employees reporting to marketing who are responsible for the worldwide distribution of products. About 30% of the products are shipped to independent distributors, and an additional 30% are shipped to about 200 OEMs (original equipment manufacturers). Other Motorola units purchase about 15% of the products. The remainder are shipped directly to domestic and international customers.

UDS Motorola has about 10 major competitors for various product lines. The company views product development as critical to future success. Existing product lines are subject to significant price competition because of the level of worldwide competition. The product life for new products is expected to average less than two years. The company averages a new product introduction each week. The key performance measurements for marketing are customer satisfaction and sales volume.

Quality assurance and quality control activities are combined into one department reporting to a vice-president. Quality includes customer support functions in addition to the manufacturing and purchasing activities. There are about 30 inspectors currently on the factory floor. The number of shop floor inspectors is decreasing as responsibilities are shifted to the manufacturing operators. About 20% of all purchased parts are currently certified and bypass incoming inspection. This number is expected to increase over the next year as the quality department continues to work with purchasing to certify additional vendors. There is an active total quality control program in use throughout the factory, with statistical quality control charts in use where applicable. Quality data is routinely posted in each manufacturing line. Quality problems that arise in the manufacturing process are resolved with manufacturing participation. The performance measurement system for the quality department is the attainment of a six sigma quality level. UDS Motorola reports quality measures to the Motorola company on a quarterly basis.

The design engineering function reports to a vice-president of engineering. There are over 100 engineers employed in product design activities. The company maintains a CAD-CAM system that facilitates the design of new products and the modification of existing products. Each customer product has a design configuration maintained within the CAD-CAM system, which indicates the electronic components required to assemble the product. The CAD-CAM system is updated by the design engineers as required to maintain customer specification. The requirements for the final product are downloaded on-line to the shop floor, to the robots and to the manufacturing operators who load the assembly component fixtures. There are about 14 manufacturing and industrial engineers reporting to an engineering manager and four engineering supervisors. The engineering manager reports to the vice-president of manufacturing. One supervisor is responsible for all factory manufacturing engineering activities, another is responsible for all floor industrial engineering activities and a third is responsible for equipment maintenance. The fourth is responsible for new product and manufacturing technology introduction.

There is a vice-president of finance, reporting to the company president, who is responsible for all accounting activities including cost accounting, financial reporting, accounts payable, credit and accounts receivable. There is little interaction between the Motorola headquarters and UDS Motorola except through the quarterly financial reports. The company uses a standard cost accounting method for product costing. Direct labor is approximately 3% of the total cost, material is approximately 60%, with overhead being approximately 37%.

The manufacturing organization reports to the vice-president of manufacturing. Each of the five product areas is organized as a manufacturing team. A shop supervisor manages each team using a factory-within-a-factory concept. Teams consist of the supervisor and wage employees. Staff support is available to the teams as requested by the team manager, although the staff employees continue to report to the functional managers. The second shift floating crew has two supervisors. An additional floor supervisor is assigned to a new manufacturing area that is being developed for prototype builds for modems using liquid crystal displays. Key performance measurements for manufacturing supervision are quality levels, on-time delivery, housekeeping, and safety. There is no measurement by shop area budget performance. A key area of concern is the current delivery performance of about 80% on-time shipments. The 80% delivery figure is believed to be caused by inventory errors, errors in the bills of material, changes in customer request dates, and engineering holds for design modifications.

Based on the interviews and observations the following characteristics are present at UDS Motorola:

(1) Common purchased components are assembled into finished products.

(2) Routings for components require unique processing.

(3) Component parts are common to many end items.

(4)   There are points of convergence in the routing where components are assembled into end items.

These factors, among others, lead to the conclusion that UDS Motorola can best be described as a repetitive manufacturer. Routings for all components are fixed. Five separate product layouts are utilized in the factory. Material flows through the processes without being cross-routed back to previous operations. Production and capacity are measured in terms of units per day. The overall process creates a flow of material through the facility to packaging operations. Even though the average customer order is approximately 50 units and the facility operates in an assemble to order environment, the management of the production planning and control system creates a very responsive repetitive environment.

Production planning and control methods

Background

The COPICS material requirements planning system was purchased and installed in 1983. COPICS was selected over other software available as the result of a written specification developed by the factory. The largest factor in selecting COPICS was its modularity. Modifications to the COPICS system have been made over the past several years by an in-house systems staff. In 1991, the computer system underwent a significant modification to improve on-line performance. The system is operated on a daily net change basis with weekly regeneration. The MPS module of COPICS was implemented along with the MRP calculation module. The purchasing system was written by the in-house staff to accommodate COPICS output. The shop floor control module has not been installed by UDS Motorola. Management reports that the system could be improved to be more user friendly, especially in training new employees. The output from the system is, according to management, valid, timely and very useful in facilitating management decisions. In-house training in MRP was conducted and all employees received about one hour of general education as well as specific training in their job responsibilities. MRP training is ongoing when requested.

An extensive JIT program was introduced at UDS Motorola in the mid-1980s. About 95% of all component parts are controlled by Kanban methods to bring material from purchased finished stores into the assembly area. Kanban is not used in the assembly lines since the product layout moves units in almost a continuous flow. The entire layout of the facility was rearranged as part of the JIT program. A program of employee cross-training and employee empowerment was also undertaken as part of the JIT effort. Machine set-ups were also reduced so that set-ups average about 10 minutes each. Machine set-up occurs about eight times per shift on each line.

The bills of material are believed to be about 90% accurate for each product line. Improvements are expected to occur from the inventory analysis group that is being established in the master production scheduling area. As part of the JIT program and the reconfiguration of the plant layout, the number of levels in the bills of material was reduced from ten to three. Under the former functional layout each subassembly required an additional level in the BOM as components were added. Under the revised flow layout, all components are added while the model remains in the production area. Currently the BOM levels are: (i) modem-in-process, (ii) modem and case assembly, and (iii) finished assembly and packaging. Changes in the bills of material are frequent as the result of changes in customer requirements. Change orders are primarily generated by design engineering, although industrial and manufacturing engineering also create change orders. Changes requiring the procurement of new components are reviewed by purchasing to establish an acceptable vendor and set the effectivity date. Manual data entry involving changes in the bills of material are believed to be a major source of errors, especially in the quantity per description.

Routings are believed to be approximately 100% accurate. The routing module in COPICS is currently being installed to support the addition of a finite scheduling software package. The product layout was sufficient to enable the factory to avoid using the routing module until the investigation of the finite scheduling package.

Inventory accuracy is believed to be about 95%. A cycle counting process is currently being implemented at the factory in order to avoid the annual physical inventory. The largest problem with inventory accuracy is believed to be the accuracy in the bills of material. As a matter of company policy, safety stock is used only on a few selected components that have a relatively long lead time and/or are sourced overseas. There is stocking of a few end items to support key customers although the level of inventory is not believed to be a concern. The purchasing department establishes vendor order quantities based on their analysis of vendor capability. Order policies are established by manufacturing and master production scheduling for work in process parts numbers. Only a few components have order policies other than lot for lot in daily time buckets.

Master production scheduling

The development of the master production schedule is accomplished by the company's master scheduler, who reports to the vice-president of manufacturing. The MPS is developed for about 75 base modems and major options for the next six months. The MPS is stated in days for the first four to six weeks and then for weeks through the end of six months. The MPS is a modified COPICS module and is updated continuously as new orders are received. It is regenerated into the MRP system on a weekly basis. There is a seasonal peak in November, December, and January of about 25% higher then the average. The seasonal valley occurs in June, July, and August. This seasonal pattern is included in the forecast and MPS. A forecasting software package called FOCUS is used to help develop the forecast and answer "what if" questions.

After the monthly MPS meeting, the adjusted forecast is reviewed by the five production schedulers. The forecast is then broken into more specific products by the schedulers and entered into the MPS system by part number. The MRP calculation disaggregates the MPS parts into the purchased components required to support the dates. Requirements for service parts are loaded directly into the MPS system from the order entry system. Service components are less than 5% of the total dollar sales volume.

The MPS is based on the sales forecast developed by marketing, purchasing, and the master scheduler. There is an annual forecast, which is updated on a monthly basis. The forecast is entered into the MPS for the first six months when actual orders fail to cover the planned production rate. Orders are received by the marketing department on a daily basis and are entered into an in-house written order entry system. The order entry department proposes a customer request date to the master scheduler. The master scheduler accepts the date or counter-proposes a date that has available resources for production. If accepted, the actual order will replace the forecast for the shipping date. The customer request date is accepted about 50% of the time, and it is accepted within one week about 75% of the time.

The MPS production rate is established at a quantity just below the actual labor capacity of the product lines determined by the number of workers employed. In the two older technology lines, the actual production rate is 85–92% of actual capacity. In the two newer technology lines, the actual production rate is 95–98% of actual capacity. Therefore, the lines operate with excess capacity at all times. This policy allows manufacturing to be able to respond to changes in customer orders at relatively short notice.

Production is monitored by the production schedulers on a daily basis and the results posted on charts along with the quality reports. The second shift is assigned to the product area that is in need of the additional capacity to maintain the schedule. No more than a 20% backlog is acceptable for the product lines before overtime is scheduled beyond the use of the swing shift. The backlog quantity is rolled into the current time period in the MPS system until production is sufficient to make up the backlog.

Priority planning

Priority planning is accomplished through the use of MRP's net requirements for purchased components, and for 5% of the WIP parts. MRP is used at the request of suppliers in order to give long term visibility to part requirements for the supplier's own planning purposes. This is also the reason given for the remaining 5% of the WIP parts. Kanban is used to plan priorities for about 95% of the WIP parts. All parts are identified in the bill of material and MRP system for inventory purposes. Since 5% of the WIP components are still planned using MRP, the overall system could be described as a hybrid JIT/MRP approach.

The MPS feeds the MRP module in daily time periods for the first four to six weeks where actual orders have replaced the forecast quantity. MRP accepts changes from the MPS system in a daily net change calculation with a weekly regeneration at the weekend. The shop schedule uses the actual customer ship date as its O-level (MPS level) due date. Components are then offset by lead time and netted against the inventory. All WIP inventory is placed in one bucket for netting due to short manufacturing times, rather than accounted at each workstation along the five product layout lines. The shop schedule gives the manufacturing team two weeks of production orders in a report received each day. The due dates of the orders are the actual ship dates of the customer orders. The start dates are calculated by MRP. The material release is also fed by the MRP system for all components for accounting purposes to record the move from raw materials to WIP accounts. The purchased finished stores area releases material. to the shop in accordance with the shop schedule. (The CAD-CAM system establishes the order in which the electronic components are staged on the fixture. In doing so, set-up time is minimized in the production line by choosing the most appropriate sequence of components, given a customer order.) The MRP system also establishes the part's due dates, which are fed into the purchasing system, although most vendors rely on Kanban triggers for sending replenishments.

The Kanban system controls the part priorities from the purchased finished stores areas to the five product assembly lines that are not released using the MRP system. All hardware items are controlled using Kanban. The parts on the line are monitored by a wage employee, who moves a filled bin to replace an empty bin as required on the line. The empty bin has a Kanban, which is then collected by the employee and taken to the purchased stores area. This action causes the stores employees to replace the empty bin with one filled to a predetermined level with components. The employee returns the full container to the line. All electronic components that are assembled by the robots are controlled by MRP releases; all others are planned to be controlled using Kanban.

The factory is actively exploring the implementation of a finite scheduling system to improve priority and capacity planning in the shop. Motorola, Inc. is involved at other facilities with pilot implementations. The finite scheduling system being explored is FACTOR by Pritsker, Corp. The UDS Motorola company has been to the Pritsker site and has seen the software package in operation. Management feels that the system will greatly enhance the plant's on-time delivery performance by accounting for the bottlenecks believed to exist in each line. The assembly lines were developed using line balancing methods and management feels that many operations are interactive bottlenecks. Motorola, Inc. reviewed two other finite scheduling systems, including one based on OPT, but chose FACTOR based on its capabilities and price. One complicating factor to priority and capacity planning that is causing management to implement a finite scheduling system is the amount of set-ups required during the day on each line. Set-ups are averaging about 10 minutes each due to the reduction programs that were part of the JIT program. However, the relatively small customer order quantities are causing the lines to be set up as many as 10 times per day. Management feels that an improved sequencing of orders will reduce the set-up amounts and improve delivery performance.

Capacity planning

Capacity is defined in terms of units per day on the two through-hole product layout lines and in terms of standard hours per day on the two on-board product layout lines and the board production line. The standard hours are from the industrial engineering methods sheet, which was developed at the time of product introduction and is not viewed as up to date. The factory uses a COPICS module to develop a rough-cut capacity analysis that is made in conjunction with the monthly MPS meeting. A set of five bottleneck operations are used, one per line, and the actual orders are matched against a bill of resources to determine the number of workers required for a particular line rate. The MPS line rate is adjusted to reflect the next lower level that is supported by the amount of labor to be employed. The 85–98% excess capacity is created by the calculated line rate, which is then set in the MPS. Detailed capacity requirements planning is not accomplished, although the COPICS module supports the calculations. The capacity analysis uses the six-month horizon that is also used for the MPS. Capacity is viewed by management as a function of the amount of labor employed on a line rather than in terms of the amount of capital equipment. New product introductions would cause equipment to be reviewed and adjustments made to purchase additional equipment if it were financially justified.

If capacity exceeds requirements beyond the percentages previously mentioned, the company will move employees to other lines through cross-training or will engage employees in training programs. The company has a policy that seeks to provide 40 hours of in-house training per employee per year. The next step that the company would use would be requested vacation times. There has never been a layoff at the UDS Motorola plant although there is no written policy that forbids this.

If capacity is less than the sales requirements, an attempt would be made to move workers to the affected area through cross-training. Overtime of up to 16 hours per week could be scheduled as required.

Only if sales requirements exceeded capacity by over six months would the company add new employees.

Capacity is monitored by the manufacturing teams on an ongoing basis based on the actual production accomplished during the week. The swing shift is expected to correct short-term capacity problems caused by unplanned absenteeism or by machine breakdowns. The five production schedulers also review capacity levels on an ongoing basis and make recommendations concerning workforce adjustments as required.

Priority control

Once a production order is released to the factory floor no updates to the MRP system are made except to report the finished order. The only exception is a change in the order quantity made by a customer. Priorities of the orders in process cannot be modified because of the nature of the product layout and the robotics involved in making the change. Informal coordination between the manufacturing team and the shop schedulers maintains the order priority before they are launched if the priorities change after the daily shop production schedule is printed. There is no final assembly schedule (FAS) report or FAS shortage list used to control priorities. In case of a conflict among orders for the sequence, the manufacturing supervisor and shop scheduler would establish the new sequence.

A shortage list is prepared for purchased parts. This report lists shortages for the next 15 days by part number. In addition, a daily handwritten shortage report is made by the five shop floor schedulers for use by the purchasing department. An analysis has been completed by the master scheduler to determine the causes for the purchased parts shortages. However, no pattern was identified.

The factory places great emphasis on meeting customer changes to orders if possible. The company feels that customer response is critical to its future success. Once started, a product is finished even though some excess inventory is created. Changes to customer orders may mean the launch of additional products through the production lines in order to provide the needed modems.

Capacity control

Capacity control is primarily the responsibility of the manufacturing teams. The daily production is compared to the planned daily production rate and the shop production schedule. If an adjustment to a line's capacity is needed the second shift is assigned to that area. Only if the swing shift cannot make up the needed capacity is overtime scheduled. The vice-president of manufacturing approves all requests for overtime from the manufacturing teams. Overtime is monitored on a weekly basis for each line and reported as part of the monthly budget report to the company president. The product layout allows the manufacturing supervisor to determine quickly if a machine is down. A series of lights above each machine center also alerts the supervisor to the machine's status. The status of each machine is also logged into the engineering system from the light bar and a machine time history made available on-line or on a request basis to the factory engineering manager.

The factory is implementing a method of measuring the efficiency of the five product layout lines. This implementation was the first task of the manufacturing teams and was begun four months ago. The teams are still developing the efficiency measures to be used. There are no COPICS reports that are used to control capacity at UDS Motorola.

Key problem areas by production function

Master production scheduling

The first area of concern for management at UDS Motorola involving the MPS function is the difficulty in preparing the forecast. The product line is evolving rapidly and there is significant competition in the marketplace. Additionally, new products are introduced in the field on a frequent basis. The forecast is based on the sales history, but the environment may be changing too rapidly to enable the history to be an effective basis for the future. The second area of concern is the seasonality in the product line. The company has an informal policy that minimizes the use of layoffs to smooth production requirements. (As mentioned previously, there has been no layoff of employees in the history of the company.) The seasonality presents the master scheduler with a peak and a valley of about 25% (compared with the average) to be managed. The MPS is developed to make the transitions from the peak and valley as non-disruptive as possible from the factory floor. The third area of concern is the difference between the actual customer order configuration and the forecast option quantity. Differences between the order and the forecast can cause excess inventory or expediting to occur. The fourth concern is the relatively long lead times for some purchased components, which extend beyond the actual order horizon and, therefore, require the use of the forecast quantities for purchase orders. The last concern is the identification of the reasons for the 80% on-time delivery performance for the products.

Priority planning

The first area of concern for priority planning is the amount of changes in customer orders within the MPS horizon. Changing customer requirements can cause expediting and parts shortages to occur in manufacturing. The second concern is the difference between the forecast requirements and the actual customer orders. The differences can cause parts shortages or may require extra units to be produced to meet customer demand. The third area of concern is the amount of parts shortages for purchased components. The parts shortages can cause changes to the build sequence, expediting, and rework. The fourth concern is the number of interactive constraints (sometimes called floating bottlenecks) in the product layout lines. Depending upon the product configurations, different areas can become production bottlenecks. Management believes that the line is balanced when it is implemented in such a way as to create a number of bottleneck operations. The number of bottleneck operations causes competition for resources among different customer orders with the same due date. The last concern for management in priority planning is the number of set-ups required on the five product layout lines. The amount of set-up decreases the lines' capacity and compounds the competition for the resources by customer orders.

Capacity planning

The first area of concern is the seasonality in the product lines, which causes a peak and valley of about 25% compared with the average rate of production. The peak and valley cause leveling activities in the MPS to rely on the use of a swing shift and overtime. The second concern is the existence of interactive constraints believed to exist in the product layout lines. The interactive constraints can require additional capacity to be needed in an area that is not able to be planned using current MRP methods. The third concern is the effective use of the swing shift so that overall shipping performance is enhanced.

Priority control

The first area of concern in priority control is the number of purchased parts that are short for the production lines. Parts shortages are believed to be a major contributor to the 85% shipping performance. Parts shortages can cause expediting, reprioritization of orders, and downtime on the lines. The second concern is the amount of changes in customer orders. Changes to customer orders can require the reprioritization of orders and expediting to ensure the orders are assembled correctly. The third area of concern is the frequency of set-ups required on the lines. The set-up frequency is not considered in the MRP calculation and can cause reprioritization as family groupings are attempted to reduce the number of set-ups required.

Capacity control

The first concern involving capacity control is the purchased parts availability. Part availability can cause downtime on the line and can reduce the amount of capacity available. The second concern is the amount of actual machine downtime.

Summary

The UDS Motorola facility operates with an MRP system acting as a planning framework or database, and an extensive JIT system. The MPS is developed using a modification of the sales forecast and has a six-month horizon. Customer orders replace the forecast in the first four to six weeks. The first four to six weeks in the MPS are in daily buckets. The MRP system generates a daily production schedule that is used for part of material release for accounting, and to generate purchasing requirements for long-term planning by suppliers. The MRP process also includes the capacity planning process, and its results are used in a formal monthly meeting with continuous updating as required. The manufacturing organization is responsible for capacity control through the use of a second shift crew and overtime. Priority control uses JIT as well as informal methods involving the manufacturing, master scheduling, and purchasing functions. A finite scheduling system is actively being explored for implementation this year.

The company has a highly developed total quality control program in place. The plant layout was reconfigured into five factory-within-a-factory areas. The set-ups required on the machine centers were studied and reduced. The employees were empowered and cross-trained. Machine downtime is monitored and improvements are made on a continuous basis. The manufacturing function is organized into work teams that operate to improve overall performance. Kanban is used to control and plan part priorities in 95% of the manufactured components.

Management's performance measurement system is focused on factory profitability, meeting customer demand, quality, and introducing new products. A significant expansion in overseas markets is under way.

PART IV

Optimized production technology

Overview

The major intent of this portion of the book is to introduce and review an approach to production management developed in the early 1980s – OPT – an acronym for optimized production technology†. This system has two major components, namely, a philosophy which underpins the working system, and a software package that produces manufacturing schedules through the application of this philosophy to the manufacturing system.

The OPT system generated some interesting discussion – one might even say controversy – in the literature. In our view this controversy arose from two sources. Firstly, the term *optimal* has a strict scientific meaning and it is fairly clear that OPT is not optimal in the scientific sense. Secondly, the original information on OPT talked about a *black box* secret algorithm for generating schedules. This algorithm has never been made public to our knowledge. Some authors took the view that OPT was a competitor for MRP II and JIT. Others, notably Vollmann (1986), consider OPT as an enhancement to MRP II.

It has been suggested that the major tenets of the OPT philosophy can be applied to the management of a manufacturing system without recourse to the software package. Here we shall consider these tenets, or rules as they are called, with respect to their applicability.

This part is organized into two chapters. In the first of these we cover the thinking behind OPT, and in the second we outline the operation of the software package as we understand it. We shall support this second chapter with an example similar to that used to outline the basics of MRP in Part II.

In Chapter 14, we consider the backbone of OPT – its *philosophy*. The OPT philosophy is founded on the basic assumption that the primary goal of any manufacturing business is to *make money*. OPT addresses itself to various aspects of manufacturing, from both the production and

† OPT® is a registered trademark of Scheduling Technology Group Ltd.

301

business perspectives. For example, scheduling, resource utilization, and cost accounting are all important elements of OPT. The OPT philosophy can be condensed into *rules* which must be followed to attain the primary goal of making money.

In Chapter 15 we describe how the OPT software package operates, or rather, as much of the system as can be understood from reading available documentation. The system has, as inputs, complete descriptions of the facility, the products, and the orders. OPT then produces schedules which must be followed exactly to achieve the gains that are attributed to this system. We shall complement this description of the system by manually attempting to simulate the operation of the OPT system.

Although the OPT system as such is much less widely discussed in the literature today than it was in the mid 1980s, it is clear that OPT thinking has had a major impact on the practice of production planning and control. Today "bottleneck analysis" and "bottleneck scheduling" are part of the practice of production scheduling. It is worth remembering that it was the proponents of OPT who first brought the "bottleneck" issue to the attention of the production planning and control community. For this reason alone, it is worth studying the OPT approach.

CHAPTER FOURTEEN

Optimized production technology philosophy

14.1 Introduction

In response to the continued success of Japanese manufacturing, a new approach to the management of manufacturing has been developed in the West within the last 20 years. The OPT (optimized production technology) approach contains many of the insights which underlie the Japanese Kanban system (see Part III) – an important element in just in time manufacturing.

14.2 Background to OPT

"The OPT philosophy contends that improving productivity is any step that takes the company closer to its goal" (Fox 1982a). From the OPT perspective there is one, and only one, goal for a manufacturing company – **to make money**. All activities in the business are but means to achieve this goal.

This goal can be represented by three **bottom-line** financial measurements as follows:

(1) net profit,
(2) return on investment, and
(3) cash flow.

If the business takes actions that increase each of these simultaneously then it is moving in the right direction – towards the goal of making money. From the operational point of view, OPT defines three important criteria that are useful in evaluating manufacturing progress towards this goal. These criteria are throughput, inventory, and operating expenses and are defined in the following way:

(1) **Throughput** Throughput is the rate at which the manufacturing business generates money through *selling* finished goods. It is *not* a measure of production. For example, in an automobile production plant, the manufacture of components is unimportant from the perspective of throughput as defined by OPT, since components, in general – ignoring the manufacture of spares for the purposes of the example – can only generate money for the business when they appear as part of a finished product. To generate money, finished automobiles must be sold. Therefore, throughput in the OPT sense is concerned only with the rate at which finished units are sold.

(2) **Inventory** Inventory is defined by OPT to be the raw materials, components, and finished goods that have been paid for by the business but have not, as yet, been sold. Inventory thus excludes the added value of labor and overhead in order to eliminate the distortions that may be caused by accounting profit and losses into inventory. For example, in Chapter 5, the legs, frames, and cushion material used to manufacture the stools in Gizmo-Stools Inc., plus the finished stools in stock at any moment, are all considered inventory. These are materials that have been paid for and have not yet been converted back into money through the sale of finished products.

(3) **Operating expenses** Operating expenses are defined as the cost of converting inventory into throughput. Operating expenses include the cost of direct and indirect labor, heat, light, etc., and production facilities, to mention but a few. In the example of Gizmo-Stools Inc. above, the operating expenses are a measure of the costs incurred to produce the seat of the stool, assemble the legs to the seat, paint the stool, etc. These expenses have to be recovered by the sale of finished stools.

Changes in any of these three elements, such as increasing the throughput or reducing the inventory level, result in changes in the *bottom-line* financial measurements listed above. The effects that changes in throughput, inventory, or operating expenses have on the financial measurements of net profit, return on investment, and cash flow will now be considered.

- An *increase* solely in throughput means a simultaneous increase in net profit, return on investments, and cash flow. The business is selling more finished goods while maintaining a stable level of inventory and operating expenses. This obviously means a greater influx of money, larger profits, and earlier recovery of investments.

- A similar result applies with a *reduction* in operating expenses. In this case the cost of producing the finished product is reduced while the

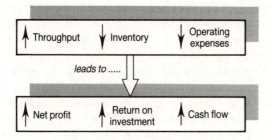

Figure 14.1 Operation measures and financial measures.

inventory and the rate at which the finished products are sold remains unchanged. It is clear that this increases cash flow, net profit, and return on investment.

- A *reduction* in inventory directly impacts return on investment and the cash flow. Here, less costs are associated with a particular period since the inventory is lower. This improves the flow of money and helps recover investment. Profit is not changed, since the cost of raw material has not changed and neither has the cost of transforming the raw material into a finished product.

Therefore, the goal of manufacturing, as seen by OPT, is to increase throughput while *simultaneously* decreasing inventory and operating expenses, as shown in Figure 14.1.

OPT, which was initially developed in Israel during the late 1970s, is an analytical technique that is designed to achieve this goal of increasing throughput and decreasing inventory and operating expenses through realistic *optimized* schedules. Closely coupled with the analytical technique is the OPT philosophy. This philosophy basically consists of 10 rules. These rules and the analytical technique have been computerized to give a software product called OPT.

The 10 rules of OPT, which form the basis of the OPT approach, may be applied to the manufacturing organization without recourse to the software system. Therefore, the rest of this chapter will be devoted to describing and discussing these rules. Chapter 15 will concentrate on the software product, OPT, and try to illustrate how it operates using an example.

14.3 The OPT philosophy

The OPT philosophy rests on the premise that the primary goal of manufacturing is to make money. To attain this goal, OPT considers activities on the shop floor to be critical. Therefore, shop floor issues, such as bottlenecks, set-ups, lot sizes, priorities, random fluctuations, and performance measurements, are treated in great depth. OPT maintains that the conventional assumptions made about the operation of the shop floor are mainly responsible for the poor performance of manufacturing in the past. The OPT philosophy incorporates 10 rules which, when followed, help move the organization toward the goal of making money. Eight of these rules relate to the development of correct schedules, while the other two are necessary for preventing traditional performance measurement procedures from interfering with the execution of these schedules.

The following subsections deal with each of these rules separately. The simple example which demonstrated the operation of MRP in Chapters 5 and 6 will be used here to highlight how some of the OPT rules can improve manufacturing performance. The example is set up to facilitate the explanation of OPT and does not represent the complexity that might appear in a real manufacturing plant.

14.3.1 Bottlenecks

A manufacturing organization can be considered as a system which transforms raw material into finished goods through the use of manufacturing resources. This general description of an organization could be applied to any facility, whether the finished goods were cars, oil, computers, etc. The manufacturing resources are crucial aspects in this process and can be considered to be anything that is required to produce the final product, whether it is a machine, an operator, space, or fixtures. All of the resources in a manufacturing facility can be classified into **bottleneck** and **non-bottleneck** resources. A bottleneck can be defined as:

> ". . . a point or storage in the manufacturing process that holds down the amount of product that a factory can produce. It is where the flow of materials being worked on, narrows to a thin stream."
>
> Bylinsky (1983)

A bottleneck could be a machine whose capacity limits the throughput of the whole production process. Similarly, highly skilled or specialized operators and/or scarce tools may be considered as bottlenecks.

Using the example from Chapter 7 where there were three work centers – assembly, painting, and inspection – it can be shown what is meant by a bottleneck. If we recall, we have two different kinds of stool – Stool A and Stool B. From Table 7.11 we see that the processing times per unit for each work center are as shown in Table 14.1.

Let us assume that each work center can work for 40 hours per week and that, in the first instance, we are only producing one type of stool. Therefore, a market demand of only 100 units in a particular week leads to the following requirements for each work center, as outlined in Table 14.2.

Table 14.1   Process times for each operation.

Assembly processing time	= 0.25 hours
Painting processing time	= 0.35 hours
Inspection processing time	= 0.20 hours

Table 14.2   Processing requirements for each work center.

Assembly hours required	= 25 hours
Painting hours required	= 35 hours
Inspection hours required	= 20 hours

Table 14.3   Processing requirements for 130 units.

Assembly hours required	= 32.5 hours
Painting hours required	= 46.5 hours
Inspection hours required	= 26.0 hours

If the market demand were for 130 units the work center requirements would be as shown in Table 14.3.

Assuming a 40-hour week, this clearly shows that the painting work center can be considered a bottleneck when the demand is for 130 units. With respect to the painting work center, the other work centers are considered as non-bottlenecks.

When we consider the manufacturing resources, some of which are bottlenecks and some of which are non-bottlenecks, certain relationships exist between the resources. OPT highlights four basic relationships that can exist between a bottleneck and a non-bottleneck. These are illustrated in Figure 14.2 (adapted from Fox 1982a).

Each of these four relationships will now be discussed in turn.

- **Type I relationship**   In this relationship, all products flow from the bottleneck to the non-bottleneck resource. This relationship occurs in the example above. Here, the painting work center may be fully utilized at 100%, but the inspection work center can only be

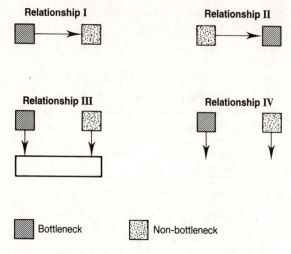

Figure 14.2 Relationships between bottlenecks and non-bottlenecks.

utilized for approximately 80% of the time. This is due to the painting work center *starving* the inspection work center of raw material. If the demand increases beyond this point, the inspection work center, in theory, is able to meet the increased work load, but it cannot because of the metering effect of the painting work center in restricting the flow of material.

- **Type II relationship** In this situation, all products flow from a non-bottleneck to a bottleneck. This again occurs in the example above, where the assembly work center feeds the painting work center. As shown above, if the assembly center is utilized approximately 71% of the time, the painting work center is already utilized 100% of the time. However, the utilization of the assembly work center could be increased to 100% provided the market demand required it, but this would lead to a continuous build-up of inventory at the painting work center. This leads to an increase in inventory without any change in throughput for the overall system.

- **Type III relationship** The third relationship is where a bottleneck work center (let us call this work center **leg-form**) and a non-bottleneck work center (let us call this work center **seat-form**) feed a common assembly work center. Let us assume that the assembly work center requires one unit from each work center to complete a product. If work center leg-form (the bottleneck) is operating at 100% utilization, we require work center seat-form (the non-bottleneck) to operate at 80% utilization to keep the assembly work center supplied with material. If, however, the demand increases we can increase the throughput of the non-bottleneck (work center seat-form) but this will lead to a build-up of inventory before the assembly work center since the bottleneck (work center leg-form) prevents an increase in throughput (in the OPT sense).

- **Type IV relationship** The final relationship exists when two work centers feed independent market demands. Again, work center leg-form (the bottleneck) is utilized 100% of the time, but unless the market demand for the products of work center seat-form increases, it (the non-bottleneck work center) is still limited to processing just 80% of the time.

In all four of the above relationships the same result was obtained, i.e. the non-bottleneck should work at a reduced level of utilization sufficient to support the bottleneck while, at the same time, preventing a build-up of WIP (work in progress) or inventory at the bottleneck station, and the bottleneck should work at 100% utilization. In reality, a manufacturing plant can be simulated by a combination of any of the above relationships. Thus, resources in a plant could either be labeled as bottlenecks or non-bottlenecks. The strategy suggested is to ensure that the bottleneck resources are fully utilized at all times. With regard to non-bottleneck resources, not all of their time can be used effectively and some of their time is therefore considered as enforced idle time. It is important to remember that in the OPT approach this *idle time* is not considered detrimental to the efficiency of the organization. If it were utilized, it would possibly result in increased inventory without a corresponding increase in throughput for the plant.

The first rule of OPT derives from this discussion and is as follows.

RULE 1

The level of utilization of a non-bottleneck is determined not by its own potential, but by some other constraint in the system.

As shown above in relationships I, II, and III, the utilization of the non-bottleneck was determined by the bottleneck and not by its own capacity. In the fourth case, the constraint applied to the non-bottleneck is the market demand.

From this discussion it is clear that non-bottleneck resources should *not* be utilized to 100% of their capacity. Rather, they should be scheduled and operated based on other constraints in the system. If this were done, the non-bottleneck resources would not produce more than the bottlenecks can absorb, thereby preventing an increase in inventory and operating expenses.

OPT deduces another rule from this discussion concerning utilization of resources:

RULE 2

Utilization and activation of a resource are not synonymous.

Traditionally, utilization and activation were considered to be the same. However, in OPT thinking, there is an important distinction to be made between doing the required work (what we should do – activation) and performing work not needed at a particular time (what we can do – utilization). Thus, it is vitally important to schedule all non-bottleneck resources within the manufacturing system based on the constraints of the system, which are usually the bottlenecks.

For example, one can operate a non-bottleneck resource at 100% utilization. However, if only 60% of the output of this non-bottleneck resource can be absorbed by the following resource, which for the purposes of this example is assumed to be a bottleneck, then 40% of the utilization of the non-bottleneck is simply concerned with building up inventory. From the point of view of the non-bottleneck resource, we could argue that we are achieving 100% efficiency. From a system point of view we are only 60% effective. We are confusing the utilization of the non-bottleneck with activation. Utilization is concerned with **efficiency**. Activation is concerned with **effectiveness**. Thinking in terms of the discussion on mechanistic and holistic approaches to problems in Part I, we could argue that, in this context, efficiency is a reductionist criterion whereas effectiveness represents a systems or holistic measure of performance.

14.3.2 Set-up times

Let us now consider another important aspect of shop floor activities, namely set-up times. The available time at any resource is split between processing time and set-up time. This is illustrated in Figure 14.3. However, there is a difference between the set-up times on a bottleneck and those of a non-bottleneck.

If we can save an hour of set-up time on a bottleneck resource, we gain an hour of processing time. Relating this to the fact that bottlenecks are a limiting constraint on other resources (and the system as a whole), an hour of production gained at a bottleneck has far-reaching implications. It can be equivalent to an increased hour of production and throughput for the total system.

At a non-bottleneck resource, we have three elements of time, namely processing, set-up, and idle time. Clearly, if we can save an hour of set-up time, we gain an hour of idle time since the bottlenecks still constrain the capability of the non-bottleneck. Consequently, an hour saved at a non-bottleneck is likely to be of no real value. There is, however, one advantage to reducing set-up times at non-bottlenecks machines. Due to a lower set-up time, more set-ups can be used and the batch or lot sizes can be reduced.

Bottlenecks

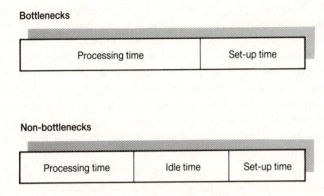

Figure 14.3   Views of time at bottlenecks and non-bottlenecks.

While a smaller lot size of itself does not increase throughput, it tends to reduce inventory levels and some operating expenses.

However, let us qualify this statement. For a specific sequence of operations to produce a specific product, a resource may be considered as a nonbottleneck. Moreover, for another sequence of operations and a different product, this same resource may be a bottleneck. Therefore, within the context of a specific schedule, saving an hour of set-up time at a non-bottleneck is *worth nothing*. On the other hand, within the context of all possible schedules, saving an hour at a resource which is a non-bottleneck in some schedules and a bottleneck in others, is equivalent to gaining an hour's production for the whole system. The next three OPT rules are deduced from the above points.

RULE 3

An hour lost at a bottleneck is an hour lost for the total system.

Therefore, to maximize system wide output, 100% utilization of all bottleneck resources should be a major goal of manufacturing.

RULE 4

An hour saved at an non-bottleneck is just a mirage.

Saving time at a non-bottleneck resource does not affect the capacity of the system, since system capacity is limited by the bottleneck resources.

OPT also maintains that the batch sizes for bottleneck resources should be as large as possible. This is in line with the thinking of the economic order quantity and economic batch quantity approaches (see Chapter 9). The reasoning behind this statement is that if we have many set-ups on a bottleneck resource, the amount of time it takes to do these set-ups is non-productive. Therefore, we try to reduce the amount of set-ups, i.e. make the batch sizes as large as possible, in order to maximize the amount of productive time at a bottleneck. However, for non-bottleneck resources, there is no significant advantage in having large batches, in fact, the smaller the better as suggested above. The obvious solution to this is to use variable batch sizes. This represents a major departure from the materials requirements planning approach where a lot sizing technique normally determines a lot size that is used for all stages of production and transportation, regardless of whether these stages represent bottlenecks or not.

RULE 5

Bottlenecks govern both throughput and inventory in the system.

Traditionally, bottlenecks were believed to limit throughput only temporarily and to have little impact on inventories. OPT argues that inventories (particularly WIP) are a function of the amount of work required to keep the bottlenecks busy.

14.3.3 Lot sizes

Another important variable to be controlled on the shop floor is lot size. This is a crucial variable that is closely linked to the inventory and throughput of the organization. Traditionally, one lot size was determined as being optimal for the manufacturing process. OPT thinking differs from this and maintains that there should be two lot sizes. To demonstrate this let us take an example.

If we examine an assembly line to determine the lot size used, there are two possible answers. On the one hand, the lot size is frequently thought of as one, where one item is moved from one assembly station to another. Alternatively, the lot size can be considered to be infinite since the products on an assembly line are very infrequently changed. Both views are correct, depending on the perspective of the viewer. When we say that the lot size is one, we are viewing the process from the standpoint of the item or product in production. If we say that the lot size is infinite, we are viewing it from the standpoint of the resource.

An analogy may be helpful. Consider a road that is so hilly and convoluted that at no time can a traveler see any other travelers either in front or behind him/her. Let us also assume that all travelers on this road are moving at the same speed. (This represents the basic operation of an assembly line.) Then, from the perspective of a particular traveler, it would seem that he/she is the only traveler on the road. This is similar to the lot size seen from the product perspective. If someone were to sit by the side of the road and watch the travelers go by, to him/her the number of travelers passing would seem infinite. This is analogous to the lot size as seen from the standpoint of the resource.

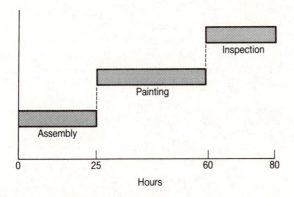

Figure 14.4 Process batch = transfer batch.

Therefore, from the OPT perspective, there are at least two lot sizes to be considered in manufacturing:

(1) The transfer batch – the lot size from the parts point of view.

(2) The process batch – the lot size from the resource point of view.

The next OPT rule is derived from this distinction.

RULE 6

The transfer batch may not, and many times should not, be equal to the process batch.

Lot splitting and overlapping of batches were traditionally discouraged in manufacturing. OPT maintains that the manner in which batches are processed is essential to the **effective** operation of a production system. Returning again to the simple example of Chapter 7, let us assume that we have to produce 100 units of Stool A. This will require processing time on the various manufacturing resources as outlined in Table 14.1. If the transfer and process batch are equal, then the batch of 100 units will not be moved to the painting work center until all the stools have been assembled. This is shown in Figure 14.4.

Figure 14.4 shows that, using this procedure, it will take two weeks for the order to be processed. If, on the other hand, the transfer batch is not equal to the process batch, then it is possible to move a part immediately to the following work center (as specified in the manufacturing routing information) once it has finished its present operation. Figure 14.5 illustrates the effect of this procedure.

The figures are not to scale but they do serve to show that there is a marked reduction in throughput time – something of the order of 40%.

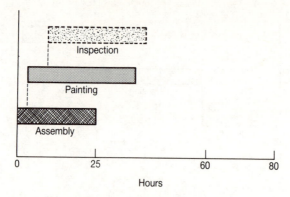

Figure 14.5 Process batch ≠ transfer batch.

This, of course, also reduces inventory and operating expenses. The dashed line showing the operation of the inspection work center in Figure 14.5 represents the fact that the painting work center is a bottleneck. As such, it can not produce enough parts to maintain full utilization of the inspection work center.

Therefore, it is argued, it is impossible to determine from the outset a single lot size that is correct for all operations. This concept is encapsulated in another OPT rule.

RULE 7

The process batch should be variable, not fixed.

This implies that the process batch size at different work centers should not be the same. Traditional manufacturing practice would suggest that, except in exceptional cases, the batch size should be fixed, both over time and from operation to operation. However, in the OPT approach, process batches are a function of the schedule and potentially vary by operation and over time.

The lot size is established dynamically for each operation and balances inventory cost, set-up costs, component flow requirements, and the needs for managerial control and flexibility. In addition, some operations might be bottlenecks and may require large process batches, while non-bottlenecks may require small process batches in order to reduce lead time and the resulting inventory.

14.3.4 Lead times and priorities

MRP, reviewed in Part II, is based on an assumption that planning lead times can be determined a priori. As seen in Chapter 5, lead times are used

Table 14.4   Calculation of production time.

Production lead time for Stool A

Batch size × Processing time per unit
100   × 0.35 hours   = 35 hours

Production lead time for Stool B

Batch size × Processing time per unit
100   × 0.35 hours   = 35 hours

---

to offset from the identified due date in order to calculate the time to start production or to release the purchase orders.

Thus, MRP uses the estimated lead time to determine the order in which jobs are processed. Priorities are assigned to jobs, and those with the higher priorities are processed first. The estimated lead time is, in turn, dependent on the estimated queuing time for each operation. Once priorities have been established, the capacity of the production process is examined to see if the plan can be met. However, the important interaction between priority and capacity is not examined. Priority and capacity are essentially considered sequentially, not simultaneously.

The example of the two stools and Gizmo-Stools Inc. will be used to clarify this point. Consider the painting work center and assume that we have two orders, one for a quantity of 100 of Stool A and a second for a quantity of 100 of Stool B. If, for argument's sake, we further assume that we have two painting work centers, then the production lead time for both batches would be as shown in Table 14.4. (Note that for the purposes of this discussion, set-up time is ignored.)

In this case, we can say that the production lead time for this work center is 35 hours. However, if, in fact, we have only one painting work center then the following applies.

If Stool A is processed first, the production lead time for Stool A is 35 hours and Stool B must wait for these 35 hours for the painting work center to become available. Thus, the overall production lead time for Stool B is, in effect, 70 hours. If Stool B is processed first, the reverse applies. Thus, if we schedule in one fashion we get one set of lead times and if we schedule in another we get another set of lead times.

This illustration demonstrates that:

- Actual lead times are not fixed.
- Lead times are not known a priori, but depend on the sequencing at the limited capacity or bottleneck resources. Exact lead times, and

hence priorities, cannot be determined in a capacity bound situation unless capacity is considered.

From this example and the points it highlights, another OPT rule is deduced.

RULE 8

Capacity and priority should be considered simultaneously, not sequentially.

So far, eight rules have been described and the thinking behind them explained. These rules focus primarily on the operation level, and particularly the scheduling of work, through the shop floor. The next two OPT rules are concerned with the performance measures used to monitor the effectiveness of the shop floor.

14.3.5   Cost accounting and performance evaluation

The rules so far are related to the development of *correct* schedules. It is important that once these schedules are developed, they are followed in detail. The OPT philosophy identifies a number of barriers to the implementation of these *correct* schedules. Some of the major obstacles are briefly described below. According to the proponents of OPT these are:

- Methods of measuring efficiency.
- The expectation of balanced plant loads.
- The so-called **hockey stick** phenomenon.

Each of these will now be discussed in turn.

Measures of efficiency

According to OPT thinking, one of the greatest threats to the use of good schedules is the *misuse* of cost accounting procedures in performance measurement systems. Cost accounting principles, when used to measure performance, are in conflict with OPT rules 3 and 4 which state that *an hour lost at a bottleneck is an hour lost for the total system* and *an hour saved at a non-bottleneck is just a mirage.* Traditional cost accounting practice does not differentiate between work at a bottleneck and work at a non-bottleneck resource. To illustrate the consequences of this, consider the situation of a non-bottleneck resource feeding a bottleneck resource in the plant.

In traditional manufacturing management practice, the supervisors of both types of resources are encouraged to seek 100% resource efficiency since, in general, they are measured by their production rates and not by how well their output impacts the output of the total manufacturing organization. If the supervisor of the non-bottleneck resource operates at full capacity this will result in a costly build-up of inventory and increased operating expenses due to the inability of the bottleneck resource to absorb the production of the non-bottleneck resource. The bottleneck supervisor should always be operating his/her resources at full capacity. The performance of the supervisor who is dealing with non-bottleneck machines should be measured, not by the amount of WIP (work in progress) he/she is responsible for creating, rather by the volume of usable product that his/her area produced.

The supervisors are also encouraged to reduce the number of set-ups on all machines, whether bottleneck or non-bottleneck, in order to increase the *efficiency* of the machines. If supervisors were encouraged to reduce the lot sizes, i.e. increase the number of set-ups on non-bottleneck machines to feed a bottleneck machine correctly, this might well result in a better flow of product to the bottleneck machines, thus ensuring that they were never starved of work (remember, an hour lost at a bottleneck resource cannot be recovered and leads to an equivalent fall in system output) as well as lower inventory levels.

The two preceding paragraphs highlight how management emphasis on certain performance measures can, in some situations, lead to overall system inefficiency. Existing conventional measures of machine and operator performance tend not to take a systems approach, that would consider the interrelationships between all of the elements of the manufacturing system.

In effect, OPT argues, cost accounting principles attempt to measure *efficiency* of resources, not their *effectiveness*. OPT argues that it is important to understand that, from the perspective of the whole manufacturing organization, it is the *effectiveness* of each resource that is important.

The expectation of balanced plant loads

Manufacturing management, certainly in the Western world, has traditionally tried to manage the operation of the production system by the control of capacity of that system. If the utilization of a given resource is considered too low or too high, schedules are changed to counteract this and to balance the load across the whole plant. This sometimes results in virtually full use of all resources, without consideration of the relationships between resources and the effect of these utilization levels on the operation of the manufacturing organization as a whole. Some of the pitfalls of this approach were pointed out in the previous section.

An alternative approach to controlling the operation of production is to consider those products that are sold, or will be sold, to customers. A manufacturing plant should produce only what is ordered by customers or what can reasonably be expected to be ordered by customers. Each work center should only produce what is required at the next work center, and so on, until the plant only produces what is required overall by customers. This reduces costly inventory, saves on operating expenses, and facilitates maximum throughput. Therefore, it is argued, one should attempt to balance the flow of products through the plant rather than the plant capacity. There is an OPT rule to this effect.

RULE 9

Balance flow not capacity.

Traditionally, the approach was to balance capacity and then to attempt a continuous flow. Line balancing is a good example of this approach. The work involved in manufacturing a product is divided into roughly equivalent elements from the capacity point of view. The resources involved in the production process are examined and their capacities balanced in order to ensure high utilization factors. Production then involves trying to create a continuous flow of material through these resources. OPT argues *against* balancing capacity and *for* a balancing of flow within the plant (similar to JIT). This involves looking at the product and ensuring that there is a continuous flow of material during production. The emphasis is on the flow of the product rather than on the resources used to produce it. This leads to the identification of bottlenecks, which can then be examined with a view towards an increase in their throughput and, consequently, the throughput of the total system.

It is important to realize that the OPT approach and the JIT approach do not advocate disregarding capacity considerations. Rather, they suggest that production is controlled by considering product flow and capacity considerations simultaneously, not sequentially, as is the case in the MRP approach.

The hockey stick phenomenon

The developers of OPT identify what they term the **hockey stick** phenomenon and argue that it is caused by the conflict between two measurement systems – cost accounting and financial performance – and is visible in most plants at the end of each financial reporting period. The hockey stick phenomenon is illustrated in Figure 14.6 (adapted from Fox 1982b).

At the beginning of each period the plant is driven by cost accounting performance measurements, which have a *local* focus, as discussed earlier. Measurements focus on machine and operator efficiency, standard times or costs to produce a part at a particular operation. To be *efficient*, large batch sizes are run through operations, regardless of whether they are bottleneck or non-bottleneck, usually resulting in the build-up of unnecessary inventory.

As the end of the financial reporting period approaches, management becomes concerned with a global measurement – the performance of the

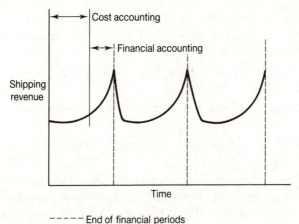

Figure 14.6 Cost accounting and financial measures.

total system. There is an enormous effort to ship products, to make more money. *Efficiencies*, the number of set-ups, etc., are no longer a consideration and, in their stead, expedited lots are split, overtime is allowed, inefficient machines are put working again – anything to increase shipments! Once this end of period is over, *local* efficiency measures take over again and the cycle repeats itself.

This method contrasts sharply with the OPT approach, which seeks to measure the performance of the plant as a whole on the basis of its raw material input and final product output, rather than by measuring only the efficiency of individual operators or machines or other elements of the subsystem. The final rule of OPT is a reflection of this thinking.

RULE 10

The sum of local optima is not equal to the optimum of the whole.

14.4 Conclusion

The preceding sections have covered the thinking behind OPT. Ten rules effectively articulate this thinking and these have been described. Effective operation of the manufacturing plant depends on the production of realistic and correct schedules.

Chapter 15 attempts to describe the software system developed by the promoters of OPT, which is based on the ideas behind the rules just described. Employing the rules outlined above will, it is argued, result in considerable improvement in manufacturing performance. However, introducing the OPT software gives one the ability to produce and follow *correct* schedules.

Questions

(14.1) How do the proponents of OPT define the terms *throughout, inventory,* and *operating expenses?*

(14.2) Identify the four basic relationships that can exist between a bottleneck and a non-bottleneck.

(14.3) "Utilization and activation of a resource are not synonymous." Explain.

(14.4) Show how bottlenecks govern the throughput and inventory of a production system.

(14.5) "Lead times are not known a priori, but depend on the sequencing of batches at the limited capacity or bottleneck resources." Can you reconcile this statement with the use of lead time offsets in MRP style systems?

(14.6) Why is it important to seek to balance flow rather than capacity in production systems?

(14.7) Explain the "hockey stick" phenomenon.

CHAPTER FIFTEEN

Optimized production technology system

15.1 Introduction

By simply applying the *ideas and rules* described in Chapter 14, "companies can improve throughput, cut inventory and increase sales..." (Bylinsky 1983). Combining the application of these ideas with the OPT (Optimized Production Technology) software system, even better results can be achieved, it is claimed. The OPT software system is based on a closely guarded algorithm which concentrates on identifying and scheduling the bottlenecks in the manufacturing system. Although the detailed operation of the software system is proprietary information, the basic operation of the software is understood. This chapter will outline how the system operates and then support this by developing OPT schedules for the example of Gizmo-Stools Inc.

15.2 The software system

In order to operate the OPT system, a complete description of the manufacturing system must be generated. This is accomplished in different stages by a module called *BUILDNET*. Firstly, a product network is constructed for each product manufactured within the organization, which shows exactly how it is manufactured and/or assembled, the resources required, etc. Figure 15.1 (Jacobs 1984) represents an illustration of such a network. The product network contains information similar to that which would be maintained in the bill of materials and routing files for a conventional MRP system. (See Chapter 8.)

At the top of Figure 15.1 are the market requirements which are linked to the various assemblies or manufactured products. These

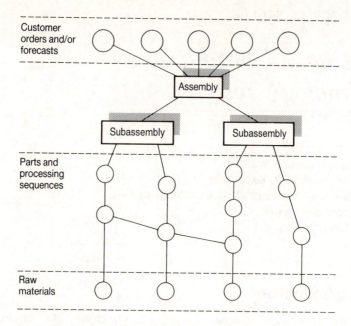

Figure 15.1 Sample product network.

products, in turn, are linked to the subassemblies from which they are assembled. The subassemblies are chained to the parts from which they are produced and the various manufacturing processes that these parts must undergo. Finally, the first manufacturing operation is tied in to the appropriate raw materials.

Detailed descriptions of each resource are then defined in OPT and combined with the product network to form an engineering network, as illustrated in Figure 15.2 (Jacobs 1984). In an initial analysis, a module called *SERVE* uses this information to backward schedule to the order due dates specified in the product network. *SERVE* assumes infinite capacity is available at each resource and uses timing information calculated from the set-up time, run time, and scheduled delay data included in the engineering network. The sole purpose of this analysis is the identification of critical bottleneck resources. A report showing utilization of each resource is developed. Those near or greater than 100% utilization are identified as bottlenecks that are important to the *SPLIT* operation performed next.

The *SPLIT* module separates the engineering network into two sections. As shown in Figure 15.3 (Jacobs 1984), the upper section includes operations that use bottleneck resources and all operations that follow the *critical* operations. The lower section includes operations that precede the critical operations, i.e. all the non-bottleneck resources between raw material acquisition and the first bottleneck resource.

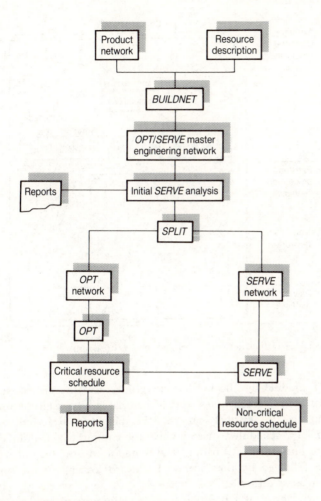

Figure 15.2   OPT/SERVE information flow.

The upper section of the engineering network is scheduled using the *OPT* module. The *OPT* forward scheduling procedure is based on a secret algorithm developed by Goldratt (1980) and takes into account the finite capacity of resources. This algorithm, as far as is generally known, is based on the rules described in Chapter 14 which deal with bottlenecks, set-ups, lot sizes, etc., to mention but a few. Once the critical part of the network has been scheduled, the non-critical or lower part of the network is scheduled using *SERVE*.

SERVE, as described earlier, is a backward scheduling procedure that assumes infinite capacity. In the initial use of *SERVE*, the due dates used are the order due dates. Now the due dates are those determined by

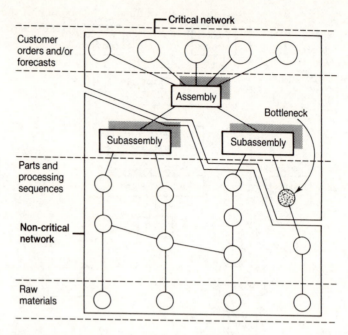

Figure 15.3 Product network – critical, non-critical split.

the *OPT* module for the bottleneck resources in the critical section. In particular, *SERVE* schedules so that material will be available for the first operation in the critical part of the network. Referred to as the *OPT/SERVE* schedules, these involve the composite schedule, developed using the finite forward loading *OPT* module on the critical part of the network, followed by the infinite, backward loading of the non-critical part, as in Figure 15.2.

When all the OPT modules have come up with a complete production schedule, the schedule is run through the program, which may locate additional bottlenecks. These may have been created in the backward scheduling of the non-critical part of the network. These bottlenecks are then resubmitted to *OPT/SERVE*. After a number of runs through the system, an OPT schedule is complete.

It is claimed that there are management parameters within OPT which permit the fine tuning of the schedule to accomplish specific objectives. These are specified by the user. For example,

"if a company's goal is to be the lowest cost producer, OPT can be told to favour minimizing set-up costs at some expense to delivery performance. However, if delivery performance is more important, the adjustment can be made so that when there is a choice, OPT will favour delivery performance over set-up costs."

Fox (1982b)

The above paragraphs have briefly outlined the operation of the OPT software in the production of schedules for the shop floor. This explanation of OPT is very simple and necessarily brief, largely because the authors do not have access to the source code of the OPT product. Section 15.3 will attempt to explain OPT using the Gizmo-Stools Inc. example that was used to explain the mechanics of MRP and of Kanban.

15.2.1   OPT as a productivity improvement tool

The developers of OPT claim that it can be used in numerous ways to improve productivity. It can be used not only as a production scheduling tool (as described above), but also as an analytical technique for "simulating, analyzing and optimizing production operations" (Fox 1982b). There are three major ways that management are using OPT to provide answers to *what if* questions.

(1)   Changing the factory load (production requirements) and studying the impact on throughput, inventory, and operating expenses, etc.

(2)   Varying the manufacturing capacity by adding or removing resources.

(3)   Modifying management policies to understand how these policies affect operating performance.

The OPT software, it is claimed, provides management with an ability to develop realistic schedules and, to a certain extent, answer *what if* questions.

15.3   An illustrative example

To explore further the application of the OPT system we will attempt to create OPT schedules manually for the example of the Gizmo-Stools Inc. stool manufacturing activity, as described originally in Chapter 5. A word of caution is in order here. The example is set up to facilitate the explanation of the logic of OPT and does not seek to present complexity and the data structures which might appear in an actual OPT installation. Furthermore, the authors are not party to the Goldratt algorithm used within OPT and hence cannot develop a complex scheduling example. Nevertheless, the example should be useful in that it allows some appreciation of the OPT and indeed the bottleneck approach to shop floor scheduling.

As described in Chapter 5, it is assumed that Gizmo-Stools Inc. manufactures two types of stool, namely, a four-legged stool and a three-legged stool. The product structures are shown in Figure 15.4.

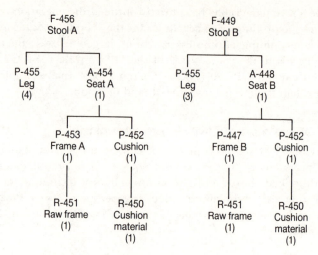

Figure 15.4 Two product structures.

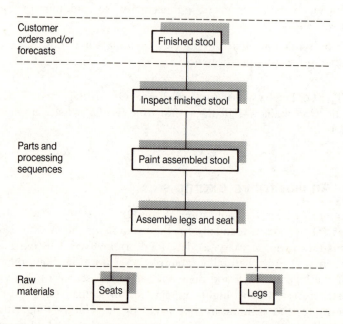

Figure 15.5 Stool product network.

From the information supplied above and the description of the process steps given in Chapter 7, the product network for the stool can be established as shown in Figure 15.5. Table 15.1 details the times for each operation and the resource which performs that operation for Stool B.

Table 15.1 Operation data to process Stool B.

Process requirements for Stool B
Number of operations 3 (All times in hours)

Operation number	10	20	30
Description	Assemble legs to stool	Paint stool	Inspect stool
Set-up time	0.5	0.75	0.5
Processing time	0.25	0.35	0.2
Operator time	0.25	0.35	0.2
Transport time	1.00	1.00	1.00
Work center	Assembly	Painting	Inspect
Next operation	20	30	Stock room

Table 15.2 Processing time at each resource.

Operation number	Resource	Time
10	Assembly	25 hours
20	Painting	35 hours
30	Inspection	20 hours

Before proceeding with the example, two points are worth noting about Table 15.1 (which contains the information required by OPT and is similar to the information required by MRP as shown in Table 7.11):

(1) Unlike the MRP explosion process, fixed recommended batch sizes do not apply in the schedule generation process within OPT. Batch sizes are considered a function of the schedule and are determined later in the detailed scheduling process.

(2) Queue delay times are not used in OPT unless they are scheduled delays within the process itself, for example, time to allow paint to dry. In contrast, MRP includes queue times in the determination of lead times as seen earlier.

15.3.1 A simple example – an order for one product

To return to the example, let us assume that at the beginning of a week we have an order for 100 units of Stool B to be delivered at the end of the same week. For the purposes of demonstrating the scheduling activity of OPT, let us also assume that sufficient raw materials are available to meet this demand. Our problem is then one of scheduling the three resources. Neglecting set-up times for the moment, the total process times required at each resource to deliver the complete order are shown in Table 15.2.

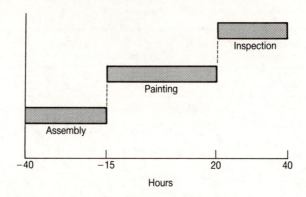

Figure 15.6 Standard MRP schedule.

If we use the standard MRP approach and, say, a batch size of 100, then in attempting to schedule this order we will produce a schedule as in Figure 15.6 which shows that we should have started this order one week ago if we are to meet the order deadline!

To meet this order using an MRP approach means *rushing* the order through the three work centers and, perhaps, interfering with other outstanding orders that are on schedule. This method of hurrying orders through the shop floor is termed *expediting* and is common in many companies. We have assumed a batch size of 100 in the above example, but there would still be a need for expediting even if the recommended batch size of 20, as used in the MRP example, were used.

If, instead, we use the OPT approach, then by backward scheduling from the order due date (see the description of the *SERVE* module above) and keeping in mind the difference between the transfer batch and the process batch, we produce the schedule given in Figure 15.7.

The important points to note about the schedule shown in Figure 15.7 are:

- The build-up of work in progress. The assembly work center produces material which will queue before the painting work center since the painting work center is the bottleneck. Similarly, the output of the painting work center initially builds up at the input to the inspection work center.

- The scheduling of this order has assumed a transfer batch of one unit which may not be realistic for many industrial situations. For example, the transfer batch in the heat treatment of parts will generally be the capacity of the oven – or the pallet that is placed in the oven – since it may not be feasible to operate the oven for single parts. Conversely, on an assembly line, the transfer batch will rarely be greater than one.

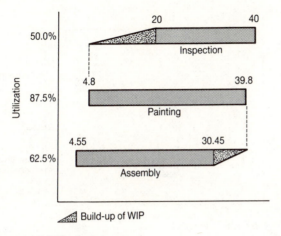

Figure 15.7   Initial OPT schedule.

The main objective of producing the above schedule is to identify the bottlenecks, and the utilization figures of each work center show that the painting resource is the bottleneck. Once the bottleneck resource has been identified, all operations after and including the bottleneck operation are combined to give the *critical network*. All operations preceding the bottleneck are termed *non-critical*. In this instance, therefore, the critical network consists of the painting and inspection work centers. The assembly work center is the non-critical network.

The critical network is now forward scheduled and the rules of Chapter 14 are incorporated into this process. These rules deal with utilization of resources, process batches and transfer batches. The non-critical network is backward scheduled in order to ensure that the bottleneck resource is not starved of material and is kept busy at all times. This results in the schedule depicted in Figure 15.8.

The dashed lines indicate that OPT schedules the inspection and assembly work centers so that they do not cause a major build-up of work in progress. Each non-bottleneck work center is scheduled to be inactive for certain amounts of time.

The next step in the OPT system is to examine the non-critical section of the network to determine if any other bottlenecks have been created by the schedule generated for the critical section. Clearly, the utilization of the assembly work center has not changed so the schedule, as given above, seems final. It should be stressed again that this example does not present the complexity that would appear in a true OPT installation.

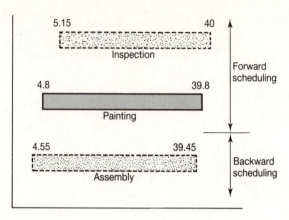

Figure 15.8 Final OPT schedule.

Table 15.3 Operation data to process Stool A.

Process requirements for Stool A			
Number of operations 3	(All times in hours)		
Operation number	*10*	*20*	*30*
Description	Assemble legs to stool	Paint stool	Inspect stool
Set-up time	0.5	0.75	0.5
Processing time	0.39	0.35	0.2
Operator time	0.39	0.35	0.2
Transport time	1.00	1.00	1.00
Work center	Assembly	Painting	Inspect
Next operation	20	30	Stock room

15.3.2 An order for two products

To illustrate how the level of complexity increases, we will consider a situation where there are orders for both types of stool. Before we do this, we shall briefly examine how an order for 100 units of Stool A would be scheduled using OPT. Table 15.3 contains the processing information for Stool A, and the major difference is that the assembly of four legs to the stool rather than three as in Stool B, takes longer. Our initial backward schedule is shown in Figure 15.9.

The points made above with respect to WIP and transfer batches also apply to this schedule. It is clear that the assembly work center is the bottleneck, so that all three operations are included in the critical network. This critical network is forward scheduled to produce the schedule in Figure

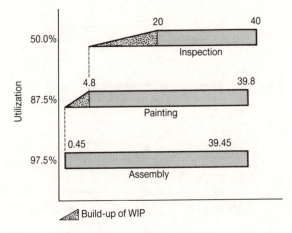

Figure 15.9 Initial OPT schedule for Stool A.

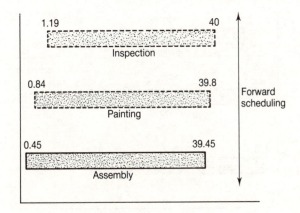

Figure 15.10 Final OPT schedule for Stool A.

15.10. The dashed lines again represent slack time, which results from the non-bottleneck work centers being scheduled in order to reduce WIP.

Returning to the situation of orders existing for both stools, let us assume that the order calls for 50 of Stool A and 50 of Stool B. Furthermore, we will assume that the order for Stool B takes priority over the order for Stool A, so that all B type stools must be produced on a work center before type A stools can be started. Backward scheduling gives a schedule as illustrated in Figure 15.11.

From this we can see that the painting operation is again the bottle-neck and causes the build-up of WIP. We therefore include the painting and inspection work centers in the critical network and forward schedule to produce a schedule as shown in Figure 15.12.

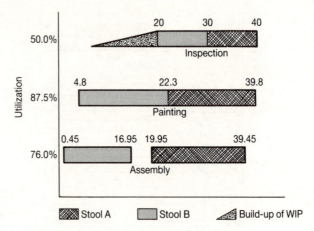

Figure 15.11 Initial two-product OPT schedule.

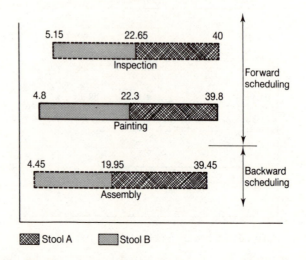

Figure 15.12 Final two-product OPT schedule.

By examining the non-critical section, we see that we may have a bottleneck in the latter half of the week but, since there is enough raw material in stock, there is no need to reschedule.

Some observations about the above example will give an indication of the complexity of such an approach. We have assumed that all of Stool B should be produced before we start on Stool A. This is not a realistic assumption since, in many cases, a small batch of B may be followed by a small batch of A, resulting in many batches overall. This *mixed model* type production might work if the set-up times involved in changing from three-legged stools to four-legged stools, and vice versa, are relatively

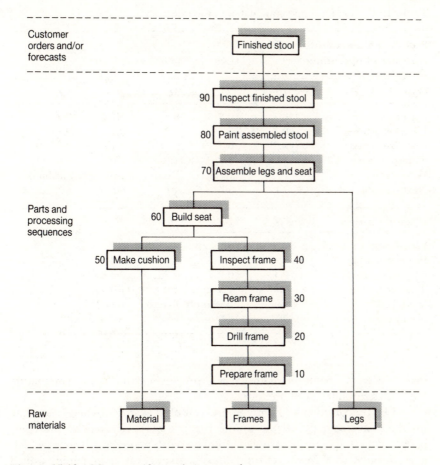

Figure 15.13 More specific product network.

short. Here again, we have assumed a transfer batch size of one as above. This batch size could be variable, i.e. one in the case of Stool A (the more difficult stool to produce) but maybe two or more in the case of Stool B. This is in direct contrast to the MRP approach where lot sizes for MRP are generally equivalent to the order quantity. OPT clearly works on the basis of variable process and transfer batch sizes.

15.3.3 A further increase in complexity

The above example involves just two very simple products and three work centers. Each product follows the same sequence through the work centers and has similar processing times (apart from the assembly operation), and each of the work centers is only visited once by a product. Therefore, it is clear that this example is trivial. A more realistic example would involve

Table 15.4 Complete operation data to process Stool A.

Process requirements for Stool A

Number of operations   9   (All times in hours)

Operation number	10	20	30	40	50
Set-up time	0.5	0.3	0.4	N/A	0.5
Processing time	0.2	0.3	0.2	0.1	0.3
Operator time	0.2	0.3	0.2	0.1	0.3
Transport time	1.0	1.0	1.0	1.0	1.0
Work center	Prep.	Drill	Ream	Insp1	Cushion
Next operation	20	30	40	50	60

Operation number	60	70	80	90
Set-up time	0.5	0.5	0.75	0.5
Processing time	0.1	0.2	0.35	0.2
Operator time	0.1	0.2	0.35	0.2
Transport time	1.0	1.0	1.0	1.0
Work center	Build	Assembly	Painting	Insp2
Next operation	70	80	90	Stock room

many different operations with varying processing times and manufacturing routes through the shop floor.

Let us consider a slightly more complex example where the seats for the stools sold by Gizmo-Stools Inc. are manufactured by the company. The seats are assembled from a cushion and a frame which goes through four manufacturing process stages – it is prepared, drilled with three or four holes, reamed, and inspected. The product network for this seat manufacturing process is shown in Figure 15.13 and the complete processing information for both types of stool is given in Tables 15.4 and 15.5.

Figure 15.14 represents the initial backward schedule designed to determine the bottleneck resources. As can be seen, three bottlenecks have been found. The unbroken lines represent the operations that are bottlenecks, whereas the broken lines are the non-bottlenecks, which should be scheduled to ensure that the bottlenecks are never starved of material. Now we will determine the process and transfer batch sizes for non-bottleneck and bottleneck resources. The process batch size will be as large as possible for a bottleneck and its transfer batch as small as possible.

This example is only for one product and it can be seen how complex the scheduling problem has become – it is both difficult and pointless to attempt to develop the complete schedule. The need for software support to develop the full schedule is clear.

Table 15.5   Complete operation data to process Stool B.

Process requirements for Stool B
Number of operations   9   (All times in hours)

Operation number	10	20	30	40	50
Set-up time	0.5	0.3	0.4	N/A	0.5
Processing time	0.2	0.3	0.15	0.08	0.4
Operator time	0.2	0.3	0.15	0.08	0.4
Transport time	1.0	1.0	1.0	1.0	1.0
Work center	Prep.	Drill	Ream	Inspl	Cushion
Next operation	20	30	40	50	60

Operation number	60	70	80	90	
Set-up time	0.5	0.5	0.75	0.5	
Processing time	0.15	0.25	0.35	0.2	
Operator time	0.15	0.25	0.35	0.2	
Transport time	1.0	1.0	1.0	1.0	
Work center	Build	Assembly	Painting	Insp2	
Next operation	70	80	90	Stock room	

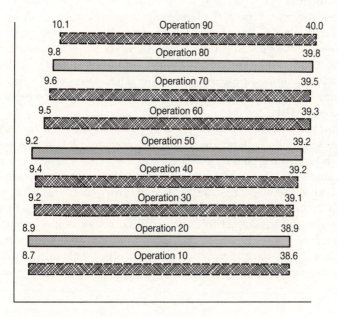

Figure 15.14   Initial schedule for the nine operations.

The above examples have shown our understanding of how the OPT software system might operate. The developers of the OPT product stress that the system will fail if the schedules it produces are not strictly followed. This is extremely important in OPT, where safety stocks or other such buffers are not tolerated.

15.4 Requirements and assumptions of OPT

Clearly OPT requires a vast amount of data to develop the product network and the manufacturing model. Not only does OPT need to know how the product is made and through what processing route it passes, it also needs to have access to accurate set-up and run times for each individual manufacturing operation, maximum stock limits, minimum batch sizes, auxiliary machines, scheduled delays, etc. The user "must already have a prodigious amount of precise data timing each step in the manufacturing process" (Bylinsky 1983). However, many companies have already assembled such data for materials requirements planning systems. Existing data structures, such as bill of materials, routings, inventories, and work center data are normally used by the OPT system.

When OPT was initially proposed, there seemed to be some suggestion that its data requirements were less rigorous than those of MRP type systems. The thinking was that one only needed accurate data on the critical or bottleneck resources and the products which visit those resources. This is not the case. Firstly, the bottleneck resources may vary from time to time as the product mix in the shop load varies. Thus one can never be sure what resource will become critical for however short a time. Secondly, given that OPT produces detailed shop schedules, it is vital that the data – particularly the process times on which this schedule is based – be accurate. If anything, in our view, the data requirements of OPT are more stringent than those of MRP.

An important aspect of the OPT approach is the need for shop floor supervisors and others (who are required to execute the schedule generated by the OPT software) to have confidence in the schedule presented to them by the computer. This confidence is clearly necessary since the schedule is expected to be followed rigorously. In our experience, this is an unusual approach to scheduling manufacturing operations and one which is at variance with the traditional freedom – indeed responsibility – of the shop floor supervisor to organize work within the area for which he/she is responsible. There have been reports of difficulties with some applications of OPT. Perhaps part of the difficulty stems from this aspect of the OPT approach.

15.5 Some views on OPT

OPT can be considered from a number of points of view. When OPT became available initially it was presented as a competitor for MRP (and MRP II) and JIT. In recent years there seems to be less emphasis on MRP versus OPT. Writers, both academic and practitioner alike, seem to be moving towards the view that the two are not incompatible.

It should also be said that when OPT was first made available, it attracted considerable criticism – and, indeed, continues to be criticized – because of the claim, implicit in its name, that it offers an optimal schedule and because of the fact that the scheduling algorithm on which it is based has never been revealed in the literature.

Lundrigan (1986) suggests that OPT brings together the best of JIT and MRP II into a "kind of westernized just in time." We agree that there is some truth in this statement, to the extent that OPT shares similar insights with JIT at the operational level, e.g. the use of small batches, the identification of transport and process batches, etc. However, OPT concerns itself with scheduling to the virtual exclusion of all else. JIT, as seen in Chapters 11 and 12, is concerned with establishing a manufacturing – indeed, a business – environment where shop floor control and, consequently, scheduling problems are minimized. We believe that JIT is much wider in scope than OPT, which concerns itself primarily with the generation of accurate shop floor schedules.

Swann (1986) argued that a company

> "may, in fact, need both tools: MRP for net requirements and OPT for realistic shop schedules. Using OPT as a scheduling tool in, for instance, a job shop, does not preclude the need for accurate bills of material and disciplined inventory planning and control. MRP is the appropriate tool to provide bill of material and inventory management features."

Vollmann (1986), coming from an academic background, offered a similar perspective and saw OPT as "an enhancement to MRP II." Vollmann argues that MRP II divides into three sections, "the front end results in the master production schedule, the engine includes *little* MRP and capacity requirements planning and the back end completes the process – out to the shop floor and vendor follow up." According to Vollmann, OPT can be used to evaluate an MPS from a capacity point of view, in order to determine its feasibility and OPT also outputs a "detailed shop schedule that concentrates on the most important resources in the factory."

We tend to agree with the points made by Vollmann, and that OPT is best considered as an enhancement to MRP II. After all, MRP II and OPT are similar in many respects. Each requires a large and complex production database. OPT requires that the process and product (i.e. bill of material) data be brought together to create the so-called product network, described earlier in this chapter. Much of basic data to achieve this is available from existing MRP II systems. The insights offered by OPT, if not the software itself, are today usefully applied in the shop floor or production activity control system.

15.6 Conclusion

This chapter has attempted to describe the production management system, OPT. Basically, OPT can be considered from two points of view – the OPT approach to manufacturing planning and control and the OPT software product.

The OPT approach to manufacturing planning and control is most often articulated in terms of 10 relatively simple rules, as outlined in Chapter 14. Many of these rules represent an implicit criticism of traditional scheduling practice and of the metrics used to measure the performance of a manufacturing system. There is no doubt that the criticism of certain aspects of traditional manufacturing practice by the developers of OPT has, over time, proved to be valid – in particular, how cost accounting metrics can lead to system inefficiencies while *increasing* individual machine utilization levels. The insights concerning the relative importance of bottleneck and non-bottleneck resources, the use of separate process and transportation batches, etc., are very valuable to anyone concerned with the scheduling of work through a manufacturing system. These insights are offered in the form of OPT rules designed to reduce inventories and operating cost while simultaneously increasing the throughput of the manufacturing plant.

The OPT rules can, of course, be implemented without recourse to the second element of OPT described in Chapter 15, namely, the software package designed to produce realistic schedules. An important point about this software system is the requirement that the schedule it generates be followed exactly. This approach may cause difficulties in manufacturing systems where, traditionally, the shop floor supervisors considered a certain level of discretion with their operations schedules to be important.

Our understanding of OPT leads to the belief that it is best considered as an enhancement to the MRP II paradigm of production management systems.

References to Part IV

Anonymous. 1984. "Competitive analysis," *Automated Manufacturing Report*, (9) Frost and Sullivan.

Bylinsky, G. 1983. "An Israeli shakes up US factories," *Fortune*, September 5th, 120–132.

Fox, R.E. 1982a. "OPT: An answer for America. Part II," *Inventories and Production Magazine*, **2**(6).

Fox, R.E. 1982b. "MRP, kanban or OPT: What's best?" *Inventories and Production Magazine*, July–August.

Goldratt, E. 1980. "Optimized production timetables: a revolutionary program for industry," in *APICS 23rd Annual International Conference Proceedings*, 172–176.

Jacobs, F.R. 1983. "The OPT scheduling system: a review of a new production scheduling system," *Production and Inventory Management*, **24**(3), 47–51.

Jacobs, F.R. 1984. "OPT uncovered: many production planning and scheduling concepts can be applied with or without the software," *Industrial Engineering*, **16**(10).

Lundrigan, R. 1986. "What is this thing called OPT?", *Production and Inventory Management*, **27**(2), 2–12.

Swann, D. 1986. "Using MRP for optimized schedules (emulating OPT)," *Production and Inventory Management*, **27**(2), 30–37.

Vollmann, T.E. 1986. "OPT as an enhancement to MRP II," *Production and Inventory Management*, **27**(2), 38–46.

PART V

PMS: a view of the future

Overview

In Part I of this book the context within which production management systems must operate was defined. The emergence of computer integrated manufacture and the extended enterprise were looked at together with the competitive pressures which push manufacturing firms to adopt integrated solutions. The key role of production management systems within integrated manufacturing was pointed out and it was argued that PMS is at the very heart of an integrated manufacturing system.

In Parts II, III, and IV three approaches to production management systems were considered. The essential assumptions behind the three approaches were explored and their main features presented with a critique of each being offered. As was seen, MRP, JIT, and OPT are not competing technologies. Each is different in terms of its scope, i.e. the range of problems it seeks to address, the types of manufacturing systems in which it has been applied, and in terms of its ability to fit into an emerging *integration* environment.

In Part V, the main weaknesses of each approach will be discussed, and the important insights which each offers will be identified. Although projecting the future is a dubious art, we shall proceed to develop an outline sketch of the attributes of an architecture for future hybrid production management systems. This, we believe, represents the most likely state toward which current systems will evolve.

In Chapter 17 we present a detailed overview of our perspective on the likely functionality in future production management systems. Our perspective is based on an overall PMS architecture which sees the manufacturing plant as a series of reasonably autonomous group technology (GT) based manufacturing cells controlled by a sophisticated shop floor control system. We view the shop floor control system as a combination of two subsystems, namely a production activity control (PAC) system which manages the flow of work through the individual GT based cells and a factory coordination (FC) system which coordinates the cells and manages the flow of work between them. We believe that the requirements planning module will translate the master production schedule (MPS) into detailed requirements for the FC system. We place great emphasis on the MPS, including its integration with customer order entry through the use of available to promise (ATP) and projected available balance (PAB) logic in the so called planning tableau.

Further, with a view to operating the existing levels of production management technology as effectively as possible, a series of key insights will be offered, which we believe our study of JIT, MRP, and OPT has uncovered.

CHAPTER SIXTEEN

MRP, JIT, and OPT compared

16.1 Introduction
16.2 The scope of MRP, OPT, and JIT
16.3 MRP, OPT, and JIT – application areas
16.4 MRP, OPT, and JIT in the new manufacturing environment
16.5 Core theories and key failings
16.6 PMS implementation issues
16.7 Conclusion
Questions

16.1 Introduction

This chapter aims to communicate an understanding of how ideas from the alternate production management paradigms – MRP, JIT, and OPT – can fit together. This problem is approached, not by attempting to force fit three competing approaches, but rather by searching out the fundamental weaknesses and strengths of each approach and then proposing a hybrid solution which addresses the requirements of PMS within an integrated manufacturing system.

The discussion begins with a review of the scope and application areas of these technologies in the context of the new manufacturing environment and considers the difficulties of designing and implementing PMS. Next, the core theories and key failings of the three paradigms are examined, focusing on the essence of the approaches, as opposed to application issues.

In Chapter 17, an attempt is made to take a very broad perspective on production management in an integrated manufacturing environment and to position the available PMS solutions against this perspective.

16.2 The scope of MRP, OPT, and JIT

We will now try to establish a framework for articulating the scope of MRP, OPT, and JIT. We do this by taking a simplified view of a manufacturing facility and neglecting, for a moment, considerations such as labor (both direct and indirect), finance, etc. We will consider the manufacturing facility as a process which produces a product from raw materials as illustrated in Figure 16.1. This allows us to view the manufacturing facility from two perspectives – from the processing viewpoint or, alternately, from the product viewpoint. We can then examine how each of the three

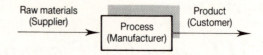

Figure 16.1   Simplified view of a manufacturing facility.

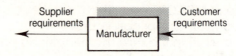

Figure 16.2   Simplified view of information flow.

major production management systems sees the manufacturing facility from these two points of view.

If we enrich Figure 16.1 and include some of the information that passes between the three main actors – the customer who requires the finished product, the manufacturer who produces it, and the vendor who supplies the manufacturer with the raw materials – we arrive at Figure 16.2.

From a management point of view it can be seen that it is mainly requirements that are passed between the actors. The MRP approach is concerned with the logistics of the manufacturing process. It takes the customer requirements for products and breaks these into time-phased requirements for subassemblies, components, and raw materials. It also seeks to schedule activities within the manufacturing process and the availability of material from vendors to produce the product on time for the customer. It can be said that MRP is really concerned with the logistics of *when*.

JIT takes a somewhat larger view and is concerned with *what* the product is, *how* the product is manufactured, and the logistics of delivering it on time to the customer. JIT seeks to develop enduring relationships with vendors and, in so far as is possible, to *influence* the vendors' manufacturing processes, in order to achieve JIT delivery of raw materials and purchased items.

OPT, in essence, is a scheduling tool and, like MRP, is mainly concerned with the logistics of *when*. However, like JIT, it takes a more granular look at the production process and produces more detailed schedules for the shop floor. OPT also seeks to influence, to a limited extent, *how* the product is manufactured, through modified process and transfer batches, emphasis on bottleneck resources, etc.

In terms of the scope of the three approaches, therefore, it may be argued that MRP and OPT are primarily concerned with *when*, whereas JIT seeks to influence the *what*, the *how*, and the *when* of manufacturing.

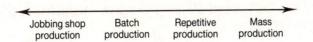

Jobbing shop
production   Batch
production   Repetitive
production   Mass
production

Figure 16.3   Continuum of manufacturing systems.

16.3 MRP, OPT, and JIT – application areas

Throughout this book, manufacturing systems have been considered to fall into three broad categories, namely, jobbing shops, batch production shops, and mass production systems. In the discussion of JIT in Part IV, this classification was widened to include repetitive manufacturing systems. We also made a distinction between customer driven systems and stock driven systems. We argued that Assemble To Order (ATO), Make To Order (MTO), and Engineer To Order (ETO) are customer driven systems.

In terms of the application of the various techniques, it is clear that people tend to associate JIT with mass production and repetitive manufacturing systems. JIT did, after all, originate in the final assembly plants of the major Japanese automotive manufacturing companies. In a similar vein, one might argue that MRP – and indeed OPT – thinking can be associated with batch production systems, given the fact that both systems tend to be concerned with a relatively large number of products, associated numbers of Bills of Materials (BOMs) and demand which is, at best, a combination of actual orders and forecasts and, at worst, a forecast. Also, it is clear from our discussions of the origins of MRP that MRP arose in Make To Stock (MTS) environments, while JIT was initially applied to ATO environments.

Given the clear distinction between JIT philosophy, JIT techniques for manufacturing process design and planning, and the Kanban system, we would like to repeat the following observation. Kanban is essentially a Production Activity Control (PAC) system which functions best in a mass production or repetitive manufacturing environment. However, the JIT philosophy and, indeed, JIT manufacturing and planning techniques, are applicable to all types of discrete parts manufacturing. Indeed, the greater the degree to which the JIT philosophy is applied and JIT manufacturing and planning techniques are used in a particular manufacturing system, the more that manufacturing system is edged along the continuum illustrated in Figure 16.3 toward becoming a simplified and, in the extreme case, a repetitive manufacturing system. We are thinking here particularly of the matching of market requirements with a well thought out product set, the ideas of modular product design, the use of JIT manufacturing planning techniques, and all of the other elements of JIT thinking discussed in Chapters 11 and 12.

16.4 MRP, OPT, and JIT in the new manufacturing environment

In Chapter 1 it was argued that modern manufacturing is faced with great challenges, particularly in terms of rapid changes in customer requirements and demands, shorter product design and life cycles, and shorter lead times for deliveries to customers.

Yamashina *et al.* (1987) argue that the JIT approach is necessary in the context of increased product variety and the need to respond rapidly to customer requirements. The argument is that in the conventional approach, the manufacturing system – by installing a buffer of finished product between itself and the market – can pursue economies of scale and not be unduly influenced by changes in the marketplace in the short term. However, since product diversity increases and customer requirements change frequently, it becomes increasingly difficult to forecast which products will be sold. Moreover, operating a *buffering* policy runs the risk of having an excess of products whose demand is falling and a shortage of products that are in high demand. Figure 16.4, based on Yamashina's original presentation, illustrates the argument.

The same argument can be made for component suppliers. The manufacturer of the finished product will not want to keep large buffer stocks of raw materials and purchased parts, for reasons of economy as well as possible obsolescence, and will tend, therefore, to put pressure on suppliers to deliver in a JIT manner. The MRP or OPT approaches, on the other hand, provide for little interaction of this type between the customer and the manufacturer.

16.5 Core theories and key failings

This section explores the core theories of the various production management paradigms – MRP/MRP II, JIT, and OPT – and highlights their key failings. By its nature, this exploration involves an attempt to summarize the important elements of the three paradigms and thus follows on from the conclusions at the end of Parts II, III, and IV of this book.

16.5.1 Requirements planning (MRP/MRP II)

The MRP/MRP II paradigm highlighted the fallacy of applying inventory control techniques to dependent demand items. Most of manufacturing activity is concerned with producing assemblies, and a bill of materials is thus a means of exploding demand from a finished product down to the components that make up the product. MRP II also showed that hierarchical planning, with multiple levels of representational detail of the manufacturing process (i.e. MPS, MRP, PAC), is a highly effective means of coping with the complexity and variety of manufacturing systems.

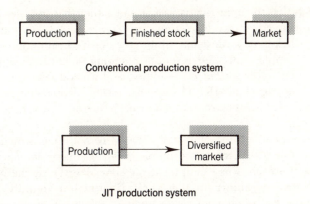

Figure 16.4 Production systems and their markets.

Another important lesson from the MRP approach is that through a computer and a manufacturing database, the work of people in many different manufacturing functions can be better coordinated, and volumes of common information can be shared. Moreover, a computer facilitates manufacturing planning to a level of detail that was never realizable before.

The MRP paradigm also stresses the role of the planner. Education must be provided to the planner. Responsibility for scheduling decisions must stay with the planner. CRP, RCCP, and bottom-up replanning were designed as tools to keep the planners in charge of the planning process.

MRP/MRP II has to be seen as a reasonably successful venture, but there are qualifications to that success. The most significant, in our view, is the fact that MRP did not attempt to address the design of the manufacturing process. This might not be seen to be such a major omission, but the lack of attention to the design of the manufacturing process itself leads to a situation where activities take place unnoticed (which are counterproductive to good manufacturing practice and hence to manufacturing system performance). For example, the BOM concept tended to encourage the development of many process stages, each with buffers separating them from the next stage. Now, there is nothing in MRP technology that requires this to be the case – it is just that MRP structures seem to guide users in this direction. In more recent times, the emergence of JIT has focused attention on the importance of looking at the basics of manufacturing engineering.

MRP, particularly in the development towards MRP II, has perhaps sought sophistication but achieved complexity instead. JIT has restored the pursuit of refined simplicity to its rightful position as a most worthy activity.

The MRP approach also has other faults. The idea of leaving the capacity management to the user has never worked very well. Perhaps it is not so much that the approach is wrong, but rather that the user is not in a position to take advantage of it. Capacity requirements planning, in many cases, overwhelms us with detail. Only now are we beginning to learn the benefits of simple aggregate resource planning (i.e. rough cut capacity planning), tools with a *what if* capability, and a good user interface. The master planning level of MRP II was never really adequate on this account. Even today, there is much more to be incorporated in terms of master planning support.

Perhaps another of the faults of MRP II is that it has grown too large. It has tried to address too many problems in too many domains with the same basic approach. For example, at the shop floor level, the production activity control capability in the MRP II system is rapidly becoming redundant because of advances in technology. Manufacturing research and development has focused, to a great extent, on sophisticated control and integration systems for the shop floor. The shop floor control module of MRP II is not a viable alternative for complex manufacturing environments. The BOM concept may have had too much influence on the design of shop floor routings, and the price is the lack of clarity in representing manufacturing process routings. Manufacturing activities form networks, not hierarchies. Moreover, batches or lots do need to be split.

There are other faults that can be laid at MRP's door. Some of these can be disclaimed. For example, although it is a fact that lead times cannot be predicted, this does not necessarily imply that average lead times cannot be used for planning purposes. In a sense, the use of planning lead times reflects the hierarchical nature of planning in MRP II. Actual lead times are a different matter. As long as the planning lead time is consistent with the average actual lead time, then the planning system will work reasonably well. This consistency can be maintained through the application of the rough cut capacity *what if* analysis (RCCP). The mistake, perhaps, is to try to drive operational control or production activity control with planned lead times.

The MRP approach to lot sizing is frequently criticized. In fairness, it seems that the MRP community always favored simplicity in lot sizing or, indeed, no real lot sizing, by matching planned orders exactly with net requirements.

16.5.2 Just in time (JIT)

As stated earlier, JIT focused attention on the pursuit of manufacturing engineering excellence. Its essence is to challenge us continuously to achieve excellence, by posing ideals such as zero set-up, zero defects, zero inventories, and zero lead time. JIT educated us to the fact that slack in a manufacturing system is bad because it allows mediocre behavior and performance to pass undetected. JIT offers a philosophy of long term commitment to incremental process refinement. In many ways, the continuing interest in Kanban as a production control technique is difficult to explain. Kanban is only a very small manifestation of what is a much deeper agenda.

JIT clearly showed us the dominance of engineering the manufacturing process, over planning production. What JIT does is attempt to convert into one large system the collection of operators, equipment, raw material, etc. that make up a manufacturing organization – with the result that the activities of all the subsystems are synchronized. With a well-designed system, control becomes a less difficult problem. In repetitive manufacturing environments, control can ultimately be exercised with a manual Kanban system.

JIT also teaches us about the value of mixing products on the same manufacturing line, without using batches. JIT locates responsibility and ownership for the manufacturing process squarely where it belongs, i.e. with the manufacturing operator. JIT also teaches us the benefits of developing flexible resources. It also shows the value of product focus and of grouping into product families to facilitate flow based production systems.

JIT, too, has its failings, though they are not as apparent perhaps as those of MRP II. There is a limit to the extent that JIT can be usefully pursued in many industries. The major JIT successes were in repetitive manufacturing situations. If the manufacturing system is discontinuous, in that demand is impossible to predict accurately and product variety cannot be easily constrained, then developing a JIT solution will be all but impossible. Moreover, it is not possible for all manufacturers to attain a position wherein their suppliers are both local and captive, since this phenomenon is very much a feature of the structure and state of Japanese industry.

16.5.3 Optimized production technology (OPT)

OPT teaches us that finite scheduling is a practical technology for scheduling manufacturing systems. It also illuminates the potential of recognizing bottlenecks, and of discriminating between bottlenecks and non-bottlenecks in attempts to manage the operations of, and the flow of materials through, the shop floor. OPT has also presented us with some very useful insights into the cost implications of scheduling decisions on the shop floor.

OPT is a proprietary technology. This, combined with the relative absence of documented case studies, naturally gives rise to some suspicion. When a technology is perceived to succeed, its success may, in fact, be due to factors other than the core technology itself, for example, the consultancy work that is tied to an OPT installation. Nevertheless, this latter criticism could be applied to MRP II. However, MRP is an open book. OPT, on the other hand – in spite of our efforts – is, to a large extent, an untold story.

One other apparent weakness of the OPT paradigm stems from the fact that it does not provide as strong a sense of hierarchical planning as, say, the MRP II paradigm. OPT also seems to emphasize a technical solution to what is really a very complex organizational, as well as technical, problem.

16.6 PMS implementation issues

There can be no illusions about the difficulty of designing and installing sophisticated manufacturing systems and, although the need for integrated manufacturing systems is accepted, there have been few such systems installed in practice.

White (1987) is of the view that "there appear to be many reasons for failing to design and implement integrated systems." White argues that the design and implementation of such systems requires a holistic approach, and that integration cannot be achieved by a design process which is essentially Taylorist in nature. In this context, there are some lessons to be learned from the experiences of those who successfully implemented JIT.

A large part of the success of the JIT approach is that it involves all of those concerned in the solution to problems. For example, in the discussion on total quality control in Chapter 12, the scientific or Taylorist approach was contrasted with the JIT approach. The JIT environment was discussed in terms of multiskilled operators, trained to carry out various tasks, and reference was made to the *mutual relief* system and the role of operators and supervisors in controlling their own environment. Clearly JIT is people centered.

In Part II we quoted St. John (1984) who regretted the fact that so much effort was devoted to the lot sizing *problem*. We believe that the emphasis on *solving* this problem is clear evidence of a *technical* and reductionist approach to production management systems.

It could also be argued that OPT is in the Taylorist tradition. OPT claims to generate an optimum schedule through its proprietary algorithm and requires that the schedule be followed in every detail. Supervisors must not, in any way, interfere with it. There is no *participation* or *learning* in this approach.

There is a framework which allows us to distinguish between the traditional Taylorist approach and the approach that JIT embodies. Gault (1984) articulated this distinction when discussing the nature of Operations Research (OR) and distinguished clearly between **technical OR** and **socio-technical OR**.

JIT represents, in some sense, a *socio-technical* approach to PMS and, indeed, manufacturing systems design and operation in general. The JIT approach to quality involves continuous improvement towards *zero defects*, with small groups actively seeking constant improvements on a broad range of issues, using the available know-how within the group. The emphasis on training and retraining of operators, on continuous improvement of the manufacturing process and on learning from past mistakes and failures to ensure that mistakes are not repeated, is further evidence of the approach.

The relative failure of many PMS installations can be explained, at least partially, in terms of the lack of a true socio-technical approach to the design and installation of these systems. Furthermore, many of the reasons normally advanced for disappointing results from PMS are evidence of an overemphasis on the technical aspects of PMS and a failure to give due regard to the social subsystem within which the technical subsystem has to function.

The socio-technical design approach argues that the autonomy of individuals, work groups, their work roles, and the social structure within which they find themselves, are components of the organization design and structure which should be addressed while the technical subsystems are under development. This approach argues that the design of the social and technical subsystems must be such as to achieve a *best fit* between the two.

We argue strongly that the design and installation of a PMS system is not a purely technical problem. We completely agree with Latham (1981) when he appeals to production and inventory management professionals to learn "additional skills, skills in dealing with the human aspects of systems." In today's manufacturing environment with a relatively small, highly trained work force, the need for this socio-technical approach is even more critical. PMS practitioners can learn much from the proponents of socio-technical design and the interested reader is referred to Cherns (1977), who lists the essential principles of socio-technical design, Trist (1982), who gives an overview and historical background to the background of the approach, and Pava (1983), who discusses the application of this approach to office system design.

16.7 Conclusion

Over time, there is no doubt that a complete PMS architecture will evolve and, indeed, we offer an outline sketch of such an architecture in Chapter 17. In the meantime we believe there are rich insights – fundamental to good production management practice – to be gleaned from a study of the JIT, OPT, MRP, and MRP II approaches to production management. We have tried to emphasize these insights throughout this book and we list them here for completeness (Shivnan *et al.* 1987).

- In designing PMS systems, it is important to adopt a design methodology which gives due consideration to the social as well as the technical subsystems of PMS.

- Product design, manufacturing system design, and layout are important in the creation of an environment which will facilitate sound production and inventory management. As Burbidge (1985) points out ". . . complex production control systems do not, and probably never can, work effectively." With intelligent product design for manufacture and assembly, it is possible, in many cases, to move in the direction of relatively simple flow based manufacturing systems. In many ways, the complexity of the production control system is dictated by the product and manufacturing system design.

- *Flow based* production systems will help shorten the production lead time and reduce inventories. Flow based manufacturing layouts are important in an era of greatly reduced product life cycles and customer expectations of rapid response to his/her demands.

- Systems designers should try to move toward decentralized planning and control which will allow greater flexibility and adaptability to changes. Ultimately, the factory should be a group of flexible manufacturing and flexible assembly cells, where each cell has been designed using group technology thinking to deal with a family of *products*. The term *product* is used rather loosely here to imply a group of identifiable assemblies or subassemblies of components. In so far as possible, production planning and, in particular, production control decisions should be passed down to the level which has access to pertinent data and knowledge.

- Production controllers should concentrate on balancing the flow of products through the plant, rather than attempting to balance plant capacity. This leads to flow based production.

- Lead times and schedules are intimately related. Lead times are a consequence of a particular schedule and cannot be used *a priori* to generate accurate operation schedules. MRP, and its use of planned lead times, is appropriate as a tactical planning procedure.

- If effort is expended on the planning procedure, then the production activity control task will consequently be easier. By the planning procedure, we mean the full gamut of manufacturing system design and planning.

- Set-up times should be reduced as much as possible and the belief that the given set-up time is immutable and a *constant* should be discarded.

- There are many types of batches or lots. In particular, there are production lots and transfer lots. In situations where large production lots are necessary, because of limitations of the manufacturing process, the use of smaller transfer batches which facilitate flow production should be considered.

- Inventories should be reduced as far as possible, and all safety and buffer stocks, which only serve to disguise problems, should be gradually reduced.

- The implementation of the above thinking requires enthusiastic support and commitment from all levels in the organization.

- Although the Kanban system is really only applicable to repetitive manufacturing situations, the JIT philosophy and manufacturing system design techniques can be applied very widely.

Questions

(16.1) "It may be argued that MRP and OPT are primarily concerned with *when*, whereas JIT seeks to influence the *what*, the *how*, and the *when* of manufacturing." Discuss.

(16.2) "Kanban is essentially a production activity control system, which functions best in a mass production or repetitive manufacturing environment. However, the JIT philosophy, and, indeed JIT, manufacturing and planning techniques, are applicable to all types of discrete parts manufacturing." Discuss.

(16.3) "There is a limit to the extent that JIT can be usefully pursued in some industries." Explain.

(16.4) "OPT is a technical solution to a socio-technical problem," Do you agree?

(16.5) "In the structure of a proposed hybrid production management system, we distinguish clearly between the strategic, tactical, and operational issues; also between the 'push' or make to stock elements and the 'pull' or customer driven elements." Discuss.

(16.6) "MRP assumes infinite capacity." Explain.

(16.7) "We consider that MRP II has sought to achieve an integrated solution without working through the strategic issues which reside above MRP and the operational issues which reside below MRP." Comment.

CHAPTER SEVENTEEN

PMS – an integration approach

17.1 Introduction

Factories today are not uniform, and there may, even within the four walls of one factory, exist the desire to adopt different production management approaches, working in coordination. We will attempt to sketch, in loose terms, the attributes of what might be called a hybrid architecture, which accommodates the needs of future manufacturing systems and also takes into account the **extended enterprise** perspective outlined earlier in Chapter 4.

We believe that MRP II will no longer exist in the form that we know it today. Nor, indeed, will OPT. There will be a manufacturing information system that will provide database support to manufacturing decision making. Scheduling routines, including infinite scheduling with decision support, and heuristic finite scheduling algorithms will be available as policy parameters within the system, to be set by the user as he/she sees fit. Because many suppliers will neither be local nor captive, MRP style batch scheduling has a clear role to play in acquiring purchased parts. A number of key suppliers will be connected to the manufacturing process by Kanban style control procedures and EDI technology.

On the manufacturing side, as we have seen, MRP will operate in non-predictable, human intensive manufacturing processes, whereas finite scheduling algorithms will be used in more predictable, machine intensive parts of the process. If sufficient refinement is achieved, then Kanban will be used for certain parts of the process.

Sitting on top of all this will be a hierarchical master planning module. This module is unlikely to use an optimizing procedure, but will instead be primarily a decision support tool, with a library of heuristics available, and will quite likely use knowledge based support to help the master planner approach the various tradeoffs that must be made. Integration with customer order entry systems will be an important aspect of systems as we evolve towards customer driven manufacturing. In fact, we will go a step further and argue that manufacturing planning and control systems will have to be integrated with distribution planning and control systems to support true customer driven manufacturing. On the shop floor level, Production Activity Control (PAC) will evolve more and more towards a communications and integration tool. Also, integration backwards into the value chain to work more closely with key suppliers will be important.

17.2 An architecture for PMS

We will try now to describe the architecture for such a hybrid PMS system and present this outline architecture in terms of a hierarchy of PMS modules, as illustrated in Figure 17.1. Our approach is to concentrate on a hybrid make to stock/assemble to order or make to order – or, indeed, engineer to order – environment which we believe will represent the majority of manufacturing plants in the medium term future. This hybrid approach reflects the emergence of customer order driven manufacturing, allowing the customer a degree of customization, and the attempt by manufacturers to retain some degree of stability and the advantages of economy of scale through the manufacture for stock of shared or common components and subassemblies.

Figure 17.1 represents a first version of the architecture. It reflects a situation where a factory has been decomposed in so far as possible into a series of Group Technology (GT) based production cells, where each cell is responsible for a family of its products, components or processes and is controlled by a PAC system. Another possibility is that each group is actually geographically dispersed – that is, there are a number of different focused factories. The factory coordination module ensures that the individual cells/factories interact to meet an overall production plan (see Bauer *et al.* 1991). Indeed, with the current trend towards the outsourcing of non-critical components and assemblies, individual manufacturing cells may well reside outside the plant, perhaps even in the plant of another enterprise.

Figure 17.2 illustrates a somewhat modified view of the architecture for PMS. This view is useful in understanding how hybrid – in this case, a hybrid of make to stock and assemble to order – manufacturing systems operate. As suggested in the figure, there may be a "push" subsystem to deal with make to stock items and a "pull" subsystem to deal with the customer specific items and final assembly, if appropriate, operating synchronously. The key point is that production of the customer specific element of the product can only commence when a firm customer order has been received. As indicated in Figure 17.2, the customer order entry function must be integrated with the PMS; in this case it is seen interacting with the PMS modules at two different levels.

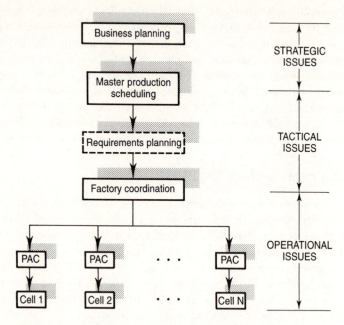

Figure 17.1   An architecture for production management systems.

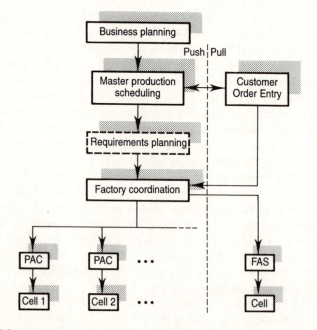

Figure 17.2   Architecture for PMS in hybrid environments.

An example of this is the case where there is demand for a semi-customized product, of which only a certain portion is standard and needs to be exploded from the MPS level downwards. (It should be noted that requirements planning in the architecture is only a calculation step, and is therefore surrounded by a dotted line in the figures.)

Figure 17.1 illustrates an outline architecture for production management systems which extends from the strategic to the operational level. These levels represent different planning horizons. The length of the time horizons depend on the production environment under consideration. The strategic planning horizon may cover one to five years, tactical planning a month to a year, and operational planning real time to one week.

The types of issues involved in each level include:

(1) **Strategic issues:** Strategic production management issues relate to:
- the determination of the products to be manufactured,
- the matching of products to markets and customers' expectations, and
- the design of the manufacturing system, to ensure short production lead times and sufficient flexibility to facilitate the production of the required variety and mix of products for the market.

(2) **Tactical issues:** Tactical issues relate to the generation of detailed plans to meet the demands imposed by the long range production plan, involving the breakdown of the products in this plan into a feasible master production schedule. This master production schedule is then further broken down into assemblies, subassemblies, and components, and a time phased plan of requirements, which is realistic in terms of capacity and material availability, is created.

(3) **Operational issues:** Operational PMS issues essentially involve taking the output from the tactical planning phase, e.g. the planned orders from an MRP system, and managing the manufacturing system in quasi real time to meet these requirements.

At the business planning stage emphasis is placed on planning in terms of aggregated product families or modules. The master production scheduling phase attempts to plan according to end items that are shipped to the customer. Even at this stage, these end items may not be the eventual product, but high level assemblies and subassemblies common to many end products, and which are configured to customer order. Requirements planning is concerned with translating the requirements for master schedule items into the corresponding time phased requirements for subassemblies, and purchased and manufactured components. Factory coordination and PAC deal mainly with controlling the operations, and the flow of work and materials associated with manufacturing the component items and assembling the finished product.

It is important to remember the business context of today's manufacturing plants. In today's manufacturing environment, the customer is coming closer to the producer of the products. Most companies are being forced to move away from making products to replenish the supply after they have been consumed by customers. Customization to consumer needs is the emerging trend. We are moving towards one-of-a-kind production (OKP) (see Wortmann 1990). This emerging trend has given rise to the merging of different techniques in the production management field. An example of this is the use of the master schedule to plan at an option level, and the application of JIT principles to create the final assembly schedule for production and, ultimately, the product for the customer. In effect, this is the situation depicted in Figure 17.2.

Each of the main building blocks in the hierarchy of Figure 17.2 will now be described in detail. We will concentrate on business planning, master production scheduling, factory coordination, and PAC. We consider that the role and scope of MRP will be somewhat reduced, and before discussing the main building blocks within the PMS architecture we will briefly outline our thinking on requirements planning.

17.3 Requirements planning – a lesser scope for MRP

Requirements planning resides in the tactical level of the PMS hierarchy. It involves Materials Requirements Planning (MRP) and some elements of Manufacturing Resource Planning (MRP II), the latter essentially being an extension of the former.

It is worth reiterating the formal definitions of key terms. MRP II has been defined by APICS as:

> "A method for the effective planning of all the resources of the manufacturing company. Ideally it addresses operational planning in units, financial planning in dollars, and has a simulation capability to answer "what if" questions. It is made up of a variety of functions, each linked together: business planning, production planning, master production scheduling, material requirements planning, capacity requirements planning and the execution systems for capacity and priority. Outputs from these systems would be integrated with financial reports, such as the business plan, purchase commitment report, shipping budget, inventory production in dollars etc. Manufacturing resource planning is a direct outgrowth and extension of MRP. Often referred to as MRP II (cf. closed-loop MRP)."

MRP II is an extension of MRP features to support many other manufacturing functions beyond material planning, inventory control and Bill of Material (BOM) control. MRP II evolved from MRP by a gradual series of extensions to MRP system functionality. These extensions included business planning, master production scheduling, Rough Cut Capacity Planning (RCCP), Capacity Requirements Planning (CRP), and PAC.

Certain assumptions underlie the effective operation of MRP II (Jones and Roberts 1990). These are:

(1)   The availability of basic and accurate data is ensured.

(2)   Complex production planning and control systems can be used.

(3)   The expertise needed to implement effective MRP II systems exists.

(4)   The disciplines required to implement MRP II systems can be enforced.

(5)   The manufacturing environment and the procedures used can be modified to suit the MRP II system.

(6)   Lead times can be specified and (for optimal use) the overall product delivery time will be longer than the composite lead times of components.

MRP II attempts to address all of the main time frames involved in the PMS. It covers the long, medium and short term planning horizons. However, this is not necessarily a good approach because we cannot assume that the same techniques are applicable across these different time frames. In the long term horizon, when dealing with both make to stock and customer driven systems, we rely heavily on forecasts, whereas in the shorter term, requirements are more specific and predictable, and can often be calculated with a very high level of confidence and accuracy.

For example, in medium term planning, average lead time values may be seen as adequate when developing master schedules and exploding them downwards into MRP planned order quantities. However, in the short term, where we seek to schedule the flow of work through the shop floor, finite scheduling techniques such as OPT are needed to create finite schedules. In the long term planning horizon, the use of planning BOMs (see Section 17.5.1) is necessary for the calculation of forecasts and the generation of master schedules, whereas in the medium term detailed BOMs are required in order to, for example, accept customer orders and perform pegging of critical resources and components to individual orders.

Many reasons have been advanced for the poor performance of some MRP systems in practice (see Plenert and Best 1986). Some of these relate to the need for widespread education in MRP thinking and to the necessity for top management commitment to ensure success. Others are more technical in nature and include:

- **Lead times:** MRP assumes production lead times to be known and fixed. Each product is given a pre-defined production lead time. These times are estimates; unfortunately, MRP users often treat them as being very precise.

- **Design/quality:** The areas of production environment design and attention to quality issues are not addressed by the installation of an MRP system. MRP systems tend to assume that the environment exists as is, and is not subject to change. This gives rise to the need for a **production environment design** element in the factory coordination subsystem.

- **Infinite capacity:** MRP assumes infinite capacity, i.e. when a master production schedule is derived, all resources being used in the plant can be assumed to offer at least sufficient capacity to fulfill that schedule. This is based on the premise that the plan has already been passed through RCCP and therefore must be achievable. Both JIT and OPT schedule production assume limited capacity. In JIT the kanban card is used to control capacity, and in OPT bottleneck scheduling is used.

- **Batch sizing:** Many implemented MRP systems tend to use the ideas of economic batch quantities after calculating the planned order quantities. Batches are larger than is necessary in order to offset the supposed costs of set-up and inventory. JIT and OPT have overcome the batch size problem. In JIT, the strategy is to reduce all set-up times to a minimum; OPT computes variable batch sizes.

While agreeing that these are issues which lead to MRP/MRP II failure, we believe that the problems are more basic. We consider that MRP II has sought to achieve an integrated solution without working through the strategic issues which reside above MRP or the operational issues which reside below MRP. In our view, the requirements planning module consists essentially of a basic BOM processor with standard features such as lead time offset and pegging. Other support tools are also required to support the requirements planning activity, including:

- **Pre-processing:** The pre-processor should have the ability to help the user to identify the critical parts and constraints in the system. This module would create **bills of critical parts** and **bills of critical constraints** to be used in partial BOM explosion processes.

- **Development of planning BOMs:** As well as performing BOM explosion processes, the requirements planning function should also have the capability of defining planning BOMs (see Section 17.5.1) for use in the system. One such type of planning BOM would be one which would relate all components/parts to their parent items, along with their associated aggregated *quantity per* and lead time values. This type of planning BOM (assuming that it is up to date) can be of great use in easing the computation process, when we need only look at particular components requirements.

- **Purchased components analysis:** This module would only explode the purchased components in each of the BOMs. This is useful for manufacturing companies that do not have long lead times on in-house assemblies and whose main problems may arise from purchased components. A facility should be made available to allow the user to identify all of the purchased components and to create planned orders for these components only, without having to carry out all of the processing normally associated with an MRP explosion. This involves having a series of special *quantity per* and lead time relationships in the database for these purchased components. (Development of the planning BOMs mentioned above would really be a prerequisite for this task.)

- **Critical component analysis:** As with the purchased parts, there may be a need to explode the requirements for the critical manufactured and assembled parts in the various products. These will have been defined by the pre-processing system. Critical components could be defined based on their expected very long lead times, or perhaps their restricted availability, or even their high cost.

- **Modular BOM analyzer:** This piece of software would analyze a series of BOMs to produce a common and unique series of BOMs. This process is termed modularization. (See Higgins 1991.)

- **Lot sizing:** Some lot sizing algorithms could also be made available as part of the requirements planning system.

- **Pegging facilities:** *Where used* and top-down pegging facilities would have to be supplied to aid in customer order acceptance functions, material availability checking, etc.

In summary, we see the requirements planning subsystem as a BOM processor with extra functionality in terms of support tools for planners, as outlined above. We will now return to describing the main blocks of Figure 17.2, with an emphasis on master production scheduling and factory co-ordination.

17.4 Business planning

Business planning deals with the long term activities of a manufacturing organization. It develops the plans necessary to drive the sales, manufacturing, and financial groups within an organization. These plans define markets to be addressed, products to be manufactured, required volumes and resources, and the financial impact of meeting the overall objectives set by strategic planning within the organization.

Business planning involves two main tasks:

(1) The formation of a manufacturing strategy.
(2) The development of a long term production plan.

A manufacturing strategy is formed by the decisions taken in, and in connection with, manufacturing which have a strategic influence on the company's competitive approach. The purpose of a manufacturing strategy is to direct the company's manufacturing resources in such a way as to support competitive ability.

The firm's manufacturing strategy is devised to help the firm win orders. Traditionally, the main areas examined include price and quality. In today's manufacturing environment competitiveness is often measured on the basis of delivery times and performance. The development of a firm's manufacturing strategy must reflect well the needs of the market in terms of price, quality, delivery lead times, and flexibility.

17.4.1 Long range production planning

Long term production planning involves the development of a quantitative set of numbers relating to production over, say, a six month to five year horizon. This numeric data may be quite aggregated in nature, and provides the input for the master scheduling process.

The production plan reflects the desired aggregate output from manufacturing necessary to support the company's overall financial objectives. It may be stated in terms of the monthly or quarterly sales output for the company as a whole, or for individual plants or businesses, in terms of the number of units to be produced in each major product line for the period in question. It is frequently based on forecast data. This production plan is an initial attempt at describing the demand pattern over a long time horizon. It is then the task of the master scheduling function to develop a response to this perceived demand.

The long range production plan provides a direct and consistent dialogue between manufacturing and top management, as well as between manufacturing and the other functions. It is important that the unit of measure employed is understandable to the non-manufacturing executives of the company as well as to manufacturing and the master production scheduler. Choosing meaningful groups to plan by requires a thorough knowledge of the plant's manufacturing process. These groupings are seldom the same ones used by the marketing department or the inventory control system. The groups must be meaningful in terms of demand on the manufacturing facilities (Plossl and Wight 1967). Companies can state their production plans in any one or more of a number of ways, including monetary values of total monthly or quarterly output, total output broken down by individual plants or by major product lines, total units per product line, or capacity related measures such as direct labor hours, tons of product, etc.

The long range production plan needs to be expressed in meaningful units, but it also needs to be expressed in a manageable number of units. In most of the literature, 10–15 family groups seems to be the commonly agreed number. Product family structuring involves a large initial effort, but after this initial effort it is only a matter of identifying into which product family an item will be included. How should parts be grouped together? Gessner (1986) argues that items may be grouped into a family because: they use the same resource, they have the same sales trends, or for any reason that causes a grouping that is significant to the company. Gessner also considers that the creation of product families should be the first step in production planning.

The time horizon appropriate for the long range production plan is driven by such factors as implementation time for new resources, planning time increments, resource availability, existing customer orders, etc. The planning horizon starts from the current date. The production plan sends targets down to the MPS. The time buckets used can be either monthly or quarterly. Taking a five year horizon, for example, the type of bucket used might vary as follows: first year in months, second year in quarters, third year in semiannual quantities, fourth and fifth years as annual quantities.

Long range production planning strategies
Orders are frequently subject to substantial fluctuation, and the question arises as to how these fluctuations should be absorbed. These fluctuations must be considered when planning in the first and second years of the planning horizon, where the buckets are sufficiently small to be affected. As the planning buckets increase in size these fluctuations should not be an influencing factor. There is a consensus among authors (e.g. Holt *et al.* 1960; Vollmann *et al.* 1988), about the alternative ways (strategies) of responding to such fluctuations. Typical strategies include:

- The **chase strategy:** Vollmann *et al.* define a chase strategy as follows: no inventories are held and production chases sales. When this strategy is employed, the manufacturing organization monitors demand closely and modifies production rates up and down in order to satisfy requirements. This has the obvious consequence of production nervousness, where employment and overtime levels are unpredictable, with associated fluctuations in productivity levels. There is erratic demand for raw materials and equipment capacity. The chase strategy is very often not an option for the continuous flow manufacturer or where plant and equipment are designed and developed to run at particular production levels.

- The **level strategy:** Vollmann *et al.* define a level strategy as follows: production is at a constant uniform rate of output, with inventory build-ups and depletions. It is also known as the inventory absorption strategy. It allows the manufacturing organization to retain relatively stable employment and overtime levels, as production rates are kept almost constant. However, it drives up inventory carrying costs, storage costs, material handling costs, and capital investment costs (storage facilities).

The chase and level strategies can be broken down into three pure alternative strategies. A chase strategy may be implemented by following either of the first two strategies, while a level strategy may be implemented by following the third. Each of these three individual strategies will now be outlined:

(1)   Production is maintained by increasing or decreasing the work force in precise adjustment with order fluctuations: an increase in orders is met by hiring, and a decrease in orders is accompanied by layoffs. However, training and reorganization are usually required when the work force is expanded, and terminal pay and loss of worker morale frequently occur when the work force is contracted. Since plant and equipment are fixed in the short run, a change in the work force may decrease labor productivity. This cost can be avoided by maintaining the plant and equipment necessary for peak employment, or by paying the premiums involved in second and third shift operation. A similar problem of imbalance may arise when the total work force fluctuates, but some components of the work force – supervision, for example – cannot easily be changed.

(2)   The work force is kept constant, adjusting production rate to orders by working overtime and short time, accordingly. This alternative realizes the ideal work force situation by absorbing fluctuations in orders with corresponding fluctuation in overtime work, without changing the size of the work force. However, since there is an upper limit to what can be produced by working overtime, the necessity for meeting peak orders governs the size of the work force. When orders fall to lower levels, overtime is eliminated, but with a further fall in orders idle time occurs; i.e. there is not enough productive work to keep the work force busy throughout the regular work week.

(3)   A constant work force and a constant production rate are maintained, allowing inventories and order backlogs to fluctuate. Big upward swings in inventory necessitate large storage facilities, large amounts of working capital, and other direct costs, and create risks such as obsolescence. Big downward swings of inventory, culminating in large backlogs, impose intangible costs on the company – poor delivery performance may lead to a loss of sales.

Obviously, none of these strategies effectively counteracts the fluctuating demand problem for the manufacturing organization. However, a hybrid combination of the three may be more effective. Order fluctuations should be absorbed partly by inventory, partly by overtime, and partly by hiring and layoffs, and the optimum mix of these factors will depend upon the costs in any particular factory.

17.5 Master production scheduling

The Master Production Schedule (MPS) is a statement of the anticipated manufacturing schedule for selected items by quantity per planning period (Fogarty and Hoffman 1983; Higgins and Tierney 1990; Higgins *et al.* 1991). It is a response to the forecast demand described by the production plan, and the actual demand in terms of received customer orders. Often, it is a listing of the end items that are to be produced, the quantity of each item to be produced, and the required schedule for delivery to the customer. End items may be products, major assemblies, groups of components, or even individual parts used at the highest level in the product structure. The MPS provides the basis for making customer delivery promises, utilizing the capacity of the plant effectively, attaining the strategic objectives of the business as reflected in the production plan, and resolving tradeoffs between marketing and manufacturing. Unlike a forecast of demand, the master schedule represents a management commitment, authorizing the procurement of raw material and the production of component items.

APICS considers the terms *master production schedule* and *master schedule* to be synonymous and defines them as: "The anticipated build schedule for those items assigned to the master scheduler. It represents what the company plans to produce expressed in specific configurations, quantities and dates." However, Everdell (1987) defines the master schedule as referring to "presentation of information that expresses how a master scheduler has decided to satisfy the demand placed on the 'end item' by determining production quantities to be completed on specific dates." Everdell also uses the APICS definition of master production schedule and presents the term *master schedule* in terms of the inputs and outputs of the master scheduling process.

In our view, master production scheduling is the linking pin between the marketing and sales (sales forecasting and customer order promising), manufacturing (operations), and engineering (product and process design) functions. The MPS function should aim to develop and maintain a manufacturing plan which is satisfactory for all three functions. This concept is illustrated in Figure 17.3, which suggests a **planning board** comprising personnel from all three departments taking part in the master scheduling process.

In order for MPS to work effectively as the linking pin for the three departments, the MPS items should be the common denominator. However, the different departments may not be able to work at the MPS item level. The sales function tends to work with sales or customer items,

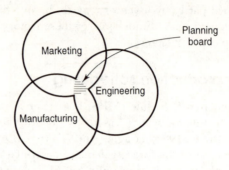

Figure 17.3 Planning board as linking pin.

while forecasts may be released by the marketing department at a product family level. In order to achieve integration between the departments it may be necessary to use planning BOMs.

17.5.1 Planning BOMs

As indicated in Chapter 5, a BOM defines a listing of all of the subassemblies, intermediates, parts, and raw materials that go into a parent assembly, showing the quantity of each required to make the assembly. A planning BOM is any use of the BOM approach to support the planning, as opposed to the building, of products. APICS defines the planning BOM as "an artificial grouping of items and/or events in bill of material format, used to facilitate master scheduling and/or material planning." The modular BOM and the super BOM are the two principal types of planning BOMs.

Modular BOMs

A modular BOM is a type of planning bill which is arranged in product modules or options. It is often used in companies where the product has many optional features, e.g. automobiles. Choosing the appropriate master scheduling unit affects the way the bills of materials are structured, and vice versa, since each master scheduling unit is also the highest level item in a bill of material. Modularization of BOMs involves the breaking down of products into options or modules, which, in various combinations, determine the final products. Each module consists of stand-alone subassemblies, or of kits of parts that cannot be put together until final assembly (Wemmerlov 1984). There are two objectives in modularising the BOM:

(1)   To disentangle combinations of optional product features.
(2)   To segregate common from unique parts in the BOM.

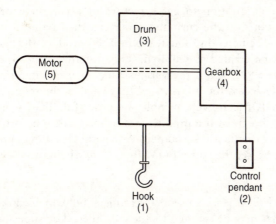

Figure 17.4 Typical hoist assembly (Orlicky *et al.* 1972).

The first objective seeks to facilitate forecasting, while the second seeks to minimize inventory investment in components which are common to more than one optional unit.

The classic example used in the existing literature of the need for a modular BOM structure is the hoist example popularized by Orlicky *et al.* (1967). Figure 17.4 represents a hoist used to handle material in a factory. Of the five elements, there is one hook, five motors, three drums, four gearboxes, and two control pendants. The total number of combinations implies that 120 ($5 \times 3 \times 4 \times 2 \times 1$) possible models can be ordered, assuming that all options are technically feasible. Clearly, it is possible to write a BOM for each of the models, but it would not be practical to manage all of these bills. Suppose there is an expected demand of 20 hoists per week. It would – for all practical purposes – be impossible to predict which 20 hoists out of 120 possibilities customers will want to buy in any given week.

One solution is to establish the MPS at the option or module level, using modular BOMs. Rather than maintaining bills for individual end products, the BOM is restated in terms of the building blocks, or modules, from which the final product is assembled. With this approach the total number of BOMs is:

1 (common module) + 5 (motors) + 3 (drums) + 4 (gearboxes) +
2 (pendants) = 15 MPS items

Of course, we are making an implicit assumption here that the final hoist can be assembled from the various modules within the customer lead time. Typically, in such situations finished product definitions are developed using a menu selection sheet, requesting the user to specify the motor, drum, gearbox, and control pendant options. The menu sheet could be used as a sales order entry sheet, or simply as a request form for engineering or accounting to get a picture of a complete product. The selection of options on the customer order can then be used to generate a BOM for this specific end product. No finished product BOMs are needed as they can all be created as required. This minimizes the amount of data stored, and yet allows all of the various functions, including sales, manufacturing etc. to access the information they need in the required format.

Modular BOMs are very flexible and powerful. They work extremely well when the design of the product is also modular. The problem is that sometimes the variants are so numerous that they become almost unmanageable. In that case, the super BOM format may be more useful.

Super BOMs

The super bill is in essence a pseudo or artificial bill which contains the various options that may be selected by the customer. The super bill is a planning bill, located at the top level in the structure, which ties together various modular bills to define an entire product or product family. The super bill is identified by a phantom level in the structure. It will be used as a planning tool, and, as such, it can never be built or bought, and on-hand inventory will never exist for it. The *quantity per* relationship of super bill to modules represents the *forecast percentage of demand* of each module. The master scheduled quantities of the super bill explode to create requirements for the modules, which are also master scheduled.

Some confusion exists in the literature in the use of BOM terminology, particularly for terms such as *option*, *variant*, etc. We adopt the following definitions. A BOM module is a standard self-contained unit or item, which can be used in combination with other units. An option represents a unique module that has no constituent components common to any other module. An option belongs to a group, from which one of the options in the group *must* be selected to assemble or build the finished product. A variant is a module that contains some components that are constituents of other variant modules. A series of variants contains the same core parts. The finished product *must* also contain one selection from each series of variants. An attachment is an option which may or may not be selected to define the finished product. The term *attachment* would apply to add-on options, maintenance kits, and service or spare parts. A super BOM links all of the modules that are used to produce a family of end items, by indicating the average usage of each module in the family of finished items.

The super bill describes the related options or modules that make up the average end item. For example, an average car might have 2.6 doors, 4.2 cylinders, 0.3 air conditioners, etc. This end term ("average car") is impossible to build. However, using BOM logic, it is very useful in planning and master production scheduling. BOM processing requires that the super bill is established in the product structure files as a legitimate single level BOM. This means that the super bill will show all the possible options as components, with their "average usage." The logic of BOM

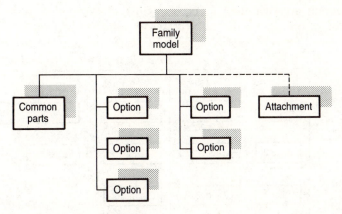

Figure 17.5 Super bill of material.

processing allows "average usage" values for single level component usage. The super bill combines the modules, or options, with the average usage rates to describe the "average end product." The BOM logic should be so defined to force arithmetic consistency in the mutually exclusive options, for example the sum of two possible engine options must be equal to the total number of cars to be assembled.

Figure 17.5 is an example of a super BOM. The first step to establishing a super BOM is to assign a model part number to the product family. This part number is used to identify the family and form the attachment point for the super BOM structure relationships. It also serves as the entry point for the shipment plan or production plan in terms of the number of units within the family.

A part number to identify all parts common throughout the family is now structured under the model part number. This part number is defined as a dummy or pseudo part number since it cannot be built. Under this part number is a list of part numbers always used on any model structure for the family. This allows MPS planning to relate to one part number for the parts structured below it, and to plan those parts in matched sets through MRP.

The model part number also has a series of part numbers structured under it, which relate to options within the family. As shown in Figure 17.5, there is a series of option part numbers attached to the model. When shown in a vertical relationship, one option must be selected from the list to build a configuration of the model. These option part numbers may define a stocked part number. They may also be pseudo part numbers which define a part list that, when combined with a portion of the common parts, provides the unique product.

Figure 17.6 represents a super BOM definition for the hoist referred to earlier. Master schedule planning would be accomplished at the part number level below the model number; common parts, motor, drum, etc.

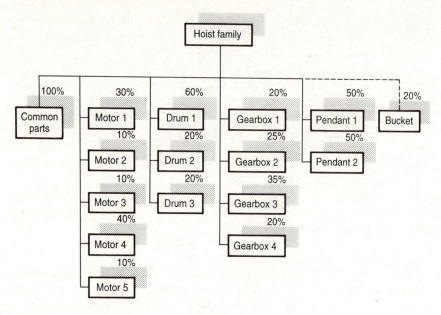

Figure 17.6   Hoist super bill of material.

Structured under the pseudo part number for common parts are all the components and subassemblies required to make any model of the hoist. The options are then structured in a vertical relationship to illustrate that a selection of one must be made to complete the hoist assembly. The bucket option is linked with a dotted line to signify that it is an attachment. The customer decides whether or not the bucket should be included.

Figure 17.6 may also be described as a percentage BOM. The percentage number refers to the ratio of each variant compared to the usage of the parent item. Rather than make forecasts of the production requirements for the 15 modules/variants, the percentages on the super bill are used to generate the master schedule from the forecast at the module level. Percentage BOMs are usually used when the number of options or variants is too high for them to be forecast as individual items. Using the super BOM approach, marketing could furnish a model forecast and a best estimate on the percentage use of options and attachments. A computer program can be used to generate the option forecast using the model forecast and option percentages.

When structuring the super BOM, other considerations include special capacity constraints related to a customer specification, inventory investment requirements, and the competitive lead time situation. Often, a unique product definition will contain a special process which is defined by the customer order. An example may be the printing of the customer information on the product before shipment. Under this condition, a pseudo part number may be included in the super BOM to specify the capacity center required to process the product before shipment. This provides visibility of capacity requirements and commitments.

The definition of the super BOM and the lower level items should also consider inventory investment. The goal is to develop a complete separation of optional parts from the common parts, and only expend resources to match the two groups of parts when actual customer orders are in place. However, if the optional parts are relatively inexpensive, it may be better to invest in extra inventory and always plan for their use rather than making the separation. Competitive lead time is another consideration in the structure analysis. There may be no choice but to build the product on the likelihood of sales, in order to match or beat the competition's quoted delivery time. This type of analysis must continue throughout the life cycle for a family of products.

17.5.2 MPS in practice

In our experience very few companies operate satisfactory MPS systems. The situation in terms of industrial practice can be summarized as follows:

- Few companies use the MPS as an order acceptance tool. Given the trend towards customer driven manufacturing and the emerging requirement in many industrial sectors for customized products, the MPS and customer order promising subsystems need to be better integrated.

- Capacity is often the only constraint which is taken into account in any analysis of the MPS. However, in many manufacturing situations the accurate identification of other constrained resources is necessary to develop a successful MPS system, e.g. long lead time or expensive components. Short simulation runs (analysis of the loads on constrained resources) may help to find a first pass satisfactory MPS. Other simulations which take more time (e.g. full BOM explosion) should only be initiated when they are relevant and when sufficient time is available. The use of time consuming simulation tools should be avoided, through correct identification and understanding of the constrained resources and an appropriate choice of MPS items.

- It appears that manufacturing planners would like to have full links between forecast, orders, scheduled item, and customer data, thus enabling reporting and planning to be prioritized by end item, by family, by order, or by customer.

- It appears that manufacturing planners would like to have the ability to see which shop orders are linked to particular customer orders and vice versa.

- MPS planners do not have access to good support tools to create appropriate planning BOMs.

- Many MPS planners do not have the ability to deal with variable time buckets and fences.

The current lack of sophisticated information systems in the area of master scheduling often results in poorly developed and managed schedules. The MPS system should be a decision support system which facilitates the preparation and management of a flexible MPS. This MPS can then establish investment levels for expected orders to meet shorter manufacturing lead times, and enable the enterprise to deal with unexpected changes to the schedule/plan within those shorter lead times.

17.5.3   A framework for MPS

In this section, we offer a framework for the development, verification, and implementation of the MPS. The proposed MPS framework describes the inputs, outputs, and constraints of the system and the basic building blocks in the MPS process. The building blocks include a customer order entry module, forecasts, a long range production plan, a facility to deal with qualitative data on product life cycles, competing products, etc., a master schedule generator, an MPS analyzer and performance monitor to deal with constraints, and, finally, a series of independent tools to support the initial decision making process. This MPS framework is an attempt to define the structure of an MPS system suitable for use in hybrid manufacturing environments.

Figure 17.7 illustrates the three main time zones in the PMS hierarchy. At the interface between business planning and MPS, the constituents of the demand change. Time buckets shorten and the items under consideration typically change from product family demand to MPS item demand. This is usually achieved via a dissagregation of the long range production plan. In the business planning time zone, demand data is almost always based on forecasts, with the exception being those customer orders that have very long lead times. In the MPS zone, there is usually a

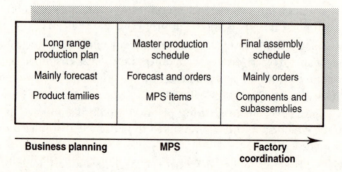

Long range production plan	Master production schedule	Final assembly schedule
Mainly forecast	Forecast and orders	Mainly orders
Product families	MPS items	Components and subassemblies

Business planning   MPS   Factory coordination

Figure 17.7   Main MPS time zones.

mixture of forecasts and orders. MPS items are scheduled and customer order promising is performed based on available to promise logic. The factory coordination time zone typically deals with the final assembly schedule. This zone can be viewed as the "'frozen" segment of the MPS, or that segment of the MPS which as been exploded by a BOM explosion module in requirements planning. The location of the "change points" along the time axis directly relates to the definition of the customer order decoupling point. (See Chapter 1.)

As indicated earlier, Figure 17.7 is a generic representation of the main PMS time zones suitable for hybrid manufacturing environments. The correct identification and positioning of the customer order decoupling point and the items used in each time zone are of great importance for any production management system. As indicated in Chapter 1, many companies are now moving towards a hybrid form of manufacturing environment. Consequently, flexibility in dealing with the positioning of the customer order decoupling point is essential. An example of the flexibility required could be the use of the master schedule to plan at an option level, and then the use of JIT principles to create the final assembly schedule for production. In this case the customer order could enter the system at two different levels (see Figure 17.2), i.e. the customer orders come in at MPS level but also at the shop floor level in the case of a hybrid push/pull environment (Bose and Rao 1988), where some components of the products are customized and some are standard.

Figure 17.8 gives an indication of the workings of an MPS system. It highlights the closed loop nature of the MPS process, i.e. how the development of an actual MPS feeds the requirements planning/factory coordination activities, thereby updating the actual constraints which are taken into account in the development of the next MPS. In order to develop a realistic MPS, it is imperative that the process incorporates the widest possible range of inputs from the organization's functions. These inputs can be seen entering the master schedule generator in Figure 17.8. The possible conflicting nature of these inputs, in addition to the constraints imposed from the lower levels (requirements planning, factory coordination, PAC), creates a requirement for a simulation or *what if* analysis to be executed on the proposed MPS, in order to find the "optimal" solution. Therefore, it may take several iterations of the process to arrive at such a solution. Also, this simulation takes place in a pre-processing environment, i.e. simulation occurs prior to a full BOM explosion. Furthermore, the simulation should focus on key constraints and financial inputs. Financial analysis generates information on how proposed MPS changes impact costs, e.g. cost penalties incurred with vendors when agreements are violated. This rapid response generation adds to the dynamic nature of the process.

In Figure 17.8 information which flows from business planning is represented in two building blocks, i.e. quantitative data, in the form of a long range production plan which states product family, quantities, and

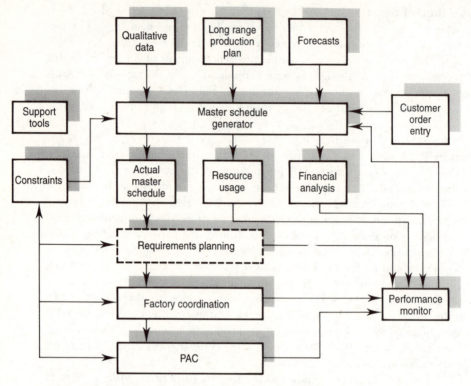

Figure 17.8 The overall MPS framework.

time periods, and qualitative data, which sets guidelines with respect to policies, on issues such as inventory levels, overtime, and subcontracting within which the MPS must operate.

Feedback to higher levels of the planning hierarchy need only happen when conflicts occur within the MPS which cannot be resolved without violating one of the long term constraints, e.g. if real demand exceeds the capacity to supply and the guidelines for subcontracting do not allow external sourcing, then the conflict would have to be referred up the planning hierarchy.

As indicated earlier, the requirements planning module contains a BOM explosion processor with standard features such as lead time offset, lot sizing, pegging, and order policies, which have a significant impact on the operational aspect of the business. However, since a full BOM explosion is time consuming and would thus inhibit the MPS process, it is envisaged that a pre-processor should be used to help select and explode critical assemblies and subassemblies.

In the same way that business planning sends qualitative data into the MPS, the MPS sends a more refined version of this qualitative data, in the form of rules on how to solve conflicts, e.g. the use of overtime, priorities with respect to production costs, individual customers, WIP levels, etc., to the factory coordination level. Factory coordination feeds short term data back to the MPS. This data is in two forms: (i) actual performance and real-time data such as interruptions, breakdowns, efficiencies and actual lead times, and (ii) data on priority conflicts which cannot be solved at the factory level.

The main aspects of the MPS framework can be summarized as follows:

- The use of qualitative data from the strategic planning levels. This is one of the most important features in the framework, and it is the prime contributor to integration with the business planning function.
- The direct linkage with the customer order entry function.
- The use of lower level constraints and historical data in the generation of the MPS.
- Financial analysis of the master production schedule.
- Measure of performance analysis based on metrics of interest to the master scheduling function and guidelines from the strategic levels.
- A series of support tools to aid in the MPS design and management processes.

The "static" view of the main MPS building blocks, presented in Figure 17.8, depicts the main modules connected with the core MPS generation system. However, in order to understand the MPS process more fully, the dynamics of the process must be reviewed in some detail.

The dynamic management of the MPS is illustrated in Figure 17.9. This diagram attempts to depict the dynamic nature of the MPS development process, and, in addition, the ongoing update process that occurs during the entry of customer orders. The MPS generator is termed a *planning table*. The planning table is the process which allows the MPS to act as the linking pin between the sales, manufacturing, and engineering departments.

For reasons of clarity, certain important features have been omitted from this figure. One of these features represents the use of a common database. A common database ensures an integrated system, which takes into account higher and lower level objectives, guidelines, and constraints. The customer order entry system sends requests to the planning table. These requests are in the form of customer order details, and may involve the entering, modification, or cancellation of customer orders. The planning table can return promise date information to the customer order entry function. Another important feature which is omitted from the figure is concerned with feedback to the strategic planning levels.

After the generation of an initial MPS, a series of MPS analysis tools are used to assist the master scheduling personnel in the authorization of this MPS. The output of the MPS analysis level is represented by a series of reports. These reports are evaluated, and the MPS can be either rejected

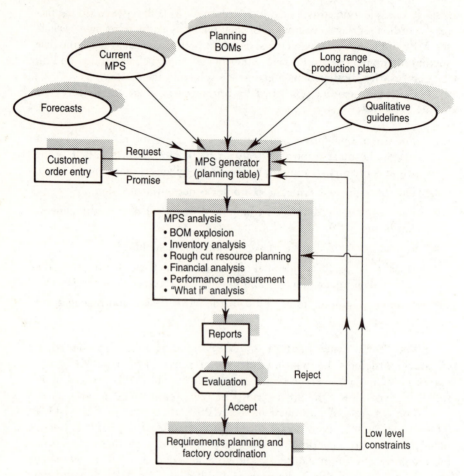

Figure 17.9 Dynamic management of the PMS.

or accepted. Rejection of the MPS creates feedback to the MPS planning table, which results in a closed loop MPS development process.

The first stage is the *development of the MPS*, which is concerned with knowing what, when, and how much to schedule. This is addressed by support tools for identification of the MPS items and time fences, and the MPS generator (planning table). The second stage, which is concerned with *MPS verification and validation*, is addressed by the use of planning BOMs to ensure proper translation between the long range production plan and demand forecast at the business planning level, and the corresponding items at the MPS level. The validation of the MPS is directly related to the MPS analysis and evaluation process of Figure 17.9. Finally, *MPS maintenance and change management* is addressed by the dynamic management proposed in Figure 17.9. This includes the incorporation of constantly changing demand, the rolling forward of the plan in time, and the downloading of schedules to the lower levels.

In the remainder of this discussion on MPS, we will concentrate on two important issues, namely the choice of MPS items and the use of the MPS tableau or planning table.

17.5.4 The choice of MPS items

MPS items may be scheduled as product groups, individual products, or parts of products (components and subassemblies). The greatest benefits of MPS can be attained when the grouping of products can be maximized. This grouping involves the effective use of planning BOMs. One objective of planning BOMs is to change the overall shape of the product BOM structure to narrow the range of items which are controlled by the MPS. Generally, the MPS controlled items are at the narrowest point of the BOM structure. This can be seen in Figure 17.10, which illustrates typical varieties of BOM structures for MTS, MTO, and ATO environments. In the MTS environment, there is typically a wide range of raw materials and a small range of finished products. MTO is typically the reverse situation, and ATO is a combination of a large number of raw materials and a wide range of finished products.

Constrained resources

MPS is concerned with the management of the constrained resources of the factory in response to a demand forecast. Therefore, it is important to identify the constrained resources as quickly and as accurately as possible in order to enable a proactive planning approach. If material supply is a constraint, the company should attempt to identify the actual purchased items constraining the flexibility of the MPS. The critical nature of these purchased parts is determined by the purchasing and production lead times, compared with the standard market lead time of the product. All purchased items which have to be ordered before the standard market lead time are subject to speculation, because ordering is based upon forecasts without the actual demand picture being known. Purchased items which can be ordered within the standard market lead time do not constrain the flexibility of the MPS, as purchase to customer order is possible.

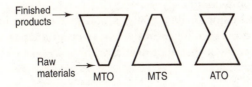

Figure 17.10 Typical BOM structures.

Purchased parts which are required across the product range and whose required volume is reasonably high are likely to have a very stable demand pattern and a reasonably small chance of obsolescence. These can be dealt with through the use of a safety stock. The purchased parts which cause the greatest problems are those which are variant (i.e. not common to many of the products within the product range) and expensive, and whose purchase lead time is in excess of the anticipated customer lead time for the product. Such parts have to be ordered in anticipation of an order.

Safety stock is not the only method of reducing the complexity of the MPS process. Other approaches, such as the use of commonality analysis and the investment diagram, may also be used. These will now be discussed in more detail.

Commonality analysis

Commonality analysis involves a systematic study of the component commonality across the range of product structures for the purpose of identifying appropriate MPS items. The output of this analysis in its simplest form can be in the style of reports summarizing the common and unique assemblies and components (both purchased and manufactured) across the product range. Identifying the common and unique elements is also quite beneficial in deciding whether or not certain items are critical. However, uniqueness is only one criterion for placing an item on the critical list – other criteria include the length of the lead time for the item, its cost, certain physical characteristics (e.g. bulkiness, which might make it difficult to store or transport), the number of available suppliers, etc.

As a first step in identifying critical and non-critical parts, it is useful to perform a common/unique analysis and to apply planning rules to these two categories. For example, on critical unique items, flexibility can be negotiated and thus become part of a basic ordering agreement with a supplier. A second step in identifying critical/non-critical items might involve performing a Pareto or ABC analysis, based on cost and lead time. Combining the common/unique analysis with the ABC classification can result in a more refined approach to planning. For example, unique A class parts (in a Pareto sense) would clearly require more careful planning than common A class parts.

Applying the other two previously identified criteria of physical characteristics (say, bulkiness) and the number of suppliers leads to a further refinement of the critical items list, and may result in the addition of items to the list which were previously classed as non-critical with respect to cost, lead time and commonality.

As well as commonality analysis and the correct identification of constrained resources, another important concept that is useful in MPS analysis is that of the investment diagram.

The investment diagram

The investment diagram provides a profile of cost build-up for a particular product range or product family, i.e. once the first purchase order is placed

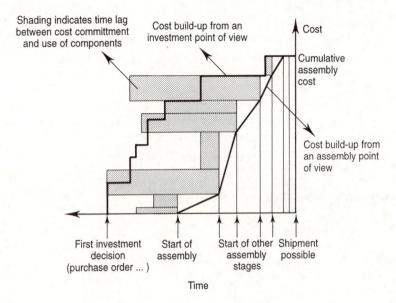

Figure 17.11 Typical investment diagram profile.

for a component of a product and the first value adding operations are performed on the raw material, an investment risk is incurred. The investment diagram profile helps to focus attention on those items which contribute a major part to the build-up of cost and which, through careful planning, can be managed so that the greatest build-up occurs in the period where customer orders are firm, therefore minimizing risk. The investment diagram may be used at the MPS level to make decisions on planning time fences and MPS items.

An investment diagram provides a clear view of the cost build-up for a particular end product or product family. The cost build-up is considered as soon as the first purchase order is placed, since this represents an investment decision with which there is an associated risk. Increased cost build-up occurs as soon as assembly begins and value is added to the raw components. Thus, there are two graphs to be represented in the investment diagram – the purchase order commitment graph and the assembly cost graph. These are illustrated in Figure 17.11.

The risk associated with investment decisions depends mainly on the cost of the components and the component lead time. An "ideal" investment diagram profile with respect to risk is illustrated in Figure 17.12, where the long lead time items are also low cost items, thereby resulting in a reduction of the risk.

Alternatively, a highly undesirable profile results when expensive items are also long lead time items, as illustrated in Figure 17.13. In this scenario, the high investments are made early on and thus the risk is increased. The expensive long lead time items are classed as critical, due to

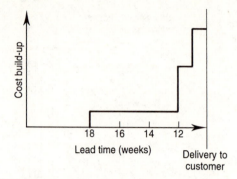

Figure 17.12 "Ideal" investment diagram profile.

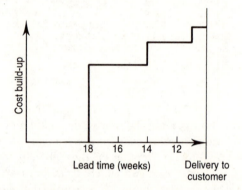

Figure 17.13 "Undesirable" investment diagram profile.

the fact that the risk associated with these parts is high, as a result of their high cost and their long lead time.

To reduce risk, expensive items are committed to as close as possible to the delivery date, i.e. reduce their lead times in order to reduce the dependence on forecasts and forecast error, or increase the firm period within which customer orders cannot be changed. This risk can be reduced and the profile of the investment diagram can be greatly modified by performing a common/unique analysis on the long lead time expensive items. By definition, if an item is common across a range of products, then a long lead time item has a smaller risk attached to it than one which is unique to a product, since the common item may be used on another product if the forecast on one product or order is incorrect. Therefore, shorter lead times should be negotiated on the unique parts in order to reduce the risk. This in turn influences the profile of the investment diagram and improves it, as illustrated in Figure 17.14.

Clearly, the investment diagram approach can be used to create a view of where the greatest cost build-up occurs, and therefore indicate where to focus the most careful planning attention. Improving the cost

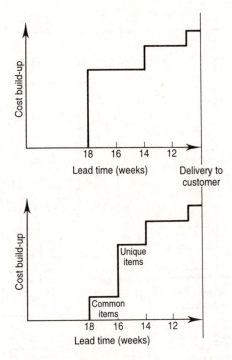

Figure 17.14   Effects of commonality analysis.

build-up profile means getting the major build-up to occur close to the customer delivery date.

17.5.5   The MPS planning table

In this section we describe the main ideas and concepts behind the MPS planning table. We will also, through a simple example based on the products we used earlier to describe the MRP approach, illustrate in simplistic terms the use of this planing table. The MPS planning table is the core system used by senior planners to develop, validate, and maintain the MPS. The main requirement for the planning table is that it should enable the process of **concurrent planning** via the use of an easy to use, menu driven, multiple windows based user interface. Concurrent planning should allow different users to access the system simultaneously, and also access the same updated information in different formats.

A planning table may be visualized as illustrated in Figure 17.15. The planning table is basically a tabular representation of the MPS, which provides information for the manufacturing and sales functions. The entries in the planning table show clearly the nature of the MPS as the linking pin between the different functions. The demand forecast is an input coming from marketing. The customer orders (allocated, reserved, and unplanned) are an input from sales. The MPS (firm and unplanned) is approved by

Planning table window

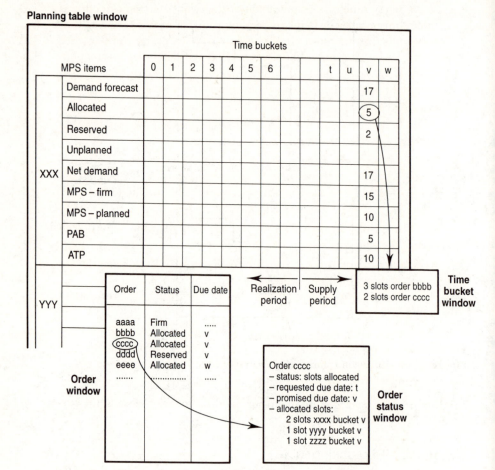

Figure 17.15 Typical planning table layout.

marketing, sales, and manufacturing, and drives the manufacturing operations. Projected Available Balance (PAB) is used to check for availability of MPS items, and Available to Promise (ATP) is the starting point for all customer order promising activities in the sales department. The layout of the MPS planning table is frequently adapted to particular manufacturing environments or specific business requirements.

The planning table lists all numbers according to a series of time buckets. The idea of the time bucket is to group forecast numbers, customer order numbers, and production or MPS numbers in specific periods of time. Some of the parameters and entries used in the planning table are:

- **Safety stock and safety time:** The objective of maintaining the PAB above a certain margin is expressed through the use of safety stock, safety time or a combination of the two. Safety stock defines a minimum number of items to be kept available in stock. Safety time represents the minimum number of future time buckets to be covered by the PAB. The concept of safety stock is typically used in situations of relatively stable demand, while the concept of safety time is used more frequently where seasonal demand is the norm.

- **Forecast time fence:** The forecast time fence is the period within which only orders and not forecasts are taken into account in order to determine the net demand.

- **Reservation time fence:** The reservation time fence is the period within which no customer order slots can be reserved. Only firm customer orders can be accepted for allocation within this time fence.

- **MPS time fence:** The MPS time fence is the time horizon within which the MPS remains firm. A management decision is needed to change the schedule within this time fence.

- **Available to promise time fence:** The ATP time fence is the period within which no additional orders may be accepted. This time fence may be considered as the minimum customer order lead time.

The idea of time fences is to gradually firm up demand and production. This is necessary in order to start production, finalize the purchase schedules, and purchase the short lead time items. The ATP time fence should be greater than or equal to the forecast time fence, since the net demand within the ATP time fence may only be based upon order information and not upon forecast information.

- **Forecast:** This represents the demand forecast for the MPS item. If the main objective is to ship products, the demand forecast should relate to a forecast of units to be shipped. If the objective is to get products into a finished products warehouse, the demand forecast should relate to a forecast of units to be produced and made available for further shipment activities.

- **Slots allocated:** Customer orders are converted into a set of MPS item requirements. Each of the accepted customer orders (orders with promised due dates) consumes slots for each required MPS item. These are termed *allocated slots*.

- **Slots reserved.** Slots reserved are similar to allocated slots, but are concerned with bid orders, i.e. orders for which management wishes to guarantee resource availability without being certain whether the order will become firm.

- **Unplanned slots:** Unplanned slots are also similar to allocated slots, but represent orders which have occurred unexpectedly and hence were not included in the forecast calculations.

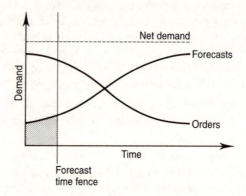

Figure 17.16 Graphical representation of net demand.

- **Net demand:** The net demand line is calculated based upon forecast and slot allocation information (allocated, reserved, unplanned). This represents the expected demand on the basis of which the MPS is determined and checked. Net demand may be described more clearly by looking at Figure 17.16. In this diagram, net demand is seen as a combination of forecasts and orders. In the short term, net demand is composed primarily of orders. Within the forecast time fence, forecasts may not be taken into account in the calculation of the net demand.

- **MPS – firm:** A firm MPS item manufacturing order is an order which has been released and documented, and may well be in production. Therefore, all changes to this line of the MPS planning table must be by manual intervention. Orders may be "firmed" to act as a mechanism to "freeze" the MPS on a longer horizon.

- **MPS – planned:** A planned MPS item is a manufacturing order which has been automatically calculated or manually manipulated during the development of an MPS. The value for time bucket i is calculated as follows:

$$\text{MPS}[i] \text{ planned} = \text{SS} + \text{Net\_Demand}[i] - \text{PAB}[i-1] - \text{MPS}[i] \text{ firm}$$

(Equation A)

where SS is the safety stock and $\text{PAB}[i-1]$ is the projected available balance for the previous time bucket.

If we use the safety time constraint, then SS = 0 and $\text{MPS}[i]$ planned is calculated as follows:

$$\text{MPS}[i] \text{ planned} = \sum_{j=1}^{i+\text{ST}} \text{Net\_Demand}[j] - \text{PAB}[i-1] - \text{MPS}[i] \text{ firm}$$

(Equation B)

where ST is the safety time value.

If both SS and ST are in operation then we simply take the maximum of the two, i.e.:

$$MPS[i] \text{ planned} = MAX[Equation(A), Equation(B)]$$

- **Projected available balance (PAB):** The projected available balance represents the projected number of available MPS items at the end of each planning time bucket. This projected figure is calculated by taking into account the PAB for the previous time bucket, the production (MPS figures), and the net demand. $PAB[i]$ is calculated by setting the SS value as the target as follows:

$$PAB[i] = SS = PAB[i-1] + MPS[i] \text{ planned} + \\ MPS[i] \text{ firm} - Net\_Demand[i]$$

(Equation C)

- **Available to promise (ATP):** The available to promise calculation expresses the number of MPS item slots which are actually available to be promised to incoming customer orders. The ATP is computed based upon production (MPS figures), the slot allocation information (allocated, reserved, unplanned), and the opening PAB. ATP is calculated using the following two equations:

$$ATP[1] = PAB[0] + MPS[1] \text{ planned} - \\ MIN(Customer\_Orders[1], Net\_Demand[1])$$

(Equation D)

$$ATP[i] = MPS[i] \text{ planned} - \\ MIN(Customer\_Orders[i], Net\_Demand[i])$$

(Equation E)

In summary then, there are six main lines involved in the MPS planning table. These are as follows:

(1) The demand forecast line is a direct input from the sales/market forecasting department. This frequently has to be disaggregated from a product family forecast to an MPS item forecast through the use of planning BOMs.

(2) The customer slots are directly input by the sales department. This involves the use of sales planning BOMs to translate sales items into MPS items. These planning BOMs are typically single level BOMs.

(3) The net demand line is calculated as a function of lines (1) and (2), based on the time fence information and the forecast consumption rule used.

(4) Both MPS lines (firm and planned) are calculated during the MPS generation stage and are fed directly to requirements planning.

(5) The PAB line is a useful way to measure the performance of the MPS system, and to project availability.

(6)   The ATP value is used by the sales department to facilitate customer order promising.

An example of the use of the MPS planning table

In this section we outline through a worked example the operation of the MPS planning table. Using the example of the stools originally used in Chapter 5 we have demand forecasts and orders for stool A and stool B as shown in Figure 17.17.

For stool A we have no demand forecasts for time buckets 1 and 2 because these time buckets are inside the forecast time fence and therefore only customer orders are used in calculating the net demand. For these two time periods the net demand is simply the sum of the allocated, reserved, and unplanned customer orders. In time buckets after the forecast time fence, we are using the maximum of demand forecasts and the sum of allocated, reserved, and unplanned customer orders to determine net demand. Thus, we can see in time bucket 4 that the demand forecast of 35 stools is larger than the sum of customer orders, in this case 25 stools. Depending on the specific situation different algorithms can be used in determining net demand. One may wish to take a weighted average of the forecasts and orders, giving more credence to orders in the nearer time buckets and putting more weight on the forecasts as one goes farther out in time. The same logic is applied in determining the net demand for stool B.

Time buckets											
Stool A									Safety stock =		**20**
	0	**1**	**2**	**3**	**4**	**5**	**6**	**7**	**8**	**9**	**10**
Demand forecasts				40	35	45	25	20	30	25	30
Allocated		35	25	15	10	5					
Reserved				5	10	20	10				
Unplanned			5		5			20			
Net demand		35	30	40	35	45	25	20	30	25	30
MPS firm		10									
MPS planned		0	20	40	35	45	25	20	30	25	30
PAB	55	30	20	20	20	20	20	20	20	20	20
ATP		20	0	20	10	20	15	0	30	25	30
Stool B									Safety stock =		**30**
	0	**1**	**2**	**3**	**4**	**5**	**6**	**7**	**8**	**9**	**10**
Demand forecasts				10	15	20	35	40	50	45	55
Allocated		30	20	25	20	5					
Reserved				5	10	10	5				
Unplanned			10	35							
Net demand		30	30	65	30	20	35	40	50	45	55
MPS firm		15									
MPS planned		10	30	65	30	20	35	40	50	45	55
PAB	35	30	30	30	30	30	30	30	30	30	30
ATP		15	0	0	0	5	30	40	50	45	55

Figure 17.17   The MPS planning table.

Also in Figure 17.17 we can see that there are predefined Safety Stock limits for stool A and stool B: 20 and 30 units, respectively. This figure is used above in the calculation of the planned MPS figure, following Equation A. For stool A we have a firm manufacturing order in time bucket 1 for 10 units. Taken together with the starting projected available balance of 55 units, we determine the planned manufacturing order for time bucket 1 as follows:

MPS planned in time bucket 1 = safety stock + net demand in time bucket 1 − initial projected available balance − any firm orders in time bucket 1

MPS planned in time bucket 1 = 20 + 35 − 55 − 10 = −10

Since this is a negative number, the MPS planned order for time bucket 1 is zero. In time bucket 2 the calculation is as follows:

MPS planned in time bucket 2 = safety stock + net demand in time bucket 2 − projected available balance in time bucket 1 − any firm orders in time bucket 2

MPS planned in time bucket 2 = 20 + 30 − 30 = 20

And so on across all the time buckets of the MPS planning table.

When the planned MPS order for a particular time bucket is determined, the projected available balance can be calculated. Put simply, it is determined by taking the projected available balance from the previous time bucket, adding any planned and firm MPS orders and subtracting the net demand for that time bucket, as in Equation C. Thus in Figure 17.17 for stool A in time bucket 1 the calculation is as follows:

PAB in time bucket 1 = 55 + 10 − 35 = 30

Now we can also calculate the available to promise given that the planned orders have been determined. Following Equation E and taking the planned MPS orders, we subtract the minimum of net demand and customer orders, which is the sum of the reserved, allocated and unplanned orders.

This is how the calculations in the MPS planning table are done, and the complete table for the 10 time buckets is created in such a manner. As we have pointed out, this table represents the linking pin in the PMS and effectively represents a forum where sales, marketing, and production personnel can communicate their requirements.

In Figure 17.18 we have a number of windows which provide different perspectives on the basic information displayed in the planning table. The first is the order window. This displays the information in the planning table in terms of the customer orders, lists the order number, its status − whether allocated, reserved or firm − and its due date. This window provides valuable information for sales and customer service personnel and provides a window to the manufacturing plan for the customer.

Order window							
Order	**Status**	**Due date**					
CD54-A	Firm	4/12/95					
FG65-B	Allocated	5/12/95					
DS34-A	Reserved	6/12/95					
Time bucket window				**Time bucket window**			
Bucket 7:				**Bucket 3:**			
Allocated:				Allocated:			
20 to order DS34-A				15 to order CD54-A			
				Reserved:			
				5 to order FG65-B			
Order status window							
Order: DS34-A							
Status: allocated							
Requested: 2/10/95							
Promised: 6/12/95							
Allocation:							
20 stool A Bucket 7							

Figure 17.18   The MPS planning table.

The next two windows are examples of a time bucket window. This details the breakdown of all customer orders in a particular window. It identifies which order each unit of net demand is allocated against.

The final window is the order status window and presents all the information about a single order, its number, its status, when it was requested, when it is promised, and how the components of the order are being fulfilled and in which time bucket.

Each of these windows provides a different perspective on the basic information in the MPS planning table, but, most importantly, they provide this information in a manner that is of use to the particular end user. This allows the planners to ensure that there is only one source of planning information, i.e. the MPS planning table.

Now that we have developed a simple MPS, we will look at how the planning table is used to react to changes in customer orders or revised demand forecasts. In Figure 17.19 we have a new situation, where an unplanned customer order in time bucket 7 for 20 units of stool A has appeared. If we compare the figures in this table with the original table (Figure 17.17) we see that there were 20 units of stool A available to

Stool A								Safety stock =		20	
Time Buckets	0	1	2	3	4	5	6	7	8	9	10
Demand forecasts				40	35	45	25	20	30	25	30
Allocated		35	25	15	10	5					
Reserved				5	10	20	10				
Unplanned			5		5			20			
Net demand		35	30	40	35	45	25	20	30	25	30
MPS firm		10									
MPS planned		0	20	40	35	45	25	20	30	25	30
PAB	55	30	20	20	20	20	20	20	20	20	20
ATP		20	0	20	10	20	15	0	30	25	30

Stool B								Safety stock =		30	
	0	1	2	3	4	5	6	7	8	9	10
Demand forecasts				10	15	20	35	40	50	45	55
Allocated		30	20	25	20	5					
Reserved				5	10	10	5				
Unplanned			10								
Net demand		30	30	30	30	20	35	40	50	45	55
MPS firm		15									
MPS planned		10	30	30	30	20	35	40	50	45	55
PAB	35	30	30	30	30	30	30	30	30	30	30
ATP		15	0	0	0	5	30	40	50	45	55

Figure 17.19   The MPS planning table.

promise in time bucket 7. Now that we have an order for 20 units, we can fulfill this order from the available to promise items, but this reduces the new ATP to zero, as indicated in Figure 17.19. We do not need to increase the planned MPS figure.

Now we look at another situation, depicted in Figure 17.20. We have an unplanned order for 35 units of stool B in time bucket 3. In this instance the available to promise is zero, so the master planner will have to modify the plan to accommodate the customer order. In this particular instance the net demand for this time bucket increases to 65 units, and this in turn increases the planned MPS order from 30 to 65 units so that the customer order can be fulfilled.

The added value of the MPS planning table lies in its ability to deal with changes in the original conditions on which it was built. As the master planner can change the size of the planned order that will be released to manufacturing, there is also flexibility to the time buckets when an order is fulfilled. When such a scenario occurs, the sales and marketing people responsible for interfacing with the end customer can easily and quickly determine through the order status, time bucket, and order windows the exact situation with respect to any order.

Stool A — Time buckets — Safety stock = 20

Stool A	0	1	2	3	4	5	6	7	8	9	10
Demand forecasts				40	35	45	25	20	30	25	30
Allocated		35	25	15	10	5					
Reserved				5	10	20	10				
Unplanned			5		5			20			
Net demand		35	30	40	35	45	25	20	30	25	30
MPS firm		10									
MPS planned		0	20	40	35	45	25	20	30	25	30
PAB	55	30	20	20	20	20	20	20	20	20	20
ATP		20	0	20	10	20	15	0	30	25	30

Stool B — Safety stock = 30

Stool B	0	1	2	3	4	5	6	7	8	9	10
Demand forecasts				10	15	20	35	40	50	45	55
Allocated		30	20	25	20	5					
Reserved				5	10	10	5				
Unplanned			10	35							
Net demand		30	30	65	30	20	35	40	50	45	55
MPS firm		15									
MPS planned		10	30	65	30	20	35	40	50	45	55
PAB	35	30	30	30	30	30	30	30	30	30	30
ATP		15	0	0	0	5	30	40	50	45	55

Figure 17.20   The MPS planning table.

17.5.6   A note on product distribution issues

Throughout our discussion on MPS we have been referring to customer order entry as if customer orders could be directly input to the master scheduling process. Of course, life is rarely so simple. For many products the end user or end customer lies at the end of a complex distribution channel. The manufacturer passes products to distributors or wholesalers, who in turn pass them to retailers, who supply the end user. Today many business analysts think of the flow of material between suppliers and their ultimate customers as passing through a pipeline or channel. People refer to the *customer pipeline* or the *distribution channel*. A set of linkages is established through which product is supplied to the customer. In today's customer driven manufacturing world, where customers' preferences change frequently and product life cycles are reducing, competitive advantage is gained through having a pipeline or channel which facilitates very fast throughput of product, and also very fast and accurate feedback of data on customer needs and market trends to the manufacturing plant. The availability of **Electronic Data Interchange (EDI)** and bar coding technology facilitate this fast throughput. Hence the notion of the extended enterprise, and the importance of taking a value stream analysis approach. (See Chapter 4.)

Just as MRP based approaches are used to plan and schedule the flow of material through the manufacturing plant, Distribution Requirements

Planning (DRP) and Distribution Resource Planning (DRP II) approaches are available to plan and schedule the flow of product through the pipeline of manufacturers, distributors, wholesalers, retailers, and on to the end customer. DRP and DRP II are, however, beyond the scope of this book. The reader interested in further details of these approaches is referred to Martin (1993) and Farmer and van Amstel (1991).

In the past, DRP systems and MRP style systems were developed in isolation, purchased by different divisions of companies, and run as separate systems. Today, with the emphasis on customer driven systems, the availability of EDI technology, and the emerging thinking on the extended enterprise, system developers are combining DRP and MRP thinking into integrated systems.

17.5.7 Concluding comments on MPS

The MPS function is the main linking pin between the marketing/sales, engineering, and manufacturing departments. This link is typically managed by a team of personnel from the different departments. This team is referred to as a planning board. The planning board needs to have a sophisticated planning system to aid them in the MPS management process. Such a system might include an MPS planning table of the type shown in Figures 17.17, 17.18, and 17.19. Some important techniques for improving the design of the MPS system include commonality analysis and investment diagrams. The proper identification of the constrained resources can be of great benefit in providing a more accurate picture of manufacturing operations. The MPS planning table was introduced as the basis for using the MPS as the common denominator between the marketing, sales, engineering, and manufacturing departments.

17.6 Operation level issues – factory coordination and PAC

Looking back to Figures 17.1 and 17.2, it is clear that we consider the factory to be composed of a series of mini focused factories or product based manufacturing cells. We believe that the degree to which such cells are *autonomous*, and the extent to which the factory can be so decomposed, will depend primarily on the product/process market situation and the degree to which the JIT philosophy and the ideas of group technology (see Chapter 11) can be successfully applied.

Operational production management system issues essentially involve taking the output from the tactical planning phase, e.g. the planned orders from a requirements planning system, and managing the manufacturing system in quasi real time to meet these requirements. Our view is that in the future, it will be necessary to have a PAC system for each cell and a higher level controller to coordinate the activities of the various manufacturing cells.

It is important to distinguish between the two levels of operational production management. The need for a factory coordination (FC) system arises from the fact that the factory is now seen in terms of a series of well-defined product oriented cells, or mini factories, rather than as a single unit. This concept of a factory being composed of a series of cells is in accord with the reference models of the US National Bureau of Standards (see Jones and McLean 1986) and the work of the International Organization for Standardization (see ISO 1986). Further, it accords well with modern thinking on the design and layout of manufacturing systems. (See, for example, Schonberger 1987; Burbidge 1986.)

Before offering a detailed architectural view of the PAC and factory coordination systems, we will take a functional perspective indicating the type of functionality which might exist within typical real world systems. We will start by looking at the lower level PAC systems within the individual cells.

17.6.1   A functional view of PAC

Harhen and Browne (1984) argued that the PAC system includes the following activities:

- Manufacturing order approval and release.
- Operation scheduling and loading.
- Material staging and issue.
- Priority control in work in progress (WIP).
- Capacity control in WIP.
- Quality control in WIP.
- Manufacturing order close.
- Process evaluation in terms of labor, equipment, and materials.

PAC thus involves a set of decision making activities which are supported by an effective data collection and monitoring subsystem. Later in this chapter we will present an architecture for PAC which will indicate the various modules within a PAC system and how these modules relate to each other. Earlier (Chapter 3), we stated that the PAC subsystem is key to the realization of integration at the operational level. Given the range of activities that PAC is involved with, in terms of approving and releasing orders, scheduling, and loading batches, etc., it is clear that this is so. PAC interacts with the storage and materials handling systems, the individual manufacturing, assembly and testing workstations, and the production database in order to "know" where each batch should be routed to and how they should be processed, etc. It is clear that the data and information flow system must "mirror" the physical work flow through a cell. PAC facilitates this data and information flow. When a batch finishes an operation on a workstation, the PAC system, through recourse to the process planning file in the production database, identifies its next operation. It then determines how the batch should be transported to the operation, perhaps in the case of an automated manufacturing environment instructing an **Automatically Guided Vehicle (AGV)** to move it there. Prior to releasing the batch to the next operation, it checks material availability, where appropriate, and, if necessary, arranges to have the relevant materials released from WIP or raw materials stores and made available to the workstation.

In the case of a **Computer Numerically Controlled (CNC)** workstation operating in a **Distributed Numerical Control (DNC)** environment, the PAC system should know the appropriate part program through its access to the production database, and be capable of routing this part program to the CNC workstation. In the case of a test workstation, it is clear that the PAC system must be in a position to deal with the consequences of a component or a product failing a test, identifying where the failed item should be routed, understanding what action to take in the case of multiple failures, etc. Seen in this light, the PAC system is the "intelligence" which manages the flow of work through the manufacturing system and organizes the data flow which integrates the various devices on the shop floor, including the workstations, the transport devices, the materials handling systems etc. It is in this sense that we argue that PAC realizes integration at the shop floor or operational level of the factory. (See Chapter 3.)

PAC, then, has two major elements:

(1)   A decision making element.

(2)   A data collection and reporting element.

The decision making element relates to "deciding" which jobs should go to which workstations and when, determining which transport device should be used to move semi-finished batches and materials between workstations, identifying what course of action to take when a batch fails a quality test, dealing with workstation breakdown, etc. Clearly, PAC decision making must be supported by accurate and timely recording and reporting of data on shop floor operations. The shop floor is a dynamic area in which the work force, workstations, materials, tools, transport devices, part programs, etc. are coordinated by the dispatching, routing, and monitoring of individual batches and jobs. Unless the PAC system is made aware of individual events as they take place, and thus has a real time and accurate picture of the shop floor status, it cannot make good decisions on the flow of work through the shop floor. Traditionally, shop floor data collection involved manual recording of data on the shop floor by production operators, and, in more recent times, batch updates to computer databases which were on-line but not necessarily real time. In this environment it is very difficult to create effective PAC systems, particularly when we are dealing with the variety and complexity inherent in today's production systems.

Now, however, automatic data capture equipment allows data to be captured and transmitted in real time with a reading accuracy far greater than that of manually recorded and transmitted data. Within a work cell it is possible to capture data automatically or semiautomatically using sensors. Methods available include bar coding, Optical Character Recognition (OCR), Magnetic Ink Character Recognition (MICR), magnetic stripe, and, increasingly, direct voice input. By simply placing a bar code on a component it is possible to track it automatically from the time it enters at the receiving bay, through its various processing and storage stages, until it is assembled into a product and shipped from the plant.

Furthermore, it is clear that the data flow between the shop floor and the PAC system is **bidirectional**; data emanating from the PAC system is **instructive**, i.e. instructions to a human operator or a piece of equipment to carry out an operation, or perhaps process aids to support an operator in a particular task. The data required to support PAC can be classified as being either **static** or **dynamic**. Static data comprises product structures, bill of material data, process routings, data on individual workstations, material points of storage and use, etc. This data is normally updated on-line via a terminal. Dynamic data is that data emanating from the shop floor which is used by the PAC system to keep track of activities on the shop floor. Dynamic data, to be up to date and therefore effective, must be collected in real time. Dynamic data capture systems may be classified according to collection mode: manual, i.e. keyboard entry, semiautomatic via, for example, bar code wanding terminals, and automatic, where no intervention is required from the user. The dynamic data to be collected includes the following:

- Product tracking data.
- Labor, material, and equipment tracking data.
- Inspection and quality data.

It is easy to underestimate the difficulties and complexities associated with, first, defining the precise level of data collection which is necessary to support PAC, and, second, putting in place the appropriate data collection and reporting systems. In an early paper Awad (1980) argued that "data collection is the weakest link in the data processing system. Besides being time-consuming and error-prone, it amounts to between 30 and 50 per cent of processing costs."

Data is collected for three reasons:

(1)   To support the decision making aspects of PAC.
(2)   To facilitate post production analysis, i.e. daily or weekly reporting.
(3)   To ensure traceability.

Traceability implies the possibility of tracing problems with materials or work practice all the way back to source, whether that source be within the manufacturing plant or the supplier of raw materials. Thus, if a component or subassembly fails in service, it becomes possible to locate other products from the same batch, whether they be in work in progress or at a customer's site. In this way a company may be able to recall products that may be faulty before the fault manifests itself, avoid possible product liability claims, and protect its market image.

In Section 17.6.3, we will present a PAC architecture which distinguishes clearly between the decision making and historical reporting roles of PAC.

17.6.2   A functional view of factory coordination

As indicated earlier, our model of a factory is that of a series of product based cells operating in a continuous flow manufacturing environment. As quoted earlier, Gallagher and Knight (1973) define group technology as "a technique for identifying and bringing together related or similar components in a production process in order to take advantage of their similarities by making use of, for example, the inherent economies of flow-production methods." Group technology principles are applied to define appropriate part and assembly families. These families, which share common design and manufacturing attributes, are associated in turn with particular manufacturing cells in the plant. Within each cell the workstations are organized, as far as possible, in such a manner that the products of the cell flow through the cell in a continuous flow manner. This type of layout is referred to as a **product based layout**. Similarly, the individuals cells are positioned in such a way as to facilitate the flow of products between them.

A result of this redefinition of the factory as a series of product based cells is a considerable reduction in the complexity of product flow through the factory, compared to traditional process oriented layouts. However, it is unlikely that we will be able to define cells which are completely independent. Perhaps cells will have to share expensive workstations and facilities. Certainly, we would expect that the products of one cell will be used in another cell; we might, for example, have cells which manufacture components that are assembled together in later assembly cells. This interaction between cells creates the need for a higher level PAC or FC system. Thus, the FC system coordinates the product flow between cells within the manufacturing plant, by providing a bridge between the requirements planning system which sits above it and the individual PAC systems which are below it. From the point of view of the factory coordination system, the individual cells are "work centers" and the FC system must manage the flow of work between them. The FC system must be aware of the likely completion dates of batches or jobs within each cell so that it can schedule availability of the batch or job at the next cell to which it is to be routed. Thus, the FC must manage the flow and transport of batches between cells.

17.6.3   An architectural view of PAC

Within the ESPRIT (European Strategic Programme for Research and Development in Information Technology) COSIMA (COntrol Systems for Integrated MAnufacturing) project an architecture for PAC has been defined. (See Bauer *et al.* 1993.) In this context an architecture is that which allows us to identify and prescribe the basic building blocks of a PAC system and the interrelationships between these building blocks. COSIMA has defined PAC as being composed of five basic building blocks:

(1)   A scheduling building block – the scheduler.

(2)   A dispatching building block – the dispatcher.

(3)   A monitoring building block – the monitor.

(4)   A producing building block – the producer.

(5)   A moving building block – the mover.

In general terms, the scheduler takes the list of required orders produced by the factory coordination system and develops schedules for each individual work center based on the known manufacturing process routings and expected available capacity at the work centers. This schedule acts as a short term plan. The planning horizon varies depending on the manufacturing environment, but typically might be in the range of one shift to one week. The scheduling function is important because it represents the only true planning activity within the PAC system.

The dispatcher could be described as a real-time scheduler which assigns jobs to workstations based on real-time information, including the present status of the shop floor, and on the priorities set by the scheduler. The dispatcher thus seeks to realize the plans developed by the scheduler. If the manufacturing plant works exactly as planned, i.e. there are no machine breakdowns, no unexpected operator absences, materials are available in the quantities and the quality expected, operations take the amount of time and capacity which was planned, etc., the dispatcher simply implements the plan of the scheduler, without any modifications. However, it is more likely that the manufacturing plant will not run exactly as expected and the dispatcher will have to interpret the schedule and modify it if necessary. The dispatcher will need sufficient functionality or intelligence to deal with predictable unexpected events on the shop floor. Further, the dispatcher will have to be able to determine if at any stage the planned schedule becomes infeasible, and notify the scheduler accordingly. The scheduler in turn will notify the factory coordination system, in case there are ramifications for other cells within the manufacturing plant.

Relevant data is captured as the manufacturing process proceeds, and, through the monitor, data is made available and information is fed back to the scheduler and dispatcher. The monitor fulfills three roles:

(1) It provides real-time data on the status of the manufacturing system to the other building blocks, in particular to the dispatcher and scheduler. As individual events take place on the shop floor – e.g. a batch starts an operation at a workstation, a batch is moved from one location to another on the shop floor, an item or a batch fails a test routine – the monitor notifies the dispatcher. In this way the dispatcher is able to make real time decisions using up-to-date information.

(2) It provides the basic data from which historical reports of the performance of the manufacturing system can be generated. Thus, at the end of the shift or the week the monitor should be able to generate reports on the delivery performance of the manufacturing system, the level of work in progress over the week, the utilization of various workstations, etc.

(3) It provides for specialist requirements in areas such as traceability. Within certain industrial sectors, for example the health care products sector, manufacturers are obliged by the appropriate regulatory authorities to maintain detailed records on individual items and batches as they pass through the manufacturing system, in order to facilitate product recall or diagnosis of the causes in the case of products in the field failing to meet stringent quality requirements.

As has been indicated, the dispatcher is made aware of the real-time status of each resource and batch in the manufacturing cell by the monitor. In this way the dispatcher may issue direct instructions to the movers and producers. The mover, in response to requests from the dispatcher, coordinates the flow of material from one workstation to another, or between the workstations and the storage points. It translates the dispatcher's instructions into direct instructions for the individual transportation devices. In the case of an automated Flexible Manufacturing System (FMS), the transportation devices may be, for example, Automatically Guided Vehicles (AGV) or computer driven conveyers. In such cases the mover must be aware of the status and location of each AGV, and the paths which the AGVs may take within the FMS. Further, if the FMS contains more than one AGV, then the mover must have sufficient functionality to ensure that the AGVs do not collide within the system. In the case of a largely manual system, where perhaps operators are responsible for transporting WIP, tooling, fixtures, etc., around the cell, one could envision the operation of the mover in terms of a set of instructions being made available to the operator, perhaps through a visual display unit.

The dispatcher also issues instructions to the producers. The producers may be considered as virtual workstations. On receipt of instructions from the dispatcher the producer, in the case of CNC machines, downloads the appropriate part program to the actual machine and issues the detailed instructions to the machine in terms of set-up, material availability, etc.

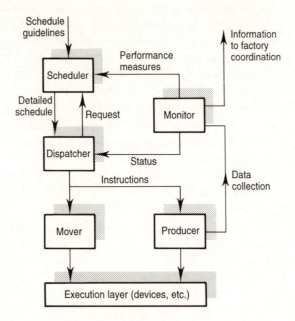

Figure 17.21   Production activity control.

Figure 17.21 indicates, in general terms, the relationship between the various building blocks within a PAC system. It further indicates the type of data which is required to support the PAC system. As is clear from this figure, PAC is a data rich activity. Data such as process routings, process and set-up times, etc. are required to allow the scheduler, dispatcher, and monitor to operate effectively. Further, as was indicated in the discussion of the monitor, PAC generates a large amount of data. It is clear that a large amount of data is collected by the data collection system, and this data must be made available, in quasi real time, to the dispatcher in particular. This transfer of data between the various building blocks of PAC is achieved through the use of an Application Network (AN). The AN (see Bauer *et al.* 1993) provides transparent data communication to permit data packages to flow between the various building blocks. A building block may request some type of data from the AN, the AN determines the source building block for that data, requests the data, and delivers it to the requesting building block. In this way the AN facilitates the integration of the various building blocks into an integrated PAC system.

In Figure 17.21 we distinguish between the data collection activity and the actual monitor building block. The design of the monitor determines what data is required to be collected. The data collection devices and associated software simply pass this data to the monitor, which then makes it available to other building blocks or in regular management summary reports as required.

It is important to understand that the precise implementation of each building block is not at issue here. In fact, no comments are being offered here about the desirability or otherwise of using particular algorithms or heuristics in order to develop schedules or to dispatch the batches through the cells. The important point is that, whatever approach is used to realize any particular building block within the architecture, the basic functionality of the building block remains the same, as does its relationship to the other building blocks.

Over the years there has been much debate about the role of finite scheduling in production management systems. One could argue that infinite scheduling is appropriate at the tactical planning level of PMS, i.e. at the requirements planning stage. However, finite scheduling, perhaps using techniques such as the OPT scheduler, may well be possible, and indeed desirable, at the FC and certainly at the PAC level.

Also, it is perhaps worth emphasizing that these three building blocks – i.e. the scheduler, dispatcher, and monitor – need not necessarily be software modules, although this might well be the case in many instances. One could imagine the work cell supervisor, or indeed the work cell team, scheduling and dispatching work through the cell, perhaps using perhaps manual or computer based decision support tools. Jackson and Browne, for example, describe an interactive scheduler using a computer based Gannt chart (Jackson and Browne 1989).

A final point: the application of JIT ideas, in pushing the manufacturing system towards simplification, tries to create a manufacturing environment within which the problems of scheduling and dispatching are greatly reduced. This makes the problems of PAC relatively simple, so much so that in the extreme case a manual dispatching and moving system – namely, Kanban cards – may be used.

17.6.4   An architectural view of FC

As indicated earlier, we visualize a typical manufacturing environment as consisting of a number of group technology cells, each controlled by a PAC system. The factory coordination system organizes the flow of products throughout a factory and ensures that production in each cell is synchronized with the overall production goals of the factory.

Traditionally, the design of the production environment was considered separate from the control of product flow through it. However, it is clear that there is a close relationship between the two, as Lubben (1988) argued when he wrote that "the physical layout significantly influences the efficiency of the production system." Within the factory coordination architecture, we recognize a link between the tasks of production environment design and control, as illustrated in Figure 17.22. The production environment design module helps to reduce the variety of possible production related problems by organizing the manufacturing system, as far as possible, into a product based layout, and allocating new products to

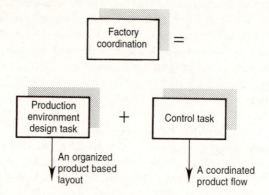

Figure 17.22 The link between production environment design and control.

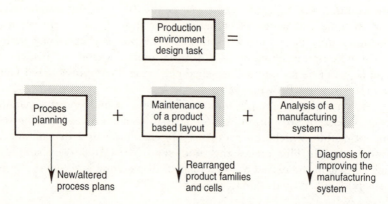

Figure 17.23 The production environment design task within factory coordination.

product families. The control module provides guidelines and goals with which each work group can manage its activities and deal with any problems that occur within its scope of responsibility.

Using an initial product based layout, the production environment design module integrates new products into the production environment with minimal disruption and reorganization to the existing product based structure. The various procedures involved in production environment design may include the following (Figure 17.23):

(1) The generation and detailing of process plans for new products. The idea here is to take the available process plan as created by the manufacturing engineers and, where appropriate and necessary, choose alternate resources (perhaps alternate machines or routings through the cell in the case of bottlenecks on the first choice machine or routing).

(2)   The maintenance of a product based layout. As indicated earlier, product life cycles are reducing and new product introductions are more frequent than before. This module seeks to maintain the product or group technology based layout as the product mix changes over time.

(3)   The analysis of a production system. Data generated or collected by the individual PAC monitors provides a rich source of data on the performance of the shop floor, and should be constantly analyzed to detect areas where continuous improvement is possible – perhaps identifying set up times which are too long, scrap rates which are too high, or thoughput times or machine waiting times which are too long – and alerting the manufacturing engineers.

The main purpose of the control task is to coordinate the activities of each PAC system through the provision of schedule and real-time control guidelines, while recognizing that each PAC system is responsible for the activities within its own cell. The time horizon for the flow of products by the control task varies, depending on the manufacturing environment. However, it is influenced by the time horizon of the MPS, since the goal of the control task is to satisfy the production requirements and constraints set by the MPS. The control task involves developing schedule guidelines using a factory level scheduler, implementing these guidelines, and providing real-time guidelines for each of the PAC systems using a factory level dispatcher, and monitoring the progress of the schedule using a factory level monitor. The FC control task is in many ways a higher level version of a PAC system (Figure 17.24).

We consider that there are three individual building blocks associated with the FC control task:

(1)   A scheduler which develops a schedule that each PAC system uses as a guide when developing its own schedule.

(2)   A dispatcher which controls the movement of material between cells on a real time basis and communicates with each PAC dispatcher.

(3)   A monitor which observes the status of the entire factory based on information coming from each PAC monitor.

In addition to these three basic building blocks, each cell on the shop floor may be regarded as a virtual producer, because each cell receives guidelines on its production activities from the factory level dispatcher. In relation to the movement of material between cells, there may be two different types of mover.

The first type of mover, the PAC mover, which is used to organize materials handling within the cell, can also coordinate the materials movement between cells, provided that the material handling between cells is a simple task. Information on the next cell on a product's process routing can

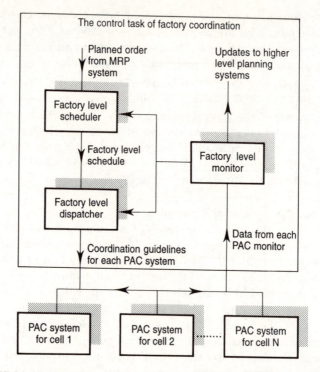

Figure 17.24 Data exchange between the control task of factory coordination and a numbr of PAC systems.

be given to the mover by the particular PAC dispatcher of the cell which the batch is leaving.

The second type of mover, the factory level mover, operates on the same principles as the PAC mover, except that it is concerned with organizing the materials flow between the cells on the shop floor. The factory level mover receives all of its instructions from the factory level dispatcher. In a shop floor, where there is a variety of materials movement between cells, there may well be a requirement for a factory level mover.

17.7 PMS and the extended enterprise

In today's business world, manufacturers seek competitive advantage by developing close commercial and electronic links with their suppliers and customers. As indicated earlier, supply chain management and integration together with customer driven manufacturing are important considerations. The extended enterprise facilitated by the emerging tele-computing infrastructure results in partnerships between suppliers, manufacturers, assemblers, distributors, and customers. Clearly the production

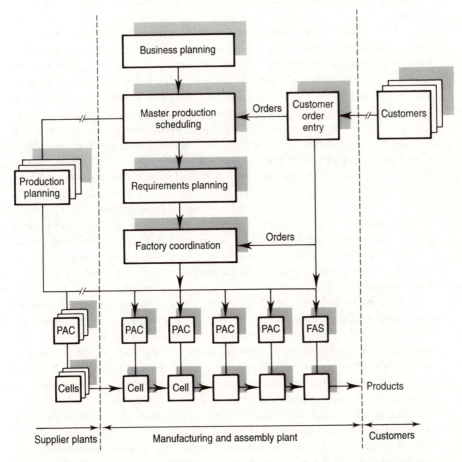

Figure 17.25 The extended PMS.

management system must manage the flow of material and product through this chain.

In this section we will look at the integration of suppliers into the manufacturing and product final assembly system. In our experience the supply chain to large manufacturers tends to be dominated by small manufacturing enterprises who supply specialized components and subassemblies. As was indicated earlier in our discussion on lean supply chains (see Chapter 4), competitive advantage is achieved by integrating these suppliers into the activities of the final assembly plants.

The outline structure of a production management system to ensure the management of the supply chain is presented in Figure 17.25. The figure presents our understanding of the role that the production management system plays in coordinating the supply of materials from key subsuppliers and suppliers, and in coordinating the flow of customer orders into the system.

The environment depicted is clearly an extended enterprise style situation in that close relations exist between the suppliers and the manufacturing and assembly plant. Of course it is not a true extended enterprise in that it does not necessarily include shared product design, etc. Looking at the supply side initially, it is suggested that there are electronic links (in reality EDI connections) between the main suppliers and the main plant. The production planning functions within the supplier plants are assumed to have strong relations with the planning (in fact master production scheduling) people of the main plant, who share with them information on the likely pattern of future demand (both firm and forecast) to allow the suppliers in turn to plan their production. On a day-to-day basis, the operational planning system of the main plant (the factory coordination system) sends precise orders to the suppliers to ensure availability of components and subassemblies to its manufacturing and assembly process. This call off of supplies in effect results in a situation where the external suppliers are treated as an external "arm" of the main plant, not unlike internal manufacturing cells.

The structure and complexity of the production planning activity at the supplier plants depends very much on the structure and complexity of the products they provide. In most cases suppliers tend to be small and medium sized companies, supplying components and relatively simple assemblies, often to a relatively small number of large customers. In such cases the production planning system is relatively simple, with perhaps no necessity for a requirement planning or factory coordination module.

Figure 17.25 depicts the customer interaction in a very simplified way. No account is taken of distribution issues, and the customer (which, indeed, might well be a distribution center) interacts with the planning and control system of the product manufacturer. The environment suggested in the figure is an assemble to order (ATO) system where modules manufacture is driven by the master production schedule, based primarily on order forecasts and final assembly is driven by actual customer orders. The concept is that the modules are pulled into final assembly and are configured/assembled directly to order prior to dispatch to the customer.

17.8 Conclusion

In this chapter we presented an overview of a production management system architecture which facilitates integration forward with the customer order entry function and backward with the supply chain. We emphasized the need to consider each functional block, including business planning, master production scheduling, requirements planning, and shop floor control (factory coordination and production activity control) separately. Furthermore, we indicated our understanding of the type of functionality which is appropriate at each level of the PMS hierarchy. In particular we considered master production scheduling and shop floor control in detail. We tried to explain the role that techniques such as planning BOMs, commonality analysis, and the investment diagram can play in supporting the master scheduling function, and we showed through an example, the detailed use of the MPS planning table outlined earlier in Chapter 7. Furthermore, we presented a functional architecture for the production activity control and factory coordination modules of shop floor control. Clearly the scheduling techniques presented earlier in Chapter 10 can be used to implement the scheduler building blocks within these subsystems.

Questions

(17.1) What are the two main tasks of business planning?

(17.2) "The long range production plan needs to be expressed in meaningful units, but it also needs to be expressed in a manageable number of units." Explain.

(17.3) How would one determine the time horizon for the long range production plan?

(17.4) Distinguish clearly between a chase and level strategy for long range production planning.

(17.5) "The master production schedule is the linking pin between the marketing and sales (sales forecast and customer order promising), manufacturing (operations), and engineering (product and process design) functions." Discuss.

(17.6) What do you understand by the term *planning BOM*?

(17.7) What are modular BOMs? When and why are they used?

(17.8) How does the super BOM differ from the modular BOM?

(17.9) What does the *quantity per* relationship for the various modules in a super BOM represent?

(17.10) In the context of super BOMs, distinguish clearly between the following technical terms:

    (a) Option

    (b) Variant

    (c) Attachment.

(17.11) What is a percentage BOM?

(17.12) What do you understand by the phrase "frozen segment of the MPS"? How does this segment relate to the final assembly schedule in a hybrid MTS/ATO manufacturing plant?

(17.13) What do you understand by the phrase "closed loop nature of the MPS process"?

(17.14) In the MPS framework presented in this chapter, we identified three stages. What are these three stages and their respective roles?

(17.15) "Generally the MPS controlled items are at the narrowest point of the BOM structure." Comment on this statement in the context of an ATO manufacturing plant.

(17.16) Safety stock is one method of reducing the complexity of the MPS process. Can you identify other methods?

(17.17) How might a master production scheduler use an investment diagram?

(17.18) How does an MPS planning table support concurrent planning by the marketing, sales, and manufacturing functions?

(17.19) Distinguish clearly between the forecast time fence and the ATP time fence. Which may be greater? Why?

(17.20) In the context of the MPS, distinguish clearly between allocated slots, reserved slots, and unplanned slots.

(17.21) Define the term projected available balance (PAB). How does the PAB differ from the ATP (Available To Promise)?

(17.22) "The value added of the MPS planning table lies in its ability to deal with changes in the original conditions on which it was built." Explain.

(17.23) Distinguish clearly between the respective roles of factory coordination and production activity control.

(17.24) "PAC has two major elements, namely a decision making element and a data collection and reporting element." Discuss.

(17.25) Why is shop floor data collected?

(17.26) What do you understand by the term *traceability*, when used in the context of shop floor data collection?

(17.27) Distinguish clearly between the respective roles of the scheduler, dispatcher, and monitor in the PAC architecture presented in this chapter.

(17.28) How does the PAC monitor support shop floor data collection and reporting?

(17.29) Is finite scheduling appropriate to PAC? Why?

(17.30) "The factory coordination approach seeks to integrate the design of the production environment with the control of product flow through it." Discuss.

References to Part V

Awad, E.M. 1980. *Business Data Processing*. Englewood Cliffs, NJ: Prentice-Hall.

Bauer, A., Bowden, R., Browne, J., Duggan, J. and Lyons, G. 1994. *Shop Floor Control Systems – From Design to Implementation*. 2nd Edn. Chapman and Hall.

Bose, G.J. and Rao, A. 1988. "Implementing JIT with MRP II creates hybrid manufacturing environment," *Industrial Engineering*, September.

Burbidge, J.L. 1985. "Automated production control with a simulation capability," in *Modelling Production Management Systems*, edited by P. Falster and R.B. Mazumder. Amsterdam: North-Holland.

Burbidge, J.L. 1986. "Production planning and control: a personal philosophy," paper presented to the IFIP Working Group 5.7 meeting, Munich, March.

Cherns, A.B. 1977. "Can organization science help design organizations?" *Organisational Dynamics*, Spring, 44–64.

COSIMA Project Team. 1987. "Development towards an application generator for production activity control," in *ESPRIT 87 Achievements and Impact, Part II*, edited by The Commission of the European Communities, Directorate-General Telecommunications, Information Industries and Innovation, Amsterdam: North-Holland, 1648–1661.

Everdell, R. 1987. *Master Scheduling: APICS Training Aid*. Falls Church, VA: American Production and Inventory Control Society.

Farmer, D. and Van Amstel R.P. 1991. *Effective Pipeline Management*. Gower.

Fogarty, D. and Hoffman, T. 1983. *Production and Inventory Management*. Cincinatti, OH: South-Western Publishing Co.

Gallagher, C.C. and Knight, W.A. 1973. *Group Technology*. London: Butterworths.

Gault, R. 1984. "OR as education," *European Journal of Operational Research*, **16**, 293–307.

Gessner, R.A. 1986. *Master Production Schedule Planning*. New York: John Wiley and Sons.

Harhen, J. and Browne, J. 1984. "Production activity control: a key node in CIM," in *Production Management Systems: Strategies and Tools for Design*, edited by H. Huber. Amsterdam: Elsevier, 107–122.

Higgins, P.D. 1991. *Master Production Scheduling: A Key Node in an Integrated Approach to Production Management Systems*, Ph.D. thesis, University College Galway, Ireland.

Higgins, P.D. and Tierney, K. 1990. "Development of a framework for master production scheduling," in *Proceedings of the International Conference on Advances in Production Management Systems*, Espoo, Finland, 20–22 August.

Higgins, P.D., Tierney, K. and Browne, J. 1991. "Production management systems: state of the art and perspectives," in *Proceedings of the CAPE '91 Conference*, edited by G. Doumeingts. Amsterdam: North Holland.

ISO. 1986. *The Ottawa Report on Reference Models for Manufacturing Standards*, Version 1.1. Geneva: International Organization for Standardization.

Jackson, S. and Browne, J. 1989. "An interactive scheduler for production activity control," *International Journal of Computer Integrated Manufacturing*, **2**(1), 2–14.

Jones, A. and McLean, C. 1986. "A proposed hierarchical control model for automated manufacturing systems," *Journal of Manufacturing Systems*, 5(1).

Jones, G. and Roberts, M. 1990. *Optimized Production Technology (OPT)*. UK: IFS Publications.

Latham, D. 1981. "Are you among MRP's walking wounded?" *Production and Inventory Management*, 23(3), 33–41.

Lubben, R.T. 1988. *Just in Time Manufacturing: An Aggressive Manufacturing Strategy*. New York: McGraw-Hill.

Martin, A.J. 1993. *DRP: Distribution Resource Planning*. Revised Edn. Oliver Wight Publications Inc.

Pava, C. 1983. *Managing New Office Technology: An Organizational Strategy*. New York: The Free Press.

Plenert, G. and Best, T.D. 1986. "MRP, JIT and OPT – what's 'best'?" *Production and Inventory Management*, second quarter, 22–28.

Plossl, G.W. and Wight, O.W. 1967. *Production and Inventory Control*. Englewood Cliffs, NJ: Prentice-Hall.

Schonberger, R.J. 1987. *World Class Manufacturing Casebook: Implementing JIT and TQC*. New York: The Free Press.

Shivnan, J., Joyce, R. and Browne, J. 1987. "Production and inventory management techniques – a systems perspective," in *Modern Production Management Systems*, edited by A. Kusiak. Amsterdam: North-Holland, 347–362.

St. John, R. 1984. "The evils of lot sizing in MRP," *Production and Inventory Management*, 25(4).

Trist, E.L. 1982. "The sociotechnical perspective," in *Perspectives on Organizational Design and Behaviour*, edited by A.H. Van de Ven and W.F. Joyce. New York: John Wiley and Sons.

Vollman, T., Berry, T. and Whybark, D. 1988. *Master Production Scheduling: Principles and Practice*. Falls Church, VA: American Production and Inventory Control Society.

Wemmerlov, U. 1984. "Assemble to order manufacturing: implications for materials management," *Journal of Operations Management*, 4(4), 347–368.

White, J.A. 1987. "Integrated manufacturing systems: a material handling perspective," in *Proceedings of the 4th European Conference on Automated Manufacturing*, edited by B.B. Hundy. UK: IFS Publications, 45–56.

Wortmann, J.C. 1990. "Towards one-of-a-kind production: the future of European industry," in *Proceedings of the International Conference on Advances in Production Management Systems*, Espoo, Finland, 20–22 August.

Yamashina, H., Okumara, K. and Matsumoto, K. 1987. "General manufacturing strategy: the Japanese view," in *Proceedings of the 4th European Conference on Automated Manufacturing*, edited by B.B. Hundy. UK: IFS Publications, 33-44.

Problems

Problems (1) to (23) relate to Part II of the book (MRP and MRP II) and Problems (24) and (25) relate to Part III (JIT).

(1)   Gizmo-Stools Inc. manufactures the two stools (Stool A and Stool B) described in Chapter 5. (See Figure 5.3 for a description of the bill of materials of the two stools and Table 5.3 for the master parts data.)

Gizmo-Stools Inc. have developed the following master production schedule for a 12 week planning horizon:

Week number	1	2	3	4	5	6	7	8	9	10	11	12
Stool A	20	30	50	40	20	30	30	30	30	30	30	30
Stool B	50	40	20	30	40	30	40	40	50	40	40	40

The inventory position is as follows:

Part number	Current inventory	Allocated
F-449	150	10
F-456	170	–
P-455	360	60
P-452	200	–
P-453	30	10

There are two open or outstanding orders:

Part number	Scheduled receipt	Due date
R-450	100	1
R-451	100	1

Generate the planned orders for the following items: A-454, P-447, and P-455.

(2) At the beginning of week 2, an unexpected order is received by Gizmo-Stools for 10 of Stool A. Using a net change approach, recalculate the planned orders for item P-455.

(3) At the beginning of week 3, the supplier of P-455 suddenly informs Gizmo-Stools that he has just had a serious fire at his plant and will be unable to supply this part for four weeks. What effect, if any, will this have on the production of Gizmo-Stools? Assume that no alternative source of supply is available.

(4) Based on the experience of the fire at its suppliers premises, Gizmo-Stools decides to review its inventory policy and to use a safety stock policy from now on. Looking ahead from week 4, Gizmo-Stools decides to hold a safety stock of 100 of Stool A and 120 of Stool B. Generate the planned orders for R-451 and R-450 based on this new policy.

(5) Was Gizmo wise to implement such a safety strategy? Could you advise a better strategy?

(6) Consider the planned orders for item P-455 generated in Problem (1). The supplier of P-455 now insists that all orders to him are in multiples of 50, i.e. the purchasing lot size must be a multiple of 50. Revise the planning of item P-455, taking account of this new constraint.

(7) Consider the following master schedule data for Stool A/part number F-456.

Week number	1	2	3	4	5	6	7	8	9	10
System forecast	70	70	70	70	70	70	70	70	70	70
Manual forecast	75	70	60	60	80	80	60			
Actual orders	70	60	40	30	50	35	35		10	

Assume the following:

(a) The starting inventory is 50.

(b) The company has committed to make 60 of Stool A per week in weeks 1 to 3 inclusive and 80 per week in weeks 4 to 8 inclusive.

(c) The planner uses the following simple rules to calculate total demand. In weeks 1 and 2, he assumes that actual orders constitute total demand. In weeks 3 to 6 inclusive he bases his assessment on the manual forecast or the system forecast, whichever is greater. In the remaining weeks he uses the system forecast.

Based on these procedures, generate a full MPS tableau of the type shown in Table 7.2. In particular, generate the projected inventory row and the cumulative ATP row.

(8) Consider the following master schedule data for Stool B.

Week number	1	2	3	4	5	6	7	8	9	10
System forecast	200	200	200	220	220	220	200	200	200	220
Manual forecast	190	160	180	180	190					
Actual orders	180	170	100	80	90	–	–	20	–	10

Assume the following:

(a) The starting inventory is 120.

(b) The company has committed to make 180 per week of Stool B for weeks 1 to 3 inclusive, 200 per week for weeks 4 to 6 inclusive, and 180 per week for the remaining weeks.

(c) The company is expecting a downturn in the market for Stool B and has decided on the following planning strategy to calculate total demand.

In weeks 1 and 2 it assumes that actual orders constitute total demand. For weeks where a manual forecast has been made, the lower of the manual forecast and the system forecast is to be used to estimate demand. For time buckets in which no manual forecast is available, the planner should factor the system forecast by 0.8 to estimate total demand.

Generate a full MPS tableau of the type shown in Table 7.2. In particular, generate the projected inventory and the cumulative ATP row.

(9) Consider the following Table of Net Requirements for part P-455.

Week number	1	2	3	4	5	6	7	8	9	10
Net requirements	0	0	560	630	0	460	0	880	0	950

P-455 is a purchased part. The cost of generating a purchase order is estimated to be £50 and the inventory carrying cost is estimated to be £0.10 per unit per week. The purchasing lead time is 2 weeks.

(a) Calculate the planned order receipts and the schedule of planned orders for part P-455 using the EOQ model.

(b) Calculate the planned order releases and the schedule of planned orders using the periodic order quantity model.

(c) Calculate the planned order releases and the schedule of planned orders using the part period balancing algorithm.

(10) Using the same data as in Problem (9), but with a higher cost of generating a purchase order of £60 (rather than £50) and a higher inventory cost of £0.12 per unit per week, calculate the schedule of planned order releases using the EOQ model.

(11) Using the same data as in Problem (9), but with a lower cost of generating an order of £40 (rather than £50) and a lower inventory carrying cost of £0.08 per unit per week, calculate the schedule of planned order releases using the EOQ model.

(12) Consider the results of Problems (9), (10), and (11). Do the results surprise you? Why?

(13) DEI Ltd wishes to select an appropriate lot sizing algorithm to use in its MRP system. A typical manufactured part can be described as follows:

Set-up cost: £75
Inventory carrying cost: £0.25 per unit per week

The demand forecast per week over the next 10 weeks is as indicated below. Further, we may assume a starting inventory of zero.

Week number	1	2	3	4	5	6	7	8	9	10
Demand	200	300	250	480	20	260	150	320	50	310

DEI Ltd have decided to limit their options to the Economic Order Quantity (EOQ) model, the Periodic Order Quantity (POQ) model, and the part period balancing procedure. Assuming that the demand patterns and the costs given above are representative, which policy would you advise? Why?

(14) The master scheduler at ABC Ltd is concerned at the quality of forecasts he is getting from the sales and marketing people. He has access to the following data for his main product.

Week number	6	7	8	9	10	11	12
Sales	180	195	185	190	180	175	190

Use the basic exponential smoothing model, and make the following assumptions:

(a)   A starting average of 190 at the end of week 5.

(b)   A smoothing constraint of $\alpha = 0.3$

Prepare a forecast of sales for week 13, as of the end of week 12.

(15) DEF Ltd would like to develop forecasting models for three of its main product families. The planners have collated the following sales data for the three product lines.

Month number number	Product family A	Product family B	Product family C
4	230	505	200
5	260	480	350
6	220	520	290
7	210	510	420
8	250	490	450
9	240	520	360
10	230	530	250

(a) Develop an exponential smoothing model for product family A, using a starting average of 240 at the end of month 3 and an α value of 0.25. Forecast the sales for month 11, as seen at the end of month 10.

(b) Develop an exponential smoothing model for product family B, using a starting average of 510 and an α value of 0.20. Forecast the sales for month 11, as seen at the end of month 10.

(c) What is the three period moving average for month 9 for product family B, made at the end of month 8?

(d) What is the four period moving average for product family C for month 10, seen at the end of month 9.

(e) Using the basic exponential smoothing model, a starting average of 280, and an α value of 0.15, forecast the sales of product family C in month 9, as seen at the end of month 8.

(16) FX Limited has gathered the following data on historical sales of its leading product.

Year	Actual sales (thousands)
1985	28
1986	32
1987	30
1988	29
1989	28
1990	31
1991	30
1992	30
1993	32
1994	29
1995	31

FX is now interested in developing a sales forecasting model to help it predict future sales. It intends to compare four models:

    (a)   An exponential smoothing model with a starting average of 28 000 and an α value of 0.25.

    (b)   An exponential smoothing model with a starting average of 28 000 and an α value of 0.40.

    (c)   A moving average model using three periods.

    (d)   A moving average model using four periods.

Which model would you advise FX to use? Use Mean Absolute Deviation (MAD) and Mean Squared Error (MSE) to support your opinion.

(17) Complete the following MPS planning record.

Item: Product A	Part number: FP-5026					
Month number	1	2	3	4	5	6
Manual forecast	60	100	120	110	120	120
System forecast	100	100	100	100	100	100
Customer orders	55	80	80	40	10	20
Total demand						
MPS						
PAB						

Assume that the product should have a safety stock of 30 and that the lead time is one month. Further, assume that the projected available balance is initially 40.

(18) Alpha Manufacturing Company manufactures a product known as the Gizmo. Alpha are interested in putting in place an MPS system to support the planning of Gizmo's production. Data has been collected on the past 10 months sales as follows:

Month number	1	2	3	4	5	6	7	8	9	10
Sales (000s)	40	46	39	38	41	42	47	46	41	48

Alpha is anxious to know which forecasting technique it should use to support the system forecast line in its MPS system. It has narrowed its options to two:

    (1)   A three months moving average.

    (2)   A five months moving average.

Using the data given above and the Mean Absolute Deviation (MAD) and Mean Squared Error (MSE) of the forecasts as criteria, which option would you recommend?

(19) Beta Manufacturing Ltd has created the following MPS records for its best selling product.

Item: Product A		Part number: FP-3051								
Month number	1	2	3	4	5	6	7	8	9	10
Manual forecast	80	90	85	90	95	100	110	100	110	110
System forecast	80	80	80	80	90	90	90	90	95	95
Customer orders	85	70	60	30	20	40	10	–	–	–
Total demand										
MPS										
PAB										
ATP										
Cumulative ATP										

Assume that the lead time for Product A is one month and that there is no safety stock. Further, assume that the starting inventory (or PAB at time 0) is 60.

(a) Complete the MPS record presented above.

(b) Assuming a **starting inventory of 160** and a product **lead time of two months**, complete the MPS record above.

(c) Assuming a **starting inventory of 100**, a product **lead time of one month**, and a required safety stock of 80, complete the MPS record.

(20) (a) Identify and clearly define five performance measures used to evaluate the performance of a scheduling system.

(b) What is meant when two performance measures (in scheduling) are termed *equivalent*?

(c) Describe the notation $n/m/A/B$ frequently used to classify scheduling problems.

(d) What do you understand by the term *heuristic*?

(e) What do you understand by the term *critical ratio* in scheduling?

(f) Under what conditions can Johnson's algorithm be used to solve the $n/3/F/F_{max}$ scheduling problem?

(21) Use Moore's algorithm to solve the following $6/1/N_T$ scheduling problem. N_T refers to the number of tardy jobs.

Job number	1	2	3	4	5	6
Due date	24	8	14	26	36	40
Processing time	8	4	8	6	6	10

(22) Use Johnson's algorithm to solve the following $4/2/F/F_{max}$ problem.

Job number	Processing time (machine 1)	Processing time (Machine 2)
1	5	7
2	8	11
3	4	9
4	5	6

(23) Distinguish clearly between the SPT, the modified SPT, and the EDD scheduling heuristics.

(24) The following table presents the monthly demand for the six products within a given product family. Assuming a 20-day working month and a 16-hour working day, develop a repetitive production schedule to meet this demand.

Product	Monthly demand
F1	4 800
F2	1 600
F3	6 400
F4	1 600
F5	2 400
F6	2 400
Demand	19 200 per month

(25) Consider the following situation. Assume that the data in Problem (1) reflects the expectation of requirements for the six products F1 to F6 inclusive at the start of the month, and that the scheduler is following the repetitive product schedule you have developed. Now assume that in the beginning of week 3, the situation changes because a major distributor changes his order. The result of this is to reduce the total demand for F3 by 800 and increase the demand for F2 by 800.

Generate a revised schedule for the remaining half of the month which accommodates this new situation.

Glossary of acronyms

ABC	Activity Based Costing
AGV	Automatic Guided Vehicle
AI	Artificial Intelligence
AMHS	Automated Materials Handling Systems
AN	Application Network
AMHSS	Automated Materials Handling and Storage Systems
APICS	American Production and Inventory Control Society
AQL	Acceptable Quality Level
AS/RS	Automatic Storage and Retrieval System
ATO	Assemble To Order
ATP	Available To Promise
BOM	Bill of Materials
BOMP	Bill of Materials Processing
CAD	Computer Aided Design
CAE	Computed Aided Engineering
CALS	Computer Aided Acquisition and Logistics Support
CAM	Computer Aided Manufacture
CAM-I	Computer Aided Manufacturing-International, Inc.
CAPE	Computer Aided Production Engineering
CAPM	Computer Aided Production Management
CAPP	Computer Aided Process Planning
CAST	Computer Aided Storage and Transportation
CAT	Computer Aided Test
CDI	CAD/CAM Data Interchange
CE	Concurrent Engineering
CFA	Company Flow Analysis
CIB	Computer Integrated Business
CIM	Computer Integrated Manufacturing
CNC	Computer Numerical Control
CODP	Customer Order Decoupling Point
CRP	Capacity Requirements Planning
CSG	Constructive Solid Geometry
DFA	Design For Assembly
DFM	Design For Manufacture
DIP	Dual In-line Package (electronic component)

DNC	Direct (or Distributed) Numerical Control
DP	Data Processing
DRP	Distribution Requirements Planning
DRP II	Distribution Resource Planning
EBQ	Economic Batch Quantity
EDD	Earliest Due Date
EDE	Electronic Data Exchange
EDI	Electronic Data Interchange
EOQ	Economic Order Quantity
ESPRIT	European Strategic Programme for Research and Development in Information Technology
ETO	Engineer To Order
FAS	Flexible Assembly System
FC	Factory Coordination
FFA	Factory Flow Analysis
FIFO	First In First Out
FMC	Flexible Manufacturing Cell
FMS	Flexible Manufacturing System
FTL	Flexible Transfer Line
GA	Group Analysis
4GLs	Fourth Generation Languages
GT	Group Technology
JIT	Just In Time
LA	Line Analysis
LRPP	Long Range Production Planning
LTPD	Lot Tolerance Percent Defective
MAD	Mean Absolute Deviation
MAP	Manufacturing Automation Protocol
MIS	Management Information Systems
MPS	Master Production Schedule
MRP	Materials Requirements Planning
MRP II	Manufacturing Resource Planning
MSE	Mean Squared Error
MTO	Make To Order
MTS	Make To Stock
NC	Numerical Control
NINQ	Number In Next Queue
OPT	Optimized Production Technology
OR	Operations Research
PAB	Projected Available Balance
PAC	Production Activity Control
PBC	Period Batch Control
PDES	Product Date Exchange Standard
PFA	Product Flow Analysis
PMS	Production Management System
POQ	Periodic Order Quantity
RCCP	Rough Cut Capacity Planning
SCARA	Selective Compliance Assembly Robot Arm
SMED	Single Minute Exchange of Dies

SMT	Surface Mounted Technology
SPT	Shortest Processing Time
TA	Tooling Analysis
TOP	The Office Protocol
TQC	Total Quality Control
VCD	Variable Center Distance (electronic component)
VLSI	Very Large Scale Integration
WCM	World Class Manufacturing
WINQ	Work In Next Queue
WIP	Work in Progress

Index